Rhetoric & Society
Edited by Wayne A. Rebhorn

Rhetoric and the Origins of Medieval Drama
by Jody Enders

Rhetoric and the Origins of Medieval Drama

JODY ENDERS

CORNELL UNIVERSITY PRESS

ITHACA AND LONDON

Copyright © 1992 by Cornell University

All rights reserved. Except for brief quotations in a review, this book,
or parts thereof, must not be reproduced in any form without
permission in writing from the publisher. For information, address
Cornell University Press, 124 Roberts Place, Ithaca, New York 14850.

First published 1992 by Cornell University Press.

International Standard Book Number 0-8014-2655-3
Library of Congress Catalog Card Number (92-2798)

Printed in the United States of America

*Librarians: Library of Congress cataloging information
appears on the last page of this book.*

⊗ The paper in this book meets the minimum requirements
of the American National Standard for Information Sciences—
Permanence of Paper for Printed Library Materials, ANSI Z39.48-1984.

To the memory of O. B. Hardison

Words are representations [*mimēmata*]; and the voice is the most mimetic element in our makeup.

—ARISTOTLE, *The Art of Rhetoric*, 1404a

Contents

Foreword

The purpose of this series is to study rhetoric in all the varied forms it has taken in human civilizations by situating it in the intellectual, social, and political contexts to which it is inextricably bound. Rhetoric and Society rests on the assumption that rhetoric is both an important intellectual discipline and a necessary cultural practice and that it is profoundly implicated in a large array of other disciplines and practices, from politics to literature to religion. Interdisciplinary by definition and unrestricted in range either historically or geographically, the series will investigate a wide variety of questions, among them how rhetoric constitutes a response to historical developments in a given society, how it crystallizes cultural tensions and conflicts and defines key concepts, and how it affects and shapes the social order in its turn. Rhetoric and Society will include books that approach rhetoric as a form of signification, as a discipline that makes meaning out of other cultural practices, and as a central and defining intellectual and social activity deeply rooted in its milieu. In essence, all the books in the series will seek to demonstrate just how important rhetoric really is to human beings in society.

Jody Enders's *Rhetoric and the Origins of Medieval Drama*, the inaugural volume in the series, shows the profound ways in which various discourses—rhetoric, law, theology, and literature, among others—interact in medieval culture. Investigating the relationship between forensic rhetoric and the drama of the period, it focuses on a neglected aspect of rhetoric, delivery (*actio*), which links it with the drama. Enders maintains that lawyers tended from late antiquity on to emphasize spectacle and aesthetic effect in the courtroom, so that the performance of forensic oratory came to resemble the drama that eventually emerged at the end of the Middle Ages. Her argument concerning the proximity of the two genres helps to account for the presence of law and legalistic debate as both thematic and structural elements in a large number of plays of the period. Her book makes an especially valuable contribution in revising the notion of origins, for it claims not so much that rhetoric is a source of the drama of the Middle Ages as that the two activities—along with such phenomena as theological debate and the Mass—are parts of a continuum of performance genres that are linked by their nature and capable of influencing one another, or even of collapsing the boundaries of genre, as a result. Finally, the book offers an important new perspective on the generally accepted view of the decline of rhetoric in late antiquity and the Middle Ages, since it shows convincingly that what is lamented as the decline of rhetoric can just as easily be celebrated as the rise of the drama.

WAYNE A. REBHORN

Acknowledgments

It is impossible to name all the scholars who have shared their ideas so generously with me, but I extend my special gratitude to Stephen Nichols, whose insights, guidance, and interest in my work have consistently challenged and inspired me. My heartfelt appreciation goes as well to Robert N. Gaines, who opened the world of rhetoric to me; and to James J. Murphy and John Ward for their continued help and support. I also give special thanks to Theresa Coletti, who read my manuscript for Cornell University Press with such care, precision, and perspicacity that she made the task of revision both a challenge and a pleasure.

The origins of this project can be traced to the late O. B. Hardison. In 1981 I had the pleasure of participating in the Folger Library Seminar "The Origins of Medieval Drama," which he taught with E. Catherine Dunn. His erudition was as dazzling in person as it remains in writing, and his ground-breaking work on medieval drama, his encouragement of younger scholars, and his munificent openness to new ideas represented our profession at its best.

I am particularly fortunate to have had the benefit of the expertise and enthusiasm of my colleague in classics Alexander P. MacGregor. To say that we collaborated on the translations from Latin would be a great understatement, so extraordinary is his gift for bringing classical texts to life in all their beauty and with all the richness of their philological and cultural contexts.

I am also indebted to the United Chapters of Phi Beta Kappa, whose award of the Mary Isabel Sibley Fellowship enabled me to devote

1986–87 to research; and to the National Endowment for the Humanities, Margaret Switten, and all the participants in the NEH Institute "The Medieval Lyric: Poetry and Music in Perspective" (Summer 1987) for much stimulating discussion on aspects of orality and literacy.

Grateful acknowledgment is due to Priscilla Ferguson, who generously spent many hours reading and discussing my work with me; to Wayne A. Rebhorn for his many insightful suggestions; to Alan Knight, Donald Maddox, Nancy Regalado, and Daniel Poirion for their help during the early stages of this project; and to Franklin Sweetser, who reviewed all the translations from Old and Middle French with me. I also thank Barbara H. Salazar for her conscientious care in editing my manuscript and Marilyn Reppa for her scrupulous assistance in its preparation. Finally, I am grateful to Marie-Odile Sweetser, Philip Watts, and all my wonderfully supportive colleagues at the University of Illinois at Chicago.

JODY ENDERS

Chicago, Illinois

Abbreviations

A.N.	Archives Nationales, Paris.
CCM	*Cahiers de Civilisation Médiévale.*
CM	*Le Cercle magique*, by Henri Rey-Flaud.
CP	*Les Clercs du Palais*, by Adolphe Fabre.
CR	*Classical Rhetoric: Its Christian and Secular Tradition*, by George Kennedy.
CRCD	*Christian Rite and Christian Drama in the Middle Ages: Essays on the Origin and Early History of Modern Drama*, by O. B. Hardison, Jr.
CSSJ	*Central States Speech Journal.*
DC	*Le Drame chrétien*, by Marius Sepet.
DSA	*Drama, Stage, and Audience*, by J. L. Styan.
EH	*Etudes historiques sur les clercs de la Bazoche*, by Adolphe Fabre.
EMI	*Elizabethan and Metaphysical Imagery*, by Rosemond Tuve.
ETF	*Etudes sur le théâtre français*, by Raymond Lebègue.
FMWR	*From Memory to Written Record*, by M. T. Clanchy.
HL	*Homo Ludens*, by Johan Huizinga.
ICMS	International Congress on Medieval Studies.
IOL	*Implications of Literacy*, by Brian Stock.
ISHR	International Society for the History of Rhetoric.
LIS	*Language Is Sermonic*, by Richard Weaver.
LM	*Les Mystères*, by L. Petit de Julleville.
LQ	*La Littérature quodlibétique de 1260–1320*, 2 vols., by Palémon Glorieux.
MFLL	*Medieval French Literature and Law*, by R. Howard Bloch.

MI	*Medieval Imagination*, by Douglas Kelly.
MLA	Modern Language Association.
NLH	*New Literary History*.
OAL	*Orality and Literacy*, by Walter J. Ong.
PDMA	*Pour une dramaturgie du Moyen Age*, by Henri Rey-Flaud.
PELR	*La Prédication en langue romane*, by Michel Zink.
PLF	*Poetic and Legal Fiction in the Aristotelian Tradition*, by Kathy Eden.
POLF	*Philosophy of Literary Form*, by Kenneth Burke.
PRL	*Poetics, Rhetoric, and Logic*, by Wilbur Samuel Howell.
QJS	*Quarterly Journal of Speech*.
REL	*Rhétorique et littérature*, by Aron Kibédi Varga.
RIMA	*Rhetoric in the Middle Ages*, by James J. Murphy.
RORD	*Research Opportunities in Renaissance Drama*.
RRT	*Rhetoric, Romance, and Technology*, by Walter J. Ong.
SCA	Speech Communication Association.
SSCJ	*Southern States Communications Journal*.
TADT	*Theatre and Dramatic Theory*, by Allardyce Nicoll.
TEF	*Le Théâtre en France: Histoire de la littérature dramatique*, by L. Petit de Julleville.
TM	*Théâtre médiéval*, by Jean-Claude Aubailly.
TRF	*La Tragédie religieuse en France*, by Raymond Lebègue.
WD	*World Drama*, by Allardyce Nicoll.
YFS	*Yale French Studies*.

Facts of publication are provided in the Bibliography.

Introduction

"If ever it seems an opportune time to intone," counseled Lucian of Samosata's outrageous protagonist,

> intone everything and turn it into song. And if ever you are at a loss for matter to intone, say "Gentlemen of the jury" in the proper tempo and consider the music of your sentence complete. Cry "Woe is me!" frequently; slap your thigh, bawl, clear your throat while you are speaking, and stride about swaying your hips. If they do not cry "Hear!" be indignant and upbraid them; and if they stand up, ready to go out in disgust, command them to sit down.... The rank and file are already struck dumb with admiration of your appearance, your diction, your gait, your pacing back and forth, your intoning, your sandals, and that "sundry" of yours; and when they see your sweat and your labouring breath they cannot fail to believe that you are... [1]

...a gifted actor?

Not at all. In the second century, Lucian was depicting one vantage point from which classical and medieval theorists viewed the interrelations between rhetoric and drama. Much to the surprise of the twentieth-century reader, the speaker in the passage above is a

---

[1] Lucian, "Professor of Public Speaking," 19–20. All footnotes include author, short title, and any relevant numbers for pages, verses, lines, or sections. In general, when a readily accessible bilingual edition of a classical work (such as those in the Loeb Classical Library) is available, I do not reproduce the original. Complete entries for works cited are found in the Bibliography. When practical, abbreviated titles are used parenthetically in the text; they are identified in the list of abbreviations.

professor of public speaking, an illustrious barrister (by his own account), illuminating here for his disciple how to become a "terrible opponent in debates." The work is a satire, to be sure, but satire presupposes recognition of its object of imitation, here the contemporary sophist. What the unethical professor of public speaking has outlined for his student is a fashionable legal rhetoric based not on equity but on theatricality. What he has chosen to impart is not a knowledge of the law but a program for histrionic performance. During classical antiquity and throughout the Middle Ages, rhetoricians (reluctantly or not) looked to the theater for guidance, many going so far as to assert the equivalency of orator and actor. The resulting generic interplay suggests a critical conflation of forensic rhetoric and drama that is of the utmost relevance to the origins of drama itself.

From the earliest Greek tragedies to the *Farce de Maistre Pierre Pathelin* to Arthur Miller's *Crucible* to the contemporary cinematic *Retour de Martin Guerre*, the exposition and resolution of juridical proceedings have always had latent if not blatantly manifest dramatic value. The suspense created by the anticipation of a verdict coaxed from arguments pro and contra has kept audiences spellbound for centuries as spectators and readers awaited that most crucial of legal denouements, judgment and the attribution of justice. Not surprisingly, two similar forensic spectacles drew a wide variety of observers to the Grand' Chambre of the Châtelet and to the *parvis* and courtyards of medieval French churches and universities. One was performed by the Basochiens, those celebrated legal apprentices whose histrionics during real and fictional cases helped to ensure their fame for satire.[2] The other was the quodlibet, the widely attended disputation that was the ceremonial rite of passage for theology students.[3] Still, those crucial junctures at which

[2]The finest introductions to the Basoche remain Harvey, *Theatre of the Basoche*; Genty, *Basoche notariale*; and Fabre's *Etudes historiques sur les clercs de la Bazoche* (1856; hereafter *EH*) and the second edition of that work, entitled *Les Clercs du palais* (1875), and *Les Clercs du Palais: La Farce du cry de la Bazoche* (1882). The latter two editions are hereafter cited as *CP*, with the publication date specified. The 1856 edition, unfortunately not readily accessible, reproduces primary sources not always included in the later editions. All translations of Fabre and other secondary sources are mine unless I indicate otherwise. W. M. H. Hummelen has analyzed a rhetorical phenomenon similar to the Basoche in "Dutch Rhetoricians' Drama"; see also his *Repertorium van het Rederijkersdrama*; and Robert Potter's treatment of Hummelen's work in "Unity of Medieval Drama," 48. See also Alan Nelson's discussion of the theatrical antics in English education in "Contexts for Early English Drama." I thank Alan Knight and Donald Maddox for sharing their insights on the Basoche with me.
[3]The quodlibet has been virtually ignored by literary critics, with the exception

scholastic discourse became a dramatic mimesis of legal rhetoric, where arguments were real enough but verdicts often fictional and even trivial, have remained virtually unexplored in studies of the theater.

Recent work on the momentous implications of *mouvance* (or the shifting interplay of generic forms) in medieval literature has only scratched the surface of what theorists of rhetoric articulated long ago, as when Plato problematized the fluidity between rhetoric and spectacle by having Socrates indict Lysias for a speech that was but an "extravagant performance."[4] Given the many transfers of the forensic rhetorical model from the courtroom to the medieval stage and the enduring popularity of debate and dialogic literature throughout the Middle Ages, it is certainly relevant to investigate precisely how such a shift from the legal to the literary register might have occurred. In keeping, then, with Ernst Robert Curtius's early declaration that antiquity "had rhetoric for a general theory of literature," I propose to show that the legal rhetoric of the courts in particular was the site of an ontological commingling of ritual and representation not unlike that which once enabled O. B. Hardison and Karl Young to discover the origins of medieval drama in the Christian liturgy.[5] After all, the orator of antiquity was first and

---

of Palémon Glorieux, whose two-volume *Littérature quodlibétique* (hereafter *LQ*) breaks new ground. More limited but still useful discussions of the quodlibet include Mandonnet, "Chronologie des questions disputées"; Löhr, *Theologische Disputationem*; Thurot, *De l'organisation de l'enseignement,* chap. 3; Kenny and Pinborg, "Medieval Philosophical Literature"; and Rashdall's discussion of testing in *Universities of Europe,* 1:452–89, along with editorial commentary by Powicke and Emden, 490–96n.

[4]Plato, *Phaedrus,* 235a. Here I extend Zumthor's notion of *mouvance* as a "fundamental instability" between oral and written (*Essai,* 65–72) to the level of genre. And for an excellent introduction to the importance of that concept in literary criticism, see the extensive inquiry into versions, *mouvance,* and *variance* (Cerquiglini, *Eloge*) in the "New Philology" issue of *Speculum* 65 (1990), esp. Stephen G. Nichols, "Introduction," 1–7, and Suzanne Fleischman, "Philology, Linguistics," 19–22. For the concept of generic fluidity, the most helpful introduction remains Jauss, "Littérature médiévale."

[5]Curtius, *European Literature,* 71. Douglas Kelly demonstrated the dependence of medieval poetics on the *trivium* in "Scope and Treatment"; and Northrop Frye defined literature as "the rhetorical organization of grammar and logic" in *Anatomy of Criticism,* 245. For the shift from ritual to representation in the origins of liturgical drama, I am referring to Hardison, *Christian Rite and Christian Drama in the Middle Ages* (hereafter *CRCD*), esp. chap. 2 on the Mass as sacred drama; Young, *Drama of the Medieval Church;* Chambers, *Mediaeval Stage;* Hardin Craig, *English Religious Drama.* Other helpful discussions of representation in medieval dramatic forms include Olson, "Medieval Fortunes of 'Theatrica' "; Axton, *European Drama;* and Hult, "Limits of Mime(sis)." The similarities of Christian representation to the Dionysian "liturgy" are described in Vince, *Ancient and Medieval Theatre,* 23, and Nicoll, *World*

foremost a legal advocate, and theorists of rhetoric often addressed his duties before those of deliberative and epideictic rhetoricians, making them the very context for the elaboration of their theories.[6] Characterized to a greater degree than the deliberative or epideictic rhetorical genres by such crucial protodramatic components as theatrical space, costume, staging, ritual conflict, audience participation, spectacle, dialogue, "imitation of action," and, most important of all, impersonation,[7] legal rhetoric emerges as one of the very

---

Drama (hereafter *WD*), 4 (unless I indicate otherwise, references to *WD* are to the second edition).

[6] For example, forensic oratory is the principal focus of both the pseudo-Ciceronian *Ad C. Herennium* (I, 18–27) and Cicero's *De inventione* (I, 6–20). For the wide dissemination of both those treatises in the French medieval university, see Clerval, *Ecoles de Chartres*, 115–17; George Kennedy, *Classical Rhetoric* (hereafter *CR*), 174–75; and Murphy, *Rhetoric in the Middle Ages* (hereafter *RIMA*), 109–14. The most useful general introductions to medieval rhetoric remain Murphy's *RIMA* and *Synoptic History*, and his bibliographies in *Medieval Rhetoric*; Kennedy, *CR*; Fumaroli, *L'Age de l'éloquence*; and Ong, *Rhetoric, Romance, and Technology* (hereafter *RRT*), esp. chap. 1. Helpful surveys of this material are found in Barthes, "L'Ancienne rhétorique"; Burke, "Rhetoric—Old and New"; and Leff, "In Search of Ariadne's Thread." And, despite their age, Curtius, chap. 4; McKeon, "Rhetoric in the Middle Ages"; Baldwin, *Medieval Rhetoric*; and Faral, *Arts poétiques*, remain invaluable. For examples of the general revitalization of rhetoric, see Perelman, *L'Empire rhétorique*, and Florescu, *La Rhétorique et la néo-rhétorique*; and for its reintegration into literary criticism, I refer esp. to the work of Aron Kibédi Varga, *Rhétorique et littérature* (hereafter *REL*); Howell, *Poetics, Rhetoric, and Logic* (hereafter *PRL*); Zumthor, "Rhétorique médiévale et poétique"; Vickers, *Classical Rhetoric*; Kelly, *Medieval Imagination* (hereafter *MI*); Hunt, "Rhetoric and Poetics"; Lewalski, "*Paradise Lost*"; Michel, *La Parole et la beauté*; and O'Malley, *Praise and Blame*.

[7] For comparisons of the forensic genre with deliberative and epideictic oratory, see, e. g., Alcuin, *Rhetoric of Alcuin and Charlemagne*, ll. 88–89; [Cicero], *Ad Herennium*, I, 2; Aristotle, *"Art" of Rhetoric*, 1358b; Quintilian, *Institutio oratoria*, III, 4. In chaps. 1 and 2, I analyze the specific dramatic components of the proposed paradigm, which is virtually identical to the one used by Hardison in *CRCD*. The most important studies on the general compatibility of law and literature remain Bloch, *Medieval French Literature and Law* (hereafter *MFLL*); Eden, *Poetic and Legal Fiction* (hereafter *PLF*); and Huizinga, *Homo Ludens* (hereafter *HL*), chap. 4; but their analyses focus more on structure/concept than on performance. Jerzy Axer is among the very few critics to discuss the "theatricalization" of forensic eloquence. In a fascinating article, "Tribunal-Stage-Arena," he essentially rejects the notion of impersonation in forensic oratory (303) but he is nonetheless committed to the "para- or quasi-theatricality" of the forensic experience (303), primarily on the level of "theatrical stylization" and audience reception (306). Also, Richard Garner has speculated on the protodramatic status of law in *Law and Society*, chap. 4; and Delachenal's early *Histoire des avocats* still offers many invaluable insights into the dramatic orality of law. Finally, Zumthor has posited a general interplay between dialogic discourse and spectacle, although he is concerned primarily with scenic transformations and the interplay of sacred and vernacular languages: see esp. his discussion of "le Grand Jeu" (441–49) in chap. 10 of his *Essai*. Similar arguments have been advanced for the protodramatic status of both Greek poetry and the *ars praedicandi*. For the former, see Herington, "Poetry as a Performing Art," in his *Poetry into Drama*, 3–40; and for the latter, see Zink, *Prédication en langue romane* (hereafter *PELR*), 365–88;

"origins" of drama. The same performative elements that rendered any delivered rhetoric "dramatic" encouraged particularly stunning generic modulations between forensic rhetoric and drama itself.

In accordance with Cicero's oft-repeated observation that "orators are the players who act real life,"[8] I reexamine medieval exploitations of legal oratory as a particularly apt point of departure for broader speculation, not so much about rhetoric *and* drama as about rhetoric *as* drama. Central to my inquiry is an examination of the *letteraturizzazione* or, for my purposes, "aestheticization" of both classical and medieval rhetorical forms; that is, according to George Kennedy, the process by which rhetorical focus shifts "from persuasion to narration, from civic to personal contexts, and from discourse to literature, including poetry."[9] For despite the assertions of Howard Harvey that the "preparation and trial of a case in the courtroom is essentially a dramatic art" and of Jean-Claude Aubailly that comical rhetorical declamation was "already dramatic in character," the full performative ramifications of those ideas have yet to be subjected to systematic generic inquiry.[10] Ultimately, the scholarly rehabilitation of the spectacular register of rhetoric allows us to formulate a systematic definition of the "natural drama" of law (Harvey 13) and to rediscover and reinterpret a hitherto unexploited corpus of commentary on the theater.

Today, even in the wake of a renewed critical interest in issues of orality and literacy, two of the rhetorical canons have been largely ignored in literary criticism: delivery (*actio, pronuntiatio,* or *hypokrisis*), which codified the rules of voice, gesture, and expression in oral performance; and, to a lesser extent, memory (*memoria*), which provided a treasure house of vivid imagery subsequently enacted during delivery.[11] Delivery was the key to the performative

---

Accarie, *Théâtre sacré*, 79; Rey-Flaud, *Cercle magique* (hereafter *CM*), 262; and Sepet, *Drame chrétien* (hereafter *DC*), 52–53. I discuss impersonation at length in chap. 1; helpful introductions to this concept can be found in Hardison, *CRCD*, 31–33; Young, 1:80–85; Hardin Craig, 2–5; Chambers 2:44–57.

[8]Cicero, *De oratore,* III, 215.

[9]Kennedy, *CR,* 5, which includes a discussion of *letteraturizzazione* and its particular importance in France. I use the term here as a synonym for the process by which literature becomes mimetic or "aestheticization"—a process that is not necessarily limited to written literature (as is often implicit in both *letteraturizzazione* and "fictionalization"). Nor is that process limited to drama, as is implicit in "theatricalization."

[10]Harvey, 19; Aubailly, *Théâtre médiéval* (hereafter *TM*), 124–26. Philippe Heuzé advanced a similar argument about ancient declamatory training in general in an unpublished paper, "Plaisir de la parole."

[11]For orality and literacy, I am referring to such crucial inquiries as Stock, *Implications of Literacy* (hereafter *IOL*); Ong, *Orality and Literacy* (hereafter *OAL*); Clan-

register of discourse, documenting the history of interplay between language, gesture, and mimetic impulse. As such, it proves the privileged locus for the actualization of what Brian Stock has termed the "cohesive whole" of speech and action in the Middle Ages (*IOL*, 15). The very existence of delivery as a rhetorical canon suggests that it was during performance that that "cohesion" actually occurred. Be that as it may, critics have tended to forsake delivery and memory, to neglect arrangement (*dispositio*), to reduce invention (*inventio*) to the study of thematics, and to privilege style (*elocutio*) to such an extent that rhetoric commonly appears but a compendium of tropes and figures—a critical phenomenon that has often obfuscated rather than illuminated the rich and complex performative functions of both rhetoric and literature. Even Roland Barthes, in the ordinarily helpful summary he provides in "L'Ancienne Rhétorique," presents only a tripartite schema of rhetoric based on invention, arrangement, and style.[12]

chy, *From Memory to Written Record* (hereafter *FMWR*); Zumthor, *La Poésie et la voix*; McLuhan, *Gutenberg Galaxy*; Hajnal, *L'Enseignement de l'écriture*; Saenger, "Silent Reading"; Gellrich, *Idea of the Book*; Havelock, *Muse Learns to Write*; Foley, *Theory of Oral Composition*; Kittay, "Utterance Unmoored"; and, of course, the pioneering works of Lord, *Singer of Tales*, and Parry, "Techniques of Oral Verse-Making." For memory as treasure house or treasure chest, see [Cicero], *Ad Herennium*, III, 28; and John of Salisbury, *Metalogicon*, trans. McGarry, 30. The most notable exceptions to the neglect of memory in literary criticism are Yates, *Art of Memory*; Carruthers, *Book of Memory*; Zumthor and Roy, eds., *Jeux de mémoire*; the early work of Helga Hajdu, *Das mnemotechnischen Schrifttum*; Ong, *RRT*, chap. 4; Eden, *PLF*, chaps. 2 and 3; Caplan, "Memoria"; and Joseph Weber, "Poetics of Memory." In my "Visions with Voices" and "Music, Delivery, and the Rhetoric of Memory" I have argued for a strong connection between mnemonics and delivery.

Rhetorical delivery per se has been virtually ignored in literary criticism. Some important exceptions include Elliot, "Medieval Acting"; Crosby, "Oral Delivery"; Pizarro's discussion of gestures in *Rhetoric of the Scene*, chap. 3; and Donald Perret's discussion of delivery and memory in chap. 2 of *Old Comedy in the French Renaissance*. Recent research in orality and literacy, however, often bespeaks similar concerns, esp. Stock's discussion of law as performance or action in *IOL*, 48–49. Finally, while the principles of memory and delivery were much codified in the rhetorical tradition, I am not implying that that tradition was monolithic or purely normative, or that it contained no internal contradictions (as Curtius amply demonstrates in his chap. 4). Far from it: divergent attitudes toward the nature, utility, and moral/philosophical value of rhetoric have sparked lively intellectual debates ever since the quarrel between rhetoric and philosophy led by Hermagoras in the second century B.C. (see Kennedy, *CR*, 89).

[12]Again we find notable exceptions, esp. with respect to *dispositio*. Among them are Kibédi Varga, *REL*; Eden, *PLF*; Howell, *PRL*; and Kelly, *MI*. While I do not seek to minimize the importance of *elocutio* (which was so crucial to the theories of Cicero, Demetrius, Theophrastus, and Augustine), style is by no means the only rhetorical canon to be of relevance to literary studies. Nor do I wish to imply that such analyses of rhetorical style as Croll's *Style, Rhetoric, and Rhythm* are not

Some years ago Rosalie Colie and Rosemond Tuve speculated that the study of literature against the background of rhetorical and logical theory was one of the most potentially rewarding approaches to the interrelations of literature.[13] Colie's intuition that "a man's rhetorical and logical training had something to do with the way he expressed his thoughts and emotions" (20–21) is only one of many insights that must now be reevaluated in the context of performance. Indeed, that insight is borne out by the classification of the mystery play as a rhetorical genre in the *Jardin de plaisance et fleur de rhétorique* (1501) and in the pronouncement of the fourteenth-century *Leys d'amor* that "la sciensa de rhetorica se fa en doas manieras de parlar, la una en proza, e l'autra en rima" (the science of rhetoric is composed of two ways of speaking, one in prose and the other in rhyme).[14] Still, while the compatibility of law and literature has been demonstrated compellingly by such scholars as Howard Bloch, Johan Huizinga, Kathy Eden, and more recently Kathryn Gravdal,[15] drama has been largely neglected, even though it is there that law and literature most fully reveal their "common fascination with problems of language: structure, rhetoric, ambiguity, interpretation, and the quest for meaning through linguistic signs" (Weisberg and Barricelli, 150). For example, although Bloch implied that law was as potentially "poetic" a ritual as religion when he argued that literary forms are "predicated upon the same model of verbal disputation as the trial" (*MFLL*, 176), he excluded drama from

---

enlightening. Rather, the present focus is intended as a partial corrective to the reduction of rhetoric to the "domain of figures" (Fumaroli, 10).

[13]Colie, "Literature and History," 20–21; and Tuve, esp. "Imagery and Logic," 370–77. Howell also spoke out compellingly against "the exclusion of rhetoric and logic from literary theory": *PRL*, 18. Other interesting attempts to minimize the pejorative connotations of rhetoric include T. S. Eliot, "Rhetoric and Poetic Drama," in *Selected Essays*, 26; and Richard Weaver's alarm at the "tide of prejudice" against rhetoric, which continues to "arouse skepticism and suspicion": *Language Is Sermonic* (hereafter *LIS*), 161.

[14]"Pro misteriis compilandis cronicis romanicis et hystoriis," in *Jardin de Plaisance*, ed. Droz and Piaget, vol. 1; *Leys d'amor*, ed. Anglade, 2:13 (for dating of *Leys* in the mid–fourteenth century, see 4:122). See also Bloch's work on this important text: *MFLL*, 180–84. Translations of primary sources in French are mine unless I indicate otherwise.

[15]Bloch, *MFLL*, chap. 4; Huizinga, *HL*, chap. 4; Eden, *PLF*, chap. 2; Gravdal, *Ravishing Maidens*, esp. her final chapter, "The Complicity of Law and Literature." See also Kibédi Varga, *REL*, 86–89; Garner, chap. 4; Squires, "Law and Disorder"; Weisberg and Barricelli, "Literature and Law"; Jackson, *Semiotics and Legal Theory*; and Posner, *Law and Literature*. Weaver describes the trial as a "supremely dramatic incident in a far longer and broader struggle between rationalism on the one hand and poetry and rhetoric (and belief) on the other": *LIS*, 176.

his compelling study of the transformation of law into a "new and meaningful poetic structure" (169). Yet, his crucial insight that one of the primary functions of legal discourse was to verbalize (and eventually to poeticize) the legal ordeal is particularly suggestive in the literal (and literary) "theatricalization" of that discourse, the *letteraturizzazione* of law into drama. In other words, the same coexistence of ritual and representation that we now imbue with dramatic significance in the liturgy proves equally significant in legal ritual.

More important still, the continuity of the rhetorical tradition in European history permits us to do far more than move the multiple origins of medieval drama back considerably; it suggests a recasting of the very terms of the debate about origins. While the disputational conflict of forensic rhetoric was not the only discourse to nurture dramatic representation, its theatricalization during centuries of performance promises to account for many of the theoretical and practical features of the various impulses to imitation within different ritual forms. A revised perception of the performance of conflictual discourse suggests a single performance continuum encompassing both law and drama. Such a recasting is intended neither to be all-inclusive nor to challenge the notion that medieval drama "originated" in the pantomime tradition or in the Christian liturgy. Rather, it expands those theories to suggest that the delivery of agonistic, forensic discourse was also the site of a noteworthy fusion of law, play, rhetoric, ritual, and poetics in early Occidental culture.

The reintegration into medieval literary studies of the concept of *actio*—with all its rich connotations of acting, authorship, legal prosecution, and authority for its *actor* practitioners[16]—thus helps to complete the generic puzzle of drama by enabling us to retrace the rhetorical channels between oral performance, law, drama, and spectacle. Consequently, even if the theatrical productions of the Basochiens, for example, appear far later than the earliest extant medieval "plays" and continue well into the Renaissance, there would be, as Kenneth Burke once noted, "no embarrassment": the performance of conflictual discourse (of which law is a crucial ex-

[16]Depending on context, *actor, acteur,* and *aucteur* may signify "author," "actor in a play," "prosecutor/lawyer," "authority," or, as I suggest here, a fluid combination of all four. See, e.g., Cicero's *Brutus,* 316; and his *De partitione,* 110; or Quintilian, II, 17.40; III, 16.17; VII, 1.38. *Acteur* and *aucteur* are also used interchangeably in such works as Gréban's *Mystère de la Passion* (discussed in my chap. 4). For a general discussion of those terms, see Chenu, "Auctor, actor, autor"; and for the continuity of that terminology in the later Middle Ages, see Delachenal, 95–96n. I address the theoretical ramifications of that interchangeability in chap. 1.

ample) would still constitute a strong and viable "hub," an Ur-form for emergent dramatic activity.[17] Medieval drama itself then appears less as a discrete series of variant "births" than as the variegated oral representation of ritual conflict in different social and historical contexts. As a cultural institution, rhetoric begins to emerge as a kind of repository for nascent theories and practices of drama which it could safely preserve and transmit—even during what many people have been wont to call the "Dark Ages" of drama.

Moreover, since the performance continuum of rhetoric extends from antiquity to the Middle Ages to the Renaissance, and indeed to the present day, such an approach also prompts a reevaluation of the critical conventions of periodization customarily invoked in discussions of early cultural history. From Plato to the distinguished Spanish humanist, Juan Luis Vives, many rhetorical theorists discuss the aestheticization of rhetoric in ways that are remarkably similar. Their shared views demonstrate that if the Middle Ages share much with classical antiquity, so does the Renaissance with the Middle Ages. The chronological boundaries involved in my use of the term "medieval" must thus be allowed to remain as fluid as the boundaries for genre, which are the proper subject of this inquiry. If anything, the history of rhetoric underscores the importance of the fifteenth century as an age of transition, allowing the *Medium Aevum* to re-present and redefine itself with its own sense of just what it means to be "in the middle."

Furthermore, while the aestheticization of rhetoric is particularly striking in the law, the history of delivery promises to illuminate the protodramatic status of other rhetorical forms as well. Given that the theory and practice of *actio* document the interdependence of oratory and acting, given that rhetoric itself has long been designated a mediatory force between thought and action, poetry and logic, delivery effects its mediatory functions even at the level of genre.[18] As a significant conduit between rhetoric and literature, law and drama, orality and literacy, *actio* offers paradigms for performance which restore the lost dynamism of early performative discourses wherever they may have appeared. At the same time, however, its attendant dramatic orality highlights a more general

<hr />

[17] Burke, *Philosophy of Literary Form* (hereafter *POLF*), 103.

[18] Frye, for example, describes rhetoric as an "intermediate territory" (331–35). See also Durand's modern formulation of its "metaphorical power of transposition (*translatio*) of meaning" as a mediator between word and action: *Structures anthropologiques*, 451–53; and Burke on theological language as a "species of symbolic action": *Rhetoric of Religion*, 38.

fluidity of medieval genres as apparently varied as the morality play
and the fool's play; the dialogue, the *tenso*, and the interior monologue; the *sermon joyeux*, the dialogic sermon, and liturgical troping; the quodlibet, the Basoche, the Dutch Chamber of Rhetoric,
and the scholastic disputers at Oxford. A revitalized understanding
of delivery as a semiotic system thus promises to elucidate how
epideictic performance, for example, interacted with lyric topoi of
praise and blame; or how the *ars praedicandi* might have shifted
generically to the *sermon joyeux*. Michel Zink (*PELR*, 365) and Henri
Rey-Flaud (*CM*, 262) have suggested that but a step was required for
a dialogic sermon to pass from the pulpit to the stage; it is reasonable
to posit that that step was delivery, which provides a readily available approach to the advent of mimetic elements in various forms
of ritual discourse.

The study of the performance of such social institutions as law,
drama, and religion thus facilitates a better understanding of the
role of ritualized discourse in the advent of literary genres that differ
yet are nonetheless intertwined. Since the juridical ritual in particular gave rise just as readily to the most devotional of mystery plays
as to the most blistering of satires, it provides a partial explanation
for many kinds of generic interplay that have been insufficiently
explained by the predictable polarities of "comic" versus "tragic,"
"popular" versus "learned," "secular" versus "Christian."[19] By comparing the performances of the archetypal conflicts of law and drama,
we may foster a new appreciation of how popular and learned forms
interacted in classical antiquity and the Middle Ages and help to
bridge the misleading ideological gap between them. Whether the
forum be the courtroom or the stage, the quodlibet or the Basoche,
the *procès de paradis* or the *Farce du pect*, the commingling of
dramatic rhetoric and rhetorical drama recalls the dramatic declamatory practices traditionally associated with the very process of conflictual inquiry, thereby prompting a refinement of Northrop Frye's
early insight that ritual is "the content of action and more particularly of dramatic action."[20]

[19]These distinctions are far more fluid than they were once thought to be, as such
scholars as Knight, *Aspects of Genre*, chaps. 1 and 5, and Aubailly, *TM*, chap. 3, have
shown. I argue the point at greater length in chap. 4. For revised views of the interrelations of early comedy and tragedy, see esp. Steiner, *Death of Tragedy*; Rodríguez
Adrados, *Fiesta, comedia y tragedia*; and Kerr, *Tragedy and Comedy*.

[20]Frye, 109. Frye, however, was concerned almost exclusively with such popular
ritualistic forms as the folk play, puppet show, pantomime, farce, pageant, and their
"descendants in masque, comic opera, commercial movie, and revue," arguing that

In order to delimit this vast subject, I focus here on law, disputation, and drama as discursive phenomena rather than as social/anthropological entities. In no way, of course, do I wish to imply that these forms are purely discursive; nevertheless, it is the performance of their conflictual languages that sheds new light on the advent of mimesis in different types of ritual agon. Although language is but one feature of the rituals in question, the performance of those rituals promises to account for many mimetic impulses during the *letteraturizzazione* of rhetoric in Europe, to which the particularly litigious dramas of medieval France provide a fascinating testimonial.

Nurtured by a complex pan-European tradition of forensic performance, by scholastic disputation, and by the histrionic Basochiens, many a medieval French dramatist transformed the trial into a rich source of literary invention. While textual analysis of the plays themselves is limited here primarily to the widespread use of forensic rhetoric in medieval France, it is intended to prompt further critical inquiry into such questions as why the French agon was more juridical than, for example, its physically combative German counterparts; why its flowering was so stunning in the fifteenth and sixteenth centuries; and why the public disputations of Oxford and the Dutch Chamber of Rhetoric might have played a less prominent role in the dramatic productions of those countries.[21] Even in France alone we find enormous complexity in the rhetoric of its drama and the drama of its rhetoric. The fifteenth century especially prompts questions about the extent to which the theatricalization of eloquence was connected to the social and political upheavals of the impending Reformation. Given Paul Zumthor's suggestion that theater is the art that is "the most receptive to changes in the social structure, and the most revelatory of those changes" (*Essai*, 447), a partial answer must lie in the changing fortunes of rhetoric during various types of *letteraturizzazione* in various cultures and contexts during its long history—a phenomenon that promises to illuminate similarities as well as differences in rhetorico-dramatic production in the countries of Europe.

"ritual analogies are most easily seen, not in the drama of the educated audience and the settled theatre, but in naive or spectacular drama" (107).

[21] See Axton's elegant argument about the Germans' predilection for physical battle play in drama (44); and Zumthor's discussion of the general response by Europe's *grands rhétoriqueurs* to the compatibility of rhetoric, poetry, and drama in "From Hi(story) to Poem," 238.

In that sense, the ideal scenario would, of course, have been to write a book that catalogued the interplay between rhetoric and the dramatic traditions of the various European vernaculars—and even of medieval Latin drama. It is well known, for example, that Oxford and Cambridge both bore witness to a rich disputational tradition and to intense dramatic activities; the evidence, as Alan Nelson has said, is "abundant, indeed overwhelming" ("Contexts," 139). Given the daunting nature of such a task, however, I have elected instead to present in detail the striking case of medieval France, where the histrionic developments in forensic eloquence are particularly easy to follow in the quodlibetal disputations of the Sorbonne and in the Basoche. The first half of the book is thus devoted to the general pan-European phenomenon and the second to the more coherent example of a single European vernacular. (The more Aristotelian among us might wish to consider this structure the statement and proof.) There is every reason to believe that the case of the French theatricalization of scholastic eloquence is by no means unique, and that a similar exploration of the phenomenon in English, German, and Dutch drama will prove equally illuminating, but I regretfully remand that exciting question to the custody of other scholars.

That such a fascinating body of evidence should have remained unexploited in literary criticism is unfortunate, if not surprising. Long held to be the enemy targeted by Victor Hugo when he called for "war against rhetoric and peace with syntax," rhetoric has not been permitted to elucidate the structure and performance of medieval drama.[22] Perhaps it is wisest to summarize the critical situation with regard to rhetoric with Aron Kibédi Varga as a "slight distortion of perspectives": the true relevance of rhetoric to the arts will become clear only when this codified social discourse is considered independently—rescued, as it were, from literary historians who "were interested only partially and partisanly in the art of eloquence, who sometimes disfigured its true scope and...forgot the essential." Kibédi Varga concurred with James J. Murphy that "a general history of rhetoric at the present time seems more or less impossible to execute," but I should like nonetheless to explore one particular aspect of that history: the role of the rhetorical tradition in the "origins" of drama.[23]

[22]Hugo, "Réponse à un acte d'accusation," l. 121, in *Poésies*, 1:642.
[23]Kibédi Varga, "L'Histoire de la rhétorique," 202–3; and see Murphy, "Historiography of Rhetoric." Important efforts to reassert the significance of rhetoric in medieval historiography include two essays in Breisach's *Classical Rhetoric and*

Nowhere has the distortion of rhetorical perspective been more damaging than in the study of medieval drama, which has been dominated by an anomalous selectivity. On the one hand, references to the "dramatic" and appealing use of legal structures in the farce and *sottie* abound; yet on the other hand, when the disputational structures of legal oratory are placed within the explicitly devotional context of the *miracle* or subordinated to the moral and apocalyptic visions of the *moralité* and the *mystère*, the combination of rhetoric and medieval aesthetics is deemed aberrant. Even though, as H. J. Chaytor pointed out years ago, there is no longer any doubt about the "rhetorical character" of early literature produced "very largely for public recitation,"[24] the critical reflex to the interplay of drama and rhetoric has tended to remain so negative that many an eminent specialist has concluded that rhetoric was somehow antagonistic to creative expression. Thanks to a series of elaborate ideological circumlocutions, a vicious circle has been perpetuated in which the interplay of rhetoric and drama is acknowledged only to be cited as a cause for the degeneration of theatrical forms.

In their edition of Arnoul Gréban's *Mystère de la Passion*, for example, Gaston Paris and Gaston Raynaud dismissed the elaborate juridical debates of the Four Daughters of God as an "interminable discussion," a "commonplace bequeathed to the poet by earlier times [which] offers us a faithful portrait of one of those scholastic disputes that filled the rue du Fouarre at that time" (xvi).[25] Yet in their hasty insistence that the *procès* was little more than a scholastic exercise, Paris and Raynaud never explored the fascinating implications of their own comparison: if scholastic disputes were popular enough to draw mobs to the rue du Fouarre, they may well have had dramatic appeal. Similarly, Harvey acknowledged enthusiastically that the Basochiens were the veritable fathers of French comedy, only to complain that they had written *moralités* "as dull as any a cleric had produced" (13). Even Allardyce Nicoll objected that in the mystery cycles, "rhetoric and intellectual argument" were only too often "substituted . . . for dramatic passion" (*WD*, 116).

Rhetorical theorists, however, have consistently asserted that the

---

Medieval Historiography: Ward, "Some Principles of Rhetorical Historiography," and Partner, "New Cornificus."

[24]Chaytor, *From Script to Print*, 10.

[25]It is interesting to compare this indictment with Burke's observation that drama draws its materials from the "interminable" conversation "that is going on at the point in history when we are born": *POLF*, 110–11.

performance of rhetoric was a passionate experience for lawyers, judges, and audiences alike. Audiences do not appear to have shared our distaste for erudition, as evidenced by a veritable medieval flowering of debate and dialogic forms.[26] Be that as it may, Adolphe Fabre blamed the deficient nature of medieval aesthetics on the law: "their pleadings, teeming with hybrid and barbarous locutions, seem, for the most part, so unintelligible today, that one is scarcely tempted to defend them" (*CP* [1882], 66–67). I shall demonstrate that the long dramatic history of forensic delivery provides their defense; and clearly they need one. For it is surely unreasonable to assume that one and the same legalistic structure would be appealing in the *Pathelin* yet a failure in the *Mystère de la Passion*, to praise the disorderly courtroom of one yet flee what Fabre calls the "frightful erudition" of the other (52). Can the triple authorial role of poet-theologian-lawyer really be distasteful in Jean de Justice's fourteenth-century *Advocacie Nostre-Dame*, as Fabre claims (45), yet pleasurable in Coquillart? While the severity of the condemnations has diminished somewhat over time, the disrepute suffered by the rhetoric of learned drama remains in urgent need of reevaluation.

In exploring the traditional interrelations of rhetoric and the stage, I argue that the tendency to oppose literature to a repressive rhetorical tradition has been just as misguided as the earlier tendency to oppose drama to a repressive liturgical tradition. It seemed to O. B. Hardison that E. K. Chambers's view that "drama originated *in spite of* Christianity, not *because* of it," was "unlikely to encourage scholars to seek explanations of the form or effect of medieval drama within the framework of medieval Christianity";[27] in the same way, the widespread perception of rhetoric as antagonistic to the "mimetic instinct" failed to encourage scholars to seek the origins of medieval drama within the framework of the rhetorical tradition. While there is some historical evidence of a perceived enmity between medieval law and literature—the thirteenth-

[26]For a fascinating discussion of medieval debate in its juridical context, see Bloch, *MFLL*, 167–88. Other helpful treatments of debate and *disputatio* include Ong, *Ramus*, chap. 7; Walther, *Das Streitgedicht;* Raby, *History of Secular Latin Poetry,* 2:282–308; Bossy, "Medieval Debates;. and more recently, Kendrick, *Game of Love,* chap. 1; Lerer's discussion of the disputational models in Cicero and Augustine in *Boethius and Dialogue,* 32–56; Brault on debate as a "literary genre in its own right" in *Song of Roland,* 1:181.

[27]Hardison, *CRCD,* 15–16 (emphasis mine). See also Prosser's astute observation that the "equation of drama with 'amusement' in opposition to religion" has blinded us to the "fusion of doctrine and drama": *Drama and Religion,* 189.

century Radulphus Belvacensis warned dolefully that "the days will come, woe to them, when law will obliterate the study of letters"[28]— the competition between the two disciplines appears to derive less from mutual exclusivity than from their fundamental similarities. Once rhetoric is released from a teleological tyranny akin to that which long obscured the nascent dramas of the medieval liturgy, there emerges a new perception of disputational discourse as particularly nurturing of emerging dramatic forms, a perception that the Muse has not, in fact, been "prostituted" in the courtroom:

> There exist certain monstrous couplings that nature finds repugnant, marriages of reason that the imagination cannot conceive.... Who among us has not seen pieces of poetry enclosed in a vase ... pitiful poetry, tortured by a barbarous father like a contorted clown being forced to go through a narrow hoop! We will seek out and ask the clerics, jurists, and even poets of a certain renown, whether or not they have in fact prostituted the muse by delivering her (as it were) to the caresses of the legal process.   [Fabre, *CP* (1882), 37–38]

In direct contrast to the modern tendency to dismiss any hint of the learned disputational register as pedantry, the study of delivery allows us to restore early dialogic forms to their initial sociocultural importance.

In a Folger Library seminar he taught with E. Catherine Dunn in 1981, the late O. B. Hardison dubbed medieval drama a "many-headed beast" whose origins were to be found in unexpected places. One such place is the rhetorical tradition. What is at stake here, then, is nothing less than the demystification of the medieval literary enterprise itself through the restoration of rhetoric as one of its most viable systems of norms. The study of medieval literary production in particular—still reeling from the effects of the art-for-art's-sake movement—can profit enormously from such a demystification. For even though the very process of rhetorico-literary invention was largely normative, criticism of medieval literature has tended to be profoundly influenced by what Marc Fumaroli has identified as the wish to "detach the legalistic aspects of scholastic rhetoric and emphasize the *variables* more than the invariant *norms* of the arts of speaking and writing" (7). By concentrating on the

---

[28]Radulphus Belvacensis as quoted by Gerald de Barri in Paetow, *Arts Course at Medieval Universities*, 27. In his own discussion of Gerald and of Henri d'Andeli's "Bataille des VII Ars," however, Paetow concluded that the heyday of law precipitated the "utter decline" of literary studies (18). Quotations from Andeli are from Paetow's edition of the *Battle of the Seven Arts*.

normative system of forensic oratory and its medieval continuations in the courtroom, in the disputational forum, and on the stage, I show that pro and contra argumentation became infused with a series of mimetic elements that supplied the foundation for new rhetorico-theatrical forms. In other words, though J. L. Styan once praised drama as the genre that "borrows from a dozen other arts ... [yet] owes allegiance to none," one art to which it initially owed great allegiance was rhetoric.[29]

The chapters that follow address four aspects of the generic interplay between legal and dramatic discourse: the "protodramas" of delivery and memory, the specific dramatic criteria involved in the shifting between ritual and representation, the medieval continuations of that phenomenon in the Basoche, and the literary evidence for the legal performance continuum supplied by medieval drama. In Chapter 1 I provide a historical overview of delivery as a form of mediation between mnemonic psychodrama and histrionic performance. In their treatments of *actio* and *memoria*, classical and medieval rhetoricians alike documented a pervasive confusion between oratory and acting which substantially blurred the distinction between delivered languages of equity and pleasure. Moreover, a rich mnemonic tradition of placing moving, personified images on veritable memory stages supplied the conceptual medium for dramatic invention; delivery provided the performative method. In particular, early revelations about the stunning advent of dramatic impersonation within the forensic tradition offer a scenario for the fluidity and confusion between legal and aesthetic discourses, between rhetoric and drama. That the modern *reader* of the extant written word has tended not to share that confusion is attributable in large part to the presence of what Plato and Seneca the Elder designated long ago as the "great gulf" between oral transmission and the static written transcription.[30] Therefore, even though an anonymous fifteenth-century commentator on a mystery play noted that "il n'est poinct en la possibilité d'homme vivant sur la terre le scavoyr si bien rediger par escript qu'il fut exécuté par *effect*" (it is not within

---

[29]Styan, *Drama, Stage, and Audience* (hereafter *DSA*), 5; see also Nicoll, *Theatre and Dramatic Theory* (hereafter *TADT*), 11–13.

[30]I explore this question at greater length in chap. 1. Here I refer to Plato's famous discussion of the myth of Thamus and the disadvantages of writing in *Phaedrus*, 274; and to the difference (*discrimen*) between oral and written discourse as described by Seneca the Elder in *Controversiae*, III, Preface, 3. See also Stock's analysis of such works as the *Nibelungenlied*, in which a "considerable distance" had arisen between oral performance and written record by the thirteenth century (*IOL*, 80); and Clanchy on "the spoken word in legal prose," in *FMWR*, 220–26.

the capacity of any man alive on earth to know how to commit it to writing as skillfully as it was performed in action), the restoration of *actio* to medieval literary studies helps us to bridge that gulf today.[31]

In addition to impersonation, classical and medieval forensic oratory was characterized by such traditional cornerstones of drama as theatrical space, costume, the agon, ritual participation by spectators, audience adaptation, and finally, pity, fear, and "imitation of an action."[32] In Chapter 2 I outline how those elements inspired a shift in oratorical focus to the most representational aspects of legal ritual. The study of delivery reveals that during the *letteraturizzazione* of rhetoric, orators focused increasingly on pleasing their audiences with the aesthetic performance of a juridical agon. Our understanding of early drama must thus take into account the fact that the legal "ordeal" was far more than a popular medieval theme: its discourse constituted an enduring dialogic structure whose ludic, conflictual features were analogous to those that had once spawned early Christian and pre-Christian *ludi*.[33] As a quintessential conflation of battle and play, forensic rhetoric was the site of a transformation from a conflictual rhetoric characterized by spectacular delivery to a delivered spectacle characterized by the rhetoric of conflict. Such an extraordinary ontological interplay between dramatic rhetoric and rhetorical drama renders forensic oratory not only a likely antecedent for the countless literary debates of the Middle Ages, but as viable a protodrama as the medieval Mass or the Dionysian liturgy.

Chapter 3 is devoted to the medieval version of that phenomenon in the theater of legal erudition of the Basoche. Analyzing the same dramatic components of staging, performance, audience, conflict, imitation, and impersonation, I argue that, rather than view the Basochiens as the "creators of French comedy," as Lucien Genty does (40), we must situate them along the continuum of the theatricalization of legal rhetoric. Finally, representative medieval plays and dialogues that bear the clear imprint of their rhetorical origins are examined in Chapter 4. Harking back to the quodlibet, the Ba-

[31]"Procès verbal" of the procession that preceded a Burgundian performance of the *Mistère St Martin* (12 October 1496). The text appears in Fournier, *Théâtre français avant la Renaissance*, 174. As I show in chap. 1, similar references abound in medieval commentaries on law, the quodlibet, and drama.

[32]I discuss these famous Aristotelian cornerstones of drama (*Poetics*, 1449b–50a) at greater length in chap. 2.

[33]See, e.g., Axton's discussion of the interplay between *ludi* and *luctae*, 33 (treated in my chap. 2).

soche, and the trial for the very structure of their plots, "serious" and "comic" plays alike continued to stage the forensic protodrama. Consequently, we are justified in bringing to dramatic forms as seemingly diverse as the *Pathelin* and the *Mystère de la Passion* one and the same hermeneutic of legal rhetoric.

In the final analysis, the generic modulations of legal dialogue into protodrama provide a fascinating testimonial to medieval *mouvance* on many levels. The power of delivery to mediate between histrionic performance and the more static written legal/ literary text occurs on both the generic and the institutional levels, offering important insights into how the conflictual language of a social institution such as law was transformed into the poetry of dramatic conflict. Inasmuch as these early conflictual discourses constitute performative phenomena, they promote a refinement not only of the very notion of "origins" of drama but of the complex interactions between oral and literate discourses which inform medieval literacy.

1 Dramatic Rhetoric and Rhetorical Drama

Orators and Actors

"To be sure," Lucian of Samosata wrote, "it professes in the main to be a science of imitation and portrayal, of revealing what is in the mind and making intelligible what is obscure."[1] We know (we think) what Lucian is talking about: language. But we are wrong. He is in fact describing mimicry, in which "there is display of mind in the performance as well as expression of bodily development" (69), and in which rhetoric plays an integral part. Lucian's subject was not language as we conceive it today but the gesticular language of the mime, who is "imitative and undertakes to present by means of movements" (62). Similarly, by creating the protagonist of "A Professor of Public Speaking," who taught how legal cases might be "acted" rather than argued, Lucian elevated the entire repertoire of rhetorical delivery to a new level of importance. His lawyer was an actor, fully conscious of how the actions, gestures, intonations, costumes, and props of delivery might sway not only judge and jury but onlookers as well. His law was the very rhetoric of spectacle Plato had condemned.

According to rhetorical theory and practice, law had always been a kind of microcosmic drama that was "staged" at the time of de-

[1] Lucian of Samosata, "Saltatio" (normally translated as "dance" or "pantomime"), 36. See also the excerpted translation of A. M. Nagler in *A Source Book in Theatrical History*, 28. Recent critical works on Lucian include Branham's *Unruly Eloquence* and Lauvergnat-Gagnière's *Lucien de Samosate*.

livery. Ever since Plato, the lawmaker was thought to be engaged in a theatrical enterprise: "We are composers [*poiētai*] of the same things as yourselves, rivals of yours as artists and actors of the fairest drama [*dramatos*], which, as our hope is, true law, and it alone, is by nature competent to complete."[2] Eventually, however, forensic delivery became so theatrical that law was more than similar to drama (which orators had been consistently encouraged to imitate): it was a protodrama characterized by conflict, spectacle, impersonation, staging, costume, and audience participation. And the orator's increased preoccupation with the conception, perception, and reception of legal "performance" nurtured new dramatic forms. Rhetorical scholars are familiar with the crucial interplay between legal ritual and dramatic representation of late antiquity, but the phenomenon has been little explored by their colleagues in literature, even though a similar interplay was paramount in the "origins" of drama in the liturgy. Even in his most general history of rhetoric, *A Synoptic History of Classical Rhetoric,* James J. Murphy observed that the antiphonal exchange of pro and contra replies in the Athenian law courts had helped to give rise to Greek drama (4–5). Once dramatic delivery has been reintegrated systematically into literary criticism, a revitalized view of the generic modulations between law and literature in the very "origins" of drama is possible.

It was a time-honored tenet of *actio* that, no matter how dialectically sound the proofs arranged by *dispositio,* no matter how brilliant the rhetorical style, no matter how carefully stored in memory the fruits of invention, any speech was powerless without delivery.[3] The voice was the "index of the mind [*mentis index*]" (Quintilian, XI, 3.62); and in their commentaries on delivery, classical and medieval theorists prescribed how that correspondence between speech and action was to take place in such precise social situations as adjudication. Kenneth Burke's observation that "the body is an actor ... [and] participates in the movements of the mind, posturing correspondingly" (*POLF,* 130) would have been accepted in the Middle Ages on a formal level. When Seneca the Elder wrote that speaking

[2]Plato, *Laws* 817B, as quoted in Eden, *PLF,* 29–30.

[3]For the traditional five-part division of rhetoric, see, e.g., [Cicero], *Ad C. Herennium,* I, 3; Quintilian, *Institutio oratoria,* III, 2.1–4; Cicero, *De inventione,* I, 9; Martianus Capella, *De nuptiis,* ed. Dick, 141g. A translated excerpt of Martianus appears in Miller, Prosser, and Benson, *Readings in Medieval Rhetoric.* Similarly, Alcuin noted that after the rhetorician had ordered (*dispositio*) and stylized (*elocutio*) materials discovered beforehand during *inventio,* "the last and highest [power is] to deliver what you have fixed in the memory": *Rhetoric of Alcuin and Charlemagne,* 81–82. See also Stock on law as performance or action, *IOL,* 44–53.

in the forum was "doing something" (*ago*), and when Geoffrey of Vinsauf later noted that "force issues from the tongue for death and life inhere in the hands of the tongue as long as it enjoys the double guide of face and gesture," both were stressing the dependence of meaning on delivery.[4] Indeed, according to Geoffrey, it was the "laws" of the voice that established a concordance between delivery and content: "The voice is as it were the image [*imago*] of the thing. . . . As the subject exhibits itself [*recitator*], so the speaker exhibits his voice" (ll. 2044–45). Persuasion, be it that of the barrister or of the dramatist, was not possible until rhetoric was delivered— and delivered effectively and dramatically—

> for the nature of the speech that we have composed within our minds is not so important as the manner in which we produce it, since the emotion of each member of our audience will depend on the impression made upon his hearing. Consequently, no proof . . . will ever be so secure as not to lose its force if the speaker fails to produce it in tones that drive it home. All emotional appeals will inevitably fall flat, unless they are given the fire that voice, look, and the whole carriage of the body can give them. [Quintilian, XI, 3.2]

That is a tremendous statement, overwhelming with critical implications to be explored as readily from a dramatic perspective as from a moral one. Philologically, of course, *actio, pronuntiatio,* and especially *hypokrisis* implied impersonation and counterfeit, *hypokrisis* referring to the theatrical register of "acting" (*hypocritike*).[5] As "physical eloquence" or "styled action" (Quintilian, XI, 3.1), delivery provided the oral and visual contexts in which linguistic meaning was shaped. Since signification was considered incomplete without its interpretive histrionics, *actio* was far more than an ancillary device that could enhance verbal artistry, more than the post hoc pronunciation of a preconceived legal or literary verbal structure: it was a veritable semiotic system that communicated through the performance of linguistic signs. According to the pseudo-Ciceronian author of the widely circulated *Rhetorica ad Herennium*, such features as soft intonations, pauses, and proper breathing were

---

[4]Seneca, *Controversiae*, III, Preface, 3.12; Geoffrey of Vinsauf, *Poetria nova*, trans. Gallo, ll. 2060–64. I cite Gallo's bilingual edition (by line number), though Kopp's translation, "The New Poetics (*Poetria nova*)," is also excellent. The standard edition of Geoffrey is Faral's *Arts poétiques* (194–262). See also Cicero, *De oratore*, III, 220–23.

[5]See also Lanham's definition: "exaggerating an opponent's gestures or speech habits in order to mock him": *Handlist*, 57.

mutually interdependent with meaning, as were style and gesture (III, 22). Or as one less noble proponent of the language of gesture, Chaucer's Pardoner, once put it, "Myne handes and my tonge goon so yerne / That it is joye to se my bisynesse."[6]

On the strength of delivery, the power of words could be superseded by the power of dramatic interpretation, whatever the intended context. During performance the speaker could satirize the serious or magnify the absurd through the remarkable ability to transmute context. He could reshape the moral thrust of legal proof into a dedication to legal spectacle. Indeed, as Lucian's Professor explained, if the orator had "a very loud voice, a shameless singing delivery," and an attractive gait like his, those qualities were "sometimes sufficient in themselves" ("Professor of Public Speaking," 15). In oral rhetorical performance, where logic was necessarily linear, the intonations, gestures, costumes, colors, actions—the "dramatization" of the oration—were perceived before any other "message." Delivery thus imposed on the spoken word interpretations that were more readily perceptible than the logic of the deductive syllogism or inductive example (which necessarily progressed through chronological time):[7] it actually persuaded *before proof*, the ethical core of rhetoric. Drama is characterized by an analogous situation, in which the spectator, as Styan notes, "scarcely reasons the relationship between king and beggar before he senses it in voice, posture, costume and the physical bond between them" (*DSA*, 4).

It follows, then, that any scholarly author exposed to the rhetorical tradition, or any popular author who appreciated the practical importance of performance, might have sought to exploit the interdependence of speech and action within the social context of his own literary effort. Drama especially has traditionally exploited a complex language of performance which assaults at the level of "clothes and paint and noise [and] bombards its audience with a hundred simultaneous capsules of information" (*DSA*, 4). And part of that "bombardment"—the realistic details provided by costume, gesture, movements, and attitudes—has already helped to establish the theatricality of the medieval liturgy. Synonymous with those

[6] Chaucer, *Canterbury Tales*, in *Riverside Chaucer*, ed. Benson, Fragment VI [C], 398–99.
    [7] Though the classical rhetorician habitually reduced the complexities of the dialectician's syllogisms to the abbreviated enthymeme or the epicheireme, his logic was nonetheless linear. See, e.g., Fulbert of Chartres on how the dialectician "reduces the argument to perfect syllogisms, while the other [the rhetorician] is satisfied with less rigorously formulated enthymemes": ("Rithmus de distantia dialectice et rethoricae," in *Letters and Poems*, ed. Behrends, 267.

descriptions, however, are the commentaries provided by the rhetorical canon of delivery. So, while scholars tend to agree that a
critical apparatus based on the linear logic of cause and effect cannot
help the critic to cope with the assault of performance, the rhetorical
apparatus enables us to cope very well indeed. Since delivery supplies
considerable information about the nature, circumstances, and material trappings of histrionic performance, it is in that performative
context that the similarities of rhetoric and drama may be most fully
understood.

One of the first benefits of the reintegration of delivery into literary studies is the discovery of a vast series of critical commentaries
on the generic fluidity between rhetoric and drama—a fluidity that
is articulated most completely in the consistent analogy between
orators and actors in treatments of delivery. Paramount to the successful careers of advocates and actors alike, delivery lay at the crux
of both rhetoric and drama and often rendered distinctions between
the two discourses elusive. Rhetoricians had long compared their
activity to drama, measuring the efficacy of their own delivery
against that of the dramatic actor. Cicero, for example, insisted that
actors were to be studied as role models or "patterns" for delivery
(*De oratore*, I, 156); and Quintilian formalized the similarity between rhetoric and drama by focusing on performance: "The comic
actor will also claim a certain amount of our attention, but only in
so far as our future orator must be a master of the art of delivery"
(I, 11.2). Eventually, however, the relationship between orators and
actors became more than one of simile. Orators were more than
likened to actors: during delivery, the two types of performers were
deemed one and the same. When Tacitus remarked that the orator
"must have what I may call his stage" (oratori autem clamore plau-
suque opus est, et velut quodam *theatro*),[8] he underscored the emergence of a veritable generic confusion between actor and rhetorician
during performance. Quintilian even went so far as to describe the
entire rhetorical process in dramatic terms: "It is at the close of our
drama that we must really stir the theatre [*tunc est commovendum
theatrum*], when we have reached the place for the phrase with
which the old tragedies and comedies used to end, 'Friends, give us
your applause' " (VI, 1.52). It was no coincidence that Aristotle
deemed delivery an art "of the greatest importance," arguing that
when it "comes into fashion, it will have the same effect as acting"
(*Rhetoric*, 1404a). His consistent exploitation of examples from the

[8]Tacitus, *Dialogus de oratoribus*, 32.

theater to illustrate the techniques of the *Rhetoric* suggests a conscious linkage of rhetoric and drama—one that occurs with such frequency that it is appropriate to interpret it as a literal testimonial to the drama of rhetoric.[9]

Still, many theorists expressed discomfort with both the literary and the moral ramifications of the equation of rhetoric and drama. From the standpoint of literary genre, classical and medieval theorists had difficulty setting up and maintaining heuristic barriers between oratory and acting because they recognized that if delivery were to be effective, it had to be histrionic or, at the very least, dramatic. If they consistently asserted the importance of "physical eloquence" (Quintilian, XI, 3.2), they also betrayed their uneasiness with the resemblance of orators to actors, struggling with nuances and degrees of the dramatic in order to maintain divisions that appeared increasingly artificial. Despite his praise of the delivery of Cassius Severus, for example, Seneca found it necessary to specify that it was a delivery that "would have made any actor's reputation, without being at all reminiscent of an actor's" (III, Preface, 3). Similarly, the failure of the *Ad Herennium* author to distinguish between "conspicuous" and "inconspicuous" gestures implies that, in reality, he was unable to determine where oratory ended and drama began: "The gestures should not be conspicuous for either elegance or grossness, lest we give the impression that we are either actors [*histriones*] or day labourers" (III, 26). There was a fine line that was not to be crossed, as when one used the "dignified conversational tone": the orator was to "use the full throat but the calmest and most subdued voice possible, yet not in such a fashion that we pass from the practice of the orator to that of the tragedian" (III, 24).

Still, while Tacitus advised that "the orator ought to avoid discreditable and senseless buffoonery" (22), it was hard to draw the line between drama and oratory "where the battles of the courts [*pugna forensi*] are concerned": "It is most unbecoming for an orator to distort his features or use uncouth gestures, tricks that arouse such merriment in farce [*in mimis*]. No less unbecoming are ribald jests, and such as are employed upon the stage [Dicacitas etiam scurrilis et scenica huic personae alienissima est]" (Quintilian, VI, 3.29). For during delivery the would-be orator had learned to draw upon what may well have been the purest contemporaneous elaboration of the language of gesture: the art of mimicry.

---

[9]For a particularly insightful discussion of the *Rhetoric*, see Arnold, "Oral Rhetoric," 160; and Eden, *PLF*, 4–5.

In classical antiquity, rhetoric was conceived dramatically and mimicry rhetorically: the one art was employed to enrich, explain, and justify the other, as when Lucian collapsed visual and verbal languages in a discussion of "acting" skills: "The chief occupation and the aim of dancing, as I have said, is impersonating [*hypokrisis*], which is cultivated in the same way by the rhetoricians, particularly those who recite these pieces that they call 'exercises'; for in their case also there is nothing which we commend more highly than their accommodating themselves to the rôles which they assume" ("Saltatio," 65). By looking toward *scurrili* and *mimi* as models for perfecting the significative powers of his own language of gesture, the orator was, in fact, cultivating the very generic confusion that encouraged dramatic representation. Just as Quintilian and Cicero had advocated the study of actors, Lucian advised the mime to study the orator: "From rhetoric, however, she [mimicry] has not held aloof, but has her part in that too, inasmuch as she is given to depicting character and emotion, of which the orators also are fond" (35). The divisions between rhetoric and drama appeared all the more arbitrary and the discomfort of the classical theorist all the greater because, just as rhetoric had encroached on the province of mimicry, mimicry had encroached on that of rhetoric. Indeed, a similar phenomenon in the Middle Ages led to the fascinating refusal to allow *histriones* and *scurrae* the privilege of pleading in court.[10] Given the spectacular turn taken by oratory in the courtroom, the schoolroom, and later the Basoche, it is tempting to conclude that histrionic lawyers quite simply would not have appreciated the competition from the *histriones*.

Rhetoric and mimicry were easily paired insofar as both were believed to elicit audience response through the manipulation of logic, emotion, semantics, and verisimilitude.[11] The mime of antiquity might well have dispensed with the subtleties of dialectic as "inappropriate" ("Saltatio," 35), but he respected his verbose colleagues for their ability to convey complex material through effective nonlinguistic signs. He was no mere clown; quite to the contrary, he was a "manual philosopher"[12] who was to be "retentive of memory, gifted, intelligent, keenly inventive, and above all suc-

[10]See Chambers's discussion of the *Benedictus levita*, a "somewhat dubious collection" that may date from the reign of Louis the Pious: *Mediaeval Stage*, 1:37–38.

[11]Nagler employs those very terms in his translation of "Saltatio," 65, in *Source Book*, 29. So do Weisberg and Barricelli in "Literature and Law," 150.

[12]"Manual philosopher" is Nagler's translation (*Source Book*, 29) of "Saltatio," 69, rendered as "handiwise" in the Loeb edition.

cessful in doing the right thing at the right time" (74). Once that
view is compared with the "decline" of eloquence, the generic interplay between "decadent" rhetoric and "cultured" mimicry (81),
between the drama of rhetoric and the rhetoric of drama, is all the
more apparent. Tacitus, for example, claimed that orators "make it
their aim, by wantonness of language, by shallow pated conceits,
and by irregular arrangement, to produce the rhythms of stage-
dancing; and whereas they ought to be ashamed even to have such
a thing said by others, many of them actually boast that their
speeches can be sung and danced to" (26).

But what Tacitus considered to be an ignoble rhetorical goal be-
longed more properly to mimicry—an art whose prerequisites, Lucian tells us, included the ability to "judge poetry, to select the best
songs and melodies, and to reject worthless compositions" ("Saltatio," 74).[13] Thanks to the "singing" deliveries and "intoning" exemplified in Lucian's "Professor of Public Speaking," orators had
glorified delivery to such an extent that they had made actors their
objects of imitation and mimicry the sister art of rhetoric. That
Tacitus judged the rise of such rhetorical histrionics negatively is
self-evident; but there can be no doubt as to the popularity of the
behavior he described. By the first century, the phenomenon had
become common enough to be epigrammatic: "At Rome 'orators
speak voluptuously and actors dance eloquently' " (ut oratores nostri
tenere dicere, histriones diserte saltare dicantur [Tacitus, 26]). What
he bewailed as so "shameful and so wrong-headed but yet so common" (26) was yet so crucial to the study of the origins of drama.
For the "decline" of eloquence was actually the advent of something
else—of new dramatic forms for late antiquity and, eventually, for
the Middle Ages.

Be that as it may, despite many recent advances in theories of
medieval drama, the entire period from the fifth through the twelfth
centuries still tends to be considered something of a dramatic waste-
land. Mimicry, minstrelsy, and spectacle are often deemed "intru-
sions" into drama by the very critics who acknowledge their
importance in the origins of that genre. Even Karl Young noted with
regret that the influence of farce and pantomime in the early years
of the Roman empire had caused drama to "yield ground in popular

---

[13]In "Visions with Voices," 48–50, I argue the rich performative similarities between music, rhetoric, and drama as compared to *puys* and poetic contests. For the
interrelations of grammar and music, see esp. Treitler, "Reading and Singing," and
John Stevens, *Words and Music*, 372–86.

estimation before theatrical entertainments of a lower order."[14] Similarly, Allardyce Nicoll acknowledged somewhat grudgingly that if there were "any dramatic continuity between the world of the Greek and Roman temples and the world dominated by the fantastic imagination of the Gothic cathedral, we must look for it in the pitiful and despised gesturings of the mimes" (*WD*, 99). He was correct in letter but not in spirit.[15] An extraordinary dramatic continuity does indeed inhere in those gesturings, but there was nothing despicable about them. Spectators of both courtroom and stage apparently relished them, even though gesture was often deemed problematic from a moral standpoint.

Yet are we really to believe that throughout the "Dark Ages" of drama, when elephants, chariots, and giraffes innumerable tramped across the stage, as at the grand opening of the theater of Pompey in 55 B.C., and spectators boisterously crossed the tenuous border that separated them from the fictive "play," drama was "ruined" by the "passion for spectacle" (*WD*, 95)? During the entire period from 400 to 1050 (which Murphy has more aptly termed the "Age of Transition" [*RIMA*, 43]), was the theater really dead until it sprang newly born from the liturgy? The interrelations of rhetoric, drama, law, and mimicry suggest that the answer to those questions must be negative. Instead of maintaining, with Young, the imperviousness of liturgical drama to the "contamination of alien forms" (1:1), we might wish to reconsider the unquestionable influence of a tradition that was not, in fact, alien—the rhetorical tradition. Inasmuch as its gesticular art of delivery had consistently nurtured the fusion of ritual and spectacle, we might abandon the concept of intrusion for that of interplay. We know, moreover, that both lawyers and mimes required the "high standard of culture" outlined by Lucian, so the view that histrionics was at the bottom of the aesthetic scale is not

<hr />

[14]Young, *Drama of the Medieval Church*, 1:9.

[15]Similar remarks include Petit de Julleville's complaint that the medieval author neglected plot in order to "spread out a huge spectacle before the eyes": *Les Mystères* (hereafter *LM*), 10; Cargill's that "histrionic representation" within the liturgy caused a "further degradation of the ritual by acting": *Drama and Liturgy*, 42; Baty and Chavance's that acrobats, jugglers, magicians, and gladiators caused theater to "sink into disgust": *Vie de l'art théâtral*, 68; and Dubech, Montbrial, and Horn-Monval's characterization of early drama as "nothingness" in a "barbarian night": *Histoire générale illustrée du théâtre*, 20. In general, critics have been more receptive to the influence of mimicry in popular dramatic forms. See, e.g., Axton, *European Drama*, 17–32; Nicoll, *Masks, Mimes, and Miracles*, 135–68. My intention here is not to contest the status of mimicry as an independent origin of drama but rather to show that its conventions were nurtured and perpetuated by rhetorical delivery.

borne out by the evidence of performance. Rather, performance suggests that drama remained a dominant force even during the so-
called decadence of the theater, thanks to the *letteraturizzazione* of
forensic rhetoric.

Longinus had once cautioned that "romantic exaggeration" had
no place in oratory insofar as it caused rhetoric to exceed "the limits
of credibility, whereas the most perfect effect of imagination in
oratory is always one of reality and truth."[16] Yet excessive flights
of the oratorical imagination had become the very stuff of delivery.
As I show at greater length in Chapter 2, the most "perfect effect"
of oratory was no longer the revelation of truth but the elicitation
of pleasure during the representation of truth. By means of delivery,
rhetoric had surpassed its proper limitations, functioning simultaneously as a social institution and a form of entertainment that
sought to "win success" and to "charm" (*volputatem audientium
petere* [Quintilian, V, Preface, 1]). Though Quintilian deemed the
phenomenon "hardly worthy of a self-respecting man," he was
forced to acknowledge that moral, didactic ends had been transformed into mimetic ones, and that orators had become the "slaves
of applause": "Our modern orators...imagine that their art is
wasted unless it obtrudes itself....We are the slaves of applause
[*pendemus ex laude*] and think it the goal of all our effort. And so
we betray to the judges what we wish to display to the bystanders
[ita, quae circumstantibus ostentare volumus, iudicibus prodimus]"
(IV.2.127).

Referring to the legend that Euripedes had Furies before his eyes
during the composition of the *Orestes*, Longinus once wrote that
"our wonderful modern orators...are like so many tragedians in
seeing Furies" (15.8). Orations in which they imitated literary techniques had "a strange, outlandish air, when the texture of the speech
is poetical and romantic and deviates into all sorts of impossibilities"
(15.8). Such histrionic "deviations" of delivery may well have constituted a corruption of the generic integrity of rhetoric, but it was
a corruption that left foundations for changing aesthetic principles
of genre in its wake. A renewed concentration on delivery as a dynamic oral tradition reveals that the most logical "impossibilities"
into which oratory "deviated" were classical and medieval drama.

By cultivating a histrionic delivery, orators helped to provoke an
instability in the end, the object of imitation, and the reception of
rhetoric, collapsing during performance the ancient Aristotelian dis-

[16]Longinus, "On the Sublime," 15.8.

tinction between "the mimetic status of drama and the non-mimetic status of rhetoric" (*PRL*, 49). As Cicero had observed, orators were indeed the "players that act real life" (*De oratore*, III, 215). Like actors, they were masters of delivery on a stage of their own—often so masterly as to rival their thespian colleagues. The zeal with which they pursued that rivalry was responsible to a large degree for a certain fusion of oratory and acting—a problem whose insolubility promises to lead right to the continued development of drama from rhetorical delivery.

Still, accompanying audience delight with those generic "deviations" was an attendant moral deviation: ever since Plato, the potential of spectacle to compromise the moral integrity of rhetoric had been problematic. Because of its extraordinary power in drama, delivery was considered all the more powerful in rhetoric, where subjects were ostensibly not "fictitious." Though tragic plot and rhetorical proof both relied heavily on probability to sway their audiences (*PLF*, 36–38), rhetorical proof was believed to be easier to dramatize because of its greater verisimilitude. Quintilian argued, for example, that if effective delivery rendered dramatic "fictions" believable and moving, then its service to the truth in rhetoric should have been all the more impressive—so much so that he seconded Demosthenes in granting the palm to delivery: "Now if delivery can count for so much in themes which we know to be fictitious and devoid of reality... how much greater must its effect be when we actually believe what we hear...? We are therefore almost justified in concluding that he [Demosthenes] regarded it not merely as the first, but as the only virtue of oratory" (XI, 3.6).

A fascinating articulation of the generic fluidity between rhetoric and drama, Quintilian's statement is nonetheless problematic from an ethical standpoint. If the analogy between rhetoric and drama led certain theorists to conclude that delivery was the essence of communication, it followed that that canon was detachable from any intrinsic moral orientation: delivery served fiction as readily as nonfiction, the true as readily as the false (the classical definition of sophistry). Even though Aristotle had conceived tragedy as a form of ethical imitation (*Poetics*, 1449b), and even though Plato described his lawyers as the "authors of a tragedy (*tragōidias*) at once superlatively fair and good" (*Laws*, 817B), the morality of delivery would spark lively debate throughout antiquity and the Middle Ages, especially for Christian rhetoricians. As the performative equivalent of sophistry, dramatic delivery appeared to upset the delicate balance between rhetoric and truth which had been achieved by Aristotle and to reconfirm rhetoric's independence of ethics. The gifted orator, though not always a sophist, was always an actor.

And just as actors could secure a hearing even for "the most worthless authors" and "repeatedly win a welcome on the stage that is denied them in the library" (Quintilian, XI, 3.4), rhetoricians could win a hearing for the most worthless legal case—that is, if they delivered their arguments cleverly enough. In law, the centrality of delivery privileged the *appearance* of legal equity over its ethical substance—the same phenomenon that had once led Plato to subsume rhetoric under the more noble philosophical form of dialectic in the *Phaedrus* (268–69). Augustine, as outraged as Plato, attempted to curb the independent power of delivery by housing rhetoric in the church, transforming a civic into a Christian function and recasting the church as the ultimate juridical authority.[17] Similarly, in his twelfth-century *Compendium on the Art of Preaching*, Alanus de Insulis proposed a Christian recontextualization of forensic rhetoric when he exhorted wayward lawyers to practice their art as a divine ministration: "To supply a defense for the downtrodden in a trial is the same as to visit the prisoner in his cell ... it is feeding the hungry, giving drink to the thirsty. ... So the orator who offers counsel to a needy client in a just cause truly performs all the works of mercy. Orator, why do you fail to defend widows in their need?" (239). A linguistic version of good works, legal discourse was to reflect acts of Christian mediation between God and humankind.

Because of such lofty moral imperatives, however, Christian rhetoricians deplored the dependence of ethical content on a dramatic delivery that had no intrinsic moral identity. Such a rhetoric had long departed from its initial power to "tame" the pugnacious instincts of the first inhabitants of the earth. Cicero, for example, had theorized that a wise, persuasive, and pleasurable language had once served "the highest interests of mankind" as it propagated justice in a civilized society: "Certainly only a speech at the same time powerful and entrancing could have induced one who had great physical strength to submit to justice without violence. ... This was the way in which at first eloquence came into being and advanced to greater development." (*De inventione*, I, 3–4; see also *De oratore*, I, 30–35). For that very reason, Alcuin ennobled rhetoric in the eighth century, arguing in his dialogue with Charlemagne that civilization was born when the first eloquent man discovered in rhetoric a lin-

---

[17]See, e.g., Vance on Augustine's recontextualization of forensic rhetoric in his *Confessions: Mervelous Signals*, chap. 1.

guistic means of mediating conflict. Had rhetoric failed to be accompanied by wisdom, or had wisdom been "endowed but weakly with the gift of speech, [it] would not have been able suddenly to turn men against their previous habits, and bring them to the diverse pursuits of civilized life" (48–51). The fellow brutes eventually succumbed to the power of language and were civilized by it, "made gentle and mild from being savage and brutal" (47–48).

In light of their remarks, it is interesting to reconsider Howard Bloch's argument that such genres as lyric and epic proffered "as a cultural ideal the containment of violent impulses within the bounds of language itself" (*MFLL*, 189). Similarly, Adolphe Fabre posited a correlation in the Middle Ages between the increase in litigation and the decrease in the more violent modes of divination of a feudal system in decline—"the suppression of the ordeal, of judicial duels, of trials by fire, hot iron, or boiling water, etc." (*CP* [1875], ix). Traditionally, however, that mediatory function had been codified in theories of forensic rhetoric itself. If the dialogic patterns of vernacular lyric bespoke the "substitution of a socially sanctioned verbal ordeal for a more immediate and physical one," as Bloch maintains (176–77), then so did the disputational forensic model.

Be that as it may, the power of delivery was such that it could transmute even such a noble, "civilizing" goal. Even Augustine, while attempting to reconcile rhetoric and truth, was unable to deny the power of performance in Christian rhetoric. In an intriguing passage in the *De doctrina christiana* he implies that logical proof needs to be buttressed by written authority if it is to triumph over pleasurable oral language. Not only does Augustine attempt to imbue delivery with Christian morality; he admits a written eloquence that would prevent an inappropriate delivery from usurping a "true," ethical rhetoric:

> He shall give delight with his proofs when he cannot give delight with his own words. Indeed, he who wishes to speak not only wisely but also eloquently, since he can be of more worth if he can do both, should more eagerly engage in reading or hearing the works of the eloquent.... But those to be read or heard should be those truly recommended not only for their eloquence but also for the fact that they have written or spoken wisely.[18]

Alcuin too attempted to confine delivery to a Christian context of moral excellence, only to find himself obliged to reiterate the

[18]Augustine, *On Christian Doctrine*, IV, 5.8.

classical notion that rhetoric was ineffective without the power of delivery to fuse style, content, and performance. By redefining delivery as the "attaining of excellence in words" (1092–93) and the "regulating of the voice and body according to the dignity of thought and word" (77–79), Alcuin endeavored to change the context of performance; but he could not change performance practice. Delivery may have come to be subject (in theory) to a loftier moral excellence that made it possible to identify "inappropriate pronunciation." But as long as it maintained its power to transform the Christian ethos through histrionic performance, it could remain the heart and soul of oratory, whatever its moral and generic divagations. Like many of his predecessors, Alcuin was forced to grant the palm to delivery, the "last and highest" stage of rhetoric (81–82), whose power "surpasses the other powers of the speaker to such a degree that, in the opinion of the peerless Tully, a speech devoid of skill may nevertheless achieve merit by virtue of a speaker's excellence in Delivery, while on the other hand a speech excellent beyond description may meet contempt and mockery if it is pronounced inappropriately" (1093–98).[19]

It is no coincidence, then, that rhetoric and drama share a history of turbulent debate as to their value in society. Lucian's parody of the degeneration of the noble political goals of legal oratory under the influence of delivery may be likened to Tertullian's famous condemnation of the degeneration of religion under the influence of spectacle.[20] But where Tertullian would attempt to curb the power of spectacle by banning drama completely, Saint Augustine and his medieval followers attempted to recontextualize rhetoric, not abandon it.

If a Christian view had emerged according to which only certain kinds of speeches and actions were morally permissible, the concordance between rhetorical discourse and performance, between speech and action, remained the same. Dramatic delivery shaped meaning, often in ways deemed inappropriate; yet in classical and medieval rhetoric, interpretation remained impossible without it. Inasmuch as it remained paramount to secular and Christian rhetorics alike, delivery thus lends a certain continuity to the rhetorico-literary production of both antiquity and the Middle Ages. The

[19]Of course, not all theorists gave the palm to delivery. Martianus, for example, acknowledged its importance but considered invention more powerful: *De nuptiis*, 141g.

[20]In his *De spectaculis*, Tertullian (95–96) attempted to ban drama entirely. See also Isidore of Seville, *Isidori Hispalensis Episcopi Etymologiarum [Etymologies]*, 59.

Christian discomfort with the commingling of speech, action, and signification during oral performance could not be eased precisely because delivery could still be deployed to lend credence to any argument, whatever its intrinsic moral value. And that moral stalemate derives in part from the fact that persuasion was ultimately more firmly entrenched in dramatic performance practice than in any subsequent attempt to rationalize the morality of performance.

How is it, then, that modern critics have not shared the discomfort of the classical theorists? Even though we have come to appreciate the phenomenon of medieval generic fluidity, we seem far less appreciative when that fluidity encompasses such disciplines as rhetoric, which are not normally considered "literary." As recently as 1985, Frederic Kenyon's view that declamation had an insalubrious influence on literature was echoed by Marvin Carlson, who noted of Averroës's Aristotelian commentaries that "the replacement of spectacle [in the *Poetics*] by deliberation (*consideratio*) shows clearly how far Averroës was from a theatrical concept of tragedy."[21] But there can be little doubt that during its *letteraturizzazione*, rhetoric *was* spectacle. Indeed, as eminent a scholar as Allardyce Nicoll once sliced the hermeneutic circle of rhetoric and drama, producing a convenient but ideologically dissonant cleavage between the two disciplines according to which "the enduring theatre is educative ...not in the manner of the reasoning lecturer or of the political orator; it is educative only in the sense that it arouses our interests and stimulates our imagination" (*WD* [1949], 940). It is the study of delivery that demonstrates that imagination was as crucial to rhetoric as it was to drama. The "perfectionist" who enters the hermeneutic circle of rhetoric and drama may well feel like a blind man "feeling around the elephant of medieval literature," as Paul Theiner says, with no "omniscient narrator to tell us that the elephant is really there;" but the circle is nonetheless "hospitable to entry" and rhetoric is clearly no white elephant.[22] We might thus prefer the access offered by the most hospitable entry of all: delivery.

Ultimately, the modern dichotomy between rhetoric and drama may be explained less by something gained through centuries of civilization than by something lost; namely, the latent theatricality of oral delivery. It is well known, for example, that Aristotle gave short shrift to spectacle and song in his discussion of tragedy, where he states that "spectacle, while highly effective, is yet quite foreign

---

[21] See Kenyon, *Books and Readers*, 85; and Carlson, *Theories of the Theatre*, 33.
[22] Theiner, "Medieval English Literature," 240.

to the art and has nothing to do with poetry. Indeed the effect of tragedy does not depend on its performance by actors, and, moreover, for achieving the spectacular effects the art of the costumier is more authoritative than that of the poet" (*Poetics*, 1450b).

But even if the power of tragedy was indeed independent of performance, that of forensic rhetoric clearly was not. And even Aristotle could not deny the paramountcy of spoken language as a medium of poetic imitation. Just as songmaking and diction—the tragic "means of representation"—produced "spectacular effect," so did delivery in forensic oratory, where the representation of action was acted by living persons and "by means of language enriched with all kinds of ornament" (*Poetics*, 1449b). The persistent testimonials to the "exceptionally great usefulness" of delivery (*Ad Herennium*, III, 19) underscore the necessity of restoring *actio* to our readings of any extant literary texts that might have been performed.

Today the fundamental question, then, is: If delivery was in fact so influential in the process of signification, how may we read for it today? More to the point, how may we "hear" rhetoric—and specifically the literary rhetoric of drama—as it was delivered? Any effort to read for delivery must be accompanied by several caveats, one of which was proffered by Lucian's prolix Professor: we should not be obsessed by the printed word, for "orators are beyond all that!" (14). As Seneca noted emphatically in the tradition of Plato himself, there was a "great gulf" between oral performance and written record. Rhetoric performed was not rhetoric transcribed, and it was the absence of dramatic delivery on the page that produced that gulf: "It is impossible to judge him [Cassius Severus] from his publications, though even there one may sense his eloquence; he was far greater heard than read. It happens to almost all people that they gain from being heard rather than read, but to a smaller degree: in him there was a vastly greater gulf [*maius discrimen*]" (III, Preface, 3).

The existence of a gulf or distinction between oral performance and written record is, of course, one of the most readily apparent similarities between forensic rhetoric and drama. Critics generally agree that a play is "a code of words" (*DSA*, 6) and that that code is "*written*, not primarily for reading, but for histrionic interpretation before an assembled body of spectators" (*WD* [1949], 936; emphasis mine). Therefore, in the same way that our appreciation of the theatrical experience is flawed when it is based exclusively on a "reading," our appreciation of the rhetorical experience is flawed when we permit the original vivacity of delivery to be overshadowed by the deceptive stability of the written word. The exclusion of rhetoric as a possible origin of drama may thus derive in part from an adherence to a postmedieval aesthetic that privileges the textual artifact of a "script" that never adequately transcribes the actual dramatic experience. That state of affairs, endemic in both rhetoric and drama, may be remedied by recourse to the code that described the functions of language within oral cultures: rhetorical delivery.

In each of the rhetorical and rhetorico-dramatic forms to be investigated here—in classical and medieval legal rhetoric, in the productions of the Basoche, and in selected plays and dialogues of medieval France—delivery helps to bridge a sort of modern-day *discrimen* between a comparatively lifeless written record and an initial, dynamic oral performance. To investigate how spoken forensic rhetoric differed from the dry, telegraphic style of extant records is to investigate the gulf between dynamic oral performance and written record. And to reconstitute the interaction between those two forms is to investigate delivery.

The *Actio* of Reading

Ever since Plato's celebrated reference to written speech as but the "image" of oral discourse in the *Phaedrus* (276a), it has been a precept of rhetorical theory that speeches "lend themselves to acting."[23] What was effectively conveyed through spoken language often was opaque in written renderings, no matter how accurate the transcription. So it was that Aristotle recalled that the speech as performed contained many dramatic touches that appeared "silly" when written down. Such devices as "asyndeta and frequent repetition of the same word" were "rightly disapproved in written speech" precisely because their dramatic effect was experienced not during reading but during performance. Speeches committed to writing in which "delivery is absent do not fulfil their proper function" (1413b). Similarly, Quintilian insisted that the genius of Ciceronian style had been "frozen" (*frigere*) by written records and rendered invisible. Observing that the majority of readers considered transcribed orations to be "lacking in distinction," he admonished them

_____

[23]Aristotle, *Rhetoric*, 1413b. See Arnold's insightful discussion of that passage in "Oral Rhetoric," 160. In heading this section as I have, I mean no disrespect to Wolfgang Iser's influential work in reader-response criticism in *Act of Reading*. Rather, I wish to underscore the fundamental differences between reading silently and reading aloud in the aesthetic responses he describes.

to be aware of "how the art which is scarce detected by a reader succeeded in hoodwinking the judge" (IV, 2.59). Clearly, something was missing in the written transcription, and its absence contributed to the widening of the gulf between what a reader read and how the orator had said it in a performance unique to him. What emerges in rhetorical theory is that that something was the drama of delivery. Written discourse was "dead" because of the inevitable absence of the dramatic conditions of performance. If we are to approach written records of spoken language, it is crucial to bear in mind that what we see is not what they saw and heard.

In classical antiquity and in the Middle Ages, reading entailed actual "physical exertion, demanding the use not only of the eyes, but of tongue, mouth and throat" (*FMWR*, 217). Writing itself, recalled Istvan Hajnal, was "inseparable" from oratory, and was granted great respect because it revealed "proof of a solid oral training."[24] Moreover, if the "gulf" between oral and written existed at a time when the act of reading was literally an "act" of reading, then the need for reconstruction is all the greater today, when that act conjures visions of a solitary figure reading in silence. Even after the rise of a print culture, the rhetorical tradition itself would have ensured the orality of reading. And it is significant that even when the "reading" of a text was a performance, when speech was more formal than it usually is today and was not so sharply differentiated in form from reading, writing, and composition, the gulf persisted. Lucian's Professor, for example, counseled the extreme solution of ignoring writing completely: since the lawyer's "extemporary readiness" both excused error and procured admiration, he advised that "you never write anything out or appear in public with a prepared speech" ("Professor of Public Speaking," 20). Keenly aware that "the voice adds a force of its own to the matter of which it speaks, while

---

[24]Hajnal, *L'Enseignement de l'écriture,* as translated in McLuhan, *Gutenberg Galaxy,* 94. According to Clanchy, Latin works were "generally intended to be read aloud—hence the speeches and frequent use of dramatic dialogue in monastic chronicles": *FMWR,* 216. See also Steiner's discussion in *Language and Silence,* 251–57; Stock on the changing interrelations between oral and written discourse in the Middle Ages: *IOL,* chap. 1; Peter France on the tendency of rhetoric "to blur the distinction between the written and spoken word": *Rhetoric and Truth,* 18; Clanchy on Eadmer's characterization of his *Life of St. Anselm* as *oratio*: *FMWR,* 216; Crosby on Bede's direct address to both readers and hearers (*auditor sive lector*): "Oral Delivery," 90; Kennedy, "Forms and Functions of Latin Speech"; and Saenger, "Silent Reading." Denise Troll has delivered several unpublished papers on this subject: "Role of Monastic Silence," and "Monastic Silence and Sign Language," and "Role of Medieval Manuscript Technology." Of course, Derrida explored the entire subject of logocentrism from a modern perspective in *De la grammatologie,* esp. 149–202.

gesture and motion are full of significance [*gestus motusque signi-ficet aliquid*]" (Quintilian, XI, 3.9), theorists consistently urged readers to bridge that gulf. And if we heed their advice today, our reward is a new understanding of the interdependence of orality and literacy. For if we accept Stock's view that after the year 1000 there arose "a new type of interdependence" between oral and literate discourses, with the former beginning to "function within a universe of communications governed by texts" (*IOL*, 3), it is the study of delivery that allows us to reconstruct the channels between those two universes.

What is the case for rhetoric in general is especially so for the forensic genre. Transcribers had long committed accounts of trials to writing, but in a form that invariably imposed a new order upon the original oral pleadings. On the one hand, rhetoricians described legal delivery as a dramatic spectacle; on the other hand, official legal records reduced that spectacle to the bare bones of the logic deployed during the proceedings. The task of the medieval clerkly recorder of spoken depositions was to "extract the entire substance" in a consciously reductive written version that was "skilfully edited so as to make clear the legal points involved." In such official documents as the *Brevia placitata* and *Casus placitorum* "there is no discursiveness or repetition, for the dialogue immediately, and without preliminaries, goes straight to the legal point."[25] Indeed, training in those very practices had been canonized by early literary authority, as when Quintilian reminded future rhetoricians that by providing summaries they were "following the method adopted by Homer and Virgil at the beginning of their poems."[26] By imitating the writers of fiction during the "statement of facts," the rhetorician was in fact being trained to create logical, emotional, and imagistic credibility: "to indicate our harrowing story in outline so that it

---

[25]Hajnal, 84 (my translation); Plucknett, *Early English Legal Literature*, 106. The practice is described in such works as the pseudo-Quintilianic *Declamationes minores*, which was "designed quite consciously to show the *ossa controversiae*" of an oration: Winterbottom, "Schoolroom and Courtroom," 66. Burke distinguishes two similar phenomena in his discussion of "semantic" and "poetic" ideals. The former served to "eliminate attitude," to "*cut away, to abstract, all emotional factors that complicate the objective clarity of meaning*"; the latter attempts to "*attain a full moral act* by attaining a perspective *atop all the conflicts of attitude*": POLF, 147–48 (emphasis his).

[26]For the use of a "brief and lucid summary of the case" as a structure of epic and *roman*, see Bloch's comparison of the medieval author with the "royal inquisitor, the compiler of customals, and the early recorders of verdicts and laws"; their task was the "gathering and structuring of fragmentary testimony, legend, or procedure into a sustained narrative whole. . . . Both recognize the possibility of a logical ordering of objects and events": MFLL, 203–4.

may at once be clear what the completed picture [*imago rei*] is like to be" (Quintilian, IV, 1.34, 2.120).

Extant written accounts of legal proceedings thus bear little resemblance to the output of today's court recorders; rather, they are official résumés, *abrégés*, skillful condensations that preserve "the choice and the logical sequence of the proofs," as Roland Delachenal writes, at the expense of the "warmth of the speech."[27] They were designed to reproduce not the dramatic immediacy of performance but the logic of argumentation. The same held true for the *ars praedicandi* (whose relevance to the origins of drama has been the subject of renewed enthusiasm).[28] The conversational tone of the sermon, enlivened by participation of onlookers, was reduced to a dull transcription.[29] Nor is it coincidental that a similar discrepancy arose in the quodlibet, the principal disputational ritual of the French theology faculty, which enjoyed its heyday during the thirteenth and fourteenth centuries. Here, too, a partially impromptu oral debate (the *disputatio*) was reduced to a formal summation (*determinatio*) that was first pronounced orally and later committed to writing.[30] Just as legal résumés culled only the seminal legal points, the purpose of the reductive *determinatio* was to regroup questions that were often quite disparate by imposing a "certain logical unity" on them. What we find under the name of quodlibet are reports not of the disorderly *disputatio* but of the artificially ordered *determinatio*. "Above all," cautioned Palémon Glorieux, "it does not reproduce the capricious succession of questions raised during the public session" (*LQ*, 1:45).

The very features, then, that Aristotle had described as particularly dramatic and persuasive in oral rhetoric were deleted from written renderings, and the original legal performance was thus robbed of

[27]Delachenal, *Histoire des avocats*, 230.
[28]Evidence of this resurgence of interest in the *ars praedicandi* can be seen in, e.g., Briscoe, "Preaching and Medieval English Drama"; Zink, *PELR*; Prosser, *Drama and Religion*; and Wenzel, *Preachers, Poets, and the Early English Lyric*. See also *LM*, 35; Lanson, *Histoire de la littérature française*, 189–92.
[29]Hajnal argues that the written version of the sermon is intended "only to aid the memory by providing the cleric with materials for his future career as a priest" (84; my translation). His theory that such transcriptions were designed as aides-mémoire is consistent with Treitler's work in musicology: "Oral, Written, and Literate Process," 488–91.
[30]See Glorieux, *LQ*, 1:39–47; also Mandonnet, who observed that the written quodlibetal *quaestio* was "the transcript not of the disputation itself but rather of the Master's *determinatio*": "Chronologie," 269. I explore the dramatic nature of the bipartite quodlibetal ceremony in a forthcoming article, "The Theatre of Scholastic Erudition"; suffice it to recall here that one of the most common verbs found in extant quodlibeta is *reducere*.

its inherent drama. So it was that Guillaume Du Breuil introduced fourteenth-century readers to his *Stilus Curie Parlamenti* with the reminder that "l'en treuve en escript peu du stille de Parlement de la noble court de France, qui aucunes fois se mue et diversiffie" (in writing, one finds little of the parliamentary style of the noble court of France, which sometimes changes and varies).[31] As Walter Ong demonstrated in his ground-breaking research on the ontology of rhetoric, writing does indeed "restructure consciousness" (*OAL*, chap. 4); and it did so not only during the act of transcription but before and after it as well. Clearly the implied audiences of the written legal *abrégé* were thought to be interested in the logic and ideology—not the drama—of forensic rhetoric. And nowhere is the power of that drama more clearly seen than in the widespread medieval efforts to camouflage the orality of delivery.

Given the moral problematics of the "degeneration" of delivery into spectacle, it was logical that recorders might be instructed to excise evidence of the phenomenon from their transcriptions of civic eloquence. Medieval *abrégés* appear to perpetuate quite deliberately the gulf between oral and written language for two fundamental reasons: to preserve the moral integrity of the law as a discipline that addressed issues of equity; and, more important, to attempt to ensure the law's independence of drama. Since part of the very nature of forensic delivery was its tendency to become increasingly theatrical, the reproduction of the bare bones of legal argumentation discouraged the perception that rhetoric was a form of spectacle. Ultimately, what occurred in the legal *abrégé* was an intriguing and apparently irremediable bifurcation of oral and written language, the former having become the spectacle described by Lucian, and the latter redefined as a mode better equipped to resolve moral issues of judgment. Writing, which Augustine had recognized as the most compatible vehicle for Christian rhetoric, would eventually be advanced as the only appropriate moral vehicle for the law—a bifur-

---

[31]Du Breuil, *Style du Parlement de Paris*, 61; translations are mine. According to Aubert, editor of the Latin edition, the date of Du Breuil's entry to the bar cannot be pinpointed, but apparently his oratorical talents were already famous by the beginning of the fourteenth century: *Stilus Curie Parlamenti*, i. Despite the usual critical affirmation that the work was composed sometime after 1330, Aubert believes that Du Breuil began the *Stilus* in 1329, while he was suspended from Parliament in disgrace for his association with the ill-fated Robert d'Artois (iii–vii). The French translation dates from the end of the fourteenth century or the first half of the fifteenth (xlviii). Contemporaneous with the activities of the Basochiens, Du Breuil's work is treated at greater length in chap. 3. On the *Stilus*, see Fumaroli, *L'Age de l'éloquence*, 435–39.

cation that is especially clear in the drastic measures proposed in the fifteenth century by Thomas Basin.

Though little known by literary critics, Basin's *Projet de réforme en matière de procédure* (which first appeared in 1455) is a veritable turning point in the history of the interrelations of orality and literacy.[32] In this project for juridical reform, the author posits a direct connection between the dramatization of law and the obfuscation of legal principles, lamenting the degeneration of legal delivery into a form so ostentatious that it impeded the formation of legal judgments. The crucial role of delivery in that process is revealed by Basin's extraordinary plea that the oral component of law be eliminated entirely: "Quod longe melius fit ex scripto quam verbali placitatione lites peragi" (That it would be far better to conduct legal proceedings in writing rather than in oral pleadings [chap. 7]). Delachenal speculates that Basin proposed the change for the sake of brevity in pleadings that had become increasingly lengthy (425–26), but a closer reading of the *Projet de réforme* suggests that more fundamental issues of performance as a generic construct were involved.

Basin considered the abolition of the oral trial to be the only possible way of liberating the language of legal equity from spectacle and of limiting the host of theatrical connotations that had come to accompany the term *actor*. It was no longer possible to follow spoken legal arguments, he declared, because of the declamatory fashion in which they were delivered. Legal logic was so convoluted, so ornamental, that neither the audience nor even the judges could follow it: "Audenter enim affirmaverim cum tali *declamatione verbali*, ubi multitudo confluit negotiorum, non esse possibile debitam causarum et litigantibus gratam fieri abbreviationem" (For I would boldly affirm that, with such oral declamation, once a great crowd of people congregates, it is not possible to achieve the speediness that is due to the case and that would be welcome to the litigants [51]). Apparently the drama of legal delivery had become so distracting as to compromise the very principles of legal equity; and Basin's desire to banish it from jurisprudence is directly related to the role of rhetoric in the "origins" of medieval drama.[33]

---

[32]Basin's *Réforme* appears in vol. 4 of Quicherat's edition of the *Histoire des règnes*. Translations are mine in collaboration with Alexander MacGregor. See also Delachenal's discussion of Basin (98).

[33]Basin was not merely repeating commonplaces of antitheatrical polemic: he owned a manuscript that contained the tragedies of the younger Seneca and also treatises on medicine and canon law; see Alexander MacGregor's discussion of Vat. Reginensis 1681 in *Manuscripts of Seneca's Tragedies*, 1209–10. That Basin read the

Delivery was considerably more than an aid to persuasion: it had helped to transform law into a mimetic spectacle. Forensic oratory was so immersed in pomp, splendor, and ostentation that it could not be divested of that dramatism:

> Sed difficile atque durum erit valde nostrates, ut arbitror, a placitationis verbalis seu forensis orationis *pompa divellere,* quae *splendorem* quemdam ac *magnificentiam curiarum ostentare videtur,* et dicendi exercitationem, in qua magnus est fructus, atque orationis copiam advocatis praebere. [50; emphasis mine]

> But it will be very difficult and burdensome, in my opinion, for our colleagues to strip the pomp from their oral trials and forensic oratory, which clearly puts on display a certain splendor and the magnificence of the courts, and just as obviously provides lawyers with a practice field for oratory, in which there is considerable benefit, and an abundance of raw material for pleadings.

It was the orator's veritable obsession with audience response, Basin continued, that had encouraged him to forsake expeditious argumentation in favor of histrionic declamation. Even judges yielded to audience pressure to respond to the drama of presentation rather than to the revelation of truth, thus divorcing themselves from the moral foundations of the law:

> In plerisque curiis Normanniae observatur, quod videlicet judices ex opinione majoris numeri assistentium causas diffiniunt, quorum saepius major pars est et juris scripti et consuetudinarii penitus ignara: quod aperte et divina lege et canonica est improbatum. Dicit enim Dominus in Exodo: "Non acquiesces in judicio plurium sententiae, ut devies a vero." [61]

> In many a Norman court, one sees that judges already determine cases according to the opinion of the majority of the spectators, the largest part of whom are wholly ignorant of statute and customary law both: which is plainly reproved by both canon law and divine. For the Lord says in Exodus [23:2]: "In judgment, you will not acquiesce in the opinion of the majority, so that [as a result] you deviate from the truth."

Senecan texts carefully is indicated by extensive marginal markings. Indeed, four times in his *Apologie* Basin quotes plays that appear vividly marked in the manuscript (albeit with the occasional transformations that accompany citations from memory). Seneca's tragedies were, of course, highly rhetorical, containing many a set-piece debate; they were available in Paris from 1200 and apparently were quite popular after 1400.

Therefore, Basin concluded, the only way to reinstate Christian doctrine in the courtroom was to remove delivery as the source of that "corruption of the will" and "concupiscence" (58–59)—the latter being a cornerstone of Augustinian theory. Legal rhetoric could then be safely entrusted to a less hysterical written incarnation: "longe melius arbitror, utilius, securius atque expeditius esse, pro forensium negotiorum brevi et secura expeditione, lites ex scripto agi quam cum illa placitandi festivitate declamari" (I think it is far better—more useful, trouble-free, and efficient—for speedy and trouble-free efficiency in legal proceedings to conduct lawsuits in writing rather than to declaim them in a holiday atmosphere and style of pleading [51]). His moral solution lay in the question of performance—or, rather, in the absence of performance. By deliberately freezing dramatic delivery on the page, Basin hoped to reconstitute a language of legal equity for an audience that would no longer risk being ensnared by legal mimesis. In what may well be a reference to Revelations 22:18–19, he suggested that nothing could be added to or subtracted from a sanctified written text, uncorrupted by the extravagances of declamation:

> Nunc vero quam *secure ex scripto* magis quam aliter processus deducantur, *supervacuum* videtur *ostendere,* cum res ipsa per se ipsam satis liquido se ostendat. Quid enim tutius, quid securius et certius quam *scriptura, cui nec addi quidquam, nec detrahi potest*? Hoc enim etsi vellent facere, minime possent tabelliones sive scribae, cum et libelli, et exceptiones et caetera litium principalia instrumenta apud ipsos signata ab advocato et procuratore vel eorum saltem altero deponantur. [54; emphasis mine]

> Now, it is clearly unnecessary for me to demonstrate how much more securely a legal proceeding may be conducted in writing than otherwise, since the truth of the matter speaks for itself clearly enough. For what is more safe, what is more secure and certain than a written document [or scripture], to which one may add nothing and from which one may subtract nothing? For even though notaries and scribes might want to, they would be able to do very little, since briefs and exceptions and other principal instruments of litigation are sealed in their presence and then deposited with the advocate and procurator, or at least with one of them.

When read in the context of medieval disputation and drama, Basin's *Projet de réforme* completes the historical picture of the *letteraturizzazione* of rhetoric effected by delivery. For whether *actio* was granted the palm or hounded until it became conspicuous by its absence, it clearly carried tremendous weight as a semiotic system. Given the gulf between oral and written discourse as chronicled by rhetorical theorists, and given the work of such modern-day critics as Ong, Stock, Clanchy, Zumthor, and Cerquiglini, it is certainly appropriate to bridge that gulf today through recourse to the rhetorical canon that traditionally mediated between the two modes of transmission: delivery. Since the voice was "the intermediary between ourselves and our hearers [sic velut media vox]" (Quintilian, XI, 3.63), it was in the voice that the vivacity of eloquence inhered—whether the voice spoke orally or whether its drama remained a latent program for performance on the page.[34] In that sense, the study of delivery also promises to supply a hermeneutic framework for the transition from oral to written culture in the Middle Ages. By developing a series of critical tools to "read" for delivery today, we may thus discover new literary implications of Stock's insight that the rapprochement between oral and written language played a "decisive role in the organization of experience" (*IOL*, 3); namely, that the rapprochement effected by legal *actio* might have similarly organized the literary experience of drama.

Ultimately, once we reconsider the mediatory status of performance along with the Christian mediatory status of law, legal rhetoric emerges as a privileged discourse situated between speech, text, and dramatic action. As such, it may help us to revise Bloch's theory of a two-stage process by which oral legal discourse was transformed into the written record of medieval romance or epic. Arguing that literary exploitation of an "emerging judicial model" had fostered the "transcription of lived *aventure* into document and document into romance," Bloch traced "the conversion of immediate experience into first verbal, then written, and in both cases mediated form." But, given his own insight about the *translation* of "lived experience perceived at the ontological level of gesture, ritual, and vision" into legal document and then into literature, it is logical that that "translation" might first occur orally and dramatically during the trial itself.[35] If judicial and literary inquests did indeed constitute fundamental mediatory structures that ensured the "displacement of the physical ordeal of battle toward a verbal and, even-

---

[34]Treitler has advanced a similar argument for music notation systems as programs for performance in "Reading and Singing," 207–8; see also my "Visions with Voices," 46–47.

[35]Bloch, *MFLL*, 208. See also Zumthor on the "monumentalization" of language, *Essai*, 76–77; and Bloch, *MFLL*, 206. A similar notion was addressed by Woods in "Teaching the Tropes."

tually, written equivalent" (209), then the most crucial of those
nascent literary mediations may well have been drama. Before its
fictionalization into written romance, lived *aventure* underwent an
initial theatricalization during the delivery of forensic rhetoric. The
forensic genre needed no intermediary written stage to become literature; its most logical literary outcome was the oral, dialogic genre
of drama.

Any study of the delivery of mediatory legal discourse, however,
must be further prefaced by an analysis of the rhetorical canon that
served as the epistemological predecessor to performance: the art of
memory. If classical and medieval orators did indeed require a
"stage" on which to enact the roles they assumed, then the place
where they were able to visualize their prototypes was *memoria*,
the "guardian of all the parts of rhetoric."[36] Still, with the significant
exceptions of Frances Yates, Mary Carruthers, and Walter Ong, surprisingly few critics have attended to the process by which mnemonics provided a hermeneutic framework for the conception and
actualization of the gestures, costumes, props, and impersonation
of delivery. If delivery was the principal locus for the aestheticization
of rhetoric, its "script" inhered in the memory, which provided a
literal stage for the rhetorical protodrama. As the "unalterable mental recollection of subject matter and words found in the course of
invention" (Alcuin, 76–77) and the precursor to delivery, *memoria*
ensured the smooth transition from theory of psychodrama to histrionic practice. More important still, the passage from imagistic
language to oral, gesticular performance suggests a fundamental generic interplay between rhetoric and drama.

The Mnemonic Alphabet of Dramatic Images

In antiquity and in the Middle Ages, the skilled orator was a master
of the *ars memorandi*, by means of which he stored words, stylistic
devices, topoi, and proofs before speaking them. *Memoria*, thought
by John of Salisbury to be the "mind's treasure chest, a sure and
reliable place of safe-deposit for perceptions"[37] and by the *Ad Herennium* author to be the "treasure-house [*thesaurus*] of the ideas
supplied by Invention" (III, 28), constituted a veritable alphabet of
mental images that provided a concrete, pictorial representation of

---

[36][Cicero], *Ad Herennium*, III, 28; see also Martianus's description of memory as
a *custodian* of words and things (141g).
[37]John of Salisbury, *Metalogicon*, I, 11.

discursive order: "It is order that sustains the precepts of memory," says Martianus (176g). In accordance with Cicero's principle that "the images of the facts will designate the facts themselves" (*De oratore*, II, 354), memory served as a system of figurative "writing" that recorded and stored imagistic representations of ideas on the "wax tablets of the mind"; "for as what is written is fixed by the letters on the wax, so what is consigned to the memory is impressed on the places, as on wax or on a page; and the remembrance of things is held by the images, as though they were letters."[38]

The true power of the memory vision, however, appears only when we bear in mind that within it there inhered the potential for verbalization and actualization during delivery. As Longinus once observed, its greatest virtue was the power to concretize any "idea which enters the mind from any source," and to "engender speech" (15, 1–2). Most significant of all for the mediatory status of rhetoric is the fact that classical and medieval orators appear to have moved from "reading" an internal language of memory to speaking dramatically the words of delivery. Among the most striking accounts of that progression are those of Martianus, who practiced mnemonics in a dimly lit room by "muttering" softly to himself, and Augustine, who sang meditatively within personal memory palaces: "I can sing as much as I want, even though my tongue does not move and my throat utters no sound."[39] Since the process of mnemonic imaging anticipated the oral regeneration of the referents of those images during delivery, the *ars memorandi* might thus have helped to bridge the gulf not only between image and performance but between rhetoric and drama as well.

If we consider that during the *letteraturizzazione* of rhetoric, mnemonic mediation between pictorial representation and oral speech inspired dramatic invention as it engendered performance, we can refine Bloch's analysis of how the dual role of the *greffier* and *sage clerc* as "author and judicial scribe" of Arthurian romance situated that genre "midway between a lived but unverbalized experience and its representation in the text that we are reading" (*MFLL*, 204). For there was a rhetorical canon whose particular province was the imposition of discursive order upon precisely that sketchy domain

[38]Martianus, 177g, as translated in Yates, *Art of Memory*, 51. The wax-tablet image occurs far earlier in such works as Plato's *Theaetetus*, 191D, and far later in Machaut's *Remède de fortune*, 31–34; see my "Music, Delivery, and the Rhetoric of Memory." For the history of the wax-tablet image, see Carruthers, *Book of Memory*, 16–32.

[39]Augustine, *Confessions*, trans. Pine-Coffin, bk. 10, chap. 8. On Martianus see Yates, 52. See also my discussion of these texts in "Visions with Voices," 45–46.

between unverbalized experience, oral account, drama, and written record. The medieval model responsible for the "ordering of inchoate elements of memory or imagination into credible written form" (203) was the *ars memorandi*. By visualizing detailed memory backgrounds on which vivid characters moved about holding their special props, any orator (or any learned dramatist with rhetorical training) would have learned from the *ars memorandi* quite literally how to set the stage for delivery and drama.[40]

Frances Yates argued compellingly that the *ars memorandi* was materially reflected in the architectural construction of the sixteenth-century wooden theater, which constituted an outward concretization of inner changes within the memory of the Renaissance psyche (172). But, given that memory provided the context in which we "seem to ourselves not to be dreaming but acting [*facere*]" (Quintilian VI, 2.30), that art had extraordinary performance ramifications for dramatic construction as well. Since effective speaking required the orator to generate *visiones* or *phantasiai* "whereby things absent are presented to our imagination with such extreme vividness that they seem actually to be before our very eyes" (Quintilian, VI, 2.29–30), he resembled Lucian's pantomime in his desire to appeal to the eyes as "more trustworthy than the ears" ("Saltatio," 78). Not coincidentally, memory was the guardian of mimicry as well: "It behoves her [mimicry] to enjoy the favour of Mnemosyne ... and she endeavours to remember everything" (36). As "the magic of celestial proportion [flowed] from his world memory into the magical words of his oratory and poetry, into the perfect proportions of his art and architecture" (Yates, 172), the orator might thus have called upon the mnemonic image for the morphology not only of the physical stage but of drama itself; not only for the conceptualization of theatrical space but also for the actual production of an inchoate psychodrama. Given the Aristotelian notion that the "soul cannot think without a mental picture,"[41] and given the fundamental "medieval tendency to give a concrete and figural representation to the most spiritual of truths,"[42] it is probable that a

[40]For an example of mnemonic visualization exercises for rhetorical training, see [Cicero], *Ad Herennium*, III, 31–32. Kelly has argued the continuity of that training in "Contextual Environment"; see also Yates, 50–76.

[41]Aristotle, *De anima*, 432a. For commentary on that passage, see Yates, 32, and Eden, *PLF*, 80; and for image and imagination in a mnemonic context, see Kelly, *MI*, 45–56.

[42]See, e.g., Rey-Flaud, *CM*, 261–62, for a discussion of Jacques Le Goff, *Civilisation de l'Occident médiéval*, 444.

widespread predilection for pictorial representation would have been influential not only *as* the stage but *on* the stage.

It was well known, for example, that all images required "an abode, inasmuch as a material object without a locality is inconceivable" (Cicero, *De oratore* II, 358), and that the architectural background against which those images were placed for highlighting was a veritable memory stage: "And these backgrounds ought to be of moderate size and medium extent, for when excessively large they render the images vague.... The backgrounds ought to be neither too bright nor too dim, so that the shadows may not obscure the images nor the lustre make them glitter" (*Ad Herennium*, III, 31–32). In the Middle Ages, Martianus illustrated the mnemonic association between background and images with the legendary tale of Simonides, whose phenomenal memory had allowed him to save the day by identifying the body of each guest at an ill-fated dinner party. His "collocation" of vivid imagery within memory *loci* is rich with all the theatrical connotations of the term *colloco*, which suggested theatrical space, conflict, and writing: "These [precepts] are to be pondered upon in well-lighted places [*in locis illustribus*] in which the images of things are to be placed [*collocandae*]."[43]

Similarly, John of Garland rearticulated the classical concept of the memory background in his *Parisiana poetria* (ca. 1220), counseling that "this vacant spot is to be imagined as separated into three main sections and columns."[44] There he linked figurative writing to both oral and written literary invention by placing images within the vivid architectural context of a memory building. The first column housed animate images, the second "examples and sayings" in their pedagogical context; most interesting of all, the third column monumentalized the reconstitution of sound, housing "all kinds of languages, sounds, and voices of the various living creatures, etymologies, explanations of words, distinctions between words, all in alphabetical order" (II, 94–110). As John implies, the *ars memorandi* suggested the staging of delivery as much as it did the materiality of the stage, which was far more than a locus of passive consignment. Quintilian considered mnemonic techniques to be rhetorically ex-

[43]Martianus, 1778, as translated in Yates, 51. According to the *Oxford Latin Dictionary*, *colloco* denoted "to put or set (persons or things) in a particular place, to put in a particular position (in a speech, book, etc.) ... to station, post (troops, etc.) for practical or strategic purposes, to place in ambush."

[44]John of Garland, *"Parisiana poetria,"* II, 92–93. References to John of Garland are from Lawler's edition/translation and are given parenthetically by line number. See my discussion of this text in "Visions with Voices," 39.

pedient insofar as they endowed orators with the "power of vivid imagination, whereby things, words and actions are presented in the most realistic manner" (VI, 2.30). They had instilled a strong desire to exploit sight as the "the keenest of all our senses": "Perceptions received by the ears or by reflexion can be most easily retained in the mind if they are also conveyed to our minds by the mediation of the eyes, with the result that...we keep hold of as it were by an act of sight things that we can scarcely embrace by an act of thought" (Cicero, *De oratore*, II, 357–58). That was especially necessary in forensic oratory, where the truth was "not merely to be told, but to some extent obtruded" (non dicendum sed quodammodo etiam ostendendum est [Quintilian, IV, 2.64]). Yet the very term *ostendere* is rich in theatrical connotations, designating not only the conception of logical argumentation but its spectacular display in artistic representation. As late as the sixteenth century, one lawyer underscored the enduring power of memory to engender speech through its regenerative images which came to life before audiences:

> On a comparé...la bouche de l'homme docte et sçavant à la porte d'ung cabinet royal, car tout ainsi, que, quant la porte du cabinet s'ouvre, soubdain apparoissent et se representent devant noz yeulx milles [*sic*] belles singularitéz...tant de belles medailles antiques, tant de choses exquises, recherchées curieusement et apportees des païs loingtains et estranges, et le tout ajancé et disposé leans avec ung merveilleux ordre. [A.N., X^{ra} 5022, fol. 23, 18 April 1569, Du Faur de Pibrac as quoted in Delachenal, 259–60]

> The mouth of the learned and educated man has been compared to the door of a royal office. For, just as when the door of the office opens, suddenly there appear, representing themselves before our very eyes, a thousand beautiful and unique things, so many beautiful antique medals, so many exquisite things, sought out with curiosity and brought back from faraway and strange lands, and the whole thing structured and arranged therein with a marvelous order.

Traditionally, orators thus did far more than tell stories: they showed them. And although one way of showing the story in court was to bring "a picture of the crime painted on wood or canvas [*in tabula*]," it is significant that such pictorial exploitation of the memory image was deemed insufficient: he "who prefers a voiceless picture to speak for him...must be singularly incompetent" (quae enim est actoris infantia, qui mutam illam *effigiem* magis quam orationem pro se putet locuturam) (Quintilian, VI, 1.32–33). Therefore, when Quintilian advised that the orator "stir all the emotions" less by telling than by showing characters, "as in a picture" (non tam narraret quam ostenderet [IV, 2.113–14]), the *imago* in question was not the voiceless pictorial effigy but the vivid staging of that picture during delivery. The memory image assumed its full powers only when it "spoke" during delivery, when an orator might turn mnemonic "hallucination to some profit" by using "actions as well as words . . . to move the court to tears" (VI, 2.31, 1.30). Indeed, Longinus maintained that memory visions retained their power even in written literature, where they continued to evoke "weight, grandeur, and energy" (15, 1). Therefore, whether the image were "articulated" aloud or in writing, what better way to "show the legal story" during delivery than by tapping the pictorial resources already available within the memory? than by representing a legal action dramatically on the memory "stages" so brilliantly analyzed by Yates? After all, those stages had been visualized so painstakingly to facilitate remembrance of the appearance and, more important, of the voices of the actual characters who would grace them.

So that they might appear with greater clarity, memory images often took the form of actual characters—personified, for example, by Quintilian as "linked one to the other like dancers hand in hand" (XI, 2.20). The orator had long been advised to visualize a living person engaged in some dramatic action. In the *Ad Herennium* the Pseudo-Cicero staged a veritable theatrical production, rich with costumed characters:

> We ought, then, to set up images of a kind that can adhere longest in the memory. And we shall do so if we establish likenesses as striking as possible; if we set up images that are not many or vague, but *doing something* [*agentes*]; if we assign to them exceptional beauty or singular ugliness; if we dress [*exornabimus*] some of them with crowns or purple cloaks . . . or if we somehow disfigure them, as by introducing one stained with blood or soiled with mud or smeared with red paint, so that its form is more striking, or by assigning in certain comic effects to our images, for that, too, will ensure our remembering them more readily.   [III, 37; emphasis mine]

In her reading of that passage, Yates briefly entertained the notion of a possible relationship between memory and allegory, speculating that the *imagines agentes* might have been "moralised into beautiful or hideous human figures as 'corporeal similitudes' of spiritual intentions of gaining Heaven or avoiding Hell" (77). But in view of her own work on the conflation of memory and literary imagination

(172), it stands to reason that such personifications would occur not only in the allegorical conception of the visual arts but in that of drama as well.[45]

In that sense, by recharting the course taken by the imagistic language of memory toward the drama and dramatis personae of delivery, we also discover that taken by rhetoric toward drama. As in Dionysian ritual, the apocryphal origin of drama, those personages (like Thespis himself) took on masks, thereby rendering mnemonics a kind of primordial drama. Cicero implied as much when he wrote that "we can imprint on our minds by a skilful arrangement of the several masks [*singulis personis*] that represent them, so that we may grasp ideas by means of images and their order by means of localities" (*De oratore*, II, 359–60). The entire scope of Rosemond Tuve's work might thus be extended to drama; for, as she herself noted, "many of the critical principles discussed apply, and were applied, to images as dramatists use them" (*EMI*, v). Similarly, Kathy Eden's important work on how *phantasmatae* precipitated the legal judgments involved in tragic plot (*PLF*, 112–13) might be brought to bear on the engenderment of dramatic spectacle. Beyond the potential for iconographic representation in the plastic arts, and beyond the morphology of the physical stage, the significatory power of the personified memory image might readily have been extended to include the morphology, conception, and above all performance of early drama.

The question to be raised, then, is whether or not it is likely that the orator (upon whose consciousness the theatrical imagery of memory would have been inscribed) might have focused less on the *imagines agentes* as symbols of the proofs he intended to employ, as entries in a pictorial dictionary, than on the dramatic potential of the images themselves. Is there any evidence that a

---

[45]See also Tuve's assertion that "personification of abstractions" constituted allegory in its "most natural form": *Allegorical Imagery*, 26. See also Tuve, *Elizabethan and Metaphysical Imagery* (hereafter *EMI*), 33–35; and Michel Zink, "The Allegorical Poem as Interior Memoir." Though Muscatine did not treat *memoria* as such, he implied much the same thing in "Emergence of Psychological Allegory." In "Memory, Allegory, and Medieval Generic Structures" I argued for a connection between mnemonic *phantasmatae* and the widespread medieval tendency to represent allegory with dream visions. This notion is consistent with Bourgeault's work on the "intensely pictorial" aspect of liturgical drama ("Liturgical Dramaturgy," 130) and with Sheingorn's on its "visual syntax" ("Visual Language of Drama," 174). The interrelations of memory, literature, and iconography are far too vast a subject to be explored here, but the *ars memorandi* promises to prove equally illuminating for the connections between word and picture, literature and the visual arts, text and gloss, emblem and *sententia*.

learned author might have turned to the dramatic action that
unfolded on the memory stage as a concrete role model for the
conceptualization and production of drama? Was he encouraged
in any way to shift his perspective from an epistemological to a
dramatic view of memory? Listening to his solitary voice in silence, did the muttering Martianus see himself as a protagonist
in his own memory play, transforming himself into an actor in
his personal drama?[46] The answer provided by the history of delivery is a resounding yes.

To reshape the moral chameleon of delivery into "art," Quintilian,
for example, had counseled the orator to use "mental pictures" as
the precursors to the dramatic portrayal of emotion:

> The main thing is to excite the appropriate feeling in oneself, to form
> a mental picture of the facts [*imagines rerum*], and to exhibit an
> emotion that cannot be distinguished from the truth. The voice, which
> is the intermediary between ourselves and our hearers, will then pro-
> duce precisely the same emotion in the judge that we have put into
> it. For it is the index of the mind, and is capable of expressing all its
> varieties of feeling. [XI, 3.61–63]

Such remarkable powers of "exhibition" suggest that the culmina-
tion of the mnemonic psychodrama was the drama of delivery. When
seeking to generate strong emotions, the orator was expected to
make his own *visiones* visible to his audience. Each time classical
and medieval orators used their voices to mediate between their
mnemonic mental pictures and their audiences, they created a protodrama that was no longer latent within the memory but actualized
in language and action before spectators. They discovered in the *ars
memorandi* a cognitive process that constituted an early form of
literary invention.

Finally, of special relevance to the origins of drama is the notion
that, as the mnemonic alphabet was transformed into the interpretive language of delivery, the forensic orator did far more than create
a simple word picture: he rendered judge and spectators actual witnesses to a dramatization of the crime. His goal was "not so much
to narrate as to exhibit (*ostendere*) the actual scene, while our emotions will be no less actively stirred than if we were present at the

---

[46]For a description of the transformation of the rhetorical situation into a dramatic
one, see Arnold's discussion of how, the "conditions being those of orality, something
resembling the speaker's script is to be played ensemble despite the fact that no one
engaged in the personalized, rhetorical situation can be cast as a minor actor within
his dramatic world" (165).

actual occurrence" (Quintilian, VI, 2.32). The costumed *imagines agentes* of the *Ad Herennium* were thus recast in the dramatic roles of advocates, clients, and witnesses holding the "props" of the crimes in question:

> I am complaining that a man has been murdered. Shall I not bring before my eyes [*in oculis habebo*] all the circumstances which it is reasonable to imagine must have occurred in such a connexion? Shall I not see the assassin burst suddenly from his hiding-place, the victim tremble, cry for help, beg for mercy, or turn to run? Shall I not see the fatal blow delivered and the stricken body fall? Will not the blood, the deathly pallor, the groan of agony, the death-rattle, be indelibly impressed upon my mind?   [VI, 2.31–32]

Such tangible accounts of things seen, heard, and done in the imagistic conception of a forensic speech are reminiscent of stage directions. Not only did the advocate "see" those things on an internal memory stage; he later replayed them for an audience. So it was that Quintilian supported the introduction into forensic pleadings of such vivid props as "blood-stained swords, fragments of bone taken from the wound, and garments spotted with blood" (VI, 1.30)—in part because such exploitation of the powerful memory image helped to reenact the crime dramatically during delivery: "A powerful effect may be created if to the actual facts of the case we add a plausible picture of what occurred, such as will make our audience feel as if they were actual eyewitnesses of the scene [multum confert adiecta vieris credibilis rerum *imago*, quae velut in rem praesentem perducere audientes videtur]" (IV, 2.123). Indeed, he praised Cicero for the effective display of the "blood stains on the purple-bordered toga of Gaius Caesar," which "brought such a vivid image of the crime before their minds that Caesar seemed not to have been murdered, but *to be being murdered* before their very eyes [non occisus esse Caesar sed tum maxime occidi videretur]" (VI, 1.31; emphasis mine). Longinus, too, praised that very power in literature, where the memory image was employed to recreate events in such a way that "you seem to see what you describe and bring it vividly before the eyes of your audience" (15, 1–2).

Such reenactments, however, recall the very critical criteria that have enabled us to read extant liturgical *didascalia* as indicative of the nascent drama of the medieval church, which, in Rey-Flaud's words, "seeks no longer to represent the event, but truly to reenact it."[47] In view of Marcia Colish's important insight that in the Middle Ages the verbal and the pictorial had the same cognitive and com-memorative functions,[48] the art of memory might thus be seen as a watershed form for the rhetorical conception of how to reenact a dramatic story by showing and telling it during delivery. The stage was far more than the possible source for memory imagery that Yates recognizes (18), it was also the recipient of that imagery. When the lawyer "reenacted" a crime during forensic pleadings, he conflated performatively image, word, and commemoration in an activity that was as symbolic and inherently dramatic as the sacred "dramas" of the medieval church. In that context, it is interesting to reconsider Eugene Vance's analysis of "commemorative culture" in the *Chanson de Roland*, albeit in the specific context of epic and *roman*. For commemoration he specifies "any gesture, ritualized or not, whose end is to recover, in the name of a collectivity, some being or event either anterior in time or outside of time in order to fecundate, animate, or make meaningful a moment in the present."[49] In the law, one such process of fecundation is the *letteraturizzazione* of rhetoric into drama. And if "commemorative culture will inevitably rationalize its ideologies in the perspective of a metaphysics of signs" (375), rhetoric had its own metaphysics of signs—a visual mnemonic alphabet that had performative and dramatic consequences during delivery.

Ultimately, when training in the *ars memorandi* is considered in light of the pervasive rhetorical confusion between orator and actor, we may reasonably conclude that it prompted the orator to seek there a model for the theatricalization of delivery. It was memory that ensured the safe transmission of the notion that orators were actors playing their roles in the microcosmic drama of rhetoric; and it was there that they discovered the very foundations for dramatic invention. Even as the art of memory weakened in the later Middle

---

[47]Rey-Flaud, *Pour une dramaturgie du Moyen Age* (hereafter *PDMA*), 18. For the dramatic role of *didascalia* in extant liturgical documents, see Hardison's discussion of reenactment (*CRCD*, 23–24) and also his entire essay 2, "The Mass as Sacred Drama."

[48]In the context of Byzantine iconic epistemology, Colish argues that the icon was "strictly evocative," whereas words played an "indicative as well as a commemorative role": *Mirror of Language*, 6.

[49]Eugene Vance, "Roland, Charlemagne, and the Poetics of Memory," 374. As Vance implies, the recapturing of anterior truths depends on *visibilia*: "Original Truth that is always absent will signify or present itself partially to man in time and space by means of the words and things that constitute his palpable world" (375). Carruthers devotes the entire first chapter of her *Book of Memory* to the concept of "commemorative culture."

Ages as a result of increased interaction between oral and written traditions, such aestheticization would remain a logical consequence. After all, as early as the seventh century, Isidore of Seville confirmed Plato's predictions (*Phaedrus*, 274) about the dangers of writing, complaining that memory had come to require reinforcement by a written text: while the orator "holds the parchment the connected discourse as it were cleaves to his memory, but presently when it is laid aside all recollection vanishes."[50] Similarly, Du Breuil endeavored to commit the rules of legal style to writing in large part because "mémoire d'omme régulièrement est tantost passé" (regularly, human memory is quickly outdone [61]). But the mnemonic alphabet of imagery might yet endure in drama, where it had become the stuff of dramatic invention.

In the final analysis, Yates's "bold suggestion" that the art of memory is the critical piece that has been "left out all along the line" (79) may be restated with respect to drama studies. By virtue of his exposure to the evocative power of the memory image as a precursor to delivery, the talented rhetorician had learned to conceive a speech that was both persuasive and dramatic. Indeed, it was persuasive precisely because it was dramatic. And drama was so persuasive that the dramatic appeal of a speech eventually assumed preeminence over its probative value. A revitalized understanding of how the mnemonic image was translated into the linguistic and performative patterns of delivery thus promises to elucidate the very ontology of early drama, along with its significance in the changing interrelations between medieval literature and its performative contexts. One of those consequences, however, is so pivotal in the *letteraturizzazione* of forensic rhetoric that it merits separate consideration: impersonation. The advent of impersonation may well have been the single most important influence on the generic confusion between rhetoric and drama in antiquity and the Middle Ages.

Playing the Legal Drama: The Advent of Impersonation in Forensic Oratory

An elusive concept encompassing such features as gesture, costume, imitation, and intention, impersonation has long been cited

---

[50]Isidore of Seville, *Etymologies*, II, 2, as translated in Brehaut, *Encyclopedist of the Dark Ages*, 112.

as the sine qua non for the emergence of drama from ritual. According to Hardin Craig, genuine drama combined "in reasonable balance impersonation, dialogue, and action" (4); and for Karl Young it was "a story presented in action, in which the speakers or actors impersonate the characters concerned. Dialogue and physical movements . . . will be transformed from the *dramatic* into *drama* whenever these persons convey a story and pretend to be the characters in this story" (1:80–81). In medieval drama criticism, the identification of impersonation in such extant documents as the *Regularis concordia*, the Winchester Troper, and the *De tragoediis* by Honorius Augustodunensis (c. 1100) has proved the single most important critical criterion for the establishment of the Mass as a "sacred drama."[51] Honorius remains the quintessential example of the articulation of veritable stage directions for representing the liturgy, having described the celebrant of the Mass as a *tragicus* involved in the commemorative imitation of a dramatic Christian struggle:

> Sciendum quod hi qui tragoedias in theatris recitabant, actus pugnantium gestibus populo repraesentabant. Sic tragicus noster pugnam Christi populo Christiano in theatro ecclesiae gestibus suis repraesentat, eique victoriam redemptionis suae inculcat.

> It is known that those who recited tragedies in the theaters represented to the people, by their gestures, the actions of conflicting forces. Even so, our tragedian [the celebrant] represents to the Christian people in the theater of the church, by his gestures, the struggle of Christ, and impresses upon them the victory of his redemption.[52]

Still, while critics have taken Honorius's description of the imitation of a conflictual action to have heralded the birth of liturgical drama,[53]

[51]For analyses of impersonation and the origins of drama, see, e.g., Hardison, *CRCD*, 30–33, 187–219; Young, 1:80–85, 90–111; Hardin Craig, *English Religious Drama*, 2–5.

[52]Honorius, *Gemma animae*, as translated by David Bevington in *Medieval Drama*, 9. See also Young, 1:83; and Hardison, *CRCD*, 39–40. While the role of conflict as a sine qua non of drama has been called into question by such scholars as Michelle Gellrich (*Tragedy and Theory*), the importance of the agon in medieval drama is undisputed. For "battle play" as drama, see Axton, chap. 2; and see Knight, *Aspects of Genre*, 31, on the primordial agonistic structure of both the history and the morality play. Other dramatic criteria implicit in this commemorative imitation are discussed in chap. 2.

[53]These traditional criteria for tragedy have been explored from an Aristotelian perspective by Howell, *PRL*, 45–56; Eden, *PLF*, 30–32; Ehrlich, "Congruence of Aristotle's Rhetoric and Poetics"; and Weinberg, *History of Literary Criticism*, 1:350–52. They are discussed at greater length in chap. 2.

far less known is the existence of a parallel phenomenon within legal rhetoric. I argue here that Young's principal criterion for the transition from liturgical ritual to dramatic representation already existed in classical legal oratory: the introduction of dramatic impersonation into a receptive host form.

Long before Honorius and centuries before Christianity, rhetorical theorists had explicitly documented the presence of representation or mimesis within forensic oratory. Plato had observed that lawyers were the "authors of a tragedy [*tragōidias*]," thus elaborating a theatrical vision of law of the same breadth as that of the sacred drama of the Mass. Forensic discourse and policy were "framed as a representation [mimesis] of the fairest and best life, which is in reality, as we assert, the truest tragedy" (*Laws*, 817B). But, considered in the performative context of delivery, Plato's explicit focus on the mimetic nature of law suggests that if the celebrant of the Mass was a *tragicus* talented in the art of impersonation, so was the legal advocate of Greco-Roman antiquity. Already enjoined in handbooks to imitate actors, classical and medieval orators took that analogy to fascinating dramatic extremes. The study of delivery as a program for performance reveals that if the rise of impersonation within troping provoked a generic interplay between liturgical ritual and dramatic spectacle, it had the same effect in rhetoric.[54] Rhetorical commentaries on delivery were to the drama of the law what liturgical *didascalia* were to the drama of the medieval church.

It was not sufficient, wrote Quintilian, that the forensic rhetor merely speak on behalf of his client: he was to speak *as* his client in the most literal and literary act of representation. In a crucial passage in Book VI, Quintilian's costumed, gesticulating lawyer attempts to stir the emotions of judge and audience during delivery by "impersonating" the client, a technique known as prosopopoeia: pronouncing "fictitious speeches [*fictae alienarum personarum orationes*] supposed to be uttered, such as an advocate puts into the mouth of his client" (VI, 1.25). Through the actions and intonations of delivery, the legal advocate was pretending to be someone else: like the tragedian, he was imitating actions with the rhetorical intention of producing an emotional response in the audience.[55] And,

---

[54]For a discussion of troping, see, e.g., Ritva Jonsson, *Tropes du propre de la messe*, 9–10; Grace Frank, *Medieval French Drama*, 19–23; and my discussion of them in "Visions with Voices," 36–37; also Chambers, 2:7–11.

[55]See also Isidore's fascinating discussion of *prosopoeia*, II, 13. The "intentional fallacy" is not relevant in a discipline that has always advanced intention as one of its cornerstones. Of course, I am referring here indirectly to pathos, one of the three traditional rhetorical proofs. For its definition as opposed to logos and ethos, see, e.g.,

like the priest/*tragicus* of the medieval liturgy, he was staging a drama:

> The bare facts are no doubt moving in themselves; but when we *pretend* that the persons concerned themselves are speaking [*cum ipsos loqui fingimus*], the personal note adds to the emotional effect. For then the judge seems no longer to be listening to a voice bewailing another's ills, but to hear the voice and feelings of the unhappy victims, men whose appearance alone would call forth his tears even though they uttered never a word. And as their plea would awaken yet greater *pity* [*essent miserabiliora*] if they urged it with their own lips, so it is rendered to some extent all the more effective when it is, as it were, put into their mouth by their advocate: *we may draw a parallel from the stage*, where the actor's voice and delivery [*ut scenicis actoribus eadem vox eademque pronuntiatio*] produce greater emotional effect when he is speaking in an assumed role than when he speaks in his own character. [VI, 1.25–27; emphasis mine]

What was that if not the momentous introduction of dramatic impersonation into forensic rhetoric? Quintilian's advice that the legal advocate should identify so strongly with his client that he actually *becomes* the client indicates that prosopopoeia was as mimetic during forensic delivery as it would be centuries later during the performance of the *quem quaeritis* tropes. The stage was the model, the vehicle delivery, the intention impersonation, and the result mimesis.

One logical question that follows, then, is: How does that view differ from modern ideas about the rise of drama from the effacement of the "actual" speaker in favor of the "virtual" speaker;[56] or from Young's insistence on the necessity of *pretense* in the origins of dramatic forms? And the logical answer is that it does not. When

---

Aristotle, *Rhetoric*, 1356a; Quintilian, VI, 2.1–17. Also, I analyze the crucial term *fingere* in connection with pity and fear in chap. 2. In this connection, see also Schouler's argument for the discovery of stock character types in forensic invention: "La Classification des personnes et des faits chez Hermogène," 238–42. I am not positing Quintilian as a direct influence on medieval theories of impersonation; rather, I am situating him along the continuum of oral performance tradition. While the *Institutio oratoria* was available to the Middle Ages in the mutilist tradition (see Murphy, *RIMA*, 125–27), the "complete" work did not become available until the Renaissance.

[56]In an unpublished paper, "Elements of Rhetorical Form," Paul Campbell suggested that "dramatic discourse is a rhetorical form in which the speaker, as we have traditionally known that being, disappears. These virtual speakers are not limited to theatre, for they are found, in varying degrees of clarity, in many literary forms; but theatre is the only art in which they are openly and fully and physically enacted." See also Arnold's description of the speech act as dramatic (165).

Quintilian's lawyer/author (the actual speaker) was effaced by the litigant/protagonist (the virtual speaker), he fulfilled every criterion for drama cited by Young, who insisted that the speaker "must pretend to be the person whose words he is speaking, and whose actions he is imitating. The performer must do more than merely *represent* the chosen personage; he must also *resemble* him, or at least show his intention of doing so" (1:80). The histrionic classical rhetorician, too, did more than *represent* the litigant: he *resembled* him. Even when garbed in ceremonial legal attire that distinguished him from the litigant, Quintilian's lawyer had every *intention* (one of Young's own criteria) of playing the role of his client in order to "awaken pity":

> We must identify ourselves so strongly with the persons of whom we complain... and must plead their case and for a brief space feel their suffering as though it were our own, while our words must be such as we should use if we stood in their shoes. I have often seen actors, both in tragedy and comedy [*histriones et comoedos*], leave the theatre still drowned in tears after concluding the performance of some moving role. But if the mere delivery of words written by another has the power to set our souls on fire with fictitious emotions, what will the orator do whose duty it is to picture to himself the facts and who has it in his power to feel the same emotion as his client whose interests are at stake? [VI, 2.34–35]

In their zeal to solicit strong emotions, orators appear to have interpreted quite literally Cicero's view cited by Quintilian that "by the introduction of fictitious personages we may bring into play the most forcible form of exaggeration" (personarum ficta inductio vel gravissimum lumen augendi [IX, 1.31]). The bare facts of a case may well have been moving in themselves; but efficacious evocation of pathos and catharsis was clearly enhanced by a kind of role playing. Indeed, the orator was ideally placed to exploit theatrical talents that had been cultivated in the schools for declamation. Tapping a training that had encouraged students to give speeches "a dramatic character suited to the persons concerned" (Quintilian, IV, 1.47), the rhetorician became the inventor and player of dramatis personae. Inasmuch as it was "desirable that the student should be moved by his theme," Quintilian advised that he

> should imagine it to be true [*convenit easque veras sibi fingere*]; indeed, it is all the more desirable then, since, as a rule in scholastic declamations, the speaker more often appears as the actual litigant

than as his advocate. Suppose we are impersonating [*agimus*] an orphan, a shipwrecked man, or one in grave peril. What profit is there in assuming such a rôle unless we also assume the emotions which it involves? [VI, 2.36]

In this early articulation of a theory of dramatic illusion, Quintilian was, in fact, encouraging his disciples to exploit pity, fear, and catharsis so that they might become the histrionic counterfeiters of pathos. The key to capturing the essence of a character was to capture his emotions (Quintilian, VI, 1.25–27). Presaging the critical theories to be elaborated centuries later by a Diderot, an Artaud, or a Stanislavski,[57] Quintilian further explained that that extraordinary effect was to be achieved through a process of empathic identification with the principals of a case. Since emotions were not "transferable at will, nor can we give the same forcible expression to another man's emotions that we should give to our own" (IV, 1.47), the orator was to remedy that situation by employing techniques reminiscent of today's "method acting": he was to assume the actual feelings of the personages of the case to be tried. Where the key for Young was pretense, the key for Quintilian was "counterfeit," a talent acquired in the schools: "The prime essential for stirring the emotions of others is, in my opinion, first to feel those emotions oneself. It is sometimes positively ridiculous to counterfeit [*ridicula fuerit imitatio*] grief, anger and indignation, if we content ourselves with accommodating our words and looks and make no attempt to adapt our own feelings to the emotions to be expressed" (VI, 2.26). Again, the orator had gleaned such techniques from the mime, who habitually exceeded what Lucian called the "due limit of mimicry" ("Saltatio," 82). While "passion struck the chords of the voice" during delivery, it was important to distinguish between such true emotions as grief, anger, and indignation, which "broke out naturally" but "lacked art," and "false emotions," which were the artful results of "methodical training" and lacked the "sincerity of nature" (Quintilian, XI, 3.61–62). The orator "slipped on" (*induere*) the personalities and emotions of others like a costume (IV, 1.47) in order to be a more credible and a more pleasing speaker. Ideally, such false emotions were to appear both artful and true as the lawyer transformed pathos into his own brand of dramatic illusion through imitation and representation.

Still, the appearance of dramatic truth in conjunction with the

[57]I am referring here to Diderot's "Paradoxe sur le comédien," Artaud's *Théâtre et son double*, and Stanislavski's "method acting."

reality of emotion could also exceed its proper generic bounds. Lucian supplied a particularly striking example of such exaggeration by recounting the tale of an actor who assumed the madness of Ajax so completely that he went mad himself. To thunderous applause, the actor ran into the senatorial benches and frightened the audience, especially the "riff-raff," who "thought that sort of thing consummate mimicry of the ailment." The more enlightened members of the audience, however, "perceived clearly that what went on came from the madness of the actor, not that of Ajax. . . . Perhaps in consequence of his overdone mimicry he had fallen into the real ailment" (83–84). A master of both illusion and reality, the legal advocate moved his audiences in a similar way by "calling the dead to life" (Quintilian, IV, 1.28). Dangers of madness notwithstanding, impersonation enabled him to identify so completely with his client that he was ultimately transformed into the very object of his imitation.

As I show at greater length in Chapter 2, the literary consequence of the advent of impersonation in the courtroom was a blurring between speaker and character and between illusion and reality— two hallmarks of the early theater.[58] Indeed, Aristotle had once observed that authors habitually acted in their own tragedies (*Rhetoric*, 1403b). The power to "set our souls on fire with fictitious emotions" during forensic delivery (Quintilian, VI, 2.35) suggests that when Greek and Roman orators attempted to "resemble" chosen personages, they were consciously refocusing their attention from proof to spectacle, from speech to audience; they were taking quite literally Quintilian's characterization of law as an *imitatio veritatis* (V, 12.22).

Moreover, early theories of prosopopoeia were rearticulated in the Middle Ages by such authors as Bede, William of St. Thierry, and Origen. William, for example, described the *modus dramatis et stylus comicus* in the Song of Songs as "written in the mode of a drama and in theatrical style, as if to be recited by characters and with action"; and according to Origen, once the characters were speaking and acting for themselves, the discourse was a drama: "For we call a thing a drama, such as the enaction of a story on the stage, when different characters are introduced and the whole structure of the

---

[58]For the blurring of illusion and reality as a component of medieval drama, I refer here especially to Rey-Flaud, *PDMA*, 17–20; Knight, *Aspects of Genre*, chap. 6, on the participatory spectacle of the procession; and Potter's unpublished paper "Public Execution as a Moral Spectacle." For the confusion between ritual excess and play as revealed in Gréban, see Zumthor, "From Hi(story) to Poem," 238; and Rainer Warning, "On the Alterity of Medieval Religious Drama," 282, 285.

narrative consists in their comings and goings among themselves."[59] Reflecting the transference of dramatic theories of rhetoric to an explicitly poetic context, Geoffrey of Vinsauf also advised that the orator assume the emotions of the characters "portrayed." Once again, the actual speaker was effaced in favor of the virtual speaker as the aestheticization of rhetoric continued. Speakers were to "arise a voice full of gall, a face enraged, and turbulent gestures," for "outer motion follows the inner, and the outer and inner man are equally moved. If you play this part [*quid recitator ages*], what shall you, the speaker, do? . . . Imitate [*imitare*] genuine fury" (*Poetria nova*, 2051–53).

Finally, it is helpful to reconsider in that connection an important material element that contributed to the advent of impersonation in forensic oratory: the crucial visual cues supplied by costume. Costume, as Johan Huizinga notes, allowed the lawyer to "step outside 'ordinary' life" by transforming him "into another being"—a dramatic being. Indeed, that remains true today each time the British judge dons wig and gown, an act that resembles functionally the "dancing masks of savages" (*HL*, 77). In the same way that the wearing of ceremonial ecclesiastical vestments contributed to the nascent theatricality of the medieval Mass (Hardison, *CRCD*, 79), the ritual attire of law contributed to that of forensic rhetoric. Classical orators in their togas, academic *magistri* and students in full academic regalia, and the Basochiens (whose elegant garb is treated in Chapter 3) were transformed into "other beings" when they donned costumes that symbolized their social functions, both legal and theatrical. In fact, one of the first duties of the beginning student was to acquire the attire befitting his new role—a phenomenon that is satirized in many a medieval farce.[60]

Traditionally, the visual cues of costume, accessories, and props served the orator as a kind of physical evidence, by which to evoke strong emotions. So powerful was their appeal to the eye that Quintilian sanctioned the "custom of bringing accused persons into court wearing squalid and unkempt attire" because it allowed the orator to "reenact the crime":

> We see blood-stained swords, fragments of bone taken from the wound, and garments spotted with blood, displayed by the accusers,

[59]See Minnis's discussion of the three authors and especially of Bede's *De arte metrica* in *Medieval Theory of Authorship*, 57–58, where Bede and Origen are quoted.

[60]Two such examples are the *Farce de Maistre Mimin* and the *Farce d'un qui se fait examiner*, both of which appear in Viollet-le-Duc, ed., *Ancien théâtre français*, 2:338–59, 373–87. *Mimin* also appears in Fournier, *Théâtre français*, 314–21.

wounds stripped of their dressings, and scourged bodies bared to view. The impression produced by such exhibitions is generally enormous, since they seem to bring the spectators face to face with the cruel facts [*in rem praesentem animos hominum ducentium*]. [VI, 1.30–31]

In combination with a histrionic delivery, costume and props were easily theatricalized. Spectators were indeed brought "face to face with the cruel facts," and they found that confrontation to be as pleasing as the lawyer's regalia. Tacitus, for example, noted that the "house" of the orator was to be "pleasing to the eye"; he should "also number among his belongings both gold and precious stones, so as to make people want to...gaze with admiration" (22). And, once again, Lucian's unsavory Professor proffered detailed advice about the requisite vestimentary "equipment" that would allow his disciples to appear with all the visual immediacy of an emblem book: "Let your clothing be gaily-coloured, or else white, a fabric of Tarentine manufacture, so that your body will show through; and wear either high Attic sandals of the kind that women wear, with many slits, or else Sicyonian boots, trimmed with strips of white felt. Have also many attendants, and always a book in hand" ("Professor of Public Speaking," 15).

Such attention to wardrobe suggests a predilection for the appearance of spectacle rather than for the substance of seeking truth. Continuing his lesson, the Professor urged the orator to create just such a spectacle by bringing with him ignorance, recklessness, effrontery, and shamelessness, and leaving "modesty, respectability, self-restraint, and blushes...at home" (15). Dress became a metaphor for stylistic excess, for the preference of form over content, and for a commingling of ritual and representation within civic eloquence:

You must pay especial attention to outward appearance, and to the graceful set of your cloak. Then cull from some source or other fifteen, or anyhow not more than twenty, Attic words...and have them ready at the tip of your tongue.... Whenever you speak, sprinkle in some of them as a relish. Never mind if the rest is inconsistent with them, unrelated, and discordant. Only let your purple stripe be handsome and bright, even if your cloak is but a blanket of the thickest sort. [16]

So, while Quintilian claimed that the preoccupation with dress had initially been connected to such eminently practical concerns as Cicero's desire to "conceal his varicose veins" (XI, 3.143), oratorical dress was also part of the hermeneutics of gesture in the semiotic system of delivery. Costume was readily incorporated into the lawyer's language of gesture because of its own "natural" movement with the body:

> As the pleading develops, in fact, almost from the beginning of the *statement of facts*, the fold will slip down from the shoulder quite naturally and as it were of its own accord, while when we come to arguments and commonplaces, it will be found convenient to throw back the toga from the left shoulder, and even to throw down the fold if it should stick. The left hand may be employed to pluck the toga from the throat and the upper portion of the chest, for by now the whole body will be hot. [Quintilian, XI, 3.144–46]

But the transition from practical concerns about comfort to histrionic exploitation of dramatic gesture was simple and rapid. If manipulation of the toga was often natural and logical, it was also dramatic, serving to buttress visually the histrionic intentions of the "index of the mind." Dress followed the voice which followed the soul, and its movements were to be harnessed to the same dramatic concerns. But, as forensic speeches reached their denouements, any outrageous mien began to seem appropriate:

> And just as at this point the voice becomes more vehement and more varied in its utterance, so the clothing begins to assume something of a combative pose. Consequently, although to wrap the toga round the left hand or to pull it about us as a girdle would be almost a symptom of madness, while to throw back the fold from its bottom over the right shoulder would be a foppish and effeminate gesture, and there are yet worse effects than these, there is, at any rate, no reason why we should not place the looser portions of the fold under the left arm, since it gives an air of vigour and freedom not ill-suited to the warmth and energy of our action. When, however, our speech draws near its close, more especially if fortune shows herself kind, practically everything is becoming; we may stream with sweat, show signs of fatigue, and let our dress fall in careless disorder and the toga slip loose from us on every side. [Quintilian, XI, 3.145–148]

Both Tacitus and Quintilian took offense at what they deemed a "degeneration" of the noble, "masculine" forensic rhetoric into an "effeminate" theatrical form. "Take those gowns into which we squeeze ourselves when we chat with the court, a costume that shackles movement.... Have they not also greatly contributed to the emasculation of eloquence [*debilitatur et frangitur*]?" (Tacitus, 39).[61] But as histrionic, posing orators crossed gender lines into effeminacy, they also crossed genre lines into theater. A civic and civilizing legal oratory had become nothing more than an old suit of clothes that histrionic advocates preferred to abandon in favor of more contemporary fashions: "For what can be more distressing than to be fettered by petty rules ... or, as the Greeks say, insist on keeping the coat their mother gave them. Are we to have nothing but premises and conclusions from consequents and incompatibles?" (Quintilian, V, 14.31).

Of course, the answer supplied by the corps of theatrical orators was: Absolutely not. Premises and conclusions were inconsequential and incompatible when it came to the desire to please judge, jury, and audience with a legal mimesis. The delivery of forensic oratory demanded that the old codified rules be broken—in antiquity as well as in the Middle Ages, when an ecclesiastical community denounced a similar phenomenon. In the twelfth century, for example, Gerhoh of Reichersberg complained about the *Antichristus* plays, "in quibus viri totos se frangunt in feminas quasi pudeat eos, quod viri sunt, clerici in milites, homines se in daemonum larvas transfigurant" (in which all the men disguise themselves as women as if they are ashamed to be men; clerics are transformed into soldiers, and men into the figures of demons).[62] And, on behalf of the Paris faculty of theology, Eustace de Mesnil spoke out vehemently in 1445 against priests and clerks who appear to have learned much about dramatic impersonation and transvestism from the art of delivery, for they "may be seen wearing masks and monstrous visages at the hours of office. They dance in the choir dressed as women, panders or minstrels. They sing wanton songs ... and rouse the laughter of their fellows and the bystanders in infamous performances, with indecent gestures and verses scurrilous and unchaste" (Chambers, 1:294).

[61]While the translation "emasculate" is somewhat colorful for this particular passage, there is very little ambiguity, for example, in Quintilian's discussion of castration (V, 12.17–20). Unfortunately, this fascinating association between "male" oratory and "female" literary pleasures lies outside the scope of this book. I treat it extensively in a work in progress, "Delivering Medieval Gender." For a fascinating introduction to the interrelations between medieval rhetoric and sexuality, see Leupin, *Barbarolexis*, esp. 62–71.

[62]As quoted in Chambers, 2:99n; Axton, 45; Young, 2:411–12. See also Karl Morrison's discussion of Gerhoh in "The Church as Play"; Axton on a similar passage in Herrad of Landsberg (31); Briscoe on performance in the church ("Some Clerical Notions of Dramatic Decorum"); and Clopper, "*Miracula* and *The Tretise of Miraclis Pleyinge*," esp. 878–85, 894–95.

What then of the commonplace that Greek drama arose from the introduction of impersonation into the Dionysian "liturgy" in the sixth century B.C.? It is now widely acknowledged that when Thespis placed the mask of a historical figure over that of the god Dionysius, the choral leader of the dithyramb (*exarchos*) became an actor who might represent one or more characters as the action unfolded, and that the god whose rites were enacted became the central character in a play.[63] The use of such masks (already anticipated in mnemonics) permitted individual members of the chorus to represent others, and to foster the illusion they changed their manner of speaking to accord with the characters they represented.[64] But if, as Hardison and others have maintained, impersonation did indeed constitute the decisive step in the rise of drama, the steps taken by prosopopoeia in forensic rhetoric were surely just as decisive. What then of the "second birth" of the theater in Christian rather than Dionysian worship (Vince, 23)? If the very phenomenon that has so encouraged critics to place the origins of medieval drama within the Christian liturgy already existed in forensic rhetoric, just how many "births" of drama were there?

At the risk of positing an embarrassment of riches, I submit that the "second birth" of the theater occurred in legal oratory in much the same way that its apocryphal "first birth" did—but long before the troping of the medieval liturgy. The "antithetical splitting of the dithyrambic chorus," to which Murphy attributes the development of Dionysian drama was not required in forensic oratory:[65] it was already dialogic in structure. Indeed, the verbal antiphony of forensic oratory is a logical antecedent for the musical antiphony of troping—especially given Lucian's forensic fusion of speaking and "intoning," as well as research by musicologists on the interchangeability of *cantare* and *dicere*.[66] All such forms of antiphony—dia-

[63]Hardison discussed the role of Thespis as the "father" of impersonation in Greek ritual in a 1981 lecture at the Folger Shakespeare Library titled "Liturgy and Liturgical Drama."

[64]See Murphy, *Synoptic History*, 4–5.

[65]Ibid., 4. Research also indicates that the Bible contains similar models: see Minnis, 40–42; also Kennedy, *CR*, 120–25.

[66]For the confusion among chant, intonation, and declamation, see, e.g., Treitler and Jonsson, "Medieval Music and Language," 1. The musical antiphony of the nascent liturgical drama has been studied extensively by such scholars as Young, Hardison, Sepet, E. Catherine Dunn (*Gallican Saint's Life* and "Gregorian Easter Vespers and Early Liturgical Drama"), Fletcher Collins (*The Production of Medieval Church Music-Drama*), and many others. Because I limit my discussion to the verbal manifestations of dramatic antiphony, I do not focus here on analogous phenomena in lyric debate forms, which have been insightfully analyzed in Kendrick, *Game of Love*, 14–16; and in Bloch, *MFLL*, 167–88. Indeed, Tunison suggested as early as 1907

lectical, musical, or forensic—bespoke the ancient Greek attraction
to dramatizing antithesis which was to be perpetuated in the disputations of medieval courtroom and schoolroom. If a ritualized
Dionysian discourse "largely or wholly narrative in form" could be
transformed into dramatic, dialogic representation (*WD*, 4), then a
similar transformation from dialogic legal ritual to dramatic representation would have been all the more likely. Moreover, legal oratory came fully stocked with its own characters: judges, attorneys,
plaintiffs and defendants, witnesses. Consequently, the archetypal
ludus of the law is as compatible with medieval dramatic structure
as that of the Mass.[67]

Therefore, if we grant that liturgical drama was inspired by spectacular "dialogic poems, living (lively) teachings designed to replace
virtues and vices, crimes and exploits, either real or imaginary, before the eyes of new generations" (*DC*, 52–53), then we may reasonably ask why the only arena in which the transition from
dialogue to drama should occur would be the church. It is logical
that, rather than traverse an intermediary stage in the liturgy, some
miracles and mystery plays might have originated directly from
other "living teachings," such as legal dialogue. Indeed, in the 1950s
Istvan Hajnal speculated that it was in the "lively science" of medieval canon law that one might "seek the first experimentation
with literature in the vernacular" (82). And as recently as 1985 William Davenport theorized that the "main connecting-link between
drama and academic philosophy was debate."[68] Although (within
the admittedly modest scope of his project) he offered no explanation
as to precisely how "a learned drama could have been born" through
the academic training of theologians and lawyers (96), that explanation inheres in the study of the dramatic orality of delivery. The
literary reconstruction of dramatic elements of delivery demonstrates the extent to which rhetoric and drama were indeed "inter-
penetrating and intertwining forms" and validates hitherto untested
hypotheses about the "natural drama of law."[69]

Ultimately, by restoring delivery to our readings of legal and dramatic discourse, we enhance our understanding of the generic in-

---

that the "lively dialogue" of "disputing troubadours" was a paradigm for drama:
Dramatic Traditions of the Dark Ages, 181–203.

[67]For the Mass as archetypal *ludus*, see Rey-Flaud, *PDMA*, 83; Axton, chap. 4;
Hardison, *CRCD*, 77–79, 187–92; and Young, 1: chap. 2.

[68]Davenport, *Fifteenth-Century English Drama*, 96.

[69]Campbell, "Elements of Rhetorical Form."

terplay between early forms of ritual and representation. A mimetic forensic rhetoric does not preempt the liturgy or mimicry as origins of drama, but rather resituates those ritualized discourses along a single performance continuum—a continuum that then encourages us to recast our entire concept of origins. Once that continuum has been reestablished, and once delivery is approached as an entire gamut of theatrical cues for oral tradition, a new perception of the connections between rhetoric, law, mimicry, dialogue, and the "origins" of drama is possible. What I propose, then, is a systematic reevaluation of the aspects of delivery that assisted in the dramatization of legal rhetoric and that promise to account for the popularity of so many legal structures in medieval drama. Reconsidered in light of the long *letteraturizzazione* of rhetoric, the Basochiens may well continue to appear to be the "fathers of French comedy," but by no means are they the first fathers.

In the final analysis, the troping of the medieval liturgy appears no longer as an isolated phenomenon but as a single manifestation of many sorts of mimetic impulse, some of which had been nurtured and perpetuated within the law courts. The advent of impersonation within the rhetorical tradition provides a more reasonable scenario for the emergence of liturgical drama than pure chance or happy coincidence.[70] For if those dramatic criteria were already in place in the ritualized rhetoric of law, then their subsequent appearance in the medieval liturgy does not constitute a break in tradition but makes for a certain coherence in tradition. Thus, we need not accept Young's emphatic assertions that the Latin drama of the church lent itself to "treatment in isolation," that there was no "continuation of an ancient tradition," and that "no importation" or "other dramatic tradition engendered it, or dictated its form or content." Medieval liturgical drama was not, as he claims, a "spontaneous new birth and growth within the confines of Christian worship"; it did not emerge ex nihilo; it was not, as Hardin Craig asserts, a completely independent development, a "special act of invention" (4). Even Bloch was so careful not to fall into the trap of *Geistesgeschichte* that he finessed the question of influence by positing the presence of a "polyvalent mental structure whose transformational effect was felt in seemingly divergent areas of cultural and social life" (*MFLL*, 175). But the dramatic history of forensic rhetoric clar-

[70]To Hardin Craig, for instance, "impersonation, action, and dialogue happened to come together" (4).

ifies just how easily such a "polyvalent mental structure" could have come to be and remained in place. An enlightened appreciation of the polyvalence of dramatic delivery legitimizes discussions of the reciprocal influence of legal and literary performance one on the other.

2 From Legal Ritual to Dramatic Representation in Classical Antiquity and the Middle Ages

"Your public speaker," wrote Tacitus, "can't get along without 'hear, hear,' and the clapping of hands. He must have what I may call his stage."[1] By the time he penned his dialogue on the decline of eloquence in the first century, Tacitus no longer considered lawyers to be orators. But what were they? Call the "good speakers of the present day 'pleaders,' 'advocates,' 'counsel,' " he insisted, "—anything rather than 'orators' [causidici et advocati et patroni et quidvis potius quam oratores vocantur]" (1). In fact, the entire discussion opens with Aper indicting Maternus because of his participation in the ultimate metamorphosis of the legal discipline, the abandonment of law in favor of dramaturgy: "You have not had enough of those tragedies of yours? Otherwise you would not turn your back on your profession of speaker and pleader, and spend your whole time with plays" (3).

The veritable obsession of the legal advocate with the histrionic ramifications of his duty as *actor* had provoked a shift in focus within rhetoric. No longer the noble civic and political tool described by Cicero and even less the dialectically oriented Platonic quest for truth, forensic oratory had been invaded and transformed by a rhetorical imperative not unlike that of the earliest sophists: the all-encompassing desire to please audiences. That particular manifestation of *letteraturizzazione* bespeaks a profound transmutation from speech-centered theories of rhetoric to audience-centered the-

<hr>

[1]Tacitus, *Dialogus de oratoribus*, 39.

ories, from a didactic concentration on the logic of speeches to their mimesis and reception as drama. Aper called in vain upon the powers of his own rhetoric to persuade Maternus to forsake "the narrow sphere of pleading at the bar" and to "cultivate the gift of utterance in its higher and holier form" (4). The "lower," more appreciated form of legal eloquence was dramatic spectacle.

In view of the proliferation of mimetic elements in delivery, there can be no doubt as to the dramatic quality of forensic rhetoric. The question to be addressed next, however, is whether the specific features that rendered it dramatic could in fact have contributed to its aestheticization into drama. Karl Young, for example, once speculated briefly that such dialogic genres as the *chanson à personnages*, *aube, tenson,* and *conte* might have undergone a dramatization similar to that of the medieval liturgy. Although he conceded the possibility that separate speakers might have taken the various roles during performance, he concluded that that supposition was not provable: "In spite of all the dramatic possibilities here, none of these particular literary diversions can be called a play."[2] But literary recourse to conventions of delivery supplies the needed proof. Indeed, *actio* itself emerges as a prototype of many dramatizations of ritual in antiquity and the Middle Ages—such as the Dionysian liturgy, the Roman forum, the Christian liturgy, the Dutch Chamber of Rhetoric, the disputational spectacle of the quodlibet, and the rhetorico-dramatic antics of the Basochiens.

The intense critical scrutiny drama has received for centuries now has given rise to a widely accepted view that that genre originated, in Nicoll's words, "without any conscious planning... with three main characteristic features: (a) the mingling of audience and actors; (b) the establishment of a series of platforms or small structures indicating special localities... and (c) the utilization of the space between these platforms or structures as an acting area" (*WD*, 107). No student of classical and medieval rhetoric can fail to recognize that those generic building blocks were all present in forensic oratory. By including with those features the respect requested by early theorists for the "gulf" between oral performance and written record, and also for the theatricality of the primordial agon (as described, for example, by Honorius),[3] I propose to explore precisely how drama might have emerged from legal and legalistic discourse. In the most

[2] Young, *Drama of the Medieval Church*, 1:10.
[3] Honorius, *Gemma animae*, trans. Bevington in *Medieval Drama*.

literal sense, the courtroom was the rhetorician's "stage," and his "drama" was rhetoric.

Orators continued their avid imitation of actors throughout antiquity and the Middle Ages by deliberately privileging spectacle over proof in three areas that suggest the very conditions under which drama is known to have emerged: (1) the creation of a predisposing theatrical space in the courtroom, assisted by such material trappings as costume and props; (2) the role of conflict as both a quintessential dramatic plot and a sine qua non of early drama; and (3) the interaction between audience participation in ritualized courtroom battle play and the aestheticization of the legal agon. I do not wish to imply that this paradigm represents the complete generic picture of drama (such considerations as temporality, for example, might have been included as well), yet recourse to early analogies between rhetoric and drama in all three areas promises to aid in the pursuit of generic models that take into consideration more of what we know about medieval plays than earlier classifications do and resolve anomalies. Since the rhetorical corpus supplies extensive documentation as to how and why the orator exploited theatrical conventions, any subsequent conclusions about the inherent theatricality of rhetoric will not have derived from a post hoc imposition of a modern literary construct. It will then be possible to arrive at a historically justified definition of forensic spectacle that is considerably less impressionistic than Harvey's "drama of law," and to analyze the momentous ramifications of the rhetorical tradition in the very creation of literary genres.

It is difficult, of course, to separate the three interrelated dramatic features under consideration here. Still, since the whole is better apprehended through an analysis of its parts, I treat them initially as such—but with the Ciceronian caveat that "a division into parts is more indefinite, like drawing streams of water from a fountain."[4] Like any paradigm, the model of theatrical space, conflict, and audience adaptation/reception may occasionally appear somewhat arbitrary. It suffices, however, to bear in mind the extent to which its components are intertwined. Their connections are not linear and diachronic, but concentric and synchronic. Additionally, while I felt some temptation to proceed chronologically, I have opted instead to consider simultaneously classical and medieval views of the

[4]Cicero, *Topica*, 7.33–34.

drama of rhetoric the better to convey the continuity of the theatricalization of eloquence.

The first criterion is the privileged theatrical space of legal performance—the temenos, a "sacred spot cut off and hedged in from
the 'ordinary' world," as Huizinga says (*HL*, 77). It was the orator's
exploitation of that space as his personal stage that provoked the
transformation of the courtroom into what Kenneth Burke would
later term the "predisposing structure of the *ground* or *scene* upon
which drama is enacted" (*POLF*, 106). By considering the shape of
the actual courtroom along with such attendant material trappings
as costume, makeup, and props, I argue that the legal conflict was
similarly enacted within a predisposing material space that nurtured the histrionic performance of a primordial drama. Whether
the disputational struggle was performed in the Ciceronian courtroom, the rue du Fouarre, the Châtelet, or the Pré-aux-Clercs, the
arena in which it unfolded was as crucial to the legal protodrama
as it was to the "theater of the church" once described by Honorius.
Critics have long been fascinated by the semiology of the egalitarian
"magic circle" of the medieval stage, in which each person became,
in Rey-Flaud's words, "the repository of the collective gaze."[5] But
the circular theater was by no means the only arena in which such
magic could take place. Magic could be made in the temenos of
law, too.

The dramatic conflict of forensic rhetoric constituted a microcosmic conflictual drama with an agon for its plot—as did its medieval disputational analogues in the quodlibet and the Basoche. At
the same time, however, the pro and contra clashes of forensic discourse were also verbal play, sharing with such cultural institutions
as sport, sophistry, philosophy, warfare, and theology a fusion of
"glorious exhibitionism and agonistic aspiration" (*HL*, 146). Battle
and play were easily conflated in the courtroom in what may well
prove to have been its most spectacular and sporting (if occasionally
dangerous) conflict: the physical pugnacity of the *rixe*. Despite the
protestations of Christian thinkers against widespread "uncivilized"
violence, the verbal battle of law often devolved into a physical
battle, all the while maintaining its status as a ritual mode of judgment, divination, and celebration.[6] Consequently, if medieval debate

---

[5]Rey-Flaud, *PDMA*, 12; see also Southern's discussion in *Medieval Theatre in the
Round*, 70–81; Olson on the interplay between architecture and theatrics in "Medieval Fortunes of 'Theatrica,' " 272.

[6]Huizinga has demonstrated compellingly the status of early legal practice as a
combination of judgment ritual, divination, and celebration in *HL*, chap. 4. The

was "the verbal form of violence *par excellence,*" as Bloch calls it (*MFLL,* 164), then the status of forensic rhetoric as both verbal *and* physical violence rendered it a particularly compelling form of battle play, a ritual drama par excellence.[7]

That notion then helps us to contextualize the long-deplored violence of the medieval stage. For as audiences were integrated into a spectacular forensic conflict in what Rey-Flaud has called a "spectacle of participation" (*PDMA,* 17), illusion and reality became fused and confused. Like the Mass and the popular sword dance, like the medieval procession as it has been described by Alan Knight and by Bernard Guenée and François Lehoux,[8] and like medieval drama, classical and medieval legal ritual drew its audience into its proceedings and fostered lively exchanges between participants and onlookers. Moreover, forensic rhetoric exemplifies in a learned context the pervasive association of *ludi, luctae,* and *lusi* which is known to have spawned such popular "dramas" as the "Twelfth Night diversion" (c. 953) described by the Emperor Constantinus Porphyrogenitus: "two teams of masked warriors... armed with staves and shields presented a dance-combat... accompanied by stringed music, the clash of the weapons, and their own battle-songs."[9] For that reason, the conflictual forensic model is likely to prove as illuminating in the learned ratiocinations of the *procès de paradis* as it is in the domestic squabbling of the *Farce des drois de la Porte Bodès,* where its own agon was transformed into an aesthetic *imitatio veritatis,* a nascent form of dramatic unity, an "imaginary conflict."

I approach the generic interplay between law and drama through the analysis of three final features: (1) the actual "roles" played by the audience in the legal agon, not only physical but verbal; (2) the influence of their participation on a revised view of rhetorical audience adaptation; and (3) the ultimate theatricalization as that very adaptation encouraged lawyers to exploit impersonation, pity, fear, and verisimilitude for their participating audiences in a mimesis of

---

celebratory nature of medieval conflictual discourse has also been analyzed by John Ward in an unpublished paper, "Education in the Middle Ages and Renaissance"; Ong, *Ramus,* chap. 7; Grafton and Jardine, *From Humanism to the Humanities,* 89–97; and Garner, *Law and Society,* 97–99.

[7] For the protodramatic status of ritual battle play, see esp. Axton, *European Drama,* chap. 2; Chambers, *Mediaeval Stage,* 1:182–204; and Olson's fascinating discussion of John of Salisbury's *Policraticus* in "Medieval Fortunes," 276.

[8] Knight, *Aspects of Genre;* Guenée and Lehoux, *Entrées royales françaises.*

[9] *De ceremoniis* as cited in Tydeman, *Theatre in the Middle Ages,* 7; and see Axton, 33.

conflict—a veritable paraphrase for the conditions under which drama is known to have emerged. Classical and medieval lawyers knew what their audiences most desired—the drama of combat—and they desired to provide it. Among the "peculiar and characteristic vices of this metropolis of ours," wrote Tacitus, was the "passion for play actors, and the mania for gladiatorial shows and horse-racing" (histrionales favor et gladiatorum equorumque studia [29]). The participatory experience of forensic battle play created an aesthetic dynamic according to which audiences took pleasure in their own participation and the orator modified canonized rhetorical traditions of audience adaptation to enhance that pleasure. Once orators made conscious efforts to please and to play the participating crowd, the aims and reception of legal eloquence became transmuted: orators *impersonated* the "virtual speakers" of their discourse.

In that way they provoked one of the most stunning consequences of all in the *letteraturizzazione* of forensic rhetoric: the pathos of rhetorical pity and fear became the pathos of tragic *misericordia*; and the forensic conflict became the imitation of an agon, acquiring a nascent dramatic unity.[10] The nature of audience involvement in the medieval ludic experience might then provide a partial explanation for how an apparently prosaic ceremony such as forensic adjudication could have come to be conceived and received as spectacle. Ultimately, once aspects of theatrical space, battle play, ritual, audience participation, and audience adaptation have been reidentified within the history of forensic rhetoric, it is possible to resituate law along the same continuum that now includes such dramatic rituals as the popular sword dance and the medieval Mass. By molding their discourse to the aesthetic needs of the public, orators "enslaved" themselves to applause, nurturing a crucial interplay between legal ritual and dramatic representation; and the site of that commingling of rhetorical genre and literary genre was delivery.

Theatrical Space and the Orator's Stage

Ever since classical antiquity, forensic rhetoric has been delivered within the privileged space of a temenos. Reminiscent of both the theatrical space of Dionysian ritual and the "ecclesiastical theater"

---

[10]For pity, fear, and catharsis, see Aristotle's discussion in *Poetics*, 1449b (treated at greater length later in this chapter).

of Honorius, that temenos was demarcated for the representation of a particular type of agon: law was played out in a *vierschaar*—literally "a space divided off by four ropes or ... four benches." But whatever the geometric shape of the temenos, it was "a magic circle, a play-ground where the customary differences of rank are temporarily abolished" (*HL*, 76–77). Any understanding of the fluidity of ritual and representation in legal battle play must therefore be prefaced by a consideration of the physical space in which that agon took place. Kenneth Burke maintained that such material trappings were only "mechanistic considerations" necessary to the dramatic perspective but essentially "lifeless," a "mere property" (*POLF*, 115). I propose to show that in the courtroom there was nothing lifeless about them: stage, costume, and even makeup all contributed to the dramatization of the law.

First of all, the establishment of an architectural background has long provided crucial evidence for the emergence of drama from ritual. Nicoll, for example, argued that the earliest Greek dramas could be traced in part to the desire to "give the actors [an] opportunity for the changing of mask and dress and to provide for them an architectural background" (*WD*, 9). But if the delineation of a privileged space from the natural, ritualistic background of an open landscape helped to provoke the celebrated emergence of Greek drama from dithyrambic singing, it follows that a similar theatrical influence might have been exerted by the sacred space for law. Though the legal battle play is a far cry from the seventeenth-century *théâtre vitrine*, its temenos fulfills one of the critical criteria for the presence of drama: that the actor be separated in some way from the audience. We might then rephrase Styan's question about what qualities were brought to the dramatic experience if the play were performed "in a public street, a church or a private room" (*DSA*, 13) and inquire instead: What dramatic qualities were brought to the legal performance by the *vierschaar* or by such privileged medieval spaces for disputational battle as the Grand' Chambre of the Basochiens, the Pré-aux-Clercs, or the rue du Fouarre?

The literary properties of the temenos were as compelling to medieval commentators as they had once been to Tacitus. Lawyers had long been the envy of their poet and tragedian colleagues because their job came fully equipped with its own house to play in and with a built-in audience. Unlike their friends with a literary penchant, they were spared the inordinate trouble of rounding up an audience (*qui dignentur audire*), house, and recitation hall, and of spending money (Tacitus, 9). But perhaps the most exceptional aspect of the legal "theater" was its demarcation of the roles to be played there. Costume was the chief visual cue for the identification of judge, lawyers, and witnesses, and the legal cast of characters was also recognizable by their placement within the englobing structure of the temenos. One is reminded of Roland Barthes's analysis of how the demarcation of a privileged space for wrestling permits the recognition of the stock characters who occupy that space. The moment the competitors step into the ring, he theorized, the public is "invested" with the "obviousness of the roles": "As in the theatre, each physical type expresses to excess the part which has been assigned to the contestant.... Wrestlers therefore have a physique as peremptory as those of the characters of the *Commedia dell'Arte*, who display in advance, in their costumes and attitudes, the future contents of their parts."[11] During the theatricalization of forensic rhetoric, it was not only the wearing of ceremonial dress but the semiotics of the temenos that helped to delineate the dramatis personae of legal ritual.

One of the most concrete depictions of the interrelations between the ludic field of legal battle and the roles played in it appears in the *De necessariis observantiis scaccarii dialogus* (c. 1176).[12] In that educational dialogue, a master responds to a disciple's queries about the nature and function of the exchequer, a kind of giant "chessboard" (*scaccarius*) on which British legal battles were played out. Conjuring a vision of linear architecture that recalls the loci of the art of memory, the master is actually describing the theatrical space in which costumed characters were to wage their legal battles:

> The exchequer [chess-board] is an oblong board measuring about ten feet by five, used as a table by those who sit at it.... Over the [upper] exchequer is spread a cloth, bought in Easter term, of a special pattern, black, ruled with lines a foot, or a full span, apart. In the spaces between them are placed the counters, in their ranks.... But though such a board is called 'exchequer,' the name is transferred to the Court in session at it; so that if a litigant wins his case, or a decision on any point is taken by common consent, it is said to have happened 'at the Exchequer' of such a year. [6–7][13]

[11]Barthes, *Mythologies*, 13; trans. Lavers, 17.

[12]Written by Richard, son of Nigel [Fitzneale], Treasurer of England and Bishop of London. References are to Charles Johnson's edition/translation and are given parenthetically by page number. Moreover, the term *thesaurarius* (7) might well have recalled the *thesaurus* or "treasure house" of the *ars memorandi*.

[13]Like the rituals cited by Frye, legal spectacles were often "attached to the calendar year": *Anatomy of Criticism*, 105–7. The coincidence of the Exchequer's proceedings

In that conflation of conflict, contest, judgment, and spectacle, such vivid architecture helped the public to identify the ranks and roles of the participants. It is no coincidence that the delineation of a privileged space for dramatis personae was as integral to legal battle as it was to battle play, a phenomenon exemplified by such time-honored mises-en-scène as the judicial duel. Citing the Old Norse practice of marking out the battle ground "with wooden pegs or hazel-switches," Huizinga noted that the " 'staking out' of a place for battle is identical with the 'hedging in' (*hegen* in German) of a law court" (*HL*, 98–99). Indeed, medieval disputational spectacles were similarly inscribed, as when "loud-mouthed" theologians engaged in the conflictual quodlibetal spectacle in the streets around the Sorbonne: "in that most quiet of streets called the rue de Sorbonne, you may admire the most venerable of fathers, lords, and, as it were, the holy and divine satraps."[14] Like the memory stage with its protodramatic *imagines agentes*, the *scaccarius* housed its own *actores* who reenacted the drama of law. And, like their military and chess-piece analogues, litigators had different powers, different "moves" within their symbolic space, and were subject to different authority during their *ludi, lusi,* and *luctae:*

> For as on the chess-board the men are arranged in ranks, and move or stand by definite rules and restrictions. ... Just as on a chess-board, battle [*pugna*] is joined between the kings; here too the struggle takes place, and battle is joined [*conflictus est et pugna committitur*], mainly between two persons, to wit, the Treasurer and the Sheriff who sits at his account, while the rest sit by as judges to see and decide. [7]

But the most striking medieval attestation to the role of the temenos in law, battle, and spectacle was articulated by Isidore of Seville (ca. 570–636) in his encyclopedic *Etymologies*.[15] The work

---

with Easter is consistent with a similar commingling of drama, disputation, and ritual in both the quodlibet (held at Advent and Lent) and popular drama. Tydeman, for example, observed that Christianity "endeavoured to assimilate the old heathen festivals into the new patterns of worship by ensuring that the dates on which the church commemorated the significant events in the Christian calendar coincided with the old pre-Christian ceremonies" (12).

[14]Jean de Jandun, *De laudibus Parisius* (1323), as quoted in Le Roux de Lincy and Tisserand, *Paris et ses historiens*, 38–41; translation mine.

[15]References to Isidore of Seville's *Etymologies* are to the standard edition by W. M. Lindsay, *Isidori Hispalensis Episcopi Etymologiarum*, and are given parenthetically by section number. Bk. 18 appears in vol. 2. All translations are mine in collaboration with Alexander MacGregor, with the exception of a few selected passages that were translated by Brehaut in *Encylopedist of the Dark Ages*. They are indicated as his in the text. See also the bilingual Latin/Spanish edition, *Etymologías*, ed. Oroz Reta and Marcos Casquero.

is considered crucial by medievalists by virtue of its wide dissemination in universities, yet Isidore's fascinating discussion *"de bello
et ludis"* (bk. 18) has gone virtually unnoticed.[16] Inasmuch as it
constitutes one of the most remarkable extant testimonials to the
equivalence of verbal and physical warfare and of law and drama,
Book 18 merits extensive consideration from a rhetorico-dramatic
perspective. There Isidore conflates historically (and, of course,
etymologically) warfare, law, judgment, drama, sport, and spectacle,
articulating a complex relationship shared by sixty-nine fields as
seemingly diverse as wars and ball playing. As his attention shifts
almost imperceptibly from warfare (1–14) to forensic rhetoric (15)
to spectacle (16) to sport (17–26) to the circus (27–41) to the theater
(42–51) to the amphitheater (52–69), his exposition is rendered coherent by a focus on the theatrical space in which each combat ritual
is played out. Even if the many subjects strike the twentieth-century
reader as strange bedfellows, they would scarcely have appeared so
to future medieval readers trained in the agonistic exhibitionism of
the medieval university, who took Isidore as philological gospel.
The interrelations of war and play far surpass philological compatibility here; rather, they suggest a conception of battle play as a
theatrical form of judgment ritual. Isidore's passage from bloody to
bloodless to playful or "pretend" conflicts is so stunning that "De
bello et ludis" serves as an ideal point of departure for the study of
the interplay between ritual and representation in legal battle play.
It may be seen as emblematic of a more significant interplay between
conflictual discourse and mimesis, between law and the very
"origins" of drama.

After treating various aspects of warfare (victory, trumpets, types
of weaponry), Isidore analyzes briefly the term "helmet" in "De
galeis" (14). Though his subsequent treatment of litigation in "De
foro" (15) may seem somewhat abrupt to the modern reader, the
logic of that transition is consistent with the medieval concept of
battle as conflictual judgment ritual and also as play. From the battlefields of warfare Isidore proceeds logically to the ludic field of the
legal battle:

> Forus est exercendarum litium locus, a fando dictus (sive a Foroneo
> rege, qui primus Graecis leges dedit). Qui locus et Prorostra vocatur
> ab eo quod ex bello Punico captis navibus Carthaginensium rostra

---

[16]The principal exception is Glending Olson, who treats Isidore briefly in his
"Medieval Fortunes" (268, 270). For the dissemination of Isidore in the Middle Ages,
see *CR*, 18.

ablata sunt, et in foro Romano praefixa, ut esset huius insigne victoriae. Constat autem forus causa, lege et iudice.   [15]

The forum is the place for the working out of lawsuits. Its name derives
from *fari* [speak] (or from King Foroneo, who was the first to give laws
to the Greeks). This place is also called the "prorostrum" owing to
the fact that the prows taken from Carthaginian ships captured in the
Punic War [*sic*] were set up in the Roman forum to commemorate
this victory. The forum, then, is a place of lawsuit, law, and judgment.

Initially Isidore's reference to the bellicose origins of the very
terminology of jurisprudence and his subsequent transition to the
concept of spectacle (16) underscore the conflictual nature of legal
battle play. Defense and victory (*insigne victoriae*) constitute the
ends of law and words its weaponry, emerging now as the verbal
analogues for the arms he has just discussed. Both modes of warfare
were played out, of course, in a temenos—the battlefield in one case,
the forum in the other. Isidore thus demonstrates that law func-
tioned as the verbal equivalent for such conflictual judgment rituals
as the *combat singulier* or the judicial duel. His analysis supplies
the historical justification for Huizinga's characterization of warfare
as a kind of "trial by battle" (*HL*, 93) and Bloch's mediated ordeal
(*MFLL*, 164).

Next (and centuries before Barthes) Isidore moves to a consideration of the legal roles delineated by the space for the conflict he
has just described. As was the case in many an early drama, there
was a stock cast of characters. In fact, Bernard Schouler has argued
that those "character types" were to be found in the elaborate series
of legal questions (*staseis*) that lay at the foundation of forensic
discourse as Hermogenes described it.[17] The most important member of the cast was the judge—to be so named only if he were indeed
the incarnation of justice:

In omne autem iudicium sex personae quaeruntur: iudex, accusator,
reus et tres testes. Iudex dictus quasi ius dicens populo, sive quod iure
disceptet. Iure autem disceptare est iuste iudicare: non est autem
iudex si non est in eo iustitia.   [15]

For in every trial, six persons are involved: the judge, the accuser, the
defendant, and three witnesses. The judge is so called because he
"dispenses justice" to the people or because he "decides rightly." For
to decide rightly is to judge justly: and he is no judge if there is not
justice in him.

[17]Bernard Schouler, "Classification des personnes," 239.

More interesting still is the fact that Isidore's inquiry into the principal legal players is immediately followed by "De spectaculis" (16), a transition that suggests that the ritual of legal judgment was not only conflictual but theatrical. Legal oratory emerges as a spectacular *ludus* as entertaining as any sporting event:

> Dicta autem spectacula eo quod hominibus publica ibi praebeatur inspectio. Haec et ludicra nuncupata, quod in ludis gerantur aut in cenis. Ludorum origo sic traditur: Lydios ex Asia transvenas in Etruria consedisse duce Tyrreno, qui fratri suo cesserat regni contentione. [16]

> These are called "spectacles" because something is presented there for the public to look at. They are also called "plays" [*ludicra*] because they are "played out" on stage. The traditional origin of these "plays" is that the Lydians [*ludi* < *Lydii* (sic)], refugees from Asia Minor, settled in Etruria under their leader, Tirennus, who had lost to his brother in a struggle over the throne.

In that definition of contentious spectacle, Isidore cites Varro in order to analyze the interrelations of *ludi, lusi,* and *luctae.* Physical and legal warfare constitute analogues for the play fighting connected to such spectacular forms as religious and popular festivals. In fact, E. K. Chambers cited those very elements as indicative of a "far from rigid code of village ethics" that lay somewhere "on the border line between play and jurisprudence" (1:152). All were pleasing to the public, and all could be reshaped by mimetic ends:

> Igitur in Etruria inter ceteros ritus superstitionum suarum spectacula quoque religionis nomine instituerunt. Inde Romani arcessitos artifices mutuati sunt; et inde ludi a Lydis vocati sunt. Varro autem dicit *ludos a luso vocatos,* quod iuvenes per dies festos solebant ludi exultatione *populum delectare.* Unde et eum lusum iuvenum et diebus festis et templis et religionibus reputant. Nihil iam de causa vocabuli, dum rei causa idolatria sit. [16; emphasis mine]

> And so, among other rites in Etruria connected with their superstitions, they also instituted spectacles under the pretext of religion. The Romans had actors brought in from Etruria on loan; consequently, "plays" [*ludi*] are so called from the Lydians [i.e., the Etruscans]. Furthermore, Varro says that "plays" [*ludi*] are so called from "entertainments" [*lusi*], because on holidays young men habitually amused the people with the verve of their play. Consequently, they considered this "play" by the youth appropriate for holidays, temples, and reli-

gious rites. We will say no more about the etymology [*causa*] of this word, since the origin [*causa*] of the practice itself is idolatry.

Like Tertullian, Isidore situates the origins of the theater in idolatry and evil. But, moral ambiguities notwithstanding, there was nothing ambiguous about the role of the temenos in the demarcation of a privileged theatrical space for spectacular, ritualistic battle play, both verbal and physical.

As Isidore moves to a discussion of sports in sections 17–26, it is his continued emphasis on the polysemous *ludus* that serves as the transition between battle and play, spectacle and sport in the gymnasium, in the circus, in the arena, or on the stage (16). Each of the phenomena treated is analyzed in relation to the locus in which it is enacted, starting with the gymnasium. After all, the term *ludus* could also mean the actual place of intellectual or physical exercise:

> Gymnicus ludus est velocitatis ac virium gloria. Cuius locus gymnasium dicitur, ubi exercentur athletae et cursorum velocitas conprobatur. Hinc accidit ut omnium propre artium exercitia gymnasia dicantur. ["De Ludo gymnico," 17]

> Athletic "play" is a glorification of speed and strength. The place where it is practiced is called the gymnasium, where athletes train and where the speed of runners is put to the test. And so it happened that school exercises in virtually all the arts are called *gymnasia*.

Granted, the *Etymologies* was a sort of dictionary that necessarily came fully equipped with its own obvious structure; yet that Isidore chose to present the relations between his entries as a progression from serious physical battle to bloodless verbal disputation to the silly dice games that end Book 18 must be considered significant. The ease with which Isidore has passed from the spectacular conflicts of warfare and law to the physical play of sports thus confirms the arguments of Huizinga and Sir William Blackstone that law was a quintessential form of battle play, and that the whole "ceremony" of the judicial duel "much resembled certain athletic entertainments at a village sports [*sic*]."[18] In addition to its meaning as the privileged locus *"ubi exercentur athletae"* (where athletes train), the gymnasium traditionally signified another forum: the public school, high school, or college. In that sense, Isidore's gymnasium conjures up for us (and doubtless for his numerous later medieval readers) no-

[18]See Huizinga's discussion of Blackstone's *Commentaries on the Laws of England* in *HL*, 94; also Olson, "Medieval Fortunes," 266.

tions of the entire scholastic arena in which such exercises as the
progymnasmata were practiced by students training in disputation
and declamation.[19] Indeed, in his satirical portrayal of the "warriors"
of the theology faculty at the University of Paris, Jean de Jandun
was bemused by a similar rhetorical "circus": "of what use, and of
what advantage to the Catholic religion such an exercise, God only
knows" (as quoted in Le Roux de Lincy and Tisserand, 40). Isidore
thus rearticulates an analogy between rhetoric and battle play which
looks backward to Plato's early equation of rhetoric and exercise in
the *Gorgias* (464–65) and forward to the still more forceful discussion
of Juan Luis Vives.

As Book 18 continues, the interplay between verbal and physical
battle play is reasserted in other sections on the conflict, spectacle,
and theatrical space of sport (18–26), including "Of Wrestling" (23),
"Of the Gymnasium" (24), and "Of Contest" (25). Implements of
battle such as the arrow (which had appeared earlier in "De sagittis,"
sec. 8) now reappear in the context of the entertaining agon of sport,
which is described as follows: "Luctatio a laterum conplexu vocata,
quibus comminus certantes innitent, qui Graeca appellatione athletae vocantur" (Wrestling is so called from grappling each other,
where the competitors engage hand to hand; these competitors are
[likewise] called "athletes" by the Greeks ["De luctatione," 23]).
The athletic struggle took place in a physical space (the *palaestra*)
that was as carefully delimited as the hedged-in trial by battle, the
juridical forum, or the *scaccarius:*

> Locus autem luctationis palaestra dicitur. Palaestram autem vel *apo
> tis pales*, id est a luctatione, vel *apo tom pallein*, id est a motu ruinae
> fortis, nominatam dicunt, scilicet quod in luctando, cum medios ar-
> ripiant, fere quatiant; idque apud Graecos *pallein* vocatur. Quidam
> opinantur artem luctandi ursorum contentione monstratam; namque
> inter ceteras feras eos solos et erigi congressos et subsidere celeriter
> ac reverti, et modo manibus temtare invicem, modo conplexu abigere
> sese more luctantium.   ["De palaestra," 24]

> Moreover, the place for wrestling is called the *palaestra*. They say it
> comes from *pale*, that is, "wrestle, struggle," or from *pallein*, that is,
> "shake and collapse," because in wrestling they practically shake
> when they grab each other around the middle; and this is called *pallein*
> by the Greeks. There are those who believe that the art of wrestling
> was suggested by bears fighting each other; for among the other wild
> beasts, they are the only ones capable of standing upright and then

[19]For a helpful discussion of the *progymnasmata*, see, e.g., *CR*, 163–64.

engaging, only to settle back on all fours and beat a hasty retreat—
now attacking with their forepaws, now pulling out of their opponent's
grasp in the manner of wrestlers.

In Isidore's conflation of learned and popular, verbal and physical
spectacles throughout Book 18, all such struggles emerge as rituals
of judgment. And among them is a theatrical agon remarkably similar to that described by Honorius. As the interrelations between
conflict and spectacle become more pronounced, Isidore focuses increasingly on the theater, turning now to the nature of an agon that
fused celebration, fighting, and theatrical space:

> Quae Latine certamina, Graeci *agonas* vocant, a frequentia qua ce-
> lebrabantur. Siquidem et omnem coetum atque conventum agona dici;
> ali quod in circulis et quasi agoniis, id est sine angulo locis, ederentur
> nuncupatos agonas putant. ["De agone," 25; emphasis mine]

> For what the Romans call *certamina* ["contests"] the Greeks call
> *agonas*, because of the throngs before which they were performed. By
> extension, all meetings and assemblies are called *agonas*; others think
> that they were called *agonas* because they were produced in a ring,
> that is, in places "without corners."

The theatricality of the agon emerges with greater clarity still as
Isidore supplies glosses on the celebratory nature of the different yet
related dramatic competitions of the circus: "Ludi Circenses sac-
rorum causa ac deorum gentilium *celebrationibus* instituti sunt:
unde et qui eos *spectant* daemonum *cultibus* inservire videntur"
(The sports of the circus were established on account of worship,
and because of the honoring of the heathen gods. Whence those who
view them seem to be furthering the worship of evil spirits ["De
ludis circensibus," 27, trans. Brehaut]). The ritual origins of the
circus and its consequent compatibility with paganism, the privileged *spatium* in which it occurs, and the presence therein of the
visual *effigies* that traditionally occupied the memory stage are then
underscored in "De circo" (28):

> Circus Soli principaliter consecratus est a paganis, cuius aedis medio
> spatio et effigies de fastigio aedis emicat, quod non putaverint sub
> tecto consecrandum quem in aperto habent. Est autem circus omne
> illud spatium quod circuire equi solent.... Fuit autem maga et ve-
> nefica et sacerdos daemonum, in cuius habitu et opera magicae artis
> et cultus idolatriae recognoscitur.

> The circus was originally consecrated by the pagans in honor of the
> sun, whose shrine stood in the middle, and whose statue stood out
> on the peak of the shrine, because they thought that the sun, whom
> they enjoyed out in the open, should not be worshiped under a roof.
> In any case, a "circus" is all the space that horses normally "circle."
> ...But she [Circe] was a sorceress and a poisoner, and a priestess of
> demons, in whose practices we may recognize both the deeds of the
> magic art and the cult of idolatry.

As Isidore terminates his treatment of the circus (28–41) with a
discussion "de coloribus equorum," the elements of war (horses,
spears, runners) are again recontextualized as play in a context that
is strikingly similar to Tacitus's grouping of the "passion for play
actors, and the mania for gladiatorial shows and horse-racing" (29).
But the Christian moral indictment of such ritual battle play is never
absent, as when Isidore exhorts his reader to avoid such bastions of
idolatry:

> Unde animadvertere debes, Christiane, quod Circum numina in-
> munda possideant. Quapropter alienus erit tibi locus quem plurimi
> Satanae spiritus occupaverunt: totum enim illum diabolus et angeli
> eius repleverunt.

> Whence you ought to notice, Christian, how many unclean gods they
> have around. Therefore the place which many spirits of Satan have
> seized shall be alien to you. For all that place the devil and his angels
> have filled. [41, trans. Brehaut]

Even though his spectacular cast of characters is remarkably similar
to that of the mystery play, Isidore insists that this was not the noble
theatrical space of the church, and that that Christian locus could
not circumscribe a pagan spectacle in the same way. Such a spectacle
was a form of cupidity to be despised: "Quod spectaculum, Christiane, odere debes, quorum odisti auctores" (Wherefore, O Christian,
you must shun the spectacle, whose creators are also to be shunned
["Quid quo patrono agatur," 51).

Given Isidore's fascinating premonition of the medieval fusion of
combat, law, disputation, spectacle, sport, and play; given Honorius's description of the Mass as a theatrical agon; and given what
we know of the pervasive confusion in the rhetorical tradition between oratory and acting, can it really be coincidental that the next
subject under discussion in "De bello et ludis" is the theater? Just
as a privileged physical space demarcated the roles played in the
dramatic "arenas" Isidore has identified thus far, so now the *thea-*

trum (like the *scaccarius*) demarcates roles, players, and audience in its own ritual space. Theater is clearly situated within the same context of "glorious exhibitionism and agonistic aspiration" (*HL*, 146) as warfare, play, law, and sport:

> Theatrum est quo *scena* includitur, semicirculi figuram habens, in quo stantes omnes inspiciunt. Cuius forma primum rotunda erat, *sicut et amphitheatri;* postea ex medio amphitheatro theatrum factum est. *Theatrum* autem ab *spectaculo* nominatum, *apo tis theorias,* quod in eo populus stans desuper atque *spectans ludos* contemplaretur. ["De theatro," 42; emphasis mine]

> A theater is where a stage building is enclosed, having a semicircular shape, in which all the spectators may stand to watch. Initially its form was circular, as with the amphitheater; but later the theater was made out of half an amphitheater. The theater is so called from the act of watching, *theoria* in Greek, because inside the theater, the people stood high up and watched the plays from there.

The subsequent analogy of the theater to the pulpit in "De scena" (43) enables Isidore to conflate all the loci for battle play he has treated in Book 18. For the term *pulpitum* denotes not only the scaffolding and platforms of the actor's stage but also the "pulpit" of preaching, public representations, lectures, and disputation:

> *Scena* autem erat locus infra *theatrum* in modum domus *instructa cum pulpito,* qui pulpitus orchestra vocabatur; *ubi cantabant comici, tragici, atque saltabant histriones et mimi.* Dicta autem scena Graeca appellatione, eo quod in speciem domus erat instructa. [43; emphasis mine]

> Moreover, the stage building was a place below the theater [proper], the size of a house built with a platform [in front], the "pulpit," which pulpit used to be called the "orchestra," where the comic and tragic poets sang, and actors and mimes danced. Moreover, it is also called the *skene* in Greek, because it was constructed to look like a house.

Book 18 of the *Etymologies* then draws to a close (44–69) with a consideration of the other modes of nonverbal spectacle mentioned in "De scena"—phenomena known to be influential in the origins of drama: music (47), impersonation (48), mimicry (49), dancing (50), the combative games of the amphitheater (52–59), and gambling or contest (60–69). In "De amphitheatro," for example, Isidore continues to foreshadow the medieval commingling of sport, battle, play,

and the very origins of drama with a discussion of yet another form
of conflictual spectacle, the gladiatoral display:

> *Amphitheatrum locus est spectaculi, ubi pugnant gladiatores.* Et inde
> *ludum gladiatorium* dictum quod in eo iuvenes usum armorum div-
> erso motu condiscant, et modo inter se aut gladiis aut pugnis certantes,
> modo contra *bestias incedentes;* ubi non odio, sed praemio inlecti
> subeunt ferale certamen. *Amphitheatrum* dictum, quod ex duobus
> *theatris* sit factum.   [52; emphasis mine]

> The amphitheater is the place for the spectacle in which gladiators
> fight. Consequently, it is called a gladiatorial "play" or "school" [*lu-
> dum*] because inside it young men learn to master the use of weapons
> with all sorts of maneuvers—sometimes fighting each other with
> swords or with their fists, at other times going up against wild beasts.
> They undergo these beastly contests not out of hatred but because
> they are enticed by the rewards. It is called an amphitheater because
> it is composed of two theaters.[20]

Even in "De orchestra" (44) Isidore concentrates on the existence
of a physical space for pugnacious spectacle. Disputation, music,
theater, and fighting are interrelated here in a way that seems to
anticipate the later *puys* and suggests the antiphonal/agonistic
origins of drama:

> Orchestra autem pulpitus erat scenae, ubi *saltator agere* posset, aut
> duo *inter se disputare.* Ibi enim *poetae comoedi* et *tragoedi* ad cer-
> tamen conscendebant, hisque *canentibus* alii *gestus* edebant. Officia
> scenica: *tragoedi, comoedi, thymelici, histriones, mimi et salta-
> tores.*   [44; emphasis mine]

> The orchestra is the platform of the stage, where one dancer could
> perform or two could compete with each other. For it was here that
> comic and tragic poets stepped up to compete, and, while they sang,
> others staged a pantomime. Theatrical occupations: tragedians, co-
> medians, musicians, actors, mimes and dancers.

There is no separation here between verbal and physical modes of
conflictual spectacle. Tragic poets, whom Isidore describes as "qui
antiqua gesta atque facinora sceleratorum regum luctuosa carmine
spectante populo concinebant" (those who sang in mournful verses

---

[20]This "bestial" register also occurs in Vives, who describes disputing students
and masters as "wild beasts": *De tradendis disciplinis,* 61. References are to Watson's
accessible translation, *Vives: On Education,* and are given parenthetically by page
number.

of the ancient deeds and crimes of wicked kings while the people watched [45]), recall Lucian's mimes, who exercised their art in the same ludic and agonistic context. The same holds true for comic actors: "Comoedi sunt qui privatorum hominum acta dictis aut gestu cantabant" (Comedians are they who represented by song and gesture the doings of men in private life [46, trans. Brehaut]). But they resemble "dueling," disputing, declaiming sophists as well. In fact, it was no coincidence that the "emergence of tournaments in their oldest and bloodiest form... coincided in time with the evil, lamented by Peter Damiani, of professional windbags who wandered about prating of their art and gaining signal victories like the Greek sophists of old" (*HL*, 155).

In the final analysis, Isidore's inclusion of forensic rhetoric in the long list of modes of battle play suggests that law must take its proper place among the ritual origins of drama. Isidore is the quintessential medieval authority on the theatricalization of rhetoric; and his etymological justification of the interplay of legal oratory, drama, battle, circus, and spectacle attests to an intellectual climate in which the drama inherent in rhetorical conflict might readily have developed into conflictual drama as such. In fact, he explicitly links spectacular conflict (be it physical or verbal) to the origins of the theater in "De horum exercitatione ludorum" (59), citing the insidious pleasure taken there by a corrupt people:

> Haec quippe *spectacula crudelitatis* et inspectio vanitatum non solum hominum vitiis, sed et *daemonum* iussis instituta sunt. Proinde nihil esse debet Christiano cum Circensi *insania*, cum *inpudicitia theatri*, cum amphitheatri crudelitate, cum atrocitate arenae, cum luxuria ludi. Deum enim negat qui talia praesumit, fidei Christiane praevaricator effectus, qui id denuo appetit quod in lavacro iam pridem renuntiavit; id est diabolo, pompis et operibus eius. [Emphasis mine]

> These spectacles of cruelty and this gazing upon vanities were established not only by the fault of men but by the command of demons. Wherefore a Christian ought to have nothing to do with the madness of the circus, with the shamelessness of the theatre, with the cruelty of the amphitheatre, with the atrocity of the arena, with the luxury of the *ludus*. For he denies God who ventures on such things, becoming a violator of the Christian faith—he who seeks afresh that which he long before renounced in baptism, that is, the devil, his parades and his works. [59, trans. Brehaut]

These objections formed the leitmotiv of the tirades launched against spectacle, drama, and law by medieval ecclesiastical au-

thorities, who condemned priests transformed into soldiers and lawyers obsessed with the spectacle of their own war of words.[21] As
displeased as Tacitus and Quintilian once had been, they lashed out
in the Provisions of Oxford (1253) and the Synods of Exeter (1384)
against the same group of *spectacula crudelitatis*—"wrestling-
matches, dancing to the singing of songs, or other disgraceful games
... theatrical plays [*ludos theatrales*] and shows by jesters" [as quoted
in Tydeman, 17]. Similar "insanities" in the quodlibet were also
indicted, as when an anonymous thirteenth-century commentator
complained that its spectacular *quaestiones* were "inutiles et su-
pervacuae, nihil pertinentes ad aedificationem fidei et morum" (useless and superfluous, in no way conducive to the edification of faith
and morals [*LQ*, 1:15]). As we shall see, forensic rhetoric, scholastic
disputation, and drama were all to become *spectacula crudelitatis*.

Ultimately, a focus on the commingling of battle, play, and spectacle in legal rhetoric illuminates the historical continuum of drama.
The rhetorical foundations for protodrama had been laid in ancient
Greece and remained strong in the medieval university, where Latin
served as "the ceremonial polemic instrument" in the "ritual combats" of Scholastic disputation (*RRT*, 17–18). Therefore, if medieval
drama was an amalgam of conflict and spectacle, an "imaginary
conflict" (*PDMA*, 78), and if forensic rhetoric was "profoundly agonistic and ludic" (*HL*, 156), it is surely profitable to compare the two
on the basis of their respective performances of conflictual discourse.
Even though many of the ludic qualities of legal rhetoric are no
longer immediately apparent in the modern courtroom (*HL*, 84),
there is a reason why the courtroom drama has remained so enormously popular over the ages, as witness the innocuous half hour
of television entertainment in *The People's Court* or the French
Affaire suivante, the presence of cameras in court for the rape trial
of a member of the Kennedy family, and the birth of Court TV, a
cable network devoted to the airing of trials. The audience reactions
observed long ago by classical and medieval rhetoricians have not
changed substantively over time: "strife is received by the audience
with great applause, for the spectacle of a fight is most pleasing to
them" (Vives, 61). The more conflictual the judgment ritual, the
more spectacular; the more spectacular, the more pleasing to the
audience; the more pleasing to the audience, the greater lawyers'

---

[21]See Axton's discussion of Gerhoh of Reichersberg (45). The expression "war of
words" is that of an anonymous thirteenth-century commentator who denounced
the degeneration of the quodlibetal disputation into *"pugnae verborum"* (quoted in
Glorieux, *LQ*, 1:15–16. Garner employs similar terminology (109).

efforts to please. When forensic rhetoric was thus turned into a battle play, it became one of the origins of drama.

Wars of Words

"The art which is the subject of our discourse," wrote Tacitus, "is not a quiet and peaceable art" (40). Indeed, when we visualize Lady Rhetoric today, the picture that often comes to mind is Martianus Capella's armor-clad maiden emerging with hypostatized verbal armor. Rhetoric was her conflict and words were her sword:

> The weapons she carried in her hands, with which she was equally adept at defending herself and at wounding her foes, shone with blinding flashes of brilliance.... She had the power, so to speak, of a queen over all things, able to lead men where she would and to hold them back when she would, to bring them to tears or to rouse them to frenzy, and to bring about a change in attitudes and convictions in governments as well as in armies at war.[22]

Classical and medieval commentators considered forensic argumentation to be the verbal analogue of physical combat; and the strength with which that image has persisted over time is directly related to the conflictual register of debate itself. Ever since Plato's Stranger described the sophist as the "profit-making type of professional of the art of eristic; eristic being a form of controversy, controversy of disputation, disputation of combat, combat of conflict, and conflict of acquisition,"[23] debate, dialectic, and disputation have been viewed as wars of words. Nowhere is that more apparent than in the pro and contra argumentation of forensic rhetoric.

Classical and medieval treatises allude frequently to the bellicose and even militaristic nature of the courtroom struggle, the *acies, agmen, pugna, altercatio*. Legal rhetoric was a conflictual engagement; it was to be equipped not with "timbrels," says Quintilian, but with "weapons" to "parry our adversary's blows before we strike him ourselves."[24] Lady Rhetoric might well have been the handmaiden of truth, but she was the weapon of truth as well. And if stylized language constituted her weaponry, then the dialogic clash of forensic speeches constituted her fiercest battle. As late as the

[22]Martianus Capella, *De nuptiis*, trans. Miller, 3.
[23]Plato, *Sophist*, 226a. See Huizinga's discussion of Plato in *HL*, 149.
[24]Quintilian, *Institutio oratoria*, V, 12.21; IV, 2.26.

Renaissance, Vives drew upon his experience at the University of
Paris to reiterate that age-old notion in the moralistic/pedagogical
context of the *De tradendis disciplinis:* "The struggle for truth may
be likened to a battle which takes place for the deliverance of truth.
But when truth has been released, forthwith arms must be laid down
and, as the spears formerly showed their glitter in the contest, they
must be lowered before their Empress."[25] If, however, Vives continued to find it necessary to remind disputers to lay down their swords,
he was responding in part to the persistent tendency of forensic
conflict to depart from the serious quest for truth and to emphasize
instead the spectacle of conflict as an end in itself. During the histrionic delivery of legal argumentation, orators came to focus more
on the drama of the conflict than on the epistemological function
of pro and contra inquiry; whence the transmutation of a theatrical
forensic conflict into a nascent conflictual drama.

Long recognized as both an integral component and an origin of
drama, the agon is a crucial criterion by which to evaluate the generic
fluidity between law and theater. Just as it was often impossible to
distinguish between dramatic rhetoric and rhetorical drama, so the
line between dramatic conflict and conflictual drama was hard to
discern. It is helpful to bear in mind Huizinga's caveat that if we
are to understand archaic justice, we must abandon our "preoccupation with ethical values" and adopt instead a conception of medieval law that is "purely agonistic" (*HL,* 78). At the same time, the
theatrical delivery of the bellicose quest for justice helped to render
law profoundly ludic as well. According to T. F. T. Plucknett, "the
whole business of pleading orally, in face of the court and with
opponents ready to pounce at any moment, was an immensely skilful and recondite game."[26] Sharing the three fundamental characteristics of play forms cited by Huizinga—the game of chance, the
contest, and the verbal battle (*HL,* 84)—legal and legalistic disputation might thus be profitably resituated within the larger ludic/
agonistic context of a medieval society that literally plays itself out
in its magic, rituals, tournaments, and military sports.[27] At the University of Paris, which was dominated by a "mixture of rhetoric,
war and play" (*HL,* 156), boys went to school "to war ceremonially

[25]Vives, *Vives: On Education,* 175. For Vives's educational training, see Guerlac's
introduction to her edition/translation of his *Adversus pseudodialecticos* and *De
causis corruptarum artium,* bk. III. References to the latter text are given parenthetically by page number.
[26]Plucknett, *Early English Legal Literature,* 103.
[27]Le Goff, *Civilisation de l'Occident médiéval,* 444.

with each other (and with the teacher)" (*RRT*, 18). The theatrical conflicts of the Ciceronian courtroom and the *progymnasmata* of the Roman schools for declamation were thus perpetuated in the medieval trivium long before the heyday of the spectacular Basoche. Seen in that light, the battle play of classical legal oratory appears as an analogue not only of the verbal and physical struggles of the Basochiens on the Pré-aux-Clercs but of the "great jousts" of the quodlibeta, where, Glorieux tells us, "adversaries" confronted one another and Thomas Aquinas patiently endured the "assaults of his challengers" (*LQ*, 1:35, 20, 33).

"Set two forces side by side," wrote Longinus in "On the Sublime," "and the stronger always borrows the virtues of the other"—a phenomenon he viewed as "natural enough" (15, 11). In the courtroom, the stronger of the legal "virtues" was the dramatic representation of conflict; the weaker was the supposed raison d'être of that conflict—the quest for legal equity. The discovery of the potential genesis of drama within the courtroom must therefore be based on the preeminence accorded to either "virtue" at any given moment. Forensic battles often erupted into actual physical struggles. It is fruitful to reconsider from that perspective the similarities between the violent forensic agon and the long-denounced violence of the medieval stage, which often represented its "fictive" subjects so graphically that it staggers the twentieth-century imagination. The intense struggles of rhetoric thus serve as a logical (if morally tenuous) bridge between forensic and dramatic "aesthetics," both of which tended to blur the distinctions between illusion and reality (again, one of the hallmarks of early drama).

Tacitus once described the orator as someone who "enters the lists of debate with all the equipment [general culture] of a man of learning, like a warrior taking the field in full armour" (in aciem omnibus armis instructus, sic in forum omnibus artibus armatus exierit [32]). He too viewed legal discourse as an "ever ready weapon" and declamatory training as a militaristic preparation against "opponents and antagonists, who fought with swords, not with wooden foils" (34). Like a squire, the young rhetorical apprentice followed his master about in an effort to become proficient in the verbal weaponry of his craft by hearing his "word-combats at first hand, standing by him in his duellings, and learning, as it were, to fight in the fighting-line" (ita ut altercationes quoque exciperet et iurgiis interesset, utque sic dixerim, pugnare in proelio disceret [34]). The school, wrote Seneca, had "always been taken to be a sort of school

for gladiators [*scholam quasi ludum esse*]" and the forum to be a
military arena (*Controversiae*, III, Preface, 13). There the future lawyer was taught to "strive for victory...and learn how to strike the
vitals of his foe and protect his own" (Quintilian, V, 12.22).

All parts of the trial were thus battles of some sort, attacks and
counterattacks with accusation the first strike and refutation the
defense (Quintilian, V, 13.11). Prosecution and defense waged verbal
warfare among themselves, as did lawyer and witness. The only
difference between the two was that "the debate is a battle between
advocates, whereas cross-examination is a fight between advocate
and witness" (VI, 4.21). Even style entered into the fray, as when
the *Ad Herennium* author noted still more graphically that "the
reiteration of the same word makes a deep impression upon the
hearer and inflicts a major wound upon the opposition—as if a
weapon should repeatedly pierce the same part of the body."[28]

Moreover, that continued to be the case throughout the Middle
Ages and as late as the Renaissance, when Vives reiterated the literal
dangers precipitated by forensic rhetoric. Of what consequence, he
asked, was it "how one person attacks another, whether it is with
the sword or with the pen, when the intention is the same? For the
most part, you injure more keenly with speech or with the pen, than
with the sword; for you only severely wound the body with the
sword, but with language you pierce even the soul" (*De tradendis*,
292–93).

Patterns of conflict were apparent not only in the rhetorical tradition but in official codifications of legal principles, as revealed in
the bellicose vocabulary of the Justinian code:

> Nec enim solos nostro imperio militare credimus illos qui gladio,
> clypeis et thoracibus nituntur, sed etiam advocatos; militant namque
> causarum patroni, qui, gloriosae vocis confisi munimine, laborantium
> spem et vitam, ac posteros deffendunt.

> For we believe that not merely those who strive with the sword, shield,
> and breastplate are soldiering on behalf of our empire—lawyers do,
> too. For the counsels in a case do *their* soldiering when, relying on
> the bulwark of a heroic voice, they defend the hope, life, and posterity
> of those in difficulties.[29]

[28][Cicero], *Ad C. Herennium*, IV, 38, on the figure of reduplication.
[29]*De advoc. divers. judiciorum* (*Code*, liv. II, tit. VII), as quoted in Delachenal,
Histoire des avocats, 138. Delachenal argues that Boutillier's rearticulation of this
bellicose vocabulary in his *Somme rurale* is a veritable word-for-word translation of
that passage.

And in medieval rhetoric, law remained a form of battle play in both schoolroom and courtroom. When Charlemagne questioned Alcuin as to how a defendant might fend off "thrusts" against him, Alcuin responded with a definition of verbal defense as a "protecting shield [that] repels a volley of destructive arrows."[30]

But perhaps the most conflictual context of all was provided by the medieval university, where, Murphy tells us, "disputation was used for instruction, for testing, for public display, for the advancement of new ideas, and ultimately for the form of written didactic works like the *Summa Theologica* of Thomas Aquinas."[31] Roman schoolboys had practiced artful legal declamation of *controversiae*, and now their medieval counterparts turned with equal brilliance to scholastic battle play, the verbal equivalent of warfare. John of Salisbury sought to teach "matched contestants [*pares*] . . . to handle their [proper] weapons and engage in verbal, rather than physical conflict [*sermones conserere*]":

> Boys at play were . . . trained in the use of weapons, and learned ahead of time, at home, when to attack or retreat from a horseman or a foot soldier, as well as when to strike with the edge or thrust with the point of his sword. In the same way the logician must become a skilled master of the instruments of his art, so that he is familiar with its principles, is amply provided with likely proofs, and is ready with all the methods of deductive and inductive reasoning.[32]

In fact, so preeminent was the bellicose context of medieval pedagogy that Abelard opened the entire *Historia calamitatum* with the vocabulary of warfare: "Since I preferred the armor of logic to all the teaching of philosophy, I exchanged all other arms for it and chose the contests of disputation above the trophies of warfare."[33] And in London, William Fitzstephen described disputing twelfth-century schoolboys as "hurtling enthymemes" while "striving against one another."[34] The medieval university became an intellectual battlefield "programmed as a form of ritual male combat

---

[30]Alcuin, *Rhetoric of Alcuin and Charlemagne*, 659–62.
[31]Murphy, "Rhetoric and Dialectic in the *Owl and the Nightingale*," 201.
[32]John of Salisbury, *Metalogicon*, 190, 198–99. See also *MFLL*, 139.
[33]Abelard, *Historia calamitatum*, 25–28. References are to Monfrin's edition; translations are from Abelard, *Story of Abelard's Adversities*, ed. Gilson, 12. See also Huizinga's discussion of how Abelard " 'pitched the camp of his school' on the Hill of St. Genevieve in order to 'besiege' from there the rival who held the chair at Paris": *HL*, 155; and Peter Cantor's description of the duties of a teacher as "to lecture, to preach, and to dispute," quoted in Murphy, "Rhetoric and Dialectic," 201.
[34]Quoted in Murphy, "Rhetoric and Dialectic," 202.

centered on disputation" (*RRT*, 17). Indeed, the mere existence of a
work such as Henri d'Andeli's *Bataille des VII ars* is evidence
enough that, thanks to disputation, the university had metamor-
phosed into a kind of Senecan arena for gladiators where wars were
fought with words:

> Ala tel cop ferir Platon
> D'un vers berseret el menton
> Qu'il le fist trestout esbahir;
> Et dant Platon par grant aïr
> Le referi si d'un sofisme
> Sor l'escu, parmi une rime,
> Qu'il le fist trebuchier el fanc
> Et le couvri trestout de sanc.[35]

And then he went with bow and verse to strike Plato with such a
blow on the chin that he knocked the wind out of him, which so
angered Plato that he struck back with a sophism on the shield, right
in the middle of a rhyme, so that he made him trip in the mud and
quickly covered him with blood.

Even the most cursory look at the four large volumes of the *Chartularium Universitatis Parisiensis* reveals how constantly the universities were embroiled in petty disputes.[36] Schooling was big
business, recalls Hajnal, and was thus characterized by numerous
"quarrels and lawsuits" of a commercial nature, "often between the
members of the college themselves."[37] Alexander Murray attributes
much of this "learned combativeness" to "the friction of any system
with moving parts," but extant medieval documents reveal a zeal
for conflict that suggests something more than minor academic ri-
valries. William of Ockham, for example, condemned the " 'detest-
able presumption' of contemporaries who 'arrogate to themselves'
the title of master, enviously 'tearing to pieces, like barking dogs,
every view dissenting from their own dogmas' " (Murray, 236). And,
again, the humanistic Vives took particular exception to the practice
of scheduling *concurrentes* (two classes on the same subject taught

---

[35]Andeli, *Battle of the Seven Arts*, ed. Paetow, 188–95.

[36]See, e.g., the following texts in the *Chartularium Universitatis Parisiensis*, ed.
Denifle and Chatelain: no. 1340, concerning a battle between soldiers and students
on the eve of St. Nicolas in Paris (1367); no. 1311, concerning the death of a student
in a fracas (1365); no. 1299, concerning the legal action taken by twenty-one masters
of theology against one of their own (1364). See also Alexander Murray's discussion
of the pugnacious tenor of the medieval university in *Reason and Society in the
Middle Ages*, chap. 10.

[37]Hajnal, *L'Enseignement de l'écriture*, 44; translation mine.

by two professors at the same hour): "I have never heard a more appropriate word," he complained, "for they do run together assuredly, and meet and fight with violent abuse, bitterness and fury" (*De tradendis*, 61). The viciousness of disputation recalled certain spectacular sporting events, as when Haimeric de Vari (a thirteenth-century chancellor of the University of Paris) launched the following critique:

> Qu'est-ce que ces luttes de savants... sinon de vrais combats de coqs, qui nous couvrent de ridicule aux yeux des laïques? Un coq se redresse contre un autre, et se hérisse.... Il en est de même aujourd'hui de nos professeurs. Les coqs se battent à coups de bec et de griffes: l'amour-propre, quelqu'un l'a dit, est armé d'un ergot redoutable.[38]

> What are these learned struggles if not actual cockfights that heap ridicule upon us in the eyes of the laity? One cock challenges another, its feathers bristling. It is the same thing today with our professors. Cocks fight by pecking and clawing at each other: pride, as someone once said, is armed with some formidable sophistry.

Yet, within an educational system where "nothing is perfectly known until it has been masticated [*trituté* (sic)] in the jaws of debate,"[39] the performance ramifications of those verbal conflicts were of crucial importance in the *letteraturizzazione* of the law. Such battle play was pleasing to watch says John of Salisbury, by virtue of its status as "make-believe warfare" (198). Indeed, sometimes the barking dogs and fighting cocks lent themselves to explicit satirical portrayal, as when Jean de Jandun mocked the theologians of the Sorbonne in his *De laudibus Parisius*. Their exaggerated verbal battles were appropriate comic subjects in part because of the pleasures derived from watching their histrionics:

> Unus quidem obicit, alter solvit; unus replicat, alter refellit. Et, ut unico dicam sermone, quidquid in talium perscrutatione problematum unus manu potenti vivificare aut fortificare nititur, alter brachio excelso interimere aut debilitare conatur, salva tamen penitus et omnino integraliter et involiabiliter articulorum fidei sincera confessione. [As quoted in Le Roux de Lincy and Tisserand, 40]

[38]As quoted in Lecoy de La Marche, *La Chaire française au Moyen Age*, 452. See also Murray's discussion of that passage, 234–37.

[39]Robert de Sorbon as quoted in Durkheim, *Evolution of Educational Thought*, 142. Robert's selection of the verb *triturer* also underscores the physical and spiritual aggressiveness that characterized scholastic disputation, including the Old Testament precept of "an eye for an eye, a tooth for a tooth."

So one of them objects, the other resolves the objection. One replies,
the other refutes. And, in a word, during the course of the debates
about these problems, everything that one of them endeavors to animate and strengthen with powerful hand, the other, his arm raised,
is bent on overturning and destroying— but not, in any event, without
first confessing fully his sincere and inviolable devotion to the integrity of the articles of faith.

Whether the context be satirical or serious, all such commentaries
indicate that conflict might become the principal focus of eloquence
during theatrical delivery. And once again, as the drama of the conflict increased, so did Christian critiques of the aestheticization of
disputational discourse. Given that, as Durkheim says, "it was far
less a question of teaching people how to reason than of teaching
them how to debate" (141), the old objections raised by Plato and
implicitly by Tacitus against a rhetoric that possessed no intrinsic
morality of its own were revived: the forensic genre had always
constituted "a sure defence and a weapon of attack withal, that
enables you with equal ease to act on the defensive or to advance
to the assault" (Tacitus, 5). If scholastic disputation had initially
been modeled on the "cooperative competition" of Platonic dialectic, which permitted ideas to "mature through 'agonistic' development," the drama of the agon had replaced that goal (*POLF*, 107).
Once again the honorable quest for truth had become a dishonorable
spectacle, a struggle so intense that it threatened a peaceful Christian
society: "If disputations are encouraged," wrote Vives, "harmony,
the chief blessing of society, receives a serious injury" (*De tradendis*,
270).

    Similarly, Thomas Basin noted that the fifteenth-century French
courtroom was dominated by a herd of unscrupulous lawyers who
bleated pomp and irrelevancies all day. Their law had little to do
with proof and everything to do with the pleasing "spectacle of a
fight" which only encouraged humankind's bellicosity:

> This corps of lawyers gnaws at, stalks, and exhausts the very essence
> of the populace. Unfortunately, the people—somewhat and even too
> litigious already by nature—are taken in and caught up in judicial
> actions and in disputes ever more numerous and almost infinite,
> thanks to the participation and the advice of lawyers (who each day
> seek only new trials) and their contagious influence [*eorum con-
> tagio*].[40]

[40]Basin, *Apologie*, 262–63; translation mine.

And earlier, in 1317, Pope John XXII had proposed a reform of the quodlibet for those very reasons, condemning the perversion of that ceremony by theologians who,

> postpositis vel neglectis canonicis, necessariis, utilibus et aedificativis doctrinis, curiosis, inutilibus et supervacuis philosophiae quaestionibus et subtilitatibus se immiscent, ex quibus ipsius studii disciplina dissolvitur. [As quoted in *LQ,* 1:57]

> postponing or neglecting doctrines that are canonical, edifying, useful, and necessary, immerse themselves instead in philosophical questions and subtleties that are idle curiosities, useless and superfluous, whereby the foundation of their discipline crumbles.

Entranced by the pleasures of a *pugna verborum,* they preferred the fighting for its own "merits": "Tamen huiusmodi quaestionibus solvendis, quas forte melius esset contemnere quam solvere invigilabunt magistri et laborabunt" (the masters stay up all night and work away at solving problems of this sort, which it would perhaps be better to scorn than to solve [*LQ,* 1:16]). Transforming argumentation into the kind of profane spectacle to which Tertullian and Isidore had so strenuously objected, they replaced moral imperatives with aesthetic ones.

The grimmest picture of all was painted by Vives, who despaired that the "wordy fighting" of scholastic "gladiatorial displays" had caused disputation and epistemological inquiry to become mutually exclusive enterprises (*De tradendis,* 291–2; also 33). It is interesting, however, that for all his objections to "strife so nefarious and impious" that it "does not become good men, much less Christians" (58), he did not withdraw his support for an abstract moral notion of disputation. He believed nonetheless that a "true and genuine rhetoric" linked to "righteousness and piety" (185) could be restored if students of law were taught to "assemble together in a peaceful and modest manner" (269). Disputation might then become a "friendly discussion [rather] than a hostile fight for victory" (269) in which "impious attacks are made on holy truth, and doubts are started in the minds of listeners, about things which ought to be held as certain, fixed and unshakable" (291).

Still, Vives was unable to resolve some of the contradictions implicit in his own findings: if the truth were in fact unshakable, then even the genuine epistemological inquiries of dialectic would be empty ones. The conflictual machinations of even the purest dialectic might similarly succumb to the pleasurable spectacle of the

conflict itself. He too was forced to acknowledge the existence of a
connection between latent aggressiveness and aesthetic pleasure:

> Such expositions should not take place in a public assembly before a
> circle of listeners of the type that invite ostentation of arguments for
> their amusement. For such exhibitions are dangerous both to those
> pronouncing a judgment, who may be rendered conceited by it, and
> to the listeners.... In the course of quarrels and disputations, the
> laws provide plenty of handles for exercises in twisting arguments,
> and thus strife is aroused, nourished and cultivated. [*De tradendis,*
> 269–70]

His conclusion? That the forensic genre was "in no wise" to be
cultivated. Like Basin before him, Vives found himself espousing a
radical solution: a moral preselection of the chosen few who were
capable of serving on the dangerous battlefield for the truth. Both
dialectic and rhetoric were to be "denied to a youth of quarrelsome
and contentious disposition, one who is suspiciously inclined towards evil; for such a youth will twist everything to that end" (177).
To Vives, words that did not serve truth were "mere bombast" (185).
But bombast—the theatrical bombast of delivered disputational discourse—was exactly what eloquence seems eternally destined to
become. The same criteria that rendered spectacular conflicts morally unacceptable rendered them aesthetically acceptable.

What was it, then, about forensic rhetoric that had rendered it so
dangerous? It seems clear that the emphasis on the histrionic over
the epistemological increased concern that legal and legalistic argumentation had become immoral and violent rituals not unlike
the theatrical spectacles they had come to imitate. Just as Gerhoh
of Reichersberg had bemoaned the transformation of clerics into
soldiers, Marlac, the *procureur général du Roi,* complained as late
as the sixteenth century that students were being transformed into
warriors:

> Ces fuitifs et simulés escholiers dont à présent l'université est pleine
> (qui, à vrai dire, sont plus discholés, brigueurs et faineants que es-
> choliers), car ils ne font que de nuit et de jour porter espées avec
> rondelles et autres bastons nuisibles, vaguer et rauder parmi les
> rues, font querelles, debats et noises, détroussent ceux qu'ils rencon-
> trent par leur chemin, ne bougent des tavernes, cabarets et jeux de
> paulmes... [Quoted in *EH,* 52]

> These false and ersatz schoolboys with which the university is cur-
> rently full—who in reality are more unschooled rowdies and loafers

> than scholars—for all they do night and day is carry swords and shields
> and other dangerous instruments, roam and prowl the streets, instigate
> quarrels, confrontations, arguments, and trouble, make trouble for
> those they meet along the way, do not move from taverns, cabarets,
> and tennis courts...

Although Quintilian had advised that "mere violence and noise"
were to be avoided in debate, he also found it necessary to reassure
his readers that there had once been a time when judges had not yet
succumbed to the spectacular charms of "unscrupulous violence":
"although annoying to one's antagonist, [it] makes an unpleasant
impression on the judge" (VI, 4.15).

But times were always changing, thanks to delivery—and thanks
to the presence of spectators who demanded an increasingly dramatic presentation. Clearly forensic conflict had always had the
potential to become an aesthetic genre, an artful, mimetic representation of the epistemological struggle for the equity it had been
designed to serve. The history of delivery suggests that the attempts
of Vives and others were destined to fail. Then as now, one of the
principal features of conflict was how easily it got out of hand. As
Burke noted of the "dramatistic view of life," the entire dialectical
process converts even the most minimal difference into an antithesis: interlocutors succumb to the " 'dialectical pressure' of their
drama to become eventually at odds in everything. No matter what
one of them happens to assert, the other (responding to the genius
of the contest) takes violent exception to it—and vice versa" (*POLF*,
139). In fact, long before Burke and centuries before Vives, Quintilian
had come to much the same conclusion, maintaining that the conflictual engagement of forensic oratory could but perpetuate itself
inexorably:

> From our answers to objections fresh objections will arise, a process
> which may be carried to some length. The strokes of gladiators [*ut
> gladiatorum manus*] provide a parallel. If the first stroke was intended
> to provoke the adversary to strike, the second will lead to the third,
> while if the challenge be repeated it will lead to the fourth stroke, so
> that there will be two parries and two attacks. [V, 13.54]

For that reason, he had cautioned the lawyer against all strong emotions, advising in particular that debaters control their "tendency
to anger; there is no passion that is a greater enemy to reason." By
allowing anger free rein, the advocate often became so involved in
the "total drama" of the agon that he lost sight of the legal point at

issue: "It often leads an advocate right away from the point and forces him both to use gross and insulting language and to receive it in return; occasionally it will even excite him to attack the judges" (VI, 4.10).

Guillaume Du Breuil offered virtually identical advice to readers of his *Stilus Curie Parlamenti*. Since anger was the natural psychological partner of conflict, it was to be avoided at all costs. To keep from being enticed "away from his subject" (*hors de sa matière* [62]), the lawyer was to keep a cool head and "refraindre et modérer le mouvement de son penser et de son cueur, que, pour petit de parolles ou autres causes, il ne s'esmeuve à ire, courroux ou discension contre les parties qui parleront à lui en conseillant leurs causes." (restrain and moderate the movement of his thoughts and emotions, lest, for a few words or other provocation, he be moved to anger, wrath, or dissension against the parties addressing him as they plead their cases [61]).

The advice of Quintilian and Du Breuil alike, however, went unheeded or, at the very least, unpracticed. Anger did indeed obfuscate the truth, and the efficacy of debate as a form of ritual divination was compromised. To some extent, that was understandable: inasmuch as debate required "a quick and nimble understanding and a shrewd and ready judgment" that few possessed, its logical foundations were easily swept away. In actual practice, "there is no time to think; the advocate must speak at once and return the blow almost before it has been dealt by his opponent" (Quintilian, VI, 4.8). For that reason, Quintilian had insisted that "the chief essential is never for a moment to lose sight either of the question at issue or the end which we have in view. If we bear this in mind, we shall never descend to mere brawling [*in rixam*]" (VI, 4.13). But *rixae* there were—violent, noisy altercations. Despite the best-intentioned efforts to avoid them, from the *Ad Herennium* to Alcuin to Vives, violent words were persistently associated with violent action in schoolroom and courtroom. Quintilian's disapproval notwithstanding, his "chief essential" had been lost. Just as stronger arts, according to Longinus, overtook weaker ones, so now the drama of conflict overtook the logic of argumentation. Faced with "brazen-faced" opponents who "bluster and bellow at us, interrupt us in the middle of a sentence and try to throw everything into confusion," the legal advocate had no choice but to enter into the fray himself: "we must nonetheless repel their onslaughts with vigour by crushing their insolence" (Quintilian, VI, 4.11).

And repel them the lawyers did. Like the disputers in Seneca's school for gladiators or the medieval students "hurtling" enthymemes, they did indeed descend to brawling. "Some go so far as to turn the debate into an open brawl [*rixentur*]. . . . You may sometimes see several persons shouting angrily at the judge" (Quintilian, VI, 4.9). Tacitus also recorded the phenomenon, criticizing the "unskilful" use of weapons by the boisterous Cassius Severus, who was "so keen . . . to hit that he quite frequently loses his balance. So, instead of being a warrior, he is simply a brawler [*non pugnat, sed rixatur*]" (26). The same result obtained in medieval legal studies, where the "genius of the contest" widened the gulf that separated bourgeois lawyers, upwardly mobile theology students, and villagers.[41] By 1450, Durkheim notes, scholastic disputation had degenerated into "slanging matches, vulgarities, insults, and threats. 'People even reached the point where they kicked, punched and bit one another.' Wounded and dead were lying on the floor" (142). This was hardly what Seneca had described as "struggling in a dream" (*in somniis laborare*): "it is one thing to fight, quite another to shadow-box [*ventilare*]" (*Controversiae*, III, Preface, 13). This was actual physical combat—so threatening that the University of Paris forbade the bearing of arms at the Fête des Fous in order to "prevent the continual battles which were the scholars' pastime, and which frequently caused the streets to run with blood" (Durkheim, 156).

Vives was justifiably concerned that teaching rhetoric and dialectic to "one who is seditious, venal, given to anger, greedy of vengeance" would be tantamount to placing "a sword in the hand of a madman" (*De tradendis*, 177). In fact, one of the most spectacular aspects of the *letteraturizzazione* of forensic rhetoric was the retransformation of verbal conflict into the same kind of physical struggle it had been intended to mediate. Quite literally, swords were replaced in the hands of histrionic madmen. Therefore, inasmuch as forensic oratory retained its potential for violence, a reevaluation of the very concept of legal and poetic mediation is in order. Bloch maintained that both law and poetry were to serve as a "nonviolent termination of a potentially violent quarrel" (*MFLL*, 174) and to "proffer as a cultural ideal the containment of violent impulses within the bounds of language itself" (189), but the "conversion" of the legal ordeal was incomplete. Illuminating in that

[41]For a discussion of the gulf between these social classes, see Murray, 231, 270–74; Genty, *Basoche notariale*, 13–15. Hajnal describes a similar situation at Oxford, where legal and commercial problems led to "frequent quarrels and even to bloody incidents—so much so that in 1329 the Pope was obliged to intervene by forbidding activities of this nature," 44; translation mine.

context is Vives's proposal for a program of physical exercise designed to help sublimate violent tendencies in "longer and more
eager walks, running, leaping, throwing, wrestling"—so long as they
were not "of a military nature" (176). Thus he shared some "modern" views of pedagogy with Rabelais and Montaigne; but pedagogy
was not a sufficient answer to the reactivation of primordial violent
impulses during intense verbal conflicts.

Needless to say, this aspect of forensic performance borders on
sociology and anthropology, both of which are subjects too vast to
be investigated here. Though no brief analysis of the anthropological
context of *letteraturizzazione* can do justice to the complexity of
the phenomenon, the discursive status of law as a *spectaculum
crudelitatis* (to borrow Isidore's term [59]) supplies particularly valuable insights into the more widespread interplay between ritual and
representation in the Middle Ages.[42] As Isidore suggested, legal battle
play was first and foremost a violent ritual of judgment. So were the
quodlibetal rite of passage and scholastic disputation in general,
which rendered combat a "necessary and admirable condition of
existence" (*RRT*, 18), a form of ritual initiation, and a perilous academic rite of passage—notions that survive in the expression *pe-
riculo facto*, still seen on modern diplomas (*RRT*, 121). As such,
disputational discourse is reminiscent of the earliest battle-play
forms of drama on the levels of both verbal and physical fighting.
With its equation of word to sword, it was as dramatic as any sword
dance, if not more so. The forensic fusion of verbal violence, physical
violence, and spectacle was virtually guaranteed a reception as
drama by medieval audiences, who had come to appreciate the same
"winning" combination in sport, scholastic disputation, mimicry,
the circus, and drama.

Moreover, where the verbal warfare of the courtroom was retransformed into the unmediated *rixe*, the same kind of reversion to
violent action also occurred in the ostensibly mediatory language
of drama. Gaston Baty and René Chavance, for example, decried
popular "imitations of veritable struggles" in which dramatic "characters" might be stabbed or burned alive on stage.[43] Even during the
grandiose processions that announced such mid-sixteenth-century

[42]The anthropological context for the emergence of drama from the shift from
ritual to representation is treated in Bloch, *MFLL*; Huizinga, *HL*; Barthes, *Mythologies*; Grafton and Jardine; Tydeman; Kirby, *Ur-Drama*; and, in a more general way,
Girard, *Violence and the Sacred*; Uitti, *Story, Myth, and Celebration*; and Caillois,
L'Homme et le sacré and *Les Jeux et les hommes*.
[43]Gaston Baty and René Chavance, *Vie de l'art théâtral*, 67.

spectacles as the *Mystère des actes des apôtres*, armed guards were often present to regulate public conduct and to protect observers from harm (Genty, 70). And, in the ultimate confusion between spectacle and reality, the role of Christ in the mystery play was occasionally assigned to a condemned man who underwent actual physical torture within the "fictive" context of the play. As a particularly harrowing example of the theater's capacity to "push to the limit the very premises upon which it is based," Rey-Flaud cites the presentation in Tournai (1549) of a biblical drama in which a criminal playing the role of Hollophernes was actually beheaded on stage, apparently in an attempt to please the visiting Philippe II. The producers' desire to "be realistic" was met with frenetic applause but Philippe remained impassive, "looking curiously at the convulsions of the decapitated man and uttering only the words: 'Nice blow' " (*PDMA*, 19).

Here theater, law, and reality have become so fused that it is impossible to determine whether the audience was applauding the death of Hollophernes or that of a criminal.[44] Granted, the forensic *rixe* may not have reached quite such extremes (though Durkheim and others submit that it did);[45] but one need but recall such spectacular medieval rituals of judgment as the Inquisition and the infamous witch trials, where pro and contra argumentation both fascinated and terrified crowds. Public executions became "veritable spectacles whose unfolding is strictly determined according to a hierarchy of characters" (*CM*, 262). The term *mystère*, derived, like *mestier*, from *ministerium*, was similarly connected to the activities of daily life (*PDMA*, 75). To a certain extent, then, all such confusion may be attributed to the familiarity of audiences with spectacular public events such as jousts, processions, public executions, dubbing ceremonies, royal entrées, carnivals, and the Mass—all of which

[44]According to Zumthor, this is a "desymbolized one-way pseudo-communication" in which "the actor takes on the latent violence of the people for whom he dies": "From Hi(story) to Poem," 238. See also Tydeman on beheadings, deaths, and reincarnations as widespread features of such popular battle-play forms as the sword dance (6–7); Axton on the "mock killing" or the "killing and resurrection of a protagonist" (36); Kirby's recasting of Frazer's argument from the *Golden Bough* that the "ur-religion of primitive peoples had been a proto-Christianity based on the 'ritual pattern' of vegetation magic centering on the Christlike image of a slain and resurrected spirit of fertility" (x); and Girard on the role of the "surrogate victim" (82–85) in the "curative measures [that] are steps in the direction of a legal system" (21). Nicoll has also analyzed the phenomenon in terms of the modern psychology of the mob, which has a "special tendency towards confusing the imaginary and the real" (*TADT*, 20).

[45]See, e.g., Durkheim, 141–60; Genty, 13–15. But, as I show in chap. 3, such extremes were not uncommon in the hysterical Fête des Fous of the Basochiens.

tended to efface the normal distinctions between ritual and "real" life (*PDMA*, 75–79). Public cruelty was habitual, and the popularity of the legal ordeal helps us to understand how "the sight of the countless tortures inflicted upon Christ remained tolerable" (*LM*, 224). The "heathen" who witnessed the vivid dramatic presentation of Gideon's fight against the Philistines in a *Ludus prophetarum* performed in Riga in 1204 feared that "they themselves were about to be slaughtered [and] began to run away" (quoted in Tydeman, 223–24); they too were unable to distinguish between the dramatic representation of conflict and the violent realities of their daily lives. One is reminded here of Lucian's tale of the actor who went mad while playing the role of Ajax ("Saltatio," 83). Inasmuch as some spectators feared that "fictive" personages might commit real acts of violence against them, the madness of this ultimate impersonation was contagious. Consequently, if the medieval "unity of play and reality is no longer accessible to our experience," as Rainer Warning suggests, greater access to that early experience may be gained through the study of delivery.[46]

Furthermore, it is well known that one of the functions of ritual violence (dramatic or otherwise) was to reinforce the social hierarchy by instilling a sense of security and "consubstantiality" (*POLF*, 107–9). The legal agon bespeaks a similar consubstantiality, integrating its audiences both physically and verbally into its own ordeal. Abundant evidence attests to the fact that whether the conflict was verbal, physical, or a mixture of the two, audiences relished these violent rituals of judgment, and that classical and medieval lawyers knew it.

Seen from that perspective, Nicoll's contention that dramatic writing "must give the audience an impression of reality, and yet it must have within itself the power of transcending reality" (*WD*, 1st ed., 929) cannot account adequately for the participatory experience of early drama. In fact, modern predilections for such transcendance have served to camouflage the profound similarities between the courtroom and the theater, both of which brought audiences into direct contact with the most complete forms of "representation." While modern sensibilities are rightly shocked by the notion that an actual execution might constitute entertainment, such striking examples of how "the symbolic act of art overlaps upon the symbolic act in life" (*POLF*, 119) encourage us to reintegrate the very agonism of legal and dramatic spectacle into the history of aesthetics. Instead

---

[46]Warning, "On the Alterity of Medieval Religious Drama," 285.

of condemning the "fuzzy and dormant sensibilities" of the medieval spectator (*LM*, 224), we might resituate such *spectacula crudelitatis* along the same continuum that includes the participatory performance of conflictual rhetoric.

Therefore, before we consider how orators exploited the aesthetic appeal of participatory conflicts in order to render their legal spectacle increasingly appealing to numerous possible audiences, it is essential to inquire first into what specific features of the legal agon encouraged its conception and reception as an aesthetic *imitatio veritatis*. Theorists of rhetoric from Plato to Vives have observed consistently that combative behavior may well have constituted one of the great abuses of argumentative rhetoric; yet at the same time, it was one of its great appeals. The paramountcy of conflict in both law and drama thus precipitates a reevaluation of the agon as a preferred object of imitation.[47] As Aristotle once observed, "we enjoy looking at accurate likenesses of things which are themselves painful to see" (*Poetics* 1448b). Similarly, in forensic rhetoric, the dialogic quest for truth had been shrouded in conflict—potentially (and often literally) painful to experience but pleasing to behold. In the same way that Seneca the Elder once grouped together "actors, gladiators and orators" (*Controversiae*, IV, Preface, 1), so did Aeschylus in the *Eumenides*, which exemplified the "aesthetic reconstruction of struggle, horror, and the tortures of remorse" (*POLF*, 153–54); and Lucian cited the mime's imitation of conflict as a crucial contribution: "How much more delightful it is to see [mimicry] than young men boxing, astream with blood, and other young men wrestling in the dust! Why, the dance often presents them in a way that is less risky and at the same time more beautiful and pleasurable" ("Saltatio," 71).

If forensic rhetoric reconstructed aesthetically a primordial agon, then, problematic though that might be, a measure of the medieval enjoyment of violence is comprehensible if we recall that conflict and its theatrical imitation were integral to the dramatic experience. The "natural drama" of law may thus be said to inhere in its status as an Aristotelian "imitation of an action" (est ergo Tragoedia imitatio operis).[48] If that action was "heroic and complete and of a certain magnitude" (*Poetics*, 1449b), then so was the forensic *imi-*

---

[47]According to Aristotle, aesthetic pleasure depended on the ready identification of the object of imitation: *Poetics*, 1448b.

[48]For a sixteenth-century translation of *Poetics*, 1449b, on how tragedy "represents men in action and does not use narrative," see e.g., Aristotle, *Poetics of Aristotle*, ed. Margouliouth, 245.

tatio veritatis performed by Quintilian's "slaves of applause" (IV, 2.127).

Serving the ends of legal equity poorly, lawyers served its drama with the consummate skill acquired in the schools of declamation. In the "mimic combats" of declamatory exercises (*pugnae simulacris*), students learned to stage and reenact the agonistic tale of a crime with a beginning, a middle, and an end (Quintilian, II, 10.7–10). The noble forensic battle for truth became an ignoble battle for applause; and the evocation of emotion through "mimic combats" and Senecan "shadow-boxing" (III, Preface, 13) became the foundation for a dramatic aesthetic. For if such histrionic battles were not serving a legal protodrama, then what could be "more ludicrous than to work oneself into a passion and to attempt to excite the anger or grief of our hearers, unless we are preparing ourselves by such mimic combats for the actual strife and the pitched battles of the law-courts?" (Quintilian, II, 10.8).[49]

So it was that Tacitus viewed the imitation of conflict as a leaf the rhetorician had taken "out of the book of stage-players [*histriones*]" (40). In fact, as Aper attempted to win Maternus back to the nobler conflicts of law, he argued that the true challenges—civic and dramatic—were to be found in the juridical arena. The dramatic conflict of law was infinitely more noble, more rewarding, more spectacular than the "tamer" physical sports: "If heaven had given you the great bodily strength of a Nicostratus, I should protest against allowing your brawny arms, framed for combats in the arena, to be thrown away on the tame sport of hurling the javelin or the discus; and in the same way now I am trying to get you away from the lecture-hall and the stage and to the forum and to the real contests of actions-at-law" (10). Aper is never able to persuade Maternus because his friend favored an analogous conflictual spectacle: drama.

As for the medieval disputational analogues of forensic oratory, Palémon Glorieux speculated that the quodlibetal conflict, in which "one seeks to unhorse one's adversaries or to discredit rivals" (*LQ*, 2:14), rendered the participants "actors" in a "two-act play" (1:21). While his penchant for the theatrical register was more a function of his own dramatic style than the result of any systematic generic analysis, his description of the quodlibet as a "spectacle that was always new and always appealing," full of surprises, reversals, discoveries, and denouements (2:13), is in fact quite consistent with

---

[49]See Winterbottom's discussion of this passage in "Schoolroom and Courtroom," 63; also Axer on audience response to such dramatic conflict in "Tribunal-Stage-Arena," 305–8.

the rhetorical protodrama to which orators would have been exposed.[50] With roles as pronounced as those of the Roman forum and of the medieval Basoche, the quodlibet provided an opportunity for students and masters to indulge in a scholastic version of the theatrical agon. Indeed, I argue in Chapter 4 that that agon provided the archetypal plot for many a medieval drama. So, while it is not my intention here to suggest that verbal and physical conflict from the legal register were duplicated in the performance practice of every medieval theatrical work, the performative forensic model of "imminent justice"—with all its attendant catharses—emerges nonetheless as a crucial locus for the conception and transmission of much of medieval dramatic production.[51]

Ultimately, if the commingling of ritualistic and representational elements helped to make drama what Burke termed a "borderline area" (*POLF*, 119), then law was a borderline area as well. As a *spectaculum crudelitatis*, it is as viable a protodrama as the Mass. That is to say, if disputation was a form of "ritual combat" (*RRT*, 17) and combat was a form of "ritual drama" (Axton, 33–35), then forensic rhetoric was clearly both. Moreover, just as mimetic elements compromised the integrity of the Mass when they were introduced but did not destroy it, so they undermined the noble purposes of legal ritual but left the ritual intact. Such striking parallels in the respective developments of legal and religious discourse may then allow us to collapse some of the misleading distinctions between popular and learned, pre-Christian and Christian traditions. For if the Christian spectacle of the Slaughter of the Innocents could be described by Arnulfus of Orléans as a recontextualization of Roman battle play (see Tydeman, 7), then the medieval recontextualization of the dramatically impersonated forensic agon suggests a larger historical interplay among numerous discursive traditions.

Finally, while the sociological ramifications of the theatricalization of eloquence lie somewhat outside the scope of this book, it is helpful nonetheless to address briefly the issue of censorship, which may well have nurtured the aestheticization of the law. Like the

---

[50]A modern equivalent of quodlibetal *peripateia* survives in the *disputatio* of the Swedish university system, where Ph.D. candidates undergo a public costumed conflict as an academic rite of passage. My thanks to Professor Stina Hansson for sharing her thoughts with me on this practice. Rhetorically, another equivalent of *peripateia* was the technique of introducing new arguments by surprise: "It is a procedure which resembles a surprise attack or a sally from an ambush" (Quintilian, VI, 4.14).

[51]For the concept of "imminent justice," see Barthes, *Mythologies*, 17; Kibédi Varga, *REL*, 86–89; Howell, *PRL*, 243. Pity, fear, and catharsis are discussed at greater length later in this chapter.

Basochiens, who would come to be known as the fathers of both
satire and censorship (Genty, 90), classical orators made public meetings "the opportunity of launching characteristically spiteful tirades
against the leading men of the state: how all this must have inflamed
the able debater and added fuel to the fire of his eloquence!" (Tacitus,
40). That was also true of the quodlibet, during which offensive
words might precipitate official punishments ranging from censure
to public apology to excommunication. A certain Ubertus Guidi, for
example, was sentenced in 1315 to ten days of bread and water for
having made heretical remarks "in conspectu multitudinis fratrum,
secularium, clericorum, et aliorum religiosorum" (in the presence
of a great number of brothers, laics, clerics, and other religious men).
Apparently the ill-fated Florentine *baccellarius* had spoken against
the "holy doctrine" of Aquinas with arrogance and pride (*superbe
et arroganter multa dixit*)—a verbal spectacle of heresy that was too
public to go unpunished.[52] Similarly, Vives noted that it was "most
dangerous to speak on almost any subject" (*De tradendis*, 291).

According to Tacitus, the art of rhetoric "comes to the front more
readily in times of trouble and unrest" (37). Faced with the decline
of their civic power in late antiquity, classical orators retreated to
the "safer arena of the schools"; the "freedom which the author of
the *Dialogus* and the philosopher in Longinus consider so essential
for good oratory was fast disappearing from Roman public life."[53]
But the potential for physical violence and the threat of censorship
compromised even the putative safety of the schools. It is reasonable
to suggest, then, that the very agonistic nature of disputational discourse would render (or seem to render) the dramatic imitation of
its conflicts safer still. In the *pugna verborum*, it was already difficult
enough to maintain control in an adversarial situation dominated
by anger. But the dramatization of forensic and disputational oratory
allowed some of that control to be regained: if its civic power had
decreased, its power of catharsis as an *imitatio veritatis* had increased. Classical and medieval disputers might thus have retreated

---

[52]Quoted in *Chartularium*, 2:174. See also Glorieux, *LQ*, 1:32.

[53]Bonner, *Roman Declamation*, 43. Similarly, Glorieux has argued that since the
quodlibet was the forum in which the great theological and political *quaestiones* of
the day were explored, it was necessarily embroiled in such political crises as the
dissolving of the Templars (*LQ*, 2:14). Moreover, the great mystery plays, like the
satirical works of the Basochiens, often became enmeshed in political controversy.
See Lebègue's argument that before they were outlawed in 1548, mystery plays were
used by Protestants and Catholics alike as "an effective means of propaganda": *La
Tragédie religieuse en France* (hereafter *TRF*), 57. For the politics of censorship in
general, see, e.g., Chodorow, *Christian Political Theory*, chap. 3.

to the inherent drama of rhetoric in order to imitate power[54]—especially in France, where dramatists reveal a veritable obsession with the juridical process that extends well into the Renaissance.

If the safety of the disputational arena had been compromised, its very dangers encouraged a fascinating return to a complex performative model that could convert the trial to drama, yet concomitantly reframe the drama as a more perfect (or even highly imperfect) juridical process. That was true, at any rate, for Accius, whose desire for control had motivated him to remain a dramatist and to avoid the "real contests" of the courtroom. What he could not control in the courtroom, he could control in his plays: "When asked why he did not turn advocate in view of the extraordinary skill in making apt replies which his tragedies revealed, [he] replied that in his plays the characters said what he himself wanted them to say, whereas in the courts his adversaries would probably say just what he least wanted them to say" (Quintilian, V, 13.43). In a stunning display of authorial self-consciousness and control, many medieval dramatists returned to the forensic protodrama, which allowed them to comment metacritically on the very origins of the discourse they were staging.

But in the end, whatever the manner in which classical and medieval orators dealt with the waning political strength of their rhetoric, their performances had become enmeshed in a conflict that held great appeal for aficionados of battle play. While it is impossible to ascertain which came first—the theatricalization of conflict or the audience demand that it be theatricalized—the degree of histrionics in the rhetorical *imitatio veritatis* was directly proportional to the positive reception generated in classical and medieval audiences. Orators were so entranced by that revised dynamic that they altered the forensic genre to provide the foundations for mimetic unity. By imitating the conflictual action of the trial through impersonation, they found a new way of exploiting pity, fear, and catharsis.

In the final analysis, it is in the performance of forensic rhetoric that the interplay between agonistic ritual and dramatic representation is most apparent, and that Eden's elegant comparison of the philosophical and conceptual similarities of law, drama, and rhetoric is most suggestive. It is there that Bloch's argument that "personal antagonism can be translated into new and meaningful poetic struc-

---

[54]Nichols, for example, discussed the power of theological authority and its ramifications for romance and epic genres in "Fission and Fusion."

ture" (*MFLL*, 169) is most relevant—but to the emergence of meaningful *dramatic* structure. If the literary performance was a "ceremonial demonstration," a "sporting version of the trial" based on
formula, gesture, and ritual (*MFLL*, 3), then the dramatically delivered trial was also a rhetorical version of literature. In light of the
long history of generic confusion between the two, the most logical
"translation" of the verbal antagonism of forensic rhetoric was
drama itself.

The Slaves of Applause

From Honorius to the present day, ritualistic discourses such as
the liturgy have always appealed (perversely or not) to the mimetic
instincts of some of the participants. In his "Dialogue on Dramatic
Poetry," T. S. Eliot's B. once pronounced such a spectator "guilty
of a *confusion des genres*" insofar as "his attention was not on the
meaning of the Mass . . . it was on the art of the Mass. His dramatic
desires were satisfied by the Mass, precisely because he was not
interested in the Mass, but in the drama of it."[55] Given the remarks
of Quintilian and Tacitus on the courtroom as theater, and given
the inclusion of the *mystère* as a rhetorical category in the *Jardin
de Plaisance*,[56] the history of rhetoric demonstrates that the liturgy
was by no means the sole ritualistic form to captivate spectators
with its inherent drama. Courtrooms had always attracted "confused" spectators/participants of another kind whose desires were
satisfied by forensic rhetoric precisely because they were interested
not in the legalities of a case but in the drama of it. Classical and
medieval spectators of forensic oratory, along with lawyers and
judges, were as confused as those who experienced pleasure in the
drama of the Church. Indeed, they were as confused as twentieth-
century aficionados of the "true-to-life" television courtroom drama,
in which the entire "plot" consists of the exposition and resolution
of a legal case.

Theater, according to Richard Southern, is "essentially a reactive
art" whose essence "lies in the impression made on the audience
by the manner in which you perform."[57] Nicoll's dictum that the

[55]T. S. Eliot, "Dialogue on Dramatic Poetry," in *Selected Essays*, 35–36.
[56]"Pro misteriis," in *Jardin de Plaisance*, ed. Droz and Piaget, vol. 1.
[57]Southern, *Seven Ages of the Theatre*, 26; see also Styan *DSA*, 25. For the lack
of separation between actor and audience in the early theater, see, e.g., Rey-Flaud,
PDMA, 15–22; Stock, *IOL*, 80–81; Lebègue, *TRF*, 52–55; Gustave Cohen, *Histoire
de la mise-en-scène*, 257–69.

presence of spectators "provides the first prime characteristic of theatrical endeavor" may be debated, but we may reasonably agree that, like drama, the theatrical performance of legal rhetoric was an "art-object being shaped to a certain extent by the spectators themselves" (*TADT*, 15–16, 27). Illuminating in that respect is Burke's rhetorical approach to literature "not as a creator's device for self-expression, nor as an audience's device for amusement or instruction, but as a communicative relationship between writer and audience, with both parties actively participating" (*POLF*, 329). Indeed, Rey-Flaud reminds us that medieval spectators "performed" at least as much as the actors (*PDMA*, 76).

I approach the generic fluidity between law and drama through the analysis of three final features: audience participation, audience adaptation, and the transmutation of legal proof into aesthetic pathos in the dramatic imitation of a conflictual action. Like medieval drama, forensic rhetoric was a communal and "consubstantial" experience, a "spectacle of participation" (*PDMA*, 17). Classical and medieval spectators were accustomed to "contributing" both physically and verbally to the disputational agon, whether it took place in the courtroom, at the quodlibet, on the Pré-aux-Clercs, or on the stage. Moreover, since the participatory, impersonated *spectaculum crudelitatis* brought audiences into direct contact with the legal cast of characters and confused virtual speaker and actual speaker, virtual fighter and actual fighter, such a phenomenon might actually have invited audiences to identify forensic rhetoric as a dramatic experience centuries before their dialogic participation in the antiphonal singing of the liturgy.

Audience participation, audience adaptation, and theatricalization are linked. In the wake of increasingly histrionic trials in antiquity and the Middle Ages, spectators came to demand that the orator tailor his discourse to their enhanced aesthetic desires. Apparently orators were only too happy to oblige. In their quest to command the "stage," to reap the social benefits of renown, and to play the crowd, they altered rhetorical intention and rhetorical end, so privileging audience adaptation that they helped to collapse the distinctions between civic and dramatic discourse, ritual and representation. In so doing, they exceeded the "proper boundaries" once identified by Longinus, replacing the didactic ends of equity with the mimetic ends of spectacle and blurring irremediably the forensic and dramatic experiences.

"Some literary forms, such as drama," wrote Frye, "remind us with particular vividness of analogies to rituals, for the drama in literature, like the ritual in religion, is primarily a social or ensemble

performance" (107). The court proceeding, too, was an ensemble
performance, in which spectators often assumed roles of their own.
Their physical participation in its *rixes* was mirrored verbally by
their intense participation in the discursive agon of forensic performance. Indeed, dramatic delivery had long gained in efficacy by
virtue of the fact that orators "may confer with our audience, ad-
mitting them as it were into our deliberations" (Quintilian, IX, 1.30).
A similar phenomenon occurred in such ancient Greek dramas as
Aeschylus's *Eumenides*, in which the Herald's final exhortation constituted an "invitation to let the stage flow over into the audience,
making participation between actors and audience complete, as they
are asked to weld their shout of approval *for* the play with a shout
that has meaning *within* the play" (*POLF*, 156). The legal advocate
thus admitted his audience into the legal mimesis in much the same
way that the performers of the Fleury *Herod* admitted the plebs into
their own dramatic story: "Let them invite the people standing
around [*populus circumstantem*] to adore the child" (quoted in Tydeman, 223); in other words, let them invite the people to participate
in the drama.

Still more to the point is the testimony offered by medieval commentators about the role of audience integration in the definition
of early drama. Origen, for example, suggested in his commentary
on the Song of Songs that the "little book" was in "dramatic form"
because of the polyvalence of possible addressees:

> It seems to me that this little book is an epithalamium, that is to say,
> a marriage-song, which Solomon wrote in the form of a drama and
> sang under the figure of the Bride.... We find the Bride speaking not
> to the Bridegroom only but also to the maidens; likewise the Bride-
> groom's words are addressed not to the Bride alone, but also to His
> friends. And that is what we meant just now, when we said that the
> marriage-song was written in dramatic form.[58]

Like the medieval audience of the *Jeu de la Feuillée*, who intervened
"with an enormous choral moan of aggressive irony" (*PDMA*, 17),
and like the twentieth-century audience that determined the ending
of the participatory Broadway smash *The Mystery of Edwin Drood*,
classical and medieval courtroom spectators and witnesses (invited
or not) often interrupted the deliberations of lawyers, thereby establishing roles of their own in the battle play. Such interplay between audience and participant may thus provide a partial response

[58]Quoted in Minnis, *Medieval Theory of Authorship*, 58.

to Styan's lament that if only the actor/audience relationship were known, it "would certainly tell us more about the working of the drama in medieval society than that relationship today would tell us about the modern theatre" (*DSA*, 19). Much of that knowledge is available in the rhetorical corpus.

Be that as it may, many critics have disdained early audience participation, as when Nicoll applauded the Elizabethan initiative to "improve" upon a histrionic legacy in which actors brought "spectators within the framework of their performances" (*TADT*, 28–29). Yet when medieval churchgoers participated in the Mass, when spectators were integrated into processions and parades, they were participating in a tradition that had been canonized far earlier within forensic rhetoric. In that context, it is revealing to reconsider Eliot's criticism of Ben Jonson for "overstepping" generic bounds. Citing the speeches of Sylla's ghost in the *Catiline* and of Envy in *The Poetaster*, he objected to the "inappropriate" integration of the audience into the dramatic experience: "Here we are spectators not of a play of characters, but of a play of forensic, exactly as if we had been forced to attend the sitting itself." However, his insistence that "it is essential that we should preserve our position of spectators" represents the antithesis of what classical and medieval disputers were striving to achieve: the integration of audience members into the dramatic reenactment of a crime.[59] The Mass and the procession were by no means the sole medieval phenomena to provide a kind of nascent dramatic unity for the participatory experiences they sanctioned. In fact, postmedieval disapproval of audience integration might even be viewed as an eloquent (albeit begrudging) testimonial to the status of forensic oratory as a participatory spectacle.

Traditionally, the audience could interfere in the trial at any time during the "very shock of battle" when "any stupid or ill-advised statement brings prompt retribution in the shape of the judge's disapproval, taunting criticism from your opponent—yes, and from your own supporters expressions of dissatisfaction" (Tacitus, 34). Once again, Lucian's Professor of Public Speaking had precious advice on that subject for his unsavory protégés. Interruption was a particularly valuable technique by which they might enhance their reputations for histrionics:

I almost omitted the thing that is most important and most needful for maintaining your reputation. Laugh at all the speakers. . . . At pub-

---

[59]Eliot, "Rhetoric," in *Selected Essays*, 28.

lic lectures, go in after everybody else, for that makes you conspicuous;
and when everybody is silent, let fall an uncouth expression of praise
which will draw the attention of the company and so annoy them
that they will all be disgusted at the vulgarity of your language and
will stop their ears. [22]

One might say that everyone in the courtroom wanted to get into
the act. Crafty witnesses posed a particular threat to the *actores*
during cross-examination, for at that time the witnesses had an ideal
opportunity to upstage counsel by playing the crowd themselves.
Quintilian thus admonished that "above all our examination must
be circumspect, since a witness will often launch some smart re-
partee in answering counsel for the defence and thereby win marked
favour from the audience in general" (V, 7.31).

In the end, audience participation was both pleasurable and dangerous because such interruptions were not just for show; responses
and reactions from "prompters" (*monitores*) actually influenced the
outcome of the trial and shaped the very "plot" of forensic oratory.
Should he fail to remain alert, the orator might often be

> forced to give a hurried assent to those who prompt him as to what
> he should say, suggestions which are often perfectly fatuous owing to
> excess of zeal on the part of the prompter. As a result it sometimes
> happens that we are put to the blush by too ready acceptance of the
> foolish suggestions of another. Moreover, we have to deal with others
> besides these prompters who speak for our ear alone.   [Quintilian, VI,
> 4.8–9]

Similarly, in the disputational analogues of the medieval university, audience participation was the very foundation for the *disputatio* portion of the quodlibet, where candidates were judged in
part on their ability to answer any question that might arise at any
moment.[60] Like his classical predecessor in the courtroom, the
spectator/questioner often sought the spotlight as much as the performers, as when an anonymous author reported that "in disputa-
tione de quolibet proponebantur a sociis decem questiones propter
duas quas proposui ego ipse" (during the quodlibetal disputation,

---

[60]Mandonnet has argued that since both the "ordinary" and "extraordinary" disputations were held before spectators, the principal difference between the two was
that in the former, the "disputed question was determined in advance by the master
who was to lead the disputation": "Chronologie," 268; also Glorieux, *LQ*, 2:11.
Additionally, Glorieux suggests that audience participation is implied by the frequent
use of the terms *communis* and *generalis* to describe the quodlibetal *disputatio* (as
opposed to *specialis, particularis*, or *privata*) (36–43).

ten questions were raised by the spectators, two of which I brought
up myself [quoted in *LQ*, 2:39]). The unpredictability of the subject,
tone, and motivation of audience intervention lent a certain suspense to the proceedings as scholastic challengers (like the *monitores* of old) helped to shape the proceedings, assuming roles of their
own in a dramatic verbal spectacle:

> The students who are engaged therein—and the spectators themselves
> who are interested inasmuch as the session is lively and the problems
> well presented—do not have here the passive attitude characteristic
> of the sermon or the lesson. They are formed by the action itself,
> whether by playing the roles of attackers, adversaries, *opponentes*, or
> of defenders, *respondentes*. [Glorieux, *LQ*, 2:28]

Ultimately, since audiences enjoyed their participation in the "spectacle of a fight" immensely, orators sought to make their own histrionic fight increasingly pleasing in a stunning transformation of
the theory of audience adaptation into a pervasive practice of crowd
pleasing.

Forensic oratory, like drama, had always had such a crowd to
please. "We know on good authority," wrote Tacitus, that "the defence of a Cornelius ... brought the whole community together *en
masse*" (39). So if the orator had his temenos, his "stage," he also
had a full house that he "could command day after day, when the
forum was packed by an audience at the same time numerous and
distinguished, when persons who had to face the hazard of a public
trial could depend on being supported by shoals of clients and fellow
tribesmen [cum clientelae quoque ac tribus et muncipiorum]" (Tacitus, 39). Similarly, the Basochien played a crowd of his own in the
Grand' Chambre, as did the *magister* of the medieval university.
Gérard de Frachet documented how Dominican teachers attracted
large audiences to ordinary disputations in which "legerunt et dis-
putaverunt in scolis, praesentibus scolaribus, et religiosis, et multis
ecclesiarum praelatis" (scholarly reading and disputing were done
in the presence of students, clergy, and numerous prelates of the
church [quoted in *LQ*, 1:21]). The quodlibet also packed the house
at the University of Paris, where other activities ground to a halt so
that the maximum number of spectators might attend: visiting dignitaries, civil and religious authorities, and students of all origins,
orders, and nationalities (*LQ*, 2:10). Rhetoric had long been shaped
by its theory of audience adaptation, and theorists had consistently
encouraged the speaker to communicate with each member of the

audience, including the rank and file;[61] yet it is clear that a veritable obsession with the audience's aesthetic demands led to renewed dramatic extremes during delivery in late antiquity and the Middle Ages.

Particularly influential in that shift in focus from legal ritual to dramatic representation was a change in the intended receiver of legal discourse. As orators helped to undermine the moral aims of eloquence during their histrionic deliveries, they set out to impress three audiences in addition to the judge. The orator, Tacitus tells us, needed to "command" his teachers, his "opponents and antagonists," and, most important, his public, "always numerous and always different, composed of friendly and unfriendly critics, who would not let any points escape them, whether good or bad."[62] From the beginning the legal advocate had been concerned with persuading his primary audience, the judge, but forensic expectations had changed. It had once been the "mark of a shrewd debater" to be able to "perceive what remarks impress the judge and what he rejects ... from his looks, and sometimes from some action or utterance" (Quintilian, VI, 4.19); now the rhetorical corpus suggests unceasingly that the orator was looking for something very specific in the eyes of his audience. He wanted far more than to "avoid boring his hearers" (Tacitus, 19): like the earliest sophists, he wanted to entertain them. He sought less the absence of boredom than the presence of delight.

Quintilian, for example, encouraged aesthetic exploitation of wit and *sententiae* to relieve "the fatigue of the judge's stomach" (IV, 2.121), "restore their flagging spirits," and "alleviate their boredom" (IV, 1.49). He was ambivalent, however, about the extent to which popular taste was to be indulged (IV, 2.122). Apparently such audience adaptation was helping to undermine the moral foundations of the law. Many a lawyer endeavored not to "burden" the judge with "all the arguments we have discovered, since by so doing we shall at once bore him and render him less inclined to believe us" (V, 12.8). After all, if the kindly disposition of the judge was so crucial to his ability and willingness to sleuth out legal truth, why disturb him with all the evidence when he might prefer a histrionic display? By the first century, it was clear that the judge who was not "in-

[61]Even Aristotle had advised that the rhetorician adapt his discourse to the "vulgarity of the hearers": *Rhetoric*, 1395b. See also Quintilian, IV, 1.34; Plato, *Phaedrus*, 277b–c.
[62]Glorieux (*LQ*, 2:11) describes the quodlibet in terms that are virtually identical to these words of Tacitus (34).

dulged" with a proper display of *actio* was a judge who was not impartial. He "travels faster than counsel, and if he cannot find something to engage his interest and prejudice him in your favour in a good-going proof, or in piquant utterances, or in brilliant and highly wrought pen-pictures, he is against you" (Tacitus, 20).

Such displays of oratorical culture were apparently "fully appreciated not only by the learned and scholarly portion of the audience, but also by the rank and file [*populus*]. They cheer the speaker from the start" (Tacitus, 32). Even if the logic of the speech remained inaccessible to unlearned spectators, they were thought to be susceptible to the very sounds of histrionically delivered language.[63] The transition from a rhetorical theory of audience adaptation to an aesthetic theory of dramatic performance required but a step; and that step was delivery. No longer content to be in the dark about the intricacies of the law, the "general audience" as well as "casual listeners who flock in and out" preferred a performance they could understand. "They will no more put up with sober, unadorned old-fashionedness in a court of law than if you were to try to reproduce on the stage [*in scaena*] the gesture of Roscius or Ambivius Turpio .... For the adornment of the poet [*poeticus decor*] is demanded nowadays also in the orator" (Tacitus, 20). As if they were at the theater, the "audience of men who, if not thoroughly ill-educated, are certainly ignorant of such arts as dialectic" (Quintilian, V, 14.29) came to "insist on a flowery and ornamental style of speaking" (Tacitus, 20). And if the legal advocate failed to meet their aesthetic expectations, if such theatricality were absent, "the crowd refuses to listen, and even their clients can scarcely put up with them" (Tacitus, 23). Not only had the orator made applause the "goal of all his effort"; the audience had come to demand that he do so, even if logical coherence were lost in the bargain.

That irrevocable compromise of proof had extraordinary literary implications: if courtroom victories depended on their literary charms for the audience, then the rhetoric of justice had tremendous power as a rhetoric of spectacle. So it was that Longinus complimented Demosthenes for sublime speeches that "dumbfound the audience" and draw "our attention ... from the reasoning to the enthralling effect of the imagination."[64] And where a more circumspect Quintilian had once declined to "deny that there is some advantage to be gained by pleasing [*in delectatione*] our audience

[63]See Romilly's discussion of the magic and music of language in Gorgias: *Magic and Rhetoric in Ancient Greece*, chap. 1.
[64]Longinus, "On the Sublime," 12.5, 15.1.

and a great deal by stirring their emotions" (V, 8.3), rhetorical documents of the first century suggest that pleasing the courtroom
crowd with the "sublimity" of those emotions was often made the
primary goal of oratory. Quintilian's statement that "the more un-
attractive the natural appearance of anything, the more does it require to be seasoned by the charm of style" (V, 14.35) was taken to
a dramatic extreme, as when the orator marked the transition from
the *exordium* to either the statement of facts or the proof with a
clever epigram, thus "seeking to win applause by this feat of leg-
erdemain [*plausum petat*]" (IV, 1.77). Though Quintilian praised
orators for imitating Ovid in their use of metaphor to weld diverse
subjects to form a whole (IV, 1.77) and to throw "a flood of light"
on subjects of real importance (V, 14.34), he also observed that *elocutio* served to disguise logical imperfections: "An argument is often
less suspect when thus disguised, and the charm with which it is
expressed makes it all the more convincing to our audience" (V,
14.35).

Therefore, despite Bloch's view of the medieval literary exploitation of the legalistic model as a new type of aesthetic, according
to which "the most convincing plea is that which can claim superior
poetic merit; and, conversely, that which is superior poetically is
the most persuasive" (*MFLL*, 180), the efficacy of poetry as an effective form of persuasion was not new at all; it may be traced to
the far earlier *letteraturizzazione* of forensic rhetoric. Indeed, extensive training in the schools for declamation had equipped future
lawyers with all the skills they required to effect that very process.
Quintilian, for example, credited the schools with the popular practice of "digressing to some pleasant and attractive topic with a view
to securing the utmost amount of favour from their audience" (IV,
3.1–2). But the ability of future lawyers to please the public and to
"flaunt their talents" (IV, 3.2) then extended inappropriately to the
law courts as a form of spectacle. "If declamation is not a preparation
for the actual work of the courts, it can only be compared to the
rant of an actor [*scenicae ostentationi*] or the raving of a lunatic"
(II, 10.8).[65] In reality, the rant of an actor in a "mimic combat" is
exactly what forensic delivery had become. Forensic conventions of
actio seem to have eliminated any hint of impropriety; or at the
very least, delivery allowed impropriety and theatricality to run
rampant. Tacitus assured his readers that there had been a time

[65]*Ostento*, of course, had both conflictual and theatrical connotations, conjuring
up visions of displays of military strength, but also of any ostentatious exhibition or
spectacle. See also Winterbottom's discussion of the brilliance (*nitor*) of declamation
(63).

when a delightful speech was no less meritorious for its ability to give pleasure (20), but that time had passed. The spirit of the anti-sophistic precept that "our delivery must be adapted to our matter" had disappeared, thanks to the widespread disregard manifested by "the majority of speakers who are used to the noisy applause of a large audience, whether it be a chance gathering or an assembly of *claqueurs*, and consequently are unnerved by the attentive silence of the courts. They feel that they have fallen short of eloquence, if they do not make everything echo with noise and clamour [*tumultu et vociferatione*]" (Quintilian, IV, 2.37).

A similar phenomenon obtained in the medieval university, where elegant performance was once thought to have buttressed pedagogical efficacy. Ideally, law, oratory, pedagogy, and theatricality, were to have been in harmony, as when one particularly gifted professor at Paris in 1177 charmed a large and varied audience with a lecture on canon law—or so the sycophantic tone implies. As he "soothed and entranced" them with the consonance of "sweetness of language" to subject matter, "such a crowd—almost all the professors with their students—collected to hear his charming voice that the largest hall could scarcely hold the audience." As the speaker interwove "apt citations from civil and canon law" into his "structured and colourful prose," his substantive interpretations, though of a "length that usually bores many people," transfixed the audience nonetheless (quoted in Murray, 230).

But, as was the case with its forensic analogues, spectacle came to overshadow pedagogy during the performance of the normal curriculum of lectures, of ordinary disputations, and of the quodlibet as well. John of Salisbury, for example, cited Quintilian, I, 3.3–5, to deplore the performance abuses that rendered disputation a quest less for truth than for applause. It was the orator's desire for an actor's reputation, he speculated, that had encouraged students to imitate the appearance of truth rather than to apprehend its substance:

> Thus emboldened, they proceed to display the full limit of their ability.... They talk at a break-neck pace, but without saying much. Their statements lack solid basis and deep roots.... So it is with minds that affect to be subtle and productive, yet lack [real] depth. "Such exhibitions evoke our applause, in view of the youth of the principals, but as progress comes to a halt, admiration fades." [*Metalogicon*, 91]

John's admiration may have faded, but that of the audience was clearly on the rise. Even the ostensibly noble, theologically moti-

vated quodlibet underwent theatricalization. Originally intended as
a "salubrious" and "honest" intellectual exercise designed for the
benefit of the academic collectivity,[66] it too was denounced by Benedetto Caetani (the future Pope Boniface VIII) for representing its
quaestiones as histrionic *fabulosa et frivola:*

> Vos, *magistri* Parysienses, stultam fecistis et facitis doctrinam scien-
> tiae vestrae, turbantes orbem terrarum.... Deberetis disputare de
> quaestionibus utilibus, sed nunc assumitis vobis fabulosa et fri-
> vola. [Quoted in Glorieux, *LQ,* 1:15]

> You Parisian masters have succeeded in making the doctrines of your
> field look foolish, and you continue to do so while you disturb the
> whole world. You should dispute about useful questions; nowadays,
> though, you take up all manner of fairy tales and trivia.

Apparently Roman lawyers and medieval disputers were not nearly
so interested in logic as they were in art. They "imagine that their
art is wasted unless it obtrudes itself, whereas as a matter of fact
the moment it is detected it ceases to be art" (Quintilian, IV, 2. 127).
Still, while their rhetoric may have ceased to be oratorical art, it
was clearly dramatic art.

Nowhere is that clearer than in Vives, who continued to take
exception to the "deference shown to the listeners who surround
the disputants" (*De tradendis,* 291). Oratory had become little more
than a pleasurable talent competition in which "only praise for wit
or cleverness is sought" (57–58), and indulging the audience had
rendered the dissemination of knowledge "theatrical" (291). Vives's
impatience with the scholastic obsession with spectacle is most
explicit in the *De causis corruptarum artium,* where he condemns
the widespread desire on the part of disputers to appeal to the "popular audience [*ad populum vero spectatorem*]."[67] In reality, Vives
is criticizing the advent of *dulcitudo* as a rhetorical end, in much
the same way that Quintilian had described *voluptas* (IV, 2.122) and
Tacitus *laetitia* and *pulchritudo* (20). His condemnation of the way
disputers had been seduced by the "pleasure of debate" (*adducti
dulcedine disputandi*) is strikingly similar to that of Benedetto Caetani on the quodlibet as *fabula:*

---

[66]One Sorbonne statute of 14 November 1344 underscores this notion by insti-
tutionalizing the convocation of students to disputations as "honest exercises" for
the benefit of the collectivity (*in collationum honestis exercitiis*). The complete text
appears in Glorieux, *Robert de Sorbon,* 224.

[67]Vives, *De causis corruptarum artium,* in "*Adversus pseudodialecticos* and *De
causis corruptarum artium,* Book III," ed. Guerlac, 147.

> To appeal to the popular audience even sometimes, forsooth, to the
> arbiter of the disputation [*altercationum arbitrum*], they made up
> ludicrous things as if in a play [*tamquam in fabula*], and with the
> same lofty and empty style, so that the common crowd would admire
> what they could not understand, and they themselves would gain a
> reputation among the people. [Vives, *De causis*, 147]

Furthermore, it appears that once audiences' demands had been
met, their appreciation was so great that it encouraged further indulgence on the part of the orator. He then yielded to one of the
most powerful motivators of all: fame. When lawyers privileged the
"taste and judgment of hearers," they "gained in grace and attrac-
tiveness" (Tacitus, 20). Playing out a legal battle for a crowd of
transfixed spectators was in fact an ideal way to distinguish oneself
verbally, physically, and aesthetically. "Think again of the incessant
public meetings... and of the glory you gained by being at daggers
drawn with them [influential people]" (Tacitus, 40). Similarly, Alexander Murray points out that within a medieval university system
that would give rise to the *concurrentes* that Vives criticized in *De
tradendis* (61), "uppish intellectuals" fighting their way up the university ladder also learned that "strength was an occasion for boast-
ing" (231). The promise of the personal validation that accompanied
fame instilled quite naturally a desire to increase one's reputation
as an orator by playing the crowd, by becoming a pleasing dramatic
personage. Indeed, the temptation appears to have been irresistible.

During their legal apprenticeship, students habitually attended
their role model wherever he appeared. "The youth had to get the
habit of following his patron about, of escorting him in public, of
supporting him at all his appearances as a speaker, whether in the
law courts or on the platform" (Tacitus, 34). Even in the good old
days of oratory, Tacitus himself was not immune to the charms of
having groupies. Being "passionately fond of rhetorical studies," he
had himself played that obsequious role as a boy, when he "made a
practice not only of listening attentively to their pleadings in court,
but also of attaching myself to them at their homes and attending
them out of doors" (2). How were contemporary lawyers to resist
what Tacitus described?

> Just look, again, at the imposing retinue of clients that follows you
> when your leave your house! What a brave show you make out of
> doors! What an amount of deference is paid to you in the law-courts!
> What a supreme delight it is to gather yourself to your feet, and to
> take your stand before a hushed audience, that has eyes only for you!

> Think of the growing crowd streaming round about the speaker, and
> taking on any mood in which he may care to wrap himself, as with
> a cloak. [6]

And what *magister* could resist the medieval counterpart of such
celebrity, as when Abelard's reputation caused students to "flock"
(*convalarent*) to his school (*Historia calamitatum*, 104); or when
twelfth-century enthusiasm for the New Aristotle led to what Louis
John Paetow termed "daring and spectacular dialectical flights
which astounded the gaping multitudes" (in Andeli, 21).

In that sense, the most striking aspect of the "decline" of rhetoric
may well be the paramountcy accorded to the needs of the audience.
The legal rhetoric described by Quintilian and Tacitus was a true
audience-centered rhetoric aimed more at winning satisfactory reception than at arriving at reasoned conclusions. While such an
"aesthetic" has often met with disapproval in modern criticism, the
Horatian view that the "internal characteristics of the poem are
determined largely, if not exclusively, by the external demands of
the audience" was crucial in the *letteraturizzazione* of the law.[68]
When legal advocates took center stage and attempted to dazzle their
audiences with a theatrical delivery, they chose that moment "for
affected modulations of the voice, throwing back their heads, thump-
ing their sides [*brachium in latus iactant*] and indulging in every
kind of extravagance of statement, language and style." The result
of that behavior? More protean rhetorical intentions and ends that
were sometimes didactic, sometimes mimetic. "While the speech,
from its very monstrosity, meets with applause, the case remains
unintelligible (deinde, quod sit monstro simile, placet actio, causa
non intelligitur" [Quintilian, IV, 2.39]).

In a stunning denunciation of the pernicious consequences of such
practices, Quintilian articulated a veritable theory of the origins of
drama within the rhetorical tradition: he described the irremediable
bifurcation of forensic oratory into histrionic "pleading" and logical
"proving." Especially in private suits, the two tasks were distributed
(most unevenly) between the actor/declaimer and the boring logician. "You will generally find that different counsel are employed
to plead and to prove the case" (Itaque videas alios plerumque iud-
iciis privatis ad actiones advocari alios ad probationem [VI, 4.7]).
When he insisted that proving "must surely be accounted the more
important" of the duties of advocacy, his words apparently fell on

[68]Weinberg, *History of Literary Criticism*, as quoted in Howell, *PRL*, 47.

deaf ears. Complain as he might that "it is a disgrace to oratory that inferior advocates should be regarded as adequate to render the greater service to the litigants" (VI, 4.7), that was precisely what had come to pass. "Some on the other hand think they have done their duty to their clients by an ostentatious and fatiguing display of elaborate declamation and straightway march out of court attended by an applauding crowd and leave the desperate battle of debate to uneducated performers who often are of but humble origin" (VI, 4.6).

The "passion for producing a thrill of pleasure [*voluptas*]" (IV, 2.122) had divided forensic oratory into two distinct parts: logic and spectacle. Or rather, the problem of genre lies in the fact that, institutionally speaking, those two parts were indistinct. Opting for the actor's mastery of his audience over the dialectician's "minute and scrupulous inquiry with a view to arriving at clear and convincing truths" (V, 14.28), the lawyer had pushed one part of legal oratory definitively into the realm of spectacle by exceeding the "limits of mere persuasion" (Longinus, 15, 11). Unless he chose representation of a spectacle over presentation of the facts, unless he "delivered" to the crowd a dramatic mimesis, his eloquence was thought to have no power at all. "Unless we attract them by the charm of our discourse or drag them by its force, and occasionally throw them off their balance by an appeal to their emotions, we shall be unable to vindicate the claims of truth and justice" (Quintilian, V, 14.29). In other words, any surviving moral and social identity within the law was utterly dependent on the protodramatic status of forensic language.

Once again Lucian's Professor had striking testimony to offer in that respect. A dismal failure as a lawyer, he was nonetheless a master of performance and of appearances, a victorious virtuoso as an actor: "I enjoy the name of a speaker, and prove myself such in the courts, generally playing false to my clients, although I promise the poor fools to deliver their juries to them. To be sure I am generally unsuccessful, but the palm-leaves at my door are green and twined with fillets, for I use them as bait for my victims" (25). Of the two possible "brides" mentioned at the end of "A Professor of Public Speaking"—drama and rhetoric—rhetoric was now the fairer of the two: her charms far outweighed those of her greatest rival, drama. If disciples followed the Professor's histrionic program, nothing could hinder them "from holding the mastery in the courts, enjoying high favour with the public, being attractive, and marrying, not an old woman out of a comedy, as did your law-giver and tutor, but Rhetoric, fairest of brides" (26).

Rhetoric, a bride? Martianus Capella's armor-clad maiden wearing a dress? This focus on the pleasure of spectacle was the ultimate indignity: the emasculation of eloquence. No longer the weapon of Ong's ritualistic male conflicts for truth, rhetoric became "flaccid and nerveless," having been relegated to the perverse arena of theatrical declamation. There it took on all the histrionic and "effeminate" colorings traditionally associated with the theater:

> Declamations, which we used to employ as foils wherewith to practise for the duels of the forum, have long since departed from the true form of pleading and, owing to the fact they are composed solely with the design of giving pleasure, have become flaccid and nerveless [*ad solam compositae voluptatem nervis carent*]: indeed, declaimers are guilty of exactly the same offence as slave-dealers who castrate boys in order to increase the attractions of their beauty [*puerorum virilitate excisa lenocinantur*]. [Quintilian, V, 12.17]

Long before Gerhoh of Reichersberg's denunciation of the transvestism of priests,[69] a livid Quintilian, while acknowledging that "this debauched eloquence . . . may please modern audiences by its effeminate and voluptuous charms, . . . absolutely refuse[d] to regard it as eloquence at all: for it retains not the slightest trace of purity and virility in itself (*ne minimum quidem in se indicium masculi et incorrupti*) (V, 12.20).

But if not rhetoric, what was it? As forensic oratory crossed genre lines into theater and gender lines into effeminacy, it was in fact a protodrama that eventually would spawn purely theatrically inspired descendants. By virtue of impersonation, conflictually structured "plot," audience adaptation, and manipulation of pity, fear, and verisimilitude, rhetoric was an origin of drama. And where orators had long plundered the riches of their histrionic colleagues, the converse phenomenon would prove equally effective: dramatists themselves would look to a theatrical rhetoric for inspiration and guidance—especially during the Middle Ages, when literary models were used in legal education, and when fictive proceedings became the training ground for the Basoche.[70] Both orator and audience had come to give such preference to the *dulce* over the *utile* that Longinus's notion that "imagination means one thing in oratory and another in poetry" (15, 2) had disappeared. If the object of the poetic

---

[69]Young, *Drama of the Medieval Church*, 2:411.
[70]For the use of literary texts in legal education, see Paetow, *Arts Course*, 23–25. I discuss the Basochial *cause fictive* in chap. 3.

imagination was "to enthral," then so too was that of a theatricalized oratory: lawyers and scholastic disputers were giving the audience what it wanted—the "spectacle of a fight" that it found so pleasing.

Performance practice had overturned the dictum that, especially during the statement of facts, "nothing must seem fictitious (*nihil videatur fictum* [Quintilian, IV, 2.126]). Indeed, delivery seemed to mandate that everything should seem fictitious. Even Quintilian confessed that the orator was actually a "spinner of fiction [fingentor]" who "should bear clearly in mind throughout his whole speech what the fiction is to which he has committed himself" (utrobique autem orator *meminisse* debebit *actione* tota, quid *finxerit* [IV, 2.90–91; emphasis mine]. And nothing can be more significant here than his emphasis on the term *fingere*, which combined notions of mnemonics, representation, impersonation, invention, law, and literary creation.[71] Eager to anticipate the mimetic unity of his rhetorical work of art, he sought to avoid the kind of "slip which is far from rare on the part of spinners of fiction" by consistently respecting the internal coherency of the fiction he presented; "for if we draw our fictions entirely from circumstances lying outside the case... above all we must see that we do not contradict ourselves" (IV, 2.89–90). Like Plato's poet, the lawyer was a "liar" subject to the "truth of the proverb that a liar should have a good memory" (quod vulgo dicitur, mendacem memorem esse opportere [IV, 2.91]). And like the Aristotelian spinner of tragic fiction, he was a master of verisimilitude: "We must take care, first that our fiction is within the bounds of possibility, secondly that it is consistent with the persons, dates and places involved and thirdly that it presents a character and sequence that are not beyond belief" (IV, 2.89). His task was to represent actions that were consistent with probabilities, possibilities, and verisimilitude in a manner strikingly similar to what Aristotle had described in his discussion in *Poetics*, 1461b:

> There are many things which are true, but scarcely credible, just as there are many things which are plausible though false. It will there-

[71]According to the *Oxford Latin Dictionary*, *fingere* had the following connotations: mnemonic: "to form or convey a mental picture of, conjure up in the mind, visualize; (of sculptors) to make a likeness of, represent"; performative: "to change one's appearance, clothes, etc., transform oneself, to modify the expression of (a face) or tone of (a voice)"; literary/inventive: "to compose (a poem and other literary works), to invent, coin; to produce artificially; to make an imitation of, counterfeit; to form out of original matter, create"; dramatic: "to make up, invent, fabricate, to make a pretence of (doing or feeling something), feign, simulate; to play the part of, pose as, imitate"; and legal: "to assume as a legal fiction."

fore require just as much exertion on our part to make the judge believe
what we say when it is true as it will when it is fictitious [quare non
minus laborandum est, ut iudex, quae vere dicimus quam quae *fin-
gimus*, credat]. [Quintilian, IV, 2.34]

Associated no longer with truth but with the appearance of truth,
forensic oratory was a "confused" genre, an *imitatio veritatis*, a
borderline area, a nascent dramatic form.

Finally, in their dramatic imitation of legal conflict, orators revealed their skill in exploiting another principal criterion of drama:
like Aristotle's tragedian, they effected catharsis through the manipulation of pity and fear to grant "relief to these and similar emotions" (*Poetics*, 1449b). Fear, for example, was considered a
particularly efficacious means of "aesthetic" proof. Quintilian noted
that "it may be necessary to frighten them [the judges] as Cicero
does in the *Verrines*" (IV, 1.20); and Tacitus declared that rhetoric
was a weapon that could "strike fear and terror in the ears of ma-
lignant foes" (5). Pity was so powerful a force in forensic rhetoric
that victory in the courts seemed doubtful if one's opponent were
an "old or blind man or a child" (Quintilian, IV, 1.42). Although
Quintilian advised that appeals to the judge's compassion (*miseratio*)
were to be used sparingly (VI, 1.28), he acknowledged that judges
were particularly susceptible to them. The orator might thus learn
to save the situation by imitating fictional models in which those
very emotions were evoked: "They invent fictitious cases and treat
them realistically on the lines which would be followed in actual
pleading" (IV, 1.43). Even though Quintilian cautioned that the use
of worst-case scenarios to frighten the judges did not "come under
the art of oratory" (IV, 1.21–22), and even though "it was wrong to
distract the judge from the truth by exciting his pity [*misericordia*],"
such distractions had become the very stuff of forensic oratory. Appeals to the emotions may well have been "disturbances of the mind
[*animi perturbatio*]," but those disturbances were consistent with
the transformed mimetic ends of oratory (V, Preface, 1).

Moreover, *metus* and *misericordia* continued to conquer medieval
audiences, not only when Lady Mercy (Miséricorde) emerged to incarnate dramatically the legal principle of *misericordia* in the *procès
de paradis*[72]—but when Martianus observed that

commoventur igitur auditores aut *miseratione* aut odio aut invidia
aut *metu* aut spe aut ira ceterisque similibus. *Miseratione*, cum cala-

[72]See, e.g., Goebel's discussion of chattel and *misericordia* in *Felony and Misdemeanor*, 238–48.

mitatem alicuis magno dolore tractamus, cum iniquitatem temporis vel periculi magnitudinem memoramus.... *Metum* vero excitari vel propriis vel communibus periculis. [163g; emphasis mine]

therefore, the audience is to be moved by pity or hatred or envy or fear or hope or anger or the like. With pity, when we respond to someone's calamity with great sorrow, or when we recall the wickedness of the age or the greatness of the danger.... Fear, however, is aroused by dangers, either personal ones or those common to all.

These are the very terms that appear in Latin translations of *Poetics*, 1449b: "non per enarrationem rei, sed *per misericordiam, metumque* factis expressum, eius modi vehementes animorum perturbationes unasquasque *purgans* expiansque" (not through narrating the thing, but through pity and fear expressed by the deeds, in that way purging and relieving all such violent disturbances of the soul [Harles ed.]); or "aequat passiones per *misericordiam* et *metum* et *purgat* illos qui patiuntur" (through pity and fear, it both regularizes the passions and also purges those who suffer [from them] [Margouliouth ed.]).

But while, in Aristotelian law and poetics, pity and fear had been subordinate to the formation of equitable judgments (Eden, *PLF*, 59–61), the phenomena described by Quintilian and Tacitus suggest that by the first century the converse was equally true: pity and fear were not aesthetic techniques subordinate to equity but legal techniques subordinate to aesthetics. In other words, what Eden has shown on the level of philosophical conception can also be demonstrated on the level of performance. By exploiting pity and fear to purge the emotions of an excessively indulged audience, the "slaves of applause" transformed forensic oratory into a legitimate sister of drama. If, as Howell says, "the process by which literature becomes mimetic is related to the process by which it awakens pity or fear or laughter, while the process by which it remains nonmimetic is related to its power to achieve rational credibility, emotional acceptance, and moral authority" (*PRL*, 55), then forensic rhetoric invariably had the potential to become mimetic. In a masterful subordination of rhetorical proof to aesthetic performance, pathos targeted pity and fear in the audience for its own sake. The ethos that had established the speaker's credibility as a logician became the glorification of reputation in and of itself. And finally, the reasoned exposition of logos had become a mimesis of its own conflictual structure, more akin to the probabilities of drama than to the certitudes of deductive reasoning. So while Howell forcefully reiterates the Aristotelian principle that the governing goal of the rhetor was only to "state the facts and prove them acceptable" (*PRL*, 56), the whole point of Lucian's satire of the "pleaders" of his day, of Quintilian's rage, of Tacitus's nostalgia for the good old days of oratory, of Basin's plea for reform was that that goal had changed radically. Classical and medieval theorists denounced the phenomenon as bad oratory, but it was clearly good drama.

Ultimately, Howell's argument that rhetorical techniques governed by persuasive intention never produce mimesis independently can be refuted by the phenomenon of delivery—the canon that could always intervene to modify rhetorical intention and that dictated that such techniques never really were independent.[73] If both orator and dramatist make deliberate a priori choices between mimetic and non-mimetic approaches to the world (58–59), and if the judgments of fictitious actions are "latent" in drama and "overt" in rhetoric (243), the theatricalization of forensic delivery blurred those very distinctions between overt and latent mimetic appeal. Reenacting their tales of crime "before the very eyes" of the audience, lawyers overtly addressed their rhetoric as spectacle in a discourse that lay somewhere between ritual, rhetoric, law, and literature. When they privileged the dramatization of a conflictual action for their participating audiences, they did not forget that the *genus iudicale* was a legal ritual; nor, however, did they forget that it could be a drama. The implicit affinity of lyric, *roman*, and scholastic and judicial debate which Bloch posits (*MFLL*, 175) is thus explicit in drama, which emerges as the most logical literary outcome for the histrionics of forensic delivery. Given the abundant evidence of the pleasures produced by deliberate mimetic intention within the rhetorical tradition, it is unreasonable for us to assume that the tales spun by orators were any less artful, any less pleasurable than those spun by the canonical literary authors—rhetorico-dramatic tales of which the Basochiens were the medieval masters.

[73]See Howell's revision of Weinberg's theories in *PRL*, 45–49. Moreover, Howell's implication that intention governed oratorical conception only before (not during or after) the speech suggests a separation of delivery from the other rhetorical canons that is unrealistic in oral societies. He seems to acknowledge that himself shortly thereafter in his discussion of the fable (60–61).

3 The Theater of the Basoche and the Medieval Dramatic Continuum

"If it was natural for the lawyers to write plays," wrote Howard Harvey, "it was equally natural for the law clerks to perform them."[1] Similarly, Adolphe Fabre observed that the influence of the Basoche on literature, satire, and spectacle was unquestionable (*CP* [1875], vii); and Lucien Genty noted that the "extreme pleasure" taken by spectators in Basochial debates was easily understood.[2] But the very ease with which we have acknowledged that pleasure has tended to mask some of the specific literary criteria that permit the identification of early rhetorico-dramatic genres. It is the history of delivery that shows just how "natural" the complicity between drama and law really was. Law students who delighted in satirizing courtroom proceedings in comic plays were participating in the long tradition of the *letteraturizzazione* of legal rhetoric. And Basochial conventions of delivery continued to provide the impetus for a theatricalization of medieval forensic ritual.

Like the protodramas of classical legal oratory and the Mass, the Basochial conflict was characterized by a proliferation of mimetic elements that stretched the very generic limits of the law. The privileged space of the legal temenos became the stage for the costumed ceremonies of the Grand' Chambre;[3] the boundary between "actor"

[1]Harvey, *Theatre of the Basoche*, 14.
[2]Genty, *Basoche notariale*, 85.
[3]For a detailed description of the architecture and physical space of the Grand' Chambre and Grand' Salle, see Delachenal, *Histoire des avocats*, chaps. 5 and 8, esp.

and "audience" was effaced by participating crowds who encouraged a renewed glorification of audience adaptation; and lawyers transformed the conflictual "action" of a crime into a nascent dramatic plot in order to please those crowds. As in Quintilian's day, law was aestheticized by virtue of an interplay between speech-centered dramatic conflict and audience-centered conflictual drama. Basochial rhetoric may thus be considered not only an influence on medieval drama but one and the same protodrama, which looks back to histrionic classical forensic oratory and concomitantly presages the juridical "plots" of many a *mystère, sottie, moralité*, and farce. While disputational forms such as those of the Basoche and the quodlibet served as the most readily accessible rhetorico-dramatic legal models for the Middle Ages, those models may be traced to the "hub" of the ritual drama of law (*POLF*, 103).

Seen from that perspective, the Basochiens were not the "creators of comedy" that Genty identified (40), and Fabre was correct only in spirit when he theorized that the Basoche, "happy rival of the [drama] of the Confrères de la Passion, is the vulgar cradle in which comedy begins to utter its first whimpers" (*CP* [1875], viii). Given the history of the *letteraturizzazione* of the law, the Basoche was by no means the only such cradle, nor was there anything vulgar about it. Rather, its theater, too, belongs to the history of mimetic activity within legal rhetoric, where the thematic, structural, and performance features of drama were already in place. A medieval recontextualization of that discourse, the Basoche too underwent an aestheticization, conflating conflict and spectacle, rhetoric and fiction in a mimetic configuration that compromised but did not destroy its host ritual.

Critics identify the heyday of the Basoche as the century between 1450 and 1550, but the generally accepted date for the founding of the Basoche du Palais is 1303, within what Genty termed the "great juridical wave" under Saint Louis and Philippe le Bel (74).[4] The professed purpose of the Basoche was the initiation of new lawyers

---

112–13 for a discussion of Viollet-Le-Duc's early *Dictionnaire raisonné d'architecture*, 8:81–84.

[4]See Genty, 73–74, for a discussion of two edicts of Philippe le Bel (1304 and 1305); also Fabre, *CP* (1875), 27, along with his detailed overview of the organization of the Basoche in his first chapter. Genty occasionally quotes Fabre without attribution: see, e.g., Genty, 77; and *CP* (1875), 34. According to Fabre, the great Paris fire of 1618 destroyed countless documents, leaving only partial evidence about Basochial practice. "Either this jurisdiction was not contested in the fourteenth and fifteenth centuries, or finally, and more probably, the palace fire of 1618 did not permit authors to reproduce the decisions of this court" (17).

into the juridical community through a required internship period. Before they were permitted to practice in Parliament, the Basochiens served as legal apprentices under the watchful eye of *procureurs* and *notaires* (Genty, 16). A kind of worldly counterpart to his clerical peer, the young apprentice renounced certain privileges in his acceptance of that office: "He had to be a bachelor, and hold no official title, be it that of lawyer or *procureur*" (*CP* [1875], 34).

The term "Basoche" itself—most commonly understood today to be the popular form of *basilique*—has revealing connotations for legal performance. Fabre's investigation of several possible etymons led him to conclude that the most likely definition was simply "maison du plaidoyer, du parler, du parloir, du parlement" (place for pleading, for speaking, for visiting, for the parliament [*EH*, 7]).[5] Since a Basoche was a hall of justice, a courtroom, or a place of conversation (*parloir*), the term immediately underscored the privileged architectural space in which medieval legal roles were delineated. Furthermore, it evoked the bourgeois context in which the organization operated: the *parloir aux bourgeois* was the medieval equivalent of today's city hall, the special province of the "Parisian bourgeoisie and municipal magistrates who legislated and ruled over legal differences among the bourgeois in their jurisdiction" (*EH*, 7–9). Therefore, *basoche* might well have suggested from the outset the conflictual nature of the entire juridical process, highlighting the friction between bourgeois law students and noble theology students (Genty, 12–13; Harvey, 11–16).

Most deserving of consideration from a performance standpoint, however, are the early insights of Pierre de Miraulmont and of Jean Du Luc, a sixteenth-century prosecutor: that *basoche* derives from the Greek *basochein*, denoting histrionics, theatricality, playfulness, and loquacity (see *CP* [1875], 4–5). That patently ludic register is consistent with the Basochial duty to organize games and recreation (Genty, 90) and allows us to situate the Basoche within the context of verbal battle play by virtue of its very name. While Fabre refuted Miraulmont's theory, insisting that it would surely have been incongruous for a nascent juridical organization to camouflage itself "clumsily" and "deliberately" with "a ridiculous title," he acknowledged nonetheless that the Basochiens were far more interesting as playful "poets and comedians than as servants of justice" (*EH*, 8–9). Yet in the explicitly rhetorical and performative context

[5]See *CP* (1875), 3–11, for an extensive treatment of the various etymologies proposed for the term *basoche* by Miraulmont in *De l'origine et l'établissement du Parlement*; also Genty, 72.

of Basochial discourse, the civic and theatrical roles were not incompatible; indeed, their commingling suggests the endurance of
the forensic conflation of civic conflict and dramatic spectacle.

As for the civic role of the Basoche, in order to "render their studies
more fruitful," Philippe le Bel appears to have granted the new legal
society a "particular and exceptional jurisdiction" in response to
earlier edicts of Philippe Auguste, Saint Louis, and Philippe le Hardi
(*CP* [1875], 9, 27). For example, certain members of the bourgeoisie,
including barkeepers, tailors, and suppliers, could plead only before
the Basochial court (22). At its inception, the Basoche was thus
endowed with a civic function as real as that of its classical legal
antecedents or of the medieval parliament, whence it borrowed "its
regulations, the names of its dignitaries, their roles, their authority,
and even their costumes" (10). Officers of the court included the
chancellor or vice chancellor, along with seven *maîtres des requêtes*,
and they appear to have held public sessions twice a week, on
Wednesday and Saturday afternoons.[6] Apparently the most common
causes for litigation there were petty disputes between cleric and
cleric or between cleric and community; demands, for example, that
books, linen, or money be returned, and that *batteries* and *rixes* be
punished (see *CP* [1875], 19).

While such causes of action struck Fabre as frivolous, the Basochial tribunal appears to have been booked solid with these small
claims during a period when "the mania for litigating was pushed
to excess" and when "each quarrel, each case was the object of a
trial that was sometimes pleaded with solemnity" (*CP* [1875], 22).
By all accounts, lawyers argued the most futile of cases at great
length before enthusiastic crowds—despite the protestations of a
Basin. Surely these cases were no less frivolous than the small claims
that flood the twentieth-century legal system; nor were they any
less entertaining than their popular and populist televised analogues.
At the very least, we may conclude that in a legal organization that
boasted as many as 10,000 members (Harvey, 17n), it must have
been a highly respected and desirable frivolity.

Finally, the aspect of the Basoche that is the most relevant to the
generic fluidity between medieval law and drama is its dual status
as both an actual judicial forum and a "fictional tribunal for laughs"
(Genty, 73) which was both famous and infamous. Harvey asserts
that "when real cases were lacking, the clerks probably tried ficti-

---

[6]Fabre says that the officers met at noon on those days: *CP* (1875), 23. Public
hearings were apparently held at 5:00 P.M. (ibid.) and later at 6:00 (Harvey, 19).

tious ones, as law student groups do to this day" (19)—though apparently there was no paucity of real cases to try. Of the two weekly sessions, it seems that one was "specially devoted to the *causes fictives*" (Genty, 83). In a declamatory tradition of their own, the Basochiens argued legal cases of their own invention by impersonating the great characters of antiquity. As Quintilian had once observed of declamatory training in the "art of debate," a student would "agree with a fellow-student on some subject, real or fictitious, and ... take different sides, debating it as would be done in the courts."[7] Even the fictive case was argued and adjudicated as though it involved real people in a real legal conflict. Bailiffs came forward to announce the case with solemnity, prosecutors prosecuted, defendants defended, audiences listened and joined in, the court recorder took notes, and judges withdrew to deliberate their verdicts and impose real sentences (Genty, 84).

In that sense, the Basoche was the site of a renewed confusion between illusion and reality not unlike that which had characterized classical forensic oratory, the Mass, and medieval drama as well. That phenomenon was nurtured in part by the fact that both real and fictive cases were heard in the same temenos: the Grand' Chambre. Indeed, Louis XII himself had guaranteed the endurance of that confusion by giving the Basochiens permission to stage their *jeux* there (Delachenal, 112). Therefore, during the heyday of the Basoche, it was less a question of transferring declamatory practices from schoolroom to courtroom than a question of fusion: during the *cause fictive*, the schoolroom for apprentices actually *was* the courtroom of the Grand' Chambre. The dual function of that privileged legal space lent a realistic air to the fictive cases and a fictive air to the real ones.

Still, within a rhetorical tradition that had always included the spectacular declamation of such forms as the mock encomium, such confusion was normal. Tacitus and Quintilian had bemoaned the bifurcation of law into logical proving and spectacular pleading, and the quodlibet had been reproached for its transformation into *fabulosa et frivola*, but the Basoche had had a frivolous and fictive side from its very advent. No bifurcation was necessary (even though the Enfants sans Souci eventually branched off to devote themselves exclusively to the theater),[8] for traditionally the Basochiens had been

---

[7]Quintilian, *Institutio oratoria*, VI, 4.21.

[8]For the association between the Enfants sans Souci and the *Confrères de la Passion*, see esp. Harvey, 23–26; Fabre, *CP* (1875), 212–63; Genty's discussion of the

pleaders and provers. Frivolity, or at least drama, was their forte. In fact, by the mid–fourteenth century they appear to have initiated a preliminary partnership with the Confrérie de la Passion.[9] And in 1400 Paris lawyers formed the Communauté des Procureurs et Avocats au Parlement to replace the Confrérie de Saint Nicolas, named for the patron saint of law and drama—and apparently of legal drama as well.[10]

Classical rhetoricians had looked to actors as role models for delivery; the actor to whom the Basochien could turn for guidance was himself. Drawing upon their disputational formation to "spin fictions," these would-be lawyers demonstrated the continued status of forensic rhetoric as an intermediary between the civic and literary worlds. Like the disputational forms before it, like the moot courts of the present day, the *cause fictive* was to become a talent competition during which the goal was less to perfect one's oratorical technique, as Genty (83) and Fabre (*CP* [1882], 41), would have it, than to prove one's talent as an actor by pleasing the audience. Extant primary sources suggest that by their fictitious lawsuits the young lawyers were attempting to make the onerous study of law attractive not only to themselves but to their audiences. A rhetorical approach to the *cause fictive* promises, then, to provide a more coherent explanation for the popularity of the Basoche—beyond its eminently practical functions of providing an opportunity to "try oneself out before the juridical public, to test one's professional force without paying too great a price" (Genty, 74). (Indeed, as we shall see, there was often a substantial price to pay for inappropriate conduct: censorship and punishment.) During the later Middle Ages and well into the Renaissance, the Basoche emerged as a watershed form that exemplified the time-honored confusion between acting and oratory and perpetuated the dramatization of the law.

Theatrical Space and Costume in the Basoche

From the official courtroom of the Grand' Chambre to the battles of the Pré-aux-Clercs, from the public spectacle of the *cause grasse*

---

founding of the first French stage in 1548 (90)—the very year that the mystery plays were being outlawed. See also Arden, *Fools' Plays*, 23–35.

[9]The *confrérie* was apparently granted its *lettres patentes* by Charles VI in 1402; see Harvey, 225; Fabre, *CP* (1875), xxi.

[10]Fabre discusses the *messe rouge* and the patronage of Saint Nicolas in *CP* (1875), 112–17; see also Harvey, 12, 179n.

to the *sermon joyeux,* the ceremonially garbed Basochiens performed law within the symbolic space of their own temenos. Like their classical predecessors, they had their stage—the theater of the Grand' Chambre—in which some seats were more desirable than others. As was the case with the apocryphal origins of Greek drama, the Grand' Chambre was characterized by a precise spatial hierarchy that bespoke an effort to separate actor from audience architecturally. Three seating divisions for "elders," lawyers, and spectators identified the functions of all present and *for* all present in the courtroom: lawyers had their own boxes (*barreaux*), and the most honored of spots were the high benches (*hauts bancs*), reserved for a select few (Delachenal, 82). "[Le] premier barreau . . . est pour les ancians advocatz plaidans ordinairement" (The first box is for the elder lawyers normally involved in pleading); the second was for peers who had come to watch."[1] The first two front benches, especially those on the left, were deemed the best seats in the house; participants sought access to them the better to see and, more important, to be seen. Although theoretically spectators and solicitors were not permitted to sit in those privileged spots, it appears that they regularly tried to do so:

> Requiert qu'il soit defendu aux solliciteurs, prebstres, escolliers, et autres manières de gens qui viennent céans pour escouter les plaidoyeries, de ne se mettre audict deuxième barreau. [A.N., X^{1a} 4899, fols. 6v–7v, 15 November 1535, as quoted in Delachenal, 86]

> Let it be forbidden that solicitors, priests, students, and other manner of people who come here to hear the trials sit in the aforementioned second box.

During the legal spectacle of Basochial pleadings, the area between the parquet and the first row of benches was to be occupied by lawyers only. But, again, that rule was largely disregarded by the curious folk who attended the hearings and participated verbally and physically in the Basochial wars of words. It was difficult to restrain the spectators because, practically speaking, the closer the range, the greater the ease of hearing the performance and perhaps of reporting on the litigation. In his epilogue to the *Arrêts d'amour,* Martial d'Auvergne lists a series of excuses for the inaccuracy of his written transcription—such personal shortcomings as fatigue and

[1]A.N., X^{1a} 4899, fols. 6v–7v (15 November 1535), quoted in Delachenal, 85. Delachenal has scrupulously reproduced most of these crucial primary sources.

logistical phenomena that were beyond his control: he can "neither report nor write" on anything else the recorder said because

> Il avoit ung peu la voix basse
> Tant qu'on ne le povoit entendre
> Et puis ma plume estoit fort lasse,
> Par quoy n'eusse sceu rien comprendre.[12]

His voice was slightly low, so much so that one could hardly hear him, plus my pen was extremely tired; and so I could not have understood a thing.

Costume, too, had its hierarchy. Surviving illuminations and woodcuts distinguish lawyers from their contemporaries, the former sporting knee-length black robes and their *bonnets de clerc,* a type of small hat or cap.[13] The first impression conveyed by the Parliamentary official or the Basochien came not from his words (although a reputation for them might certainly precede him) but from his physical appearance. Lawyers were immediately recognizable by their regalia: from *huissier* to judge, whatever the rank, whatever the legal duty, they sported costumes that signified their membership in an elite legal community—a kind of vestimentary equivalent of the heraldic coat of arms or the wooden guild sign above a medieval shop (*PDMA,* 16). To reinforce that membership, the Basochien wore his costume in court whether he was litigating or not (Delachenal, 95). In fact, Fabre concluded from his research on René Gastier's *Nouveaux styles des cours de Parlement* that Basochial garb differentiated legal personae, not only from the crowd but from each other, as the various "ranks" of the various "companies" adopted distinctive costumes (*CP,* [1875], 39).

The first *huissier,* for example, wore his *mortier* when he called cases, while his colleagues wore "appropriate" dress with the *bonnet* and *verge.* The Roi de la Basoche wore his toque in imitation of the king himself; and the chancellor donned only robe and *bonnet* (*CP* [1875], 24, 34). Therefore, as participatory a spectacle as the trials of the Basoche might have been, a sustained effort was made to distinguish the "players" from and for the crowd:

---

[12]Martial d'Auvergne, *Arrêts d'amour,* ll. 9–12; translation mine. Excerpts from this work are from Rychner's edition, which is cited parenthetically by line number.
[13]Fabre, *EH,* 113. See Delachenal's extensive discussion of costume (291–98), and of the early work of Quicherat, *Histoire du costume* (324). Reproductions of the woodcuts that identify Pathelin as a lawyer appear in *Maistre Pierre Pathelin.*

Et pour congnoistre la difference, tant d'entre tous les advocatz, que les solliciteurs et autres personnes, qui viennent pour oyr la plaidoyerie, la dicte court a enjoinct à tous les dicts advocatz, qui vouldront entrer ès bancz et barreaulx, ils apportent [*sic*], ès jours de plaidoyerie, chapperons fourréz. [A.N., X¹ᵃ 4899, fols. 6v–7v, 15 November 1535, as quoted in Delachenal, 95n, 291n]

And to distinguish among all the lawyers as well as between the sollicitors and other persons who come to hear the pleading, the aforesaid court has enjoined all the aforesaid lawyers who wish to enter the benches and boxes that, on days of litigation, they wear furry hats.

Indeed, costume was one of the first features to intrigue some fifteenth-century visitors to the French court, one of whom was particularly struck by the fact that "les conseillers portoient des manteaux, et les aucuns des mortiers avecques, et aussi les anciens advocatz de ladicte court" (the counselors were wearing coats, some of them mortarboards with them; and so were the elder lawyers of said court).[14] Similarly, Martial d'Auvergne described the presence of furry hats (*chaperons fourrés*) in his fictional court of love (Prologue, 28), along with the ermine-trimmed robe of the president (13–14).

The "physical house" of these medieval professors of public speaking was thus eminently pleasing to the eye; and they were no less impressive outside the courtroom. Philippe Le Bel had ordered that the Basochiens process in public regularly in accordance with their militaristic hierarchy. Upon the invitation of the Roi de la Basoche, they habitually divided up into companies of one hundred men, chose colonel, captain, and lieutenants, and with banners in hand "ran about the city ... on horseback, wearing magnificent costumes, preceded by drums and oboes." These processional spectacles continued well into the First Empire, and Fabre even suggested that their very purpose was simply to provide a popular spectacle. On one such occasion the Basochial officers of the Châtelet came out by the hundreds in their ceremonial red and black silks, marching to military music and carrying such props of military justice as the helmet, breastplate, and gauntlet (*CP* [1875], 38–41).

Just as Hardison analyzed the mimetic potential of ecclesiastical vestments in the liturgy (*CRCD*, 79), medieval commentators reported on a comparable phenomenon that recalls both the courtroom and the stage. In one fascinating report of a splendid preproduction

[14]A.N., X¹ᵃ 8319, fol. 89, 25 May 1487, quoted in Delachenal, 294n.

procession, André de La Vigne implied that the mere presence of costume was sufficient to transform dramatic actors into the characters they would play even before the play began:

> On fit crier à son de trompette que toutes gens ayans parsonnages du dit mistère s'assemblassent à l'eure de mydi en Lombardie chacun *acoustré* selon son parsonnage. . . . Et est assavoir qu'ilz estoient si grand train que quant *Dieu et ses Anges* sortirent du dit lieu chevaulchant après les autres, les *Deables* estoient desjà oultre la tour de la prison. [Quoted in Fournier, ed., *Théâtre français*, 173; emphasis mine]

> To the sound of trumpets, all persons having parts to play in said mystery play were ordered to assemble at the hour of noon in Lombardy, each decked out according to his role. And it must be noted that there was such a great procession that when God and his Angels left said place riding behind the others, the Devils were already beyond the prison tower.

Basochial parades reveal a confusion between actor and character in the tradition of rhetorical prosopopoeia, nurtured here by the protodramatic status of costume. Like any self-respecting advocate, the Basochien dressed for success, both inside and outside the temenos. And the splendor and pride that accompanied the wearing of ceremonial attire assumed an important role in the theatricalization of the law. Whence there begins the long history of that most coveted of vestimentary items, the furry hat. A necessary accompaniment to the wardrobe of any advocate, either the *bonnet de clerc* or the toque was required of all lawyers who presented themselves as such; even those who were not actually litigating could not take their seats without their furry hats (Delachenal, 95). The *chapperon* was thus indispensable for social as well as theatrical reasons: it ensured both public recognition and involvement (active or passive) in the proceedings. Indeed, the hat participated in the semiotics of delivery: its removal during the closing argument was part of the language of legal gesture, as was the judge's invitation (usually immediate) to put it back on—a phenomenon that is dramatized in such works as the *Pathelin* and Guillaume Coquillart's *Plaidoyés.*

Moreover, the wearing of ceremonial garb was an honor so venerated that potential confiscation of the furry hat was a potent threat. One later edict required the Basochiens to attend all proceedings, "both ordinary and extraordinary, in decent attire under penalty of confiscation of their hats," and in another of the many attempts to impose decency, officials threatened to confiscate the hats until such time as wayward apprentices performed some sort of community service (*oeuvres pitoyables*) (*CP* [1856], 24). That was a dangerous sanction, for the consequences of failing to adhere to the eternal laws of *bienséance* would be the impossibility of ever doing so again. By threatening seizure of the furry hat, government officials were actually threatening expulsion from the juridical community and from its spectacle or—just as damning—the appearance of expulsion. If lawyers wished to continue to be identified as actors in the legal profession, they had every reason to indulge the court.

The entire question of *bienséance*, however, necessarily involves the historically documented tendency of litigation to cease to be a purely civic process. Like Lucian's Professor of Public Speaking, the Basochien appears to have understood the relationship between costume and spectacular excess. Through his stunning appearance, he could redirect attention from the fictional or nonfictional question at hand to his own thespian merits. By the sixteenth century, lawyers habitually appeared in court dressed as for a theatrical spectacle. Even toward the end of that century, Parliament was still waging a losing battle against such *fantaisie*, insisting that lawyers were to dress in "modest robes and attire" or in "modest and decent attire."[15] Given the importance of costume in the continued interplay between medieval legal ritual and dramatic representation, the threat of seizure of the cap and gown was all the more menacing in that it implied not only visible exclusion from the juridical elite but also a concomitant detheatricalization.

As in Tacitus's day, a public outcry arose against the transformation of costumed pleaders into dramatic "characters." When, in the sixteenth century, the prosecutor Marlac indignantly termed them false students (*fuitifs et simulés escholiers*), he too was indicting the nefarious effects of costume. The pugnacious behavior of lawyerly gangs seems to have been nurtured by the fact that they were

> *habillez en habits* non pas de vrais escholiers, mais *deguisez* comme
> capes à l'espagnol, *manteaux* et autres *vestements* insolents et des-
> chiquetez par les *chausses* et autrement, de manière que on les jugera,
> à les voir de prime face, estre quelques avanturiers ou souldarts de
> guerre, par lesquels les bons scandalisez sont, et croit que tout le mal

[15]Ibid., 1645, fol. 193, 17 September 1574, and 5054, fols. 40v–41, 22 November 1574, quoted in Delachenal, 293–94.

d'aujourd'hui procède de tels malheureux. [Quoted in Fabre, *EH*, 52;
emphasis mine]

dressed up in clothes not of true students, but in costume, as with
Spanish capes, cloaks, and other insolent clothing, and all tattered at
their britches and elsewhere, so that on seeing them close up, one
might judge them to be a bunch of swashbucklers or mercenaries, by
whom good people are scandalized. And one might well think that
all the evil of today stems from such punks.

Like Tacitus and Quintilian, Marlac would honor them with the
name of neither lawyer nor student. But if the students weren't really
students, what were they?

The history of rhetoric suggests that, like Huizinga's judge and
Barthes's wrestler, the costumed Basochien had been transformed
into another being. Whether he were litigating, attending a trial, or
processing through the streets, he was spatially and visually endowed with a theatrical role. And like Lucian's mime, he manipu-
lated costume, sound, sight, and gesture in order to incarnate a
dramatic personage. Even Du Breuil confirmed that the physical
appearance and movements of the lawyer enhanced the efficacy of
argumentation because they helped to engender a persona: the lawyer was to have "en soy belle manière et estre de bel port, avoir le
visaige joyeulx et liez, meur et atrampé en toutes choses, courtoys
et humble à toutes gens selon l'estat de luy et de chascun" (a personal
manner and carriage that are lovely, a joyful and happy face, mature
and well versed in everything, courteous and humble with respect
to all people in accordance with his own station and theirs).[16] In
fact, so fluent were the Basochiens in the expressive language of
gesture that in 1424 the ordinarily loquacious law clerks of the
Châtelet performed a mystery play in honor of the Duke of Bedford
without uttering a single word: "et fust fait sans parler ne sans signer,
comme se ce feussent images eslevees contre ung mur" (and this
was done without speaking or movement, as if they were images
raised against a wall).[17] Trained in both memory and delivery, the
Basochiens had garnered a profound understanding of how to paint
a legal picture dramatically. Quite literally, they had their images
to cultivate during a histrionic delivery. In this medieval/Renais-
sance version of *letteraturizzazione*, they too engendered spectacle
from the ritualistic host form of the law: wearing their fantastic

[16]Du Breuil, *Style du Parlement de Paris*, 61.
[17]As quoted in Fabre, *CP* (1875), 132–33. For a discussion of mimicry and dumb
show in general, see Arden, 1–4.

disguises, they played out a primordial conflict in their own temenos; and its theatricalization was not to be stopped.

Medieval Wars of Words

In the well-known fabliau "Livre des estats du siècle," a young man tires of his knightly condition and selects another state that appears to be compatible with it; he becomes a lawyer: "Tantoust prist l'abit d'Avocat; / De Chevalier laissa l'estat" (He soon took on lawyer's clothing, leaving the station of knight behind).[18] In other words, he exchanges one mode of conflictual engagement for another.

The easy passage between those two conditions underscores the pervasive conflictual register of the law. If (like its classical analogues) the Basoche performances continued to be characterized explicitly as dramatic combat and implicitly as drama, that is due largely to their status as yet other verbal manifestations of the ritual agon. Just as Roman boys had wielded enthymemes and medieval theology students combative *quaestiones*, young law clerks now turned to a mode of verbal warfare that dramatized less the moral and philosophical controversies of law and religion than the inherently mimetic "stories" of even the most seemingly trivial of conflicts. Fabre described the *cause fictive* as a "judicial struggle" (*CP* [1875], 25); and Harvey described the royal magistrates as "a sort of black-robed militia, heroes of many a battle on the wordy fields of propaganda and diplomacy" (12). Surely both metaphors must be taken as literally as those employed by Quintilian, John of Salisbury, and Vives.

Medieval legal warfare carried the same symbolic weight as the chivalric tournament or the duel. In the tradition of Martianus and Isidore of Seville, the Grand' Chambre was a "battlefield" on which "les chevaliers sont les advocats, la lice, c'est le barreau, les armes sont les raisons de droict" (the knights are the lawyers, the battlefield is the bar, the weapons are legal rationales).[19] Organized like soldiers, the Basochiens also fought like soldiers in both words and deeds. Their trials presupposed an earlier provocation for verbal dueling and bespoke the initially violent engagement whence legal rhetoric

---

[18]The passage appears in Montaiglon and Raynaud, eds., *Receuil général*, 2:267. See also Delachenal's brief discussion of this text, 309n.

[19]Louis d'Orléans, "5ᵉ remontrance" of the "Ouvertures des Parlements," fol. 583v et passim, quoted in Delachenal, 80–81.

was thought to have originated. So ingrained in French culture was the bellicose register of the law that the fourteenth-century lawyer Jean Boutillier continued to remind readers of his *Somme rurale* that law had always been a battle:

> Or, sçachez que le fait d'advocacerie selon les anciens faiseurs de loix, si est tenu et compté pour chevalerie. Car tout ainsi comme les chevaliers sont tenus de combatre pour le droict à l'espée, ainsi sont tenus les advocats de combatre et soustenir le droict de leur pratique et science, et pour ce sont-ils appelléz en droit escrit *chevaliers de loix.* [Quoted in Delachenal, 137]

> And so, let it be known that, according to the ancient makers of law, the act of litigation is deemed and considered chivalry. For just as knights are required to fight for righteousness with their swords, so too lawyers are required to fight and uphold the law through their duties and knowledge. And that is why in written law they are called knights of law.

In one account, the Basochiens were even said to have provided actual military assistance during the 1548 revolt in Guyenne (see *CP* [1875], 43–47). Though the tale is probably apocryphal, the rumor amply demonstrates the agonistic ethos of the Basoche. A watershed form in which all the ceremonial conflicts cited by Isidore were present, it too served as the site of an ontological interplay between ritual and representation, dramatic conflict and conflictual drama.

Therefore, while Fabre suggested that the pugnacious tenor of medieval legal proceedings derived essentially from the vigor and intensity with which the Basochiens applied themselves to their studies (ibid., 25–26), it is clear that they were equally committed to the "genius" of the verbal conflict itself. The same results that had obtained in classical forms of battle play now recurred: anger and its powerful mimetic appeal came to overshadow initially civic ends. That strong emotion often led the legal advocate away from ethical substance toward a more theatrical legal battle. Du Breuil may well have sought to preserve the moral and civic imperatives of law by adhering to an abstract notion of *courtoisie*, but his strict code of ethics for the "knight of law" was impossible to maintain in practice. He insisted, for example, that legal questions were not to be obfuscated by passions; and that law, like the joust, was to be carefully orchestrated:

> Item, se doit bien garder de dire ne user de reprouches ne injures contre les curiaulx de la court, en aucune manière, ne contre sa partie ad-

verse.... Et se la partie adverse, ou son advocat, dient couvertement ou en truffant aucun mal, ou reprouches, il le doit monstrer courtoisement et sans indignacion, ou répréhencion de la court, ne des aultres qui illec seront. [62]

Item, he must be very careful not to speak or employ habitually in any way insults against the officers of the court, or against his opposing party. And if the opposing party or his lawyer should say anything offensive or reproachful, either obliquely or in jest, he must point this out courteously and without becoming indignant or blaming the court or others present.

But even Du Breuil had to admit that insults could not go unanswered. For that reason, he enjoined legal advocates never to forget the conflictual nature of their discourse. That insight would enable them to remain poised for battle through the anticipation of possible refutations and objections against them:

Et doit en grant diligence penser et soy prémunir des responses et repplicacions qui luy pourront estre faictes, dictes ou objeté[e]s de sa partie adverse, affin de faire sur ce plus chaudement repplicacions et plus briesvement. [61–62]

And with great care, he must think to arm himself against responses and objections that might be made, spoken, or raised by the opposing party, that his own retorts might be made more forceful and more brief.

But in the long run, heat and brevity proved incompatible. There came a time when the insult was so bold, the affront so great that the litigator could not remain silent. Even the most noble of legal warriors was forced to enter into the fray. So it was that Du Breuil condoned response in kind (albeit dispassionate response):

Mais se les injures sont dictes appertement et clèrement, vigoreusement et aussi appertement le doit-il monstrer et respondre et soy deffendre raisonnablement, sans soy à ire esmouvoir, affin qu'il ne perde son propos ou qu'il ne excède en aucune manière. [62]

But if the insults are made openly and clearly, then vigorously and just as openly must he point this out, and respond and defend himself reasonably, without being moved to anger, lest he lose his train of thought or the slightest degree of control.

Apparently, however, the Basochiens were unable to remain dispassionate during what Du Breuil acknowledged to be a passionate struggle. After all, it was easier to yield to the conflict than to retain and deploy all those rules of law. Not all lawyers followed the example of the dilettantish young protagonist of the "Livre des estats," who abandoned his profession when he realized that serving ethics required far more knowledge than he desired to take the trouble to acquire:

> tant de coustumes, tant de droès,
> Tant de canons et tant de loès,
> Et tant de desmandes luy baillye
> Qui il ne scet quel par qu'il alye.
> Si propousa en son courage
> Qu'il se mettroit en Mariage.
> [Montaiglon and Raynaud, eds.,
> *Receuil général*, 2:267]

so many customs, so many rights, so many canons, and so many laws, and so many demands made of him that he knows not which way to turn. So he got it into his head that he would get into Marriage.

Enjoined in heady treatises to master his passions, the lawyer received a different message entirely from that fabliau and from his audience, who encouraged him to yield to both his and theirs. Basin, for example, singled out for particular condemnation the combative Norman *haro*, a kind of legal battle cry in which alleged victims called upon their prince to rectify wrongs or avenge violence perpetrated against them: "this cry of *haro* stirs up all the *rixes*, mockery, disputes, and altercations . . . [and] it instigates the birth of all litigation."[20]

Once again, the literary result of the Basochial surrender to the passions of a litigious people echoed that of the classical law court and the rue du Fouarre: audiences were pleased with the surrender. The Basochien's motivation to heed the advice of a Du Breuil was drastically reduced by the fact that it was not only easier to yield to conflict, it was easier to please the crowd that way. As Louis d'Orléans's "5ᵉ remontrance" indicates, medieval spectators were delighted by the clash of argument with refutation, statute with statute, and passion with passion. To them, conflict was spectacle, it was sport, it was mimesis:

[20]Basin, *Apologie*, 258–61.

Est-ce pas un plaisir, quand la trompette a sonné, et que le premier huissier a appellé la cause, veoir deux champions, chacun au bout du camp, entrer en lice et rompre son bois net, et les tronsons en voler jusques au lambris de ceste chambre dorée . . . ? Est-ce pas un plaisir de les veoir avec les coustelas luysant de la raison, avec la masse de l'éloquence, se donner mille coups de coustume, mille coups de loix, se charger l'un l'autre, et faire saillir le feu de leurs armes, au plaisir et contentement des assistans? [Louis d'Orléans, "Ouvertures des Parlements," fol. 583v et passim, quoted in Delachenal, 80–81n]

Is it not a pleasure, when the trumpet has sounded and the first bailiff has called the case, to see two champions on opposite sides of the battlefield lunge into combat and break their lances clean with fragments flying all the way up to the ceiling of this golden chamber? Is it not a pleasure to see them, with their swords shining with reason and their clubs of eloquence, exchange a thousand blows of statutes, a thousand blows of law, and charge against each another, causing sparks to fly from their weapons to the pleasure and contentment of the spectators?

Medieval verbal conflict was so pleasing to eye and ear that it came to be identified less with the battle for truth than with the mimetic conventions of the battle itself—especially when that battle was grounded in the music of language. As in classical times, volume, gesture, and meaning often came together to transfix educated listeners with the resonance of conflictual legal eloquence. But medieval lawyers charmed even the uneducated audience with the mastery of a Gorgias and with the music of their own erudition. (Indeed, as I show in Chapter 4, it is the very harmony of scholastic discourse that promises to imbue many a learned play with a hitherto unperceived beauty.) Their delivery made for a pleasurable experience by virtue of its sound (if not always its substance). Such pleasures continued well into the sixteenth century, as when the lawyer Du Faur de Pibrac observed that nothing was more delightful than the language of logic:

Lorsque la bouche de l'homme sçavant se disclost et s'ouvre pour parler, ceulx qui escoutent disent: Voylà ung beau traict de Platon, en voylà ung autre d'Aristote; celluy-[ci] sent son Academie et celluy-là son lycée; bref, il n'y a object qui se présente à nos yeulx tant agreables, ne musique sy harmonieuse qui tant nous puisse delecter, *quam erudita docti hominis oratio.* [A.N., X^{1a} 5022, fol. 23, 18 April 1569, quoted in Delachenal, 260]

As soon as the mouth of the learned man is unbarred and opens up to speak, those listening say: There's a good one from Plato, there's

another from Aristotle; this one sounds like his academy and that one
like his high school. In short, there is no object to present itself before
our eyes so pleasurable or any music so harmonious that can delight
us more than the erudite discourse of the learned man.

In that respect, the Basochien was participating in a dramatic, dialogic tradition that was not unlike the antiphonal singing of the
liturgy, the musical debates of the lyric *joc partit*, the speaking and
singing presentation of medieval *puys* and poetic contests (see *MI*,
10–11), or the great half-musical, half-gesticulated tradition of mimicry as Lucian, for example, described it:

> The other performances that appeal to eye and ear contain, each of
> them, the display of a single activity; there is either flute or lyre or
> vocal music or tragedy's mummery or comedy's buffoonery. The
> dancer, however, has everything at once, and that equipment of his,
> we may see, is varied and comprehensive—the flute, the pipes, the
> tapping of feet, the clash of cymbals, the melodious voice of the actor,
> the concord of the singers.   ["Saltatio," 68]

During his apprenticeship the Basochien learned to imitate the
antiphonal conflict of law in order to sing his own legal tales. It is
no coincidence that he was nicknamed a *bec-jaune*, a young yellow-
beaked bird that had not yet grown its feathers and was not quite
ready to sing in full voice (see *CP* [1875], 36). The Basoche thus
reaffirmed the interdependence of poetry, law, music, mimicry, and
drama which had been canonized by conventions of *actio*.

Finally, in accordance with those conventions, the musicality of
conflictual language was reinforced by the equally important visual
portrayal of conflict during the *rixe*. Just as verbal conflict was pleasing to the ear, physical conflict was as pleasing to the eye as it had
been in the days of Tacitus. Sporting a furry hat and armed with
words that could wound as effectively as any sword, the Basochien
was the ultimate *acteur* and he created some of the most memorable
dramatic imitations of the agon of the Middle Ages. But for all the
free time devoted to dancing, games, and, comedy (*EH*, 1856, 40),
there appears to have been equal time for "widespread noisy crazi-
ness": "excesses were committed openly," Genty reports, "and it
was rare for games to end without the spilling of blood" (13). The
most privileged of battlefields was the Pré-aux-Clercs, where the
only games were violent ones—"regulated combats between groups,
whence people left hurt, bruised, and often mortally wounded" (15).
Within their own arena, the Basochiens took battle play to new

heights, highlighting the resemblance of law to jousting and other militaristic sports. They transformed the metaphoric armory of Lady Rhetoric into swords, sticks, daggers, and pistols as their verbal clash became a physical clash (*rixe*), particularly in the communal *folie* and violence of the Fête des Fous, which Jean Gerson described as "ritus ille impiissimus et insanus qui regnat per totam Franciam" (that most impious and insane of rituals to reign in all of France.[21] One parliamentary interdiction of March 1552 even went so far as to forbid the Basochiens (along with shop owners and other bourgeois villagers) to carry such weapons, under penalty of corporal punishment (*CP* [1875], 48–49; Genty, 13).

By restricting the bearing of arms at the Fête des Fous, such communities as the University of Paris hoped to eliminate the constant student battles. Wielding those weapons, however, were not Du Breuil's courteous knights but Tacitus's "brawlers" and Gerhoh of Reichersburg's "warriors." The bourgeois Basochiens rocked Paris with fist fights, arson, and even murder as they clashed with other citizens. Within what Ong and Huizinga characterized as the agonistic ethos of scholasticism, the *rixe* rendered initiation into the legal fraternity all the more worthy: the more violent the battle play, the greater the honor. Despite numerous sanctions, the widespread melees increased, despite Louis d'Orléans's assertion that though the Grand' Chambre was "a battlefield," it was "not to be stained red with any blood" ("c'est *le champ de bataille,* mais c'est une arène, *que nullo sanguine tincta rubet*" [quoted in Delachenal, 80]). Still, the legal conflict led to bloodshed elsewhere: the Basochial "verbalization of the ordeal" was incomplete.

Like medieval drama, then, the theatrical wars of words fought by the Basochiens fused illusion and reality in violence. The legendary tales of their military prowess were fed by their real bellicosity; and their outbreaks of physical violence signaled the presence of a ritual drama akin to the contemporaneous "spectacle of participation" of the medieval stage. Fighting their battles with both words and swords, the Basochiens were representing and reenacting the drama of the legal agon with a violence as dramatic as that which unfolded within the *cercle magique.* When conflict and spectacle fused during the *rixe* and the *cause fictive,* the Basochiens were no longer speaking on behalf of their clients (real or fictive) or merely impersonating them: they had crossed the heuristic border between virtual and actual portrayal, fusing the two identities. Whatever the

[21]Quoted in Chambers, *Mediaeval Stage,* 1:292.

initial purpose of their jurisdiction, a plethora of critiques launched
against them indicates that pleasing the crowd with a *spectaculum
crudelitatis* had become one of their primary goals. Like the rhetorical gladiators of antiquity and the fighting cocks of scholasticism, the Basochiens found themselves exploiting the theatrical
potential of violence in order to satisfy the aesthetic desires of their
demanding audiences—the same phenomenon that earlier had precipitated the vehement objections of Marlac, Du Mesnil, Gerson,
and the papal advocates of quodlibetal reform. They privileged the
agon as the end rather than the means of legal equity. Ultimately,
whether the juridical forum were the Pré-aux-Clercs, the Grand'
Chambre, or the *cause fictive*, the divisions between ritual and representation, combat and spectacle, verbal and physical battle, word
and sword, law and drama were abolished—just as they had been in
the earliest battle-play origins of drama.

In his study of the recurrence of armed combat in medieval German drama, Richard Axton speculated that the strength of the battle-
play tradition in Germany "may have been decisive in determining
the course of ecclesiastical drama there, by predisposing clerical
German dramatists to choose biblical subjects which would enable
them to present armed combat."[22] Given Kennedy's reminder that
medieval France was a particularly fertile ground for the *letteraturizzazione* of rhetoric (*CR*, 5), it is equally plausible that learned
French dramatists might have opted for dramatic plots that exemplified another ritual *ludus* well known to them: the verbal and
physical battles of adjudication. As I show at greater length in Chapter 4, the French arena for ritual combat was often the literary courtroom so vividly detailed in Gréban's *Mystère* and the *Pathelin*. The
dramatic physical struggle represented by German dramatists was
waged on the French stage not only with swords but with words.

Playing the Medieval Crowd

When we think of the courtroom today, the vision that comes to
mind tends to be the solemnity and reverence on which black-robed
judges insist as they pound their gavels and gravely demand order
in the court. There was no such order in the tribunals of the Basochiens, and there was nothing reverent about them. The tenor of

[22] Axton, *European Drama*, 44.

their proceedings suggests respect for a different kind of order—the literary order inherent in a theatrical legal agon.

Like his classical predecessor and his peers in the theology faculty at the quodlibet, the Basochien had a full house to play to in a forum that pitted lawyer against lawyer, student against student, and even public against pleaders before medieval equivalents of the "tribes" described by Tacitus.[23] During the *causes grasses* as well as the biweekly public sessions at the Châtelet, judges and lawyers from Parliament joined law clerks and lesser folk among the spectators. The operations of Parliament were a matter of national pride, and foreign dignitaries were customarily escorted to court during their official visits to witness what Delachenal described as the "imposing spectacle" of a parliamentary hearing at the palace, that "beautiful monument of civic architecture" (235). In a particularly contrived orchestration of that spectacle, Francis I once arranged to put on a veritable national show for his archrival, Charles V, ordering his magistrates to "[se] préparer à luy [Charles] faire le plus grant honneur que possible seroit: aussi qu'ilz feissent aprester quelques advocatz, et qu'il avoit l'intention l'amener [l'empéreur] veoir sa court" (prepare for him the greatest honor possible. So he had them prepare several lawyers, and he had the intention of bringing the emperor to see his court).[24]

Whether or not the histrionic behavior of legal performers can be attributed directly to the éclat inspired by the presence of such august personages, medieval and Renaissance sources alike confirm that a Basochial trial was cause for some excitement—so much excitement that the proverbial "order in the court" became irrelevant. During real or fictive proceedings, lawyers and judges alike faced constant disruptions from the more rowdy members of the audience. Like their peers at the quodlibet and the *Jeu de la Feuillée*, spectators actually participated in the legal representation in the hope that with a little luck they might shape the outcome of a trial. And like the *monitores* of classical antiquity, they turned interruption into a fine art. No fewer than six bailiffs (*huissiers*) were required to cope with the situation, two of them at the entrance (Delachenal, 99).

By the sixteenth century, parliamentary sessions that Delachenal believed had "doubtless been quite peaceful at their origin had become...almost noisy" (99). Given the disorderly conduct and violence that characterized the entire forensic tradition, however, one

---

[23]Tacitus, *Dialogus de oratoribus*, 39.
[24]A.N., X¹ᵃ 1544, fol. 57, 30 December 1539, as quoted in Delachenal, 235n.

might question how "peaceful" those sessions ever were. Matters had gotten so out of hand that legal sanctions were multiplied in an effort to diminish inappropriate conduct in the courtroom. The problem appeared to lie mostly with impetuous youths who could neither remain in their proper seats nor refrain from disturbing the litigants. Indeed, as early as the fifteenth century, parliamentary attention to the Basoche appears to have become almost exclusively negative: "The court orders issued by the magistrates for the control of play acting refer almost exclusively to plays given by the law clerks," reports Harvey (10). Whatever the nature of the disturbance, it was the young law clerks who bore the brunt of the blame: "Et quant aux jeunes advocatz, qu'ilz aient à se contenir au second bar-reau, pour escoulter..., sans faire bruict ne interrompre ceulx qui plaident." (And as for the young lawyers, they are to be confined to the second box so that they can listen—[but] without making noise or interrupting those litigating).[25] Of course, what they actually said has long since disappeared; but that they said *something* is docu-mented by the consistent desire to silence them: "La court a enjoinct à tous les advocatz et procureurs... de faire silence pendant la plai-doirie" (The court has enjoined all lawyers and prosecutors to keep silent during the pleadings).[26]

Ostensibly apprenticed to lawyers so that they might improve their skills, the Basochiens seem to have been far more interested in cultivating artistry and fame. Apparently, whenever they were present, order—or at least silence—in the court was virtually im-possible. Hence the inevitable official formulation of a request that they simply shut up: "Pareillement enjoinct [la court] aux jeunes advocatz, cependant que les aultres plaideront, escouter diligem-ment les plaidoyries qui seront faictes, leur faisant defense de parler ou *cacqueter*" (Similarly, while others are litigating, the court en-joins the young lawyers to listen carefully to the pleadings being made, and forbids them to talk or chatter).[27] True to a form that would have caused Lucian's Professor to swell with pride, they had mastered the art of self-aggrandizement. Through constant inter-ruptions, they were able to redirect attention from the case to their own persons by expressing their reactions aloud and sneaking up on those pleading cases to eavesdrop on their deliberations. In no sense were they able to keep still. When they weren't busy sticking their noses into the litigators' business, they were roaming around the

[25]Ibid., 4977, fols. 56v–57v, 21 November 1559, as quoted in Delachenal, 100n.
[26]Ibid., 4879, fol. 459v, 25 February 1535, as quoted in Delachenal, 99n.
[27]Ibid., 4907, fol. 17, 19 November 1538, as quoted in Delachenal, 100n.

courtroom: "La court a faict et faict inhibicion et deffence à tous les advocatz d'icelle, de se tenir aux fenestres et se pourmener parmi la salle, durant la plaidoyrye" (Both now and previously, the court has restrained and forbidden all said lawyers to stand by the windows and to roam around the room during the pleadings).[28] Even the solicitors (apparently somewhat more orderly than the audience) were tempted to do the same in order to launch their interruptions from point-blank range for maximum reception.

Therefore, the few remaining divisions that separated *acteur* from audience were ignored by wandering, disruptive spectators. In fact, the Basochiens actually encouraged such disruptions in the explicitly theatrical context of their own fêtes. In the same way that actors in the *Jeu d'Adam* had rushed into the audience, the Roi de la Basoche "strolled around in the crowd" (*vacabat per curiam*), apparently inviting the public to participate (*CP* [1882], vi). Although the picture of chattering, peripatetic gentlemen working the room raises a chuckle today, there was nothing droll about the menace the participatory spectacle posed to a troubled system of legal ethics. Quite literally, litigators were unable to hear themselves think: "n'ayant pu dissertement oyr et entendre, pour le peu de sillence" (unable to hear and discern things clearly because of the lack of silence).[29]

That problem was compounded by the fact that the door separating the Grand' Chambre from the Grand' Salle was normally kept open, for parliamentary and Basochial sessions were public business: an edict of 12 March 1657 decreed "que les plaidoyries ordinaires se tiendront à huis ouvert par chacune semaine deux fois" (that ordinary pleadings will be held with the door open twice a week [quoted in *EH*, 24]). The open-door policy enabled the young apprentices to compromise the seriousness not only of their own legal ritual but of Parliament's as well. Even before they claimed the Grand' Chambre from Parliament at 5:00 P.M., they made their presence known and their voices heard. And, while attempts were made to keep them at bay by postponing their séances until 6:00 P.M., the young apprentices appear to have caused such a ruckus banging their drums to announce their takeover that an official complaint was lodged on behalf of court officials, who "ne s'entendent plus l'un l'autre, et sont contrainctz abandonner leurs bancs et eulx en aller en leurs maisons, parce qu'ils ne peuvent plus rien faire" (can no longer hear one another, and are forced to leave their seats and go on home because they can no longer do anything).[30] The ears of parliamentary officials, however, were targeted far less than those of the boisterous, wandering crowd, to which the theatrical Basochial agon was increasingly directed. In view of the magnitude of such disturbances and the pleasure factor of the agon itself, it is easy to understand how the Basochiens acquired their reputation for both theater and subversion.

"If the theater had been created by the Basochiens," theorized Genty, "it is also to them that we owe censorship" (90). To a large degree, the history of the Basoche is the history of the relaxation and reinstatement of censorship. Whenever the law clerks are mentioned in official documents, it seems to be for the purpose of punishing them for such transgressions as irreverence (see Harvey, 10); and, according to Delachenal, Parliament often singled out the Basochiens in order to "strike out against the authors or actors of some satirical farce" (109). Fictive or real, Basochial trials were hardly privileged communications: their ramifications extended far beyond the momentary pleasure of a given crowd. As the constant threat of reprisals makes clear, it was not only defendants who were on trial, but lawyers as well. Even a fictional case played for laughs was potentially dangerous, especially when it became the forum for questioning royal and/or ecclesiastical authority.[31] So it was that in 1442 several law clerks found themselves dining on bread and water in prison after they made insulting allusions and performed without the court's permission (*CP* [1882], 5). Under Charles VIII, a joke in a yearly show served as the pretext for incarcerating five clerics, and in 1444 even the Faculté de Théologie intervened to censor the Basochiens (Genty, 115).

In both juridical and dramatic forums, failure to behave appropriately during a trial might thus provoke severe consequences, including possible conviction for sacrilege, heresy, or lèse-majesté:

Lemaistre, pour le procureur du Roy, presuppose que, *de jure,* le Roy en son royaume est empereur, et peut faire lois, edictz et ordonnances.... Et n'appartient à aucun de le contredire, *ymo,* quand l'on fait le contraire, c'est *incidere in sacrilegium et in crimen lese ma-*

---

[30]Ibid., 4953, fol. 36v, 13 April 1553, as quoted in Delachenal, 109n.
[31]See Harvey's discussion of the political content of Basochial satire, 221–32; also Bevington, *Action Is Eloquence,* on how social protest was channeled into "playacting through which spectators in the theater can participate in drama as a rite of passage" (138).

jestatis. [A.N. X¹ᵃ 4831, fol. 174, 22 March 1490, as quoted in De-lachenal, 203n]

Lemaistre [Le Maistre], for the King's prosecutor, assumes that, ipso facto, the King is emperor in his kingdom, and can make laws, edicts, and ordinances. And it is for no one to contradict him; indeed, when one goes against him, it is to commit sacrilege and the crime of lèse majesté.

Punishments for verbal trespasses against the king or the church might require penance by the *chevalier-ès-lois,* who could be

contrainct et condemné à amender lesdites paroles injurieuses d'a-mende honnorable, à genoulx, nue teste, et dessaint, ceans et en l'ostel episcopal de l'evesque, ou en sa chappelle, appelléz telz gens et en tel nombre que l'evesque vouldra, en lui criant mercy, et disant que faulsement et mauvaisement il a escript lesdites paroles, et aussi plai-doyé. [A.N., X¹ᵃ 4816, fols. 220–22, 18 April 1475, as quoted in De-lachenal, 201n]

constrained and condemned to retract said injurious words by re-penting on his knees, uncovered and unarmed, in the bishop's house or in his chapel, where there will have been summoned whatever number and manner of people the bishop see fit, as he begs the bishop for mercy, saying that he wrote and litigated with the aforementioned words with mendacity and malice.

Just as a hapless youth had been sentenced to ten days of bread and water for having spoken rashly and arrogantly during the quodlibet,[32] the Basochien was subject to sanctions designed to monitor the content and style of his utterances during his own perilous rite of passage.

In the tradition of Alanus de Insulis, one fascinating fifteenth-century attempt to reduce the dangers of the litigious situation priv-ileges the lawyer as a kind of social mediator whose function was interpretation (*translatio*). When David Chambellan of the Parlia-ment was indicted for having impugned the integrity of two of his peers with "calumny," he argued against the royal prosecutor Le Maistre that any lawyer was only an interpreter of the client he

[32]*Chartularium Universitatis Parisiensis,* 2:174.

represented.[33] In that capacity, he was not to be punished for verbal
offenses that had not been uttered in his own voice. Vehemently
refuting the charges that he had been "intemperate" and "depraved,"
Chambellan compared himself with Saint Jerome, who had been
accused of heresy "for having translated Greek into Latin" (426),
insisting that he too was but a translator. Moreover, he was "plus
à excuser que ung interpretateur, qui parle pour aucun qui n'entend
le langaige ouquel ung interpretateur parle, car l'interpretateur le
pourrait decevoir" (more worthy of forgiveness than an interpreter,
who speaks for someone who does not undertand the language
spoken by the interpreter; for the interpreter might deceive him
[426]). The lawyer translated not from the language but from the
opinions and the soul of another in a *translatio* that was highly
dramatic.

Chambellan was arguing for freedom of speech: it was both the
duty and the inalienable right of the lawyer to "seurement et
franchement soutenir sa querelle" (present his case safely and openly
[426]). It is reasonable to speculate, however, that one of the reasons
Chambellan's arguments did not serve to decrease the number of
sanctions was that the advent of impersonation in forensic rhetoric
had fused the voices of advocate and client. When "dangerous"
truths were delivered in accordance with rhetorical conventions of
prosopopoeia, it was a slippery task to separate the two identities.
Was it the advocate speaking? Was he simply "interpreting" for his
client? Was he impersonating him? Even Fabre invoked the name
of Thespis in his description of general histrionics in the courtroom
(*EH*, 144). Given the history of the interplay in forensic delivery
between ritual and participatory representation, the theatricalization of the legal *translatio* was a logical outcome. At a time when
his discourse was increasingly threatened by accusations of censorship, heresy, and excommunication, the *acteur* could opt for the
voice of the *tragicus*.

Therefore, however commonplace it may be to recall that controversial opinions often surface in literature in response to political
repression, that principle is operative in the rhetorico-dramatic spectacles of the Basochiens. The politics of legal performance encour-

[33]A.N., X¹ᵃ, 4831, fol. 386, 4 March 1490, pièce 25. The text of the "Réplique de
l'avocat Chambellan, accusé d'avoir porté contre deux commissaires du Parlement
des accusations calomnieuses," appears in Delachenal, 425–26. Delachenal devotes
his entire chap. 12 to a fascinating discussion of "liberté de la parole." Rita Copeland
has situated the entire notion of translation along the continuum of literary and
historical discourse in *Rhetoric, Hermeneutics, and Translation in the Middle Ages*.

aged them to cloak controversial political content in the language of satire and to take refuge in what appeared to be the representational subterfuge of drama. Naturally, drama was not the only possible vehicle for channeling protest into fiction, as David Bevington notes (138); but given the course legal rhetoric had taken once before, it was the most logical vehicle. As long as delivery remained the rhetorical canon that fused oratory and acting, it followed that lawyers might transform a compromised civic eloquence into a mimetic theatrical form. Classical forensic oratory had once retreated to the ostensibly safe arena of the schools of declamation, and so now did the Basoche when they were similarly threatened by the sociopolitical ramifications of censorship.

As in classical times, however, the "safe" arena was not so safe after all. Neither in words nor in deeds could the Pré-aux-Clercs have been considered safe by any stretch of the imagination. And as the Basochiens turned increasingly to drama, the censorship continued in that forum. So potentially mordant were their dramatic productions that on 17 August 1443 they were ordered to secure permission before performing any farce or morality play. The order was relaxed in May 1473 but reinstated in 1474 (*CP* [1882], 5–6). In 1476 Louis XI forbade all "farces, sotties, moralités or other plays under penalty of banishment" unless his permission were secured first; and in 1536 Francis I suppressed the popular *causes grasses* shortly before the great mystery plays themselves were outlawed in 1548 (Genty, 115–16). Ironically, perhaps, the menace of punishment did not curb the *letteraturizzazione* of forensic rhetoric, but rather served to nurture an ongoing theatricalization.

Redirecting attention to masterful histrionic delivery, the Basochiens drew upon their rhetorical training and upon the militaristic structure of their organization to engender the "pleasing spectacle of a fight" for their audiences. The old objections against sophistry were revived in the Middle Ages and Renaissance, but threats of reprisals against lawyers could not stop the momentum of the theatricalization of eloquence because audiences continued to demand that they be indulged with what they most enjoyed: their own participation in an intriguing conflictual action. Like their classical predecessors, the Basochiens were only too happy to accommodate them; and there was a renewal of the entire dialectic between audience adaptation, applause, and further adaptation to public taste.

Initially the medieval commitment to audience adaptation appears to have been as straightforward as Aristotle had once described it: legal language had to be understood by everyone, including the rank and file. From that early commitment to a communicative process that would ensure the attention of the judge, however, there developed a fervent desire to capture the delight of spectators who found appealing the compromise of ritual in favor of representation. Indeed, in light of contemporaneous fifteenth- and sixteenth-century commentaries on the "grandes longueurs qui sont ès procès" (great lengths found in trials),[34] such accommodation was necessary. Since the actual *plaidoyers* are not extant, Delachenal noted with regret, we "have no way of knowing if movements of eloquence came to animate such stiff argumentation, shake up this hodgepodge of texts, extract from them a lively and dazzling demonstration" (247–48). But the history of delivery suggests overwhelmingly that that is precisely what happened.

First of all, in the days before the microphone, the very difficulty of being heard forced the lawyer to speak histrionically, if only by sheer volume. Even the *courtois* Du Breuil observed that a lawyer "doit parler en toutes causes plaidées plus hault et plus vive voix qu'il n'a acoustumé en son commun parler" (in all litigation, he should speak with a louder and more lively voice than he uses in ordinary speech [62]). And as for boredom—that most nefarious of enemies—Du Breuil further maintained that the key to avoiding it was a profound intellectual understanding of the content of one's speech. Rearticulating the noble concordance between subject matter and delivery, he assured his readers that masterful oratorical presentation was to be consonant with the noble aims of legal oratory and that such lessons were to be well stored in the memory: "En prononçant ses parolles doit avoir grant cure et diligence de ses causes qu'il a à ventiller et les commender à mémoire et commender à son clerc qu'il en soit mémoratif, et qu'il l'en advertisse souvent" (In delivering his words, he must be extremely careful and cautious with respect to the cases being aired and commit them to memory and remind his clerk to be mindful of them as well and that he remind him of them often [62]). Lawyers were to trim down their speeches, omit useless words (*parrolles inutilles*), and take care not to obfuscate their speeches with too many *excurses* "affin que en trop parlant ou aultrement il n'en soit déceu" (so that by speaking too much or otherwise, he might not wind up tricked [61]). But whereas it had been desirable for the medieval lawyer to avoid boring the judge, it became more desirable still to please both him

---

[34]See Guenée, *Tribunaux et gens de justice*, 221; also Delachenal on the abundant condemnations of the prolix nature of medieval pleadings (esp. 96–100).

and the audience. Contemporary pleading practices (such as those decried by Basin) defied Du Breuil's noble prescriptions inasmuch as paramountcy had come to be accorded not to the content but to the manner of legal presentation: delivery.

One of the most intriguing features of how medieval legal delivery was adapted to audiences was the choice of a legal language. With a logic similar to that of the Proclamation of Tours of 813, which dictated that sermons be given *in rustica romana lingua* for purposes of comprehension,[35] fifteenth-century commentators took considerable pains to explain why the official language of the Parlement de Paris was to be French. As early as 1406, parliamentary officials attempted to convince the University of Paris that the importance of the cases in question called for a change in linguistic venue:

> Pour ce que la matière est grande, grosse et notable, et est expedient que chacun l'oie et l'entende, que le jour qu'ils parleront proposent en français, parce que tous ceulx qui viennent ceans oir les plaidoiries, n'entendent pas latin.[36]

> Inasmuch as the subject matter is great, lofty, and important, and it is appropriate that everyone hear and understand, the day they speak let it be in French, because not everyone who comes here to hear the pleadings understands Latin.

Le Maistre, for example, compared the dignified use of French in Parliament to the indomitable use of Latin in the Roman juridical forum. As he explained the Romans' use of the *lingua vernacula* to a group of visiting Hungarian ambassadors, he acknowledged that it was true that "la cause pour laquelle l'en plaide ceans en françoys, c'est a l'exemple des Romains" (the reason pleading is done here in French is by the example of the Romans); but he dissented from the opinion of one of his colleagues that Roman institutionalization of the vernacular had been motivated by fear of usurpation of Roman dignity by foreign tongues. Le Maistre insisted that pleading in other languages had posed no such threat to the Romans; their choice of Latin was a matter of national pride. The reason that they "ne parloient, ne ne souffroyent parler en leur Senat que en langue latine, ne fut point pour doubte de usurpacion, mais pour retenir et garder

---

[35]For a description of the Proclamation of Tours, see Glanville Price, *French Language,* 6; also my discussion of this idea in "Visions with Voices," 36–37.

[36]A.N., X¹ᵃ 4787, fol. 355v, 27 May 1406, as quoted in Delachenal, 236n. For the text of "Pourquoi l'on a toujours plaidé en français au Parlement de Paris," see Delachenal, 431–34.

leur grande et excellente dignité" ([the reason that] they did not
speak or tolerate speaking in their Senate in any language but Latin
was not for fear of usurpation but from the desire to retain and
protect their great and excellent dignity).[37] A Du Bellay *avant la
lettre*? Insofar as Le Maistre equated the dignity of French with that
of Latin, he too glorified and enriched the vernacular in France.

Still, the very pride that French medieval lawyers took in the
French language contributed to the further theatricalization of legal
eloquence. Equally illuminating in that respect is their occasional
choice of Latin as the language for pleading, even in documents that
appear to focus exclusively on language as a vehicle for comprehension. So that visiting dignitaries would understand and appreciate
the French legal contests of erudition, officials occasionally sought
to reduce the gap between legal language and showmanship by re-
verting to what was still the more "universal" language, Latin. After
all, visitors would surely be more impressed by the diplomatic show
if they could understand the language in which it was performed.
Depending, then, on who was in the audience at any given time,
the court occasionally pronounced it wise to plead in *"lingua latina,
preter morem consuetum,* mais la court l'a ainsi ordonné faire, parce
que lesdits ambaxadeurs n'entendent *gallicum sermonem, quo
cause solite sunt agi in hoc senatu"* (in Latin, contrary to usual
practice, because the aforesaid ambassadors do not understand
French, the language in which cases are normally pleaded in this
senate).[38] According to Le Maistre, such intermittent pleading in
Latin was a pleasant diversion and a courtesy that was to be extended
to foreign visitors only on a limited basis:

> Mais dit que, afin qu'il ne derogue à l'auctorité de la court, a requis
> [*sic*] qu'il luy plaise donner licence de plaider en latin pour ceste foiz,
> afin que l'ambassadeur et autres estrangiers puissent entendre ce que
> dira. . . . Seullement pour la presence dudit ambassadeur, il a encomm-
> ancé en latin.   [Quoted in Delachenal, 432]

> But he said that, in order not to compromise the authority of the
> court, he requested that he be allowed to litigate in Latin on this
> particular occasion, in order that the ambassador and other foreigners
> might understand what would be said. Only because of the presence
> of said ambassadors did he begin in Latin.

[37] A.N., X^{1a} 4828, fols. 412 et passim, 8 November 1487, as quoted in Delachenal,
235–36, 431–32.
[38] Ibid., 4842, fol. 45v, 22 December 1500, as quoted in Delachenal, 236n.

And, of course, the only possible linguistic choices for the court were French and Latin, either one of which was thought to reinforce the desired message of French national pride. One later commentator stated explicitly that lawyers could readily be available for consultations in Italian, Spanish, or German, as the occasion required:

> Soliti sumus . . . vulgari nostra Francorum lingua causas controversiasque tractare et agere, non quidem ut et aliarum expertes aut ignari; *poterit nempe Grecus, si huc adventarit, sua lingua oratorem audire; id idem Ytalus, Hyspanus aut Germanus.* [A.N., X^{ra} 4852, fol. 23, 26 November 1510, as quoted in Delachenal, 236n]

> We customarily manage and conduct trials and disputes in our own tongue, French—but not because we are unlearned or ignorant of other languages; certainly if a Greek came here, he could consult a lawyer in his own language, and likewise an Italian, Spaniard, or German.

Anything other than French or Latin would have conveyed neither the glory of France nor the glory of French nor the theatrical glory of its courts.

Interplay between French and Latin thus rendered language itself a kind of predisposing dramatic feature. Linguistic selection was associated with legal showmanship and the desire to be understood with the desire to be appreciated. Medieval use of Latin was not necessarily the exclusionary phenomenon we often deem it today; rather, it often served as a particularly courteous and effective means of reaching a targeted audience. The occasional substitution of Latin for French in Parliament thus permits a reevaluation of a widespread critical tendency to view the fifteenth century as an era that increasingly and exclusively privileged the vernacular. Clearly, the converse phenomenon (even if only temporary) could be equally significant, equally effective, and equally dramatic.

Ultimately, whatever element was stressed in the Basochial forum—the agon, personal renown, pleasing the crowd—medieval forensic rhetoric was more than communicative: it was mimetic. It is all the more likely, then, that the Basochiens' legal oratory might have come to inspire independent medieval dramatic efforts beyond those of the Enfants sans Souci. Medieval students' extensive training in disputation would have impressed upon them the dramatic potential of the rhetoric of judgment in a wide variety of contexts: in the theological discussions of the quodlibetal ceremony, in the resolution of minor disputes at the court of the Basoche, in the fantastic deliberations of the *causes fictives,* in the courtroom scenes

of *mystère*, farce, and *moralité*. If the participatory spectacle of forensic performance drew standing-room-only crowds, then the dialogic presentation of a conflictual *procès* would be more dramatic
still in the explicitly theatrical context of the medieval stage. Indeed,
exploitation of the trial in works destined for the stage would have
enhanced their dramatic value by recalling the inherent theatricality
of law itself.

It is for that reason that the scholastic literary debate can no longer
be viewed as evidence of the "decline" of imaginative literature.
Quite to the contrary, both learned and popular *procès* emerge as
exemplary forms of rhetorico-dramatic unity. There was a reason
why learned dramatists paraded their knowledge of theology, scholastic argumentation, and civil and canon law in so many mystery
plays, farces, miracles, and sotties (*ETF*, 15): because the disputational structures of forensic rhetoric were compatible with the dialogic structure of drama. Wherever disputational rhetoric was
delivered—in the courtroom, on the rue du Fouarre, in the Châtelet,
on the stage—histrionic pleaders could transform dramatic rhetoric
into rhetorical drama. It is not contradictory, then, to speak of new
types of theatricalization of legal delivery as late as the fifteenth and
sixteenth centuries; but it is also possible to move back considerably
the "origins" of medieval drama.

There is no medieval genre, wrote Bloch, "lyric or narrative, that
is not infused with at least a smattering of formal debate" (*MFLL*,
167); and nowhere is that more apparent than in the forensic structures of the most dialogic of medieval literary genres, drama. But
what he termed the "fresh dialogued patterns" of medieval French
literature were not so fresh as all that: they bespeak the long aestheticization of forensic dialogue. Similarly, Harvey suggests that it
was not coincidental that the fifteenth-century flowering of *moralités* and *sotties* coincided with the "rise of the royal magistrates
and of the professional organization of advocates, solicitors, and law
clerks" (27). But it is performative rhetoric that explains the literal
"coincidence" of law and literature. If one was "largely the product
of the other," as Harvey says (27), that phenomenon was by no means
unique to the French Middle Ages; nor was debate "institutional-
ized" by literary authors for the first time in the twelfth century,
as Bloch claimed (167). Consequently, ideas that Hardin Craig
viewed as "often interesting but to some degree irrelevant"—the
ideas that "*quêtes*, *débats*, and mere dialogues are drama or the
seeds or beginnings of drama" (19)—are of the utmost relevance. If,
as Curtius demonstrated, theory of literature and theory of rhetoric

were one and the same, criteria derived from Aristotle, Horace, and their Renaissance followers are not the "wrong equipment" for medieval drama criticism.[39] In many ways, the rhetorical tradition is the only "equipment" complex and durable enough to serve as a hermeneutic framework by which to assess the interplay between literature and the law.

[39]Hardin Craig, *English Religious Drama*, 19, 4–5. See Curtius, *European Literature and the Latin Middle Ages*, 71.

4 The Forensic Heritage in Medieval French Drama

Unless they are contemplating Thibault L'Aignelet bleating in a disorderly courtroom or the raucous students of the *Jeu de St Nicolas* outwitting each other, critics have not viewed the presence of scholastic echoes in medieval drama with enthusiasm. As appealing as the "natural comedy" of the law may appear, many have responded impatiently to its more solemn literary manifestations. When dramatists treat law satirically in a work such as the *Farce de Maistre Pierre Pathelin*, the result is deemed artful; and when they treat it seriously in such learned forms as the *procès de paradis*, it is not. In comedy the *procès* is an amusing topos, an effective stylistic vehicle for comic ridicule (*TM*, 151–60), and in the mystery and miracle plays it is evidence of poor style. Though the days may be gone when all things legal could be dismissed as banalities, as Harvey noted,[1] the notion lingers that the intricate ratiocinations of scholastic rhetoric in the Basoche, the quodlibet, and the great mystery plays of the fifteenth century were forms of obscurantism. Sympathetic to different aesthetic conventions, the modern reader has often found lifeless and pedantic the text that is "stuffed...with legal terms, formulas, procedure, and juridical definitions" (Fabre, *CP* [1882], 55). Medieval dramatists, however, found in the codified legal tradition a veritable program for dramatic conception, performance, and reception. There they discovered a remarkably effective paradigm for their own enterprise: the exploitation of the mimetic

[1] Harvey, *Theatre of the Basoche*, 5.

pleasures of the "spectacle of a fight." Moreover, it was delivery that helped to provoke the transformation of forensic conflict into the "rhetorico-legal structure" of dramatic plot—but far earlier than Kibédi Varga suggested in his discussion of classical French tragedy: "The characters accuse and exonerate one another... before a judge who is sometimes invisible, sometimes visible, but whose decision is imminent and ineluctable" (*REL*, 87). In a triumph of generic interplay, medieval dramatists often recontextualized disputational rhetoric as dramatic structure, illuminating even now its very ontology.

In other words, the same conventions that had once encouraged rhetoricians to cross over the tenuous border between law and drama now encouraged learned medieval authors to tap the microcosmic drama of law as they gave rein to their literary imaginations. Since the orator had traditionally embraced the role of actor for dramatic effect, it is logical that the converse phenomenon might be equally popular: that the dramatic actor would readily assume the role of the popular, histrionic legal advocate. I am not suggesting that familiarity with the specific rhetorical treatises cited thus far was a prerequisite for dramatic composition, but it is nevertheless highly probable that such learned authors as Gréban and Coquillart had been steeped in rhetorical principles of that sort in a medieval educational system whose influence was far more pervasive and homogeneous than it was once thought to be.[2] Nor am I implying that every medieval dramatist was influenced by the forensic model. Still, whenever that model appears, it suggests the importance of the impersonated legal agon as a veritable theory of dramatic invention for the Middle Ages.

Therefore, although the literary *procès* often seems but a stiff commonplace to the modern reader, it is in fact a complex rhetorical structure that harks back to the very origins of drama in spectacular ritual conflict. Intimately connected to the *letteraturizzazione* of rhetoric, the forensic debate was more than a lifeless, prefabricated frame into which various stories were inserted; rather, it was a dynamic and variable structure that mediated between law, debate, and drama, informing an infinite variety of literary subjects. In the particularly litigious dramatic output of medieval France, the passage from mnemonic image to dramatic image, from legal topic to

[2]The coherence of medieval educational training has been argued in Kelly, "School Arts of Poetry and Prose"; Woods, "Teaching the Tropes"; and Murphy, "Influence of Quintilian."

dramatic tale,[3] and from legal imagination to dramatic performance renders forensics the microcosmic structure around which many a dramatic effort was built. Inasmuch as both law and drama staged a dialogic agon that, through impersonation, was enacted for and adapted to a participating audience, the transference of forensic ritual to the stage had three significant literary consequences: (1) the forensic agon served as a veritable plot for many a play and dialogue; (2) its adaptability to both "learned" and "popular," "comic" and serious" forms permits the reunification of what critics have tended to separate as discrete traditions; and (3) given the time-honored connection between oratory and acting, the latent performance potential of any such trial sheds new light on that anomalous generic category known as "dialogic literature," thus prompting a reevaluation of such terms as "closet-drama" and "semi-dramatic."[4] It is a question of fluidity and focus rather than of strict generic classification.

Consequently, rather than dismiss the elaborate disputations of medieval drama as bizarre conjunctures of law, theology, and dramatic poetry, as Fabre does, or reject them as "inaccessible to the people and reserved for the elite," as Raymond Lebègue does, we can take them as a point of departure for the study of the profound influence of delivery on medieval dramatic creation.[5] Whether the setting was the courtroom or the stage, whether the courtroom was French or English, whether the *procès* took place in heaven or on earth, and whether the speaker was the caustic Basochien or the student of theology, when medieval dramatists staged a trial, they were participating in the aestheticization of rhetoric. Their own conflictual discourse continued to mediate between the legal and literary registers as the temenos of the courtroom became that of the stage, the site of a costumed, enacted participatory agon in which different roles were played.

First, then, the rhetorical conventions for the delivery of medieval debate permit the rediscovery of an early form of dramatic plot. In addition to structuring such discrete dramatic episodes as the trial

[3] I am paraphrasing the title of Vance's *From Topic to Tale,* in which he offers a compatible discussion of rhetoric in the larger debate about orality and literacy (xxiii–xxxi).

[4] Young, e.g., discusses the "semi-dramatic" in *Drama of the Medieval Church,* 1:8; Davenport discusses "closet-drama" in *Fifteenth-Century English Drama,* 92. See also Robertson, *Preface to Chaucer,* 11; Raby, *History of Secular Latin Poetry,* 308; Nicoll, *WD,* 96.

[5] Fabre, *CP* (1882), 41; Lebègue, *Etudes sur le théâtre français* (hereafter *ETF*), 15.

scene in the *Pathelin* or the debates between Jesus and the *docteurs* in the mystery plays, a forensic superstructure often provided dramatic unity to an entire work. The endurance of the legal protodrama in such social institutions as the Basoche, the quodlibet, and the Dutch Chamber of Rhetoric thus promises to supply interpretive criteria of considerably greater objectivity than the impressionistic (if enlightening) parameters once proposed by Erich Auerbach in his analysis of mimesis in the *Jeu d'Adam:* "Everything in the dramatic play which grew out of the liturgy during the Middle Ages is part of one—and always the same—context: of *one great drama* whose beginning is God's creation of the world, whose climax is Christ's Incarnation and Passion, and whose expected conclusion will be Christ's second coming and the Last Judgment."[6] Inasmuch as the "great drama" of law was older still, its verbal antiphony offers a scenario for the emergence of medieval dramatic genres from both religious and legal ritual in different yet compatible ways during their own *letteraturizzazione.* From the quodlibet to the Basoche to the stage, the myriad medieval manifestations of the verbal agon may then be viewed as recontextualizations of one and the same archetypal conflict.

Second, the *letteraturizzazione* of rhetoric has traditionally inspired rhetorico-dramatic forms as distinct in tone as the quodlibet and the *cause fictive,* the *procès de paradis* and the *cours d'amour,* the *Advocacie Nostre-Dame* and the *Farce du pect.*[7] But whoever the characters involved—the Ciceronian rhetor, the gods of classical tragedy, the Christian God adjudicating the *procès de paradis,* the comic judge of the *Pathelin* impatiently entreating the litigants to "return to their sheep," or even the modern reader supplying an individual verdict for the *moralité*—all such works dramatize the rhetoric of judgment and bespeak an ad hoc conception of the dramatic potential of the trial. The forensic model was no mere post hoc addition to such familiar stories as the Passion and the *trompeur trompé.* Quite to the contrary, it often provided extended metacommentary on the theatricalization of rhetoric. In that sense, the fundamental equivalence of farcical litigation with sheep noises in the background and serious debate about God's sacrifice of his son re-

---

[6]Auerbach, *Mimesis,* 158; emphasis mine.
[7]For a helpful introduction to the *cours d'amour,* see Rychner's introduction to his edition of Martial d'Auvergne, *Arrêts d'amour,* xxiv–xxxi. According to Harvey, the influence of legalistic debate also remained strong throughout the sixteenth century in such dramas as the *Condamnation de Banquet* (52–66).

veals the privileged status of forensic rhetoric as a form of mediation not only between rhetoric and drama but between Christian and secular traditions as well.

Even though forensic rhetoric was originally a learned form, its impact was not necessarily limited to the output of such learned authors as Gréban, who is believed to have became a bachelor of theology after participating in a quodlibet; or as Coquillart, who may well have pleaded fictive cases for the Basochiens.[8] Despite Lebègue's argument that fifteenth-century drama was not "popular theater" because the majority of its authors were "clerics, priests, canons, even doctors of theology" (*ETF*, 15), R. W. Southern had already shown that the popularity of scholastic debate "did not stop at the walls of the monasteries."[9] Since the Fête des Fous and the *causes fictives* were massive group spectacles, and since even the quodlibet drew mobs to the rue du Fouarre, the dramatic structures of forensic and disputational rhetoric were accessible to many people. Any author who had watched or participated in a trial could have called upon that experience during the artistic creation of farce and mystery play alike. Consequently, we are justified in bringing to dramatic forms as seemingly diverse as the *Pathelin* and the *Mystère de la Passion* a single hermeneutic of legal rhetoric.

The most significant contribution of rhetoric to the study of medieval drama may thus be the continued critical impetus to reconcile comic with tragic, popular with learned, secular with Christian, medieval with Renaissance forms. Even though the fluidity of those terms has been increasingly underscored by such critics as George Steiner and Alan Knight, the early confluence of tragedy and comedy becomes all the more apparent when it is resituated in the dramatic context of rhetoric.[10] Rhetoric may then serve its traditional mediatory function on the level of genre, encouraging the formulation

---

[8]Paris and Raynaud discuss extant records of Gréban's training at the University of Paris in their edition of his *Mystère de la Passion*, iii. For Coquillart, see Harvey, 71–72.

[9]R. W. Southern, *Medieval Humanism*, 12. Members of a panel on justice as spectacle at the 1991 conference "City and Spectacle in Medieval Europe" discussed the public nature of trials: Gouron, "Court Proceedings in the Public Sphere"; Potter, "Public Execution as a Moral Spectacle"; and Akehurst, "Seeing Justice Done." See also Janet Nelson, "Dispute Settlement in Carolingian West Francia," 58–59; and Wendy Davies, "People and Places in Dispute in Ninth-Century Britanny," 73–74, 82–84. Guenée provides scrupulous documentation in *Tribunaux et gens de justice*, esp. 238–50.

[10]See, e.g., Steiner, *Death of Tragedy*, on how the advent of a compensating Christian heaven brought about the "death of tragedy" (324); and Knight, *Aspects of Genre*, 2–15.

of fluid generic categories that are more consonant with medieval aesthetics. Modern partiality for farce notwithstanding, it is quite simply not consistent with the nature of histrionic delivery that conflictual discourse would be a success in comic plays and a failure in serious ones.

I propose a more subtle distinction for medieval literary works that dramatize forensic rhetoric: rather than speak of comic versus tragic or learned versus popular, or even mimetic versus didactic, we might prefer to distinguish between two interrelated modes of dramatic emphasis: the dialectical, which took the quodlibet as its model, and the rhetorical, which was inspired by the Basoche. Resting on the proverbial distinction between rhetoric as an "open hand" and dialectic as a "closed fist,"[11] such an approach allows us to differentiate between dialectical focus on the spirit of the law and rhetorical focus on the pleasures of the legal process. Since the agon was the modus operandi for forensic rhetoric and dialectic alike, it provides an eminently logical explanation for both structural similarity and tonal difference, variety and interdependence in works as apparently irreconcilable as the *Mystère de la Passion* and the *Farce du pect*. Works of the dialectical strain would encourage revelation of and reflection on moral and theological truths; works of the rhetorical strain would encourage enjoyment of the very process by which those truths were revealed. If, then, the theatrical heritage of the quodlibet is primarily dialectical and that of the Basoche primarily rhetorical, we may infer not an antithesis but an interplay, and we find it chronicled in the history of rhetoric and dialectic.[12]

The dialectical strain includes such works as the *mystères de la Passion* and the *Advocacie Nostre-Dame*, which are characterized by a self-reflexivity reminiscent of the "philosophical strand" of rhetoric as codified by Plato and Aristotle and perpetuated in the Middle Ages by canon law studies and the quodlibet.[13] Such works

[11]Isidore of Seville, e.g., examines Varro's dictum in his treatment of dialectic in the *Etymologies*; see Lindsay ed., II, 23; see also Murphy's discussion of this topos in *RIMA*, 73.

[12]This notion is consistent with Robertson's discussion of medieval dialectic as a process that "did not conform to a pattern of conflict and synthesis.... Typically, the two sides of the problem do not merge to form a new position compounded of their diversity" (11). However, differentiating between rhetoric and dialectic had sparked lively controversy ever since the very advent of a prescriptive rhetorical tradition. See, e.g., Kennedy's discussion of Plato and Aristotle as opposed to Gorgias and Isocrates in *CR*, 29–36. For the renewal of that debate in the Middle Ages, see Murphy on the efforts to classify the sciences in the twelfth and thirteenth centuries: *RIMA*, 192.

[13]For a discussion of the strands, see *CR*, 15–17.

turn inward to highlight a dialectical mode of inquiry and outward
to encourage imitation of that mode of inquiry by their audiences.
They emphasize the truthfulness of their conclusions as much as
the nobility of the methods employed to determine them. In the
rhetorical strain, however, exemplified by such works as the *Pathelin,* the *Farce du pect,* and Coquillart's *Plaidoyé d'entre la Simple
et la Rusee,* it is the absurdity of the verdict that is emphasized to
satirize a dialectical process gone awry.[14] Staging such lofty matters
as the ontological status of a fart, the return of some ill-gotten cloth,
and the sexual appetites of men and women, dramas of the rhetorical
strain are closely connected to the rhetorico-dramatic activities of
the Basochiens: they dramatize the comic degeneration of a legal
process that no longer served the Truth. By imitating the *letteraturizzazione* of the initially utilitarian legal eloquence, medieval
authors immortalized the theatricalization of a rhetoric that sought
primarily to please audiences with its own agonistic spectacle. And
the law supplied them with a never-ending stock of disputed questions for their plays.

Third and last, the forensic rhetorical model proves equally illuminating in the evaluation of the performance potential of dialogic
literature, whose history extends from Plato to Seneca and from
Lucian to the *tenso* and the *Roman de la rose.*[15] A reading of the
particularly representative *Advocacie Nostre-Dame* and Coquillart's *Plaidoyé* reveals that both works are characterized by an archetypal forensic conflict whose potential for histrionic delivery was
as great as that of the trial itself. Despite D. W. Robertson's contention that dialectic lent both scholasticism (11) and religious
drama a "curiously undramatic" quality (37), recourse to delivery
allows us to bridge the gulf between orality and literacy and to
discover that such works had the potential to move from the page
to the stage. Given the status of delivery as the animator of forensic
dialogue, such literary trials would surely have recalled histrionic
performance and thus have enhanced their protodramatic status.

---

[14]Though different in focus, Knight's "Medieval Theater of the Absurd" is helpful
in this connection.

[15]Ultimately, a similar argument might be advanced for many Latin and vernacular
dialogues from antiquity through the Middle Ages, such as Lucian's "Double Indictment," Hrotswitha's "Paphnutius," the "Getta" of Vital de Blois (later translated
by Eustache Deschamps), the *Processus iocus-serius,* Delguelville's *Pelerinage de
l'ame, Bien-Advisé, Mal Advisé,* and the *Songe du Vergier.* Unfortunately, it is not
possible to include all relevant dialogues in this book. Nor is it possible to include
lyric debates, although Raby's work on "true *Streitgedicht*" suggests a more widespread generic interplay between disputational rhetoric, drama, and lyric (2:282–308).

The reintegration of *actio* into the criticism of dialogic literature thus sheds new light on why debate was a "literary genre in its own right," as Gerald Brault asserts, and why, in a religious and didactic age, the trial was among the most enduring of literary structures, and the judge and master were surpassed as archetypal characters only by "the dying Redeemer-God," as Alan Gunn notes.[16] Wherever and whenever a dialogic forensic model is present (and however dry it may appear today), it suggests a generic *mouvance* between law and drama which promises to assist us in our efforts to assess the performance potential of rhetoric in all medieval literary genres: it accounts for both the dramatic and the very origins of drama.

The Play as Proof

Nowhere is the conflation of legal rhetoric and drama more artful than in the popular courtroom allegory known as the *procès de paradis*. The *procès* of the four daughters of God serves as one of the most striking medieval metacommentaries on the very origins of drama. In the *Mystère de la Passion* of Arnoul Gréban and that of the anonymous author from Arras, and in the *Mistére du Viel Testament*, the *procès de paradis* bespeaks the elegant commingling of a rhetorical conception of drama and a dramatic conception of rhetoric. In each work the forensic debates between Ladies Mercy, Justice, Charity, and Truth as to whether God should sacrifice his only son to save humankind provide the juridical raison d'être for Christ's Passion and the dramatic raison d'être for Passion plays, both of which are engendered through *actio*.

Be that as it may, critical response to the *procès de paradis* has been characterized largely by a bizarre dialectic of praise and denial. Gustave Lanson, Marius Sepet, Gaston Paris and Gaston Raynaud, and L. Petit de Julleville, for example, all praised Gréban's *procès* as a framing device; yet Lanson dismissed it as an all too familiar commonplace, Sepet deemed it a painful representation of a "thesis defense," Paris and Raynaud denounced it as an "interminable discussion" (xvi), and Petit de Julleville thought it was "swallowed up"

---

[16]Brault, *Song of Roland*, 1:181; Gunn, "Teacher and Student in the *Roman de la Rose*," 127; cf. Kibédi Varga on rhetorico-dramatic structure in tragedy in *REL*, 86–89, and Glorieux on the omniscient, omnipresent master/judge of the quodlibet in *LQ*, 1:33.

by Gréban's "dialogic epic."[17] Even Hope Traver mourned the burial of the four daughters of God "under a load of dialectic"—and we sense that she would have liked to say a load of something else.[18] In much the same way, then, that Chambers once downplayed his own affirmation of the dramatic potential of the liturgy, critics have acknowledged the interplay between drama and juridical rhetoric only to discard those insights when they could not reconcile them with the traditionally negative reaction against scholasticism in literature. In view of the protodramatic status of rhetoric, and the proliferation of medieval dialogues, however, it is difficult to embrace such rationales. If the performative spectacle of argumentation had inspired avid audience response for centuries, it is logical that the literary *procès* might serve much the same function—a function that is particularly artful in Gréban's fascinating rhetorical conception of drama.

Gréban

From the outset of the *Mystère de la Passion*, Arnoul Gréban equates rhetoric with drama in the structurally crucial *procès de paradis*. His four daughters appear almost immediately in the First Day (2056–3376) and briefly at the virtual halfway mark of the *Passion*, at the time of Christ's suffering in the garden (18739–886); and they return to close the play in the Final Morality (33941–4402) before a Final and Total Prologue (34403–29).[19] While their first debate comprises about 1,300 of the *Passion*'s 35,000-odd lines and the last approximately 400, Gréban employs the *procès* as a rhetorico-logical superstructure for the Passion and as a metaphor for his own aesthetic conflation of theater and rhetorical proof. *His* drama literally emerges from *their* rhetoric—a phenomenon for which the 1473 manuscript of the *Passion* provides explicit extratextual evidence:

> Et devez savoir que maistre Arnoul Gresban, notable bachelier en theologie, lequel *composa le present livre* a la requeste d'aucuns de

[17]Lanson, *Histoire de la littérature française*, 209; Sepet, *Origines catholiques du théâtre moderne*, 308–9, 334; Paris and Raynaud's introduction to Gréban, *Mystère de la Passion*, xvi; Petit de Julleville, *LM*, 245–46.

[18]Traver, *Four Daughters of God*, 8.

[19]References to Gréban's *Mystère de la Passion* are to Jodogne's edition and are given parenthetically by line number. Translations are mine. For an excellent résumé of the arguments of Gréban's three *procès*, see Traver, 82–90. And for a comparison of French and English *procès*, see Traver, chaps. 4–9. Later I also treat briefly the "Procès que a faict Misericorde."

Paris, fit ceste creacion abrègée *seulement pour monstrer la difference du peché du deable et de l'omme et pour quoy le peché de l'homme ha esté reparé et non pas celluy du deable.* [As quoted in Traver, 93n; (emphasis mine)]

And you should know that Master Arnoul Gréban, noble bachelor of theology, who composed the present book at the request of certain Parisians, made this abbreviated version of the Creation solely to demonstrate the difference between the sin of the Devil and that of man and to show why the sin of man was redeemed while that of the Devil was not.

Though this lengthy work hardly seems "abbreviated" to the modern reader, Gréban has managed nonetheless to reduce the expansive story of Christ to the answer to a single disputed *quaestio*—a practice reminiscent of both the quodlibetal disputation and the trial. Indeed, he appears to have been familiar with two specific *quaestiones* of Thomas Aquinas: "utrum voluntas daemonum sit obstinata in malo" (whether the will of demons is fixed on evil) and "utrum fuerit magis conveniens quod persona Filii assumeret humanam naturam quam alia persona divina" (whether it was more appropriate for the person of the Son to assume a human nature rather than a different person of the Trinity).[20] His own *procès* (1671–1707) is introduced in a style that closely resembles that of the quodlibetal *determinatio*, recapitulating the cause of action for man's redemption and citing previous authoritative commentaries. Moreover, in much the same way that the abbreviated *determinatio* imposed a new order on the *disputatio*, Gréban imposes a new order on the Passion play by framing it with the "arguments and defenses" (1696) of a great forensic debate: "We will argue *sic* and *non* / as Saint Thomas has treated it [the question]" (1692–93). The oral drama of that debate will then be preserved in the written account of the "present book" described earlier (Traver, 93n).

What Gréban promises is a *deduccion*, a *demonstracion*, an abridgment ("petit abregié" [9905–6]) of that great *quaestio* to be visually "witnessed" (legally/dramatically) by his audience ("verrez con-

[20]Emile Roy has argued that both Gréban and the author of the Arras *Passion* had specific knowledge of two quodlibeta of Aquinas: *Mystère de la Passion en France*, 207–8, 266. Furthermore, it seems that Gréban also knew "the *Gesta Pilati*, the *Dialogus* of the Pseudo-Anselm, the *Meditations* attributed to Bonaventura, the *Historia Scolastica* of Peter Comestor, the *Summa* of St. Thomas Aquinas, the *Postillae* of Nicolas de Lyre, the *Golden Legend*, a prose French *Passion* written in 1398 for Isabel of Bavaria, and perhaps a French version of the *Gospel of Gamaliel*": Grace Frank, *Medieval French Drama*, 184, referring to Roy, 280.

clurre en audïence" [1703]). In fact, throughout the *Mystère de la Passion*, he uses interchangeably the terms *monstrer* (to show by means of spectacle) and *demonstrer* (to prove) in a vision of drama that privileges proof as enjoyably delivered spectacle. His explicitly stated intention is to reenact the Passion for profit and pleasure ("demonstrer par doulceur" [1618]) by dramatizing a cast of the very mnemonic *imagines agentes* who have helped to preserve this crucial legal question: "we seek to show by means of characters" ("monstrer voulons, par personnaiges") (1621; see also 19965–68, 27296–99). That *monstrer/demonstrer* pair is then reinforced by the dual rhetorico-dramatic connotations of the terms *deduire/deduccion*, which signified both delightful diversion and deduction (9905; also 27301–5). *Deductio*, for example, had not only logical but militaristic, juridical, and literary connotations; it could signify the bringing of witnesses before a tribunal, seduction, and the creation of a literary composition. To Gréban, proving and pleasing, rhetoric and drama are one and the same, as they had come to be in the classical and medieval courtroom. His very vocabulary thus refutes the early critical view of Gabriel Marcel, who maintained that the essence of Christian thought was to be *montré* (shown) by the Christian dramatist, "certainly not *démontré*" (demonstrated)—an epistemological cleavage that is simply not consistent with medieval philology.[21]

Once the daughters of God prove logically (*demonstrer*) why only the sin of man is redeemable, the dramatically delivered *demonstracion* of the Passion is possible: the *deduccion* can be staged to *deduire*. But first Gréban's *personnaiges* must reemerge from the memory. As he moves from mnemonic figuration to dramatic delivery, he replaces devotional language with figural representations who take the form of exemplary characters:

> Si *monstrerons* les motz exprés,
> car la maniere du produire
> ne se puet *monstrer ne deduire*
> par effect sinon seulement
> *grossement et figuraument;*
> et, selon qu'il nous est possible,
> *en verrez la chose senssible.* [20–26; emphasis mine]

Thus we will show the very words, for the manner of presentation cannot be shown or [pleasurably] demonstrated in action if not ex-

---

[21]Marcel, *Théâtre et religion*, 77.

clusively in an oblique and figural way. And, insofar as it lies within our capacity, you will see the thing tangibly.

It is the imagistic, forensic language of the *demonstracion* that will allow Gréban to "show the words" that in turn reengender dramatic characters. In fact, "showing words" is the crux of his theory of dramatic invention (despite Maurice Accarie's discomfort with that term).[22] In a dramatic imitation of the *ars memorandi*, Gréban brings the trial and the story of Christ "devant les yeulx, / senssiblement, par parsonnaiges" (tangibly before our eyes by means of characters [19955–56]) by introducing the five litigious ladies: "S'introduirons cinq personnaiges / de cinq dames haultes et saiges... / et ce pour jugier de l'offense... / et s'elle est digne de pardon" (Thus we will introduce five incarnations of five wise and noble ladies so that they may judge the offense and determine if it is pardonable [1671–79]). Before the daughters actually come forward to adjudicate the rhetorico-dramatic question that precipitates Passion and Passion play, however, their dramatic existence is presaged by the plaintive invocations of Adam, Eve, and various Old Testament prophets. They all call for "mercy" and "justice"—the abstract qualities that will soon become tangible incarnations on the stage (1741–42, 2042, 1973).

Just as the memory image brought vivid pictures "before our eyes," so here Gréban's mnemonic language anticipates the dramatic incarnations of Justice and Mercy onstage. In a fascinating act of forensic *inventio*, he engenders *"mystère-iously"* (*par mistere* [1516]) his own *imagines agentes*, who commemorate the passage from memory to delivery and rhetoric to spectacle in the ultimate *demonstracion* of the Passion. Having been invoked repeatedly in the Prologue, the four daughters now emerge to dramatize the great agon (*ceste guerre*) between God and man (1549), until such time as Christ resolves their dispute through his Passion and Gréban through his Passion play. In a masterful Christian recontextualization of the forensic rhetorical model, Gréban thus communicates a vision of his own: as abstractions take on the "veil of human nature" ("voille de nature humaine" [1518]), legal topic assumes dramatic form. He thus supplies a gloss for the entire dramatic enterprise by producing an artistic facsimile of something that humankind can duplicate only through art: the power of logos. Gréban's intertwining of rhet-

[22]Accarie, *Théâtre sacré*, 120.

oric, memory, and allegory in the *procès de paradis* allows him to reenact the rhetorical "origins" of drama: each time the five noble ladies emerge from memory, each time they stage their *procès*, its conclusion leads to the same "event"—the literal drama of Christ's Passion.

Introducing herself as "the most merciful of all" (2077), Mercy now takes a legal and dramatic stand by petitioning the celestial court for clemency (2056–87): "pour leur bon droit maintenir, / il fault que leur *cause procure*" (to maintain their rights, I must prosecute their case [2058–59]). It is the pathos of his repentance that moves her emotionally (*"sa penitence me meult"* [2500]); but pathos also moves her juridically (*mouvoir*, from Latin *movere*) to initiate legal proceedings, to set things in motion, to disturb the established order. As she attempts to temper the old law of justice with the New Testament law of mercy, that transformation of the law is paralleled here by the generic transformation of forensic ritual into dramatic representation. The daughters' very participation in the debate transforms them from legal *actores* to dramatic ones. The very ontology of Gréban's *Passion* thus lies in his ability to transform forensic discourse into a dramatic Christian demonstration of mercy.

At the outset of the trial, Mercy's arguments appear to conform to the tradition of legal *staseis* as codified by Hermagoras and Hermogenes and disseminated during the Middle Ages in such widely circulated treatises as the *Ad Herennium* and *De inventione*.[23] She begins, for example, by acknowledging that man has, in fact, committed a crime—an argument based on juridical issue: "when there is agreement on the act, but the right or wrong of the act is in question."[24] Since Lady Mercy denies neither the commission of the crime nor the need for punishment (2141–43 or 2412), there is no question here of absolute issue, "when we contend that the act in and of itself, without our drawing on any extraneous considerations, was right." Instead, she chooses the assumptive issue, the second subtype of juridical issue, "when the defence, in itself insufficient, is established by drawing on extraneous matter" (*Ad Herennium*, I, 24). Accordingly, she calls into question the nature and motives of man's crime by comparing it to the criminal pride (2138)

---

[23]The *stasis* theory described in the technical handbook of Hermagoras of Temnos (2 B.C.) is not extant, but its influence is apparent in such works as the *Ad Herennium*, and it remained an unparalleled influence on theories of rhetorical invention until the end of the Renaissance; see *CR*, 103–5.

[24][Cicero], *Ad C. Herennium*, 5, 14.24.

of the Devil and his cohorts (2140–43). Since the Devil sinned by
lust for power (2145) and man by vainglorious desire for knowledge
(2146), the Devil's offense is unforgivable (2168–71) but man's is
"excusable / grandement par raison prouvable" (highly forgivable by
demonstrable reasons [2165–66]). She "infers from those premises"
(*desquelles premisses je infere* [2160]) that it is unfair that man's
entire progeny pay an eternal price while the Devil's punishment is
endured by the malefactor alone (2149–52).

Lady Justice perceives a logical fallacy immediately: "Cuidez
vous, pour vostre preschier, / les delivrer, quant au surplus, / pour
dire 'je le vueil,' sans plus?" (Moreover, do you think to deliver them
with your plea by saying 'I wish it' and nothing more? [2184–86]).
The message of that preaching, consistent with the *ars praedicandi*
encouraged by Christ himself, is as yet unclear to Justice the logician. As both daughters proceed to launch irrelevant ad hominem
(or ad feminam) attacks against each other (e.g., 2214–20),[25] the legal
combat that Justice has promised to wage (2188) is recontextualized
as a spectacular war of words. In a conflictual antiphony of their
own, Mercy's compassionate pleas for man's release clash with Justice's *argumens, lois actives*, and *raisons demonstratives* for his
eternal condemnation (2230–33). And though their mutual re-
proaches are not germane to the legal issue at hand, they are extremely relevant to the dramatization of the greater agon between
Justice and Mercy, between the letter and spirit of the law. Even
though traditionally pathos was thought to have worked in conjunction with logic,[26] the relentless tension here between the two
lies at the crux of both the legal and dramatic causes of action.

Yet ultimately, for all the appearance of logic, Lady Mercy's pathos
subverts the juridical process; that is, the redemption is not logically
determined by the arguments presented. Like so many scholastic
deductions, the trial was essentially over before it began, when God
admitted his preternatural inclination to indulge his merciful daughter (2092–93) and all his creation through grace (2422–23). Lady
Mercy is well aware of that, taunting Justice with the claim that
"vous n'arez raison, / tant soit estrangement prouvee, / s'i Dieu
plaist, qui ne soit sauvee" (you will never be vindicated, no matter

---

[25]For descriptions of the argumentum ad hominem, see, e.g., *Ad Herennium*, II,
44, and Cicero, *De inventione*, I, 92–94. And for a complex discussion of the avail-
ability of both texts (and commentaries on them), see John Ward's "From Antiquity
to the Renaissance."
[26]For the interplay of pathos and logic, see Fortenbaugh, "Aristotle's *Rhetoric* on
Emotions."

how strangely proved, if it please God to forgive [2236–68]). In the
end, the fact that Justice is an accomplished advocate who introduces
her premises and refutations in a logical and orderly fashion is irrelevant. She ably refutes Mercy's "three formidable points" (2243)
by maintaining that (1) man has no intrinsic merit; (2) even if he
did, the redemption would be unfeasible (2253–55); and (3) his crime
is identical to that of the Devil (2259–69). But her mastery of "legal
ceremony" (9760–63) does not allow her to triumph over Mercy's
logically inferior (but emotionally superior) appeals. Gréban has
staged the forensic model only to subvert it in favor of a new Christian legal hierarchy that privileges mercy over justice, pity over logic.
He resolves the moral dilemma of delivery by transferring the logic
of the letter of the law to the drama of the spirit of the law—a
process that engenders his own play.

As yet unaware of just what is being engendered, Lady Justice
continues to demand "equal punishment" for man under the law
(2332): "L'un, dictes vous, est importun; / *ergo* l'autre, car c'est
tout ung" (One, you say, is troublesome; ergo, so is the other, for
they are one and the same [2337–38]). In an analogy drawn from
the most terrestrial of registers, she argues that man must remain
as "hostage" (2343) in his purgatorial debtors prison, treated like
any other convict with insufficient resources (2341–47). At that
point, Lady Truth comes forward to validate mercy as a legal
principle. Despite her affirmation that an offense against the Infinite requires infinite penance (2373–76), she comes unexpectedly
to a conclusion that is logically contradictory to her own remarks:
that Mercy might well find a "much sweeter road" (2380). Here
that sweeter road is drama, ennobled by the subordination of secular rhetoric to Christian mercy. In the mediatory tradition once
described by Alanus de Insulis, Gréban's forensic rhetoric becomes
a divine ministration.

The incensed Lady Justice may well insist that "il me souffist que
mes raisons / inferent leurs conclusions / contre les dictz qu'elle
maintient" (it suffices that my conclusions follow logically from
my premises against the contentions she advances [2383–85]). But
Mercy's invocation of a "sweet judge" (2406) who will confound
Justice's laws shatters the very *staseis* she uses in her own defense.
She goes on, for example, to manipulate three of the four subtypes
of assumptive issue: "Shifting of the Question of Guilt," "Rejection
of the Responsibility," and "Acknowledgment of the Charge" (*Ad
Herennium*, I, 24). First, Mercy shifts the question (*translatio criminis*) by blaming the Devil for instigating man's crime; (2) she

attributes responsibility to the Devil (*remotio criminis*) (I, 25); and (3) she acknowledges the charge with an exculpation (*purgatio*) and a plea for mercy (*deprecatio*). Since man did not act with intent but sinned by ignorance (*inprudentia*), she may plead for mercy: "when the defendant confesses the crime and premeditation, yet begs for compassion" (I, 24):

> J'alegue a sa cause deffendre
> plusieurs poins: premier, sa noblesse,
> son ingnorance, sa foiblesse.
> J'allegue aussi qu'il estoit mis
> entre ses mortelz ennemis
> qui, par envye qu'ilz avoient,
> de tout leur pouoir le grevoient.
> J'alegue aussi, hault crëateur,
> qu'il pecha comme viäteur
> et n'estoit pas faicte du tout
> sa voye: qui l'excuse moult. [2424–34]

In his defense, I advance several arguments: first, his nobility, his ignorance, and his weakness. I also allege that he was placed among his mortal enemies who sought to harm him with all their might because of envy. I further allege, Great Creator, that he sinned as a traveler who had not yet traveled his whole path, which greatly excuses him.

With that very line of argument, however, she has already modified standard legal practice. As the *Ad Herennium* author advised, the plea for mercy was "rarely practicable" and even inadmissible in the court under ordinary circumstances (I, 24). But the *procès de paradis* is no ordinary circumstance; in God's court the plea for mercy is more than admissible: it is the most viable rhetorico-dramatic proof.

Lady Justice is quick to point out that her opponent's reasoning has "skirted its own premises" (*comme hors des termes saulte* [2458]): for man's initial nobility makes his sin all the more abominable (2460–63). She also rejects Mercy's attempts at retaliation with *remotio criminis*, "when we repudiate not the act charged but the responsibility, and either transfer it to another person or attribute it to some circumstance" (*Ad Herennium*, I, 25), and with *translatio criminis*, "when we do not deny our act but plead that we were driven to it by the crimes of others" (I, 25). Since man had free will (*franche voulenté*), he *chose* to sin (2478–79). Therefore, Lady Mercy's only recourse is to abandon logic in favor of the *pathos* of "mourning his offense" (2498). Clearly exasperated by the persistence of such emotional appeals, Justice sees no reason for further legal wrangling. Even if she were to stretch the rules, the redemption would still be impossible (2520–27). Quite unexpectedly, however, when she demands to *see* who indeed might do penance in man's place (2522–23), she precipitates her own downfall by implying that she might accept such penance. She has asked, in fact, to see the drama of the redemption with her own eyes: she has asked to see the proof of the Passion play.

Lady Mercy rises forthwith to the challenge of presenting the argument that will allow drama to stage the answer to the legal question (2544–68). Although man's crime requires infinite penance, she postulates, a being with infinite powers would be capable of paying the price (2553–58). Mercy finally presents six points in man's defense, arguing against Lady Justice's fallacious "minor premise" that man's crime is identical to the Devil's (2564–66): (1) his ignorance exculpates him (2610–12); (2) the two crimes and criminals are of different natures (2626–35); (3) man was vainglorious (2642), while the Devil lusted for power (2646); (4) unborn humans were condemned for the sins of their ancestors (2667–76) in contrast to the fact that (5) only the Devil and his cohorts have paid the price for their crime (2686–97); and (6) man's "pilgrimage" toward heaven (2710–12) had only just begun. But even though Lady Justice begrudgingly concedes her logic (2732–37), a final question of law, rhetoric, and drama remains to be resolved before the Passion can be performed: the justification of who might play the role of the redeemer (2750), which they remand to Wisdom (2865–70).

Initially Lady Wisdom rejects all the proposed redeemer candidates, including any person of the Trinity (3057–72), because none of them can suffer (3075). The inescapable conclusion is that the redeemer must be both God and man (3078–79)—a task that most befits the Son. As the "middle person" of the Trinity, he is the *ymaige* of his father (3132–33) and the natural *mediäteur* between creature and creator (3198–99). Moreover, as the incarnation of the Word, Christ will fulfill earlier prophecies (3185–90) by becoming a visible dramatic sign, and by translating prophesy into dramatic action. His incarnation thus parallels Gréban's larger enterprise, in which the incarnations of his own characters transform juridical rhetoric into didactic drama. When God agrees to the redemption, his subsequent request that man "behold" his grace is also a dramatic cue to the audience to behold the Passion play that is about to unfold:

> *Regarde* quel honneur te fais,
> *regarde* par qui tes meffais
> seront reparéz et reffaiz
> au parvenir...!
> Et *vois* que j'aray fait pour toy.
> ma grace considere et *voy*
> qui te fait plus que je ne doy:
> tu *vois le fait.* [3277–300; emphasis mine].

Behold the great honor I pay you, behold by whom your misdeeds will be atoned for and paid in full! And see what I will have done for you. Reflect upon my grace and see who does more for you than I should: you see the demonstration.

As Gréban proceeds to commemorate the Annunciation (3313–24), he is in fact celebrating the power of logos in the genesis of Christ, which is also the birth of his play. All those functions are exemplified in God's directive that Gabriel commit a performative act: "Alez exposer / en terre ce divin mistere" (Go and present this divine mystery on earth [3333–34]). That act is as iterative as the Mass inasmuch as the *procès* reenacts and commemorates the Passion and the play anew each time it is staged.

Later in the play, when God responds to the "piteous eloquence" of Christ alone in the garden (18771),[27] Lady Justice insists that she cannot relent until the pathos of the Passion has been demonstrated through visible signs of Christ's "ardent charity": "je vueil qu'il me soit *presenté* / en l'arbre de la croix pendu..., / tant que l'ame a son pere rende, / et n'est admende que j'en prende / tant qu'en ce party le *verray*" (I wish that he be presented to me hanged on the wooden cross until he offers up his soul unto his father, and there is no payment that I will accept until such time as I have seen it leave [18858–64; emphasis mine]). The audience too must witness

---

[27]It is also interesting to compare Gréban's *procès* with that of the anonymous fifteenth-century *Mystère de la Passion de Troyes* (ed. Bibolet). In that lengthy work of some 15,000 lines, a brief trial takes place only at the time of Christ's suffering in the garden (2:6723–858). While the play itself is closely modeled on Gréban's (Bibolet provides a veritable line-by-line comparison), it does not take up Gréban's complex use of the *procès de paradis* as an overarching structure and commentary on the origins of drama—at least, not in what is extant. Justice and Miséricorde are only abstract virtues, invoked, e.g., by Mary Magdalene (2:1288–99), and the initial verdict is not witnessed in this play.

the ultimate rhetorico-dramatic proof supplied by the dramatic representation of the Crucifixion and glossed in the *moralité finable*, where Christ will echo Justice's words. When God reconvenes the court at the end of the play for a divine *determinatio* (34053–108),[28] the arguments of the earlier *procès* are recapitulated (34113–15) as he asks Lady Justice the only question that can resolve the *procès de paradis* and the play. The four daughters now exchange the long-foretold kiss of peace: "*Misericordia / et Veritas obviaverunt, / et aprés, osculate sunt / sese Pax et Justicia. / David ainsi prophetiza*" (Mercy and Truth embraced and then Peace and Justice kissed as David prophesied [34338–42]). After translating this Latin phrase into French (34344–46), Gréban proceeds to the aesthetic *translatio* that is truly at stake in his own representation of *translatio criminis:* the "translation" of mnemonic into dramatic images effected by the mediatory attorney/translators once described by the lawyer Chambellan of Parliament (see Delachenal, 425–26). Not coincidentally, that was the function of metaphor (*translatio*), which was employed to place vivid mental pictures "before the eyes" (ante oculos ponendae causa [*Ad Herennium*, IV, 45]). In the same way that Ladies Mercy and Justice had been generated as *imagines agentes*, Christ now effects the ultimate *translatio* by recommitting to the collective memory the dramatic images of the pathos of the Passion and play (34222–35).

To his final query as to what more the rigorous lady can possibly desire (34236), Justice is finally tempered with Mercy as the four daughters embrace (34354–89). As the *Mystère* draws to its legal, theological, and dramatic conclusion with God's call for singing, he is also referring to the *resonance* of legal *raison* as it provides edifying entertainment with the music of its own erudition. The *concordance* is not only the legal contract; it is a divine theological harmony reminiscent of the antiphonal singing that once inspired liturgical drama:

> Angelz, pour *conclurre* le fait,
> mectez vous en belle *ordonnance*,

---

[28] If the opening *procès* recalls the quodlibetal *disputatio*, this second section recalls the *determinatio*, pronounced by the master before an audience. As was the case for the *determinatio*, God's summation is transmitted both orally (during the drama) and in writing (in the manuscript of the *Passion* itself): "Se riens avons dit ou escript / ou mal fait ou mal ordonné, / pour Dieu, qu'il nous soit pardonné!" (If, either orally or in writing, we have misrepresented or arranged improperly, may God grant us forgiveness for it [34409–11]). See Glorieux, *LQ*, 1:51–55, on the oral and written transmission of the *determinatio*.

> chantez par doulce *concordance,*
> menez joye parfaicte et plainne
> tant que la region haultainne,
> en *l'armonye de voz sons,*
> *resonne* par doulces chançons
> [34396–402; emphasis mine][29]

Angels, to conclude this case, arrange yourselves in a lovely order, sing in sweet concordance, rejoice perfectly and fully while the heavens above resonate in sweet song with the harmony of your sounds.

Forensic debate has thus allowed the iterative engenderment of the play as proof, demonstrating even today that not only is drama rhetorical but rhetoric is drama.

Finally, the "Proces que a faict Misericorde," a later reworking of Gréban's *procès de paradis,* provides striking testimony to the generic interplay between dialogue and drama.[30] In this little-studied work, an anonymous author provides a virtual word-for-word "translation" of Gréban's celestial debates, transforming them into a meditative dialogue on the Creation. It too is a *demonstracion,* as its complete title implies: "Le Proces que a faict Misericorde contre Justice, pour la redemption humaine, Lequel nous demonstre le vray mistere de l'annunciation nostre Seigneur Ihesucrist" (The trial initiated by Mercy against Justice, which demonstrates for us the true mystery of the annunciation of our Lord Jesus Christ). So although Traver has criticized the work for its many scribal errors and "misreadings"—citing only the allegorical prologue between La Terre et L'Omme as innovative (99)—the work serves as a fascinating testimonial to the *mouvance* between law, drama, and dialogue. From its opening lines, the power of divine logos functions as a metaphor for the act of literary creation, a symbol of the medieval author's predilection for *remaniements:*

> Tout n'étoit qu'une masse informe
> Ou les elemens confondus
> Sembloient dans leur course eperdus
> Combattre et s'agiter sans forme
> L'affreux cahos dans ses prisons....
> Voulant accomplir les decrets

[29]For music as a philosophical construct of divine harmony, see Stevens's helpful discussion in *Words and Music,* 372–80.

[30]The date assigned to the manuscript of the "Proces que a faict Misericorde" by the Bibliothèque Nationale is 1508. See also Traver's discussion of the work (98–99). Translations are mine.

Dieu dit un mot. De prompts effets
Signalent sa toute puissance.
Tout est dans l'ordre: tout s'avance
Au but que sa voix a prescrit. [1]

Everything was but an unformed mass where blended elements in their wayward course seemed to agitate shapelessly and to fight against the atrocious chaos of their prisons. Wishing to realize his decrees, God uttered a word. Immediate results signal his omnipotence. Everything is in order: everything moves forward toward the end which his voice has prescribed.

So it is that the *remanieur* of Gréban's *procès* engenders his own literary creation. Indeed, the narrating Earth goes on to explain that by representing (*presenter*) the horrors of man's suffering, she "takes on new life" (*me donne nouvelle vie* [1]). By extension, so does Gréban's story as it undergoes a transformation thanks to a new rhetorico-dramatic "ministration": "Et ainsi comme bonne mere / Je scay *ministrer* la matiere" (And like a good mother I know how to minister to these materials). When the Earth is inseminated by Phoebus, it is literary art that is born:

Ainsi de nous deux naist la chose
Que nature aura comprimée
Par la vertu bien imprimée
En la semence de tout le genre
Qui tousiours son semblable engendre. [2]

Thus from us two is born the thing that Nature will have compressed through her well-inscribed virtue into the seed of the entire genre, which always engenders its likeness.

This regenerative process suggests that the *semblable* of dialogue is drama, as drama is that of dialogue. Whether or not a work such as the "Proces que a faict Misericorde" was actually performed is ultimately less important than the fact that the work is artistically coherent in either incarnation, as written *livre* or as a play staged with the assistance of its didascalic commentaries. By staging allegorical *parsonnaiges* in litigation, Gréban and his *remanieurs* commemorate and resolve the Christian agon with a dramatic reunion of God and man effected by performative language. Thus ennobling *actio* itself, they stage the "spectacle of that fight"— not as an end in itself but as the most vivid representation of the confluence between the advent of Christian law and the advent of drama.

The Arras *Passion*

In the fifteenth-century Arras *Passion* (often attributed to Mercadé), the *procès de paradis* serves once again as a rhetorico-dramatic superstructure for both Passion and play.[31] It is the means by which the author translates *actio* into dramatic action. *Actores* (litigants/ actors) bring the Passion to life "before our very eyes" (16) as the Arras author engenders his own *Passion* by bridging the gulf between the legal *abrégé* and the oral drama of delivery. Whereas Gréban would devote his prologue to the story of the Fall, the Arras author begins with a resumé of the well-known verdict of the *procès de paradis* (5–17).[32] In a dramatic reenactment of that verdict, the legal *abrégé* reverts to the dialogic trial and the abbreviated *determinatio* to the lively *disputatio*. As the preacher/narrator explains, that forensic process serves to reconcile God and man by allowing the latter to relive the Christian agon through the "experience of play": "Par no *jeu* arez *congnoissance* / De sa glorieuse *naissance*. . . . / Car vous en *verrez plainement* / Par nostre *jeu l'experiment*" (Through our play you will gain understanding of his glorious birth. . . . For through our play you will see the experience completely [34–41; emphasis mine]).

Moreover, just as some fifty years later Gréban would promise to "show things through words," the Arras author manipulates artistically the performative power of logos: "Ces mots icy verrez juer" (You will see here the words played out [63]). And as Gréban's allegorical figures seemed to emerge directly from mnemonic invocation of the abstract qualities they were to incarnate, so too the Arras author privileges memory as the precursor to both legal delivery and drama. Even before the four daughters begin to litigate, they are placed within a veritable memory palace in a manner reminiscent of the detailed *didascalia* that anticipated the *ordo prophetarum*.[33] Holding symbolic props, they are *imagines agentes*,

[31]References to the Arras *Mystère de la Passion* are to Richard's edition. Traver dates the play as "possibly half a century" before Gréban's (82). Translations are mine.

[32]The first leaf of the manuscript, which is thought to contain some eighty lines, is not extant. Richard believes that the prologue to the First Day is pronounced by the same "Preacher" who introduces the subsequent days (1n). Moreover, given the references throughout the play to the *exposicion* of the "theme [*theume*] of our subject" (69), the Arras author also bridges the gulf between the transcribed sermon and conversational preaching, between the *ars praedicandi* and the lively sermon as described by, e.g., Rey-Flaud (*CM*, 262) and Young (1: 539). For an excellent resumé of the debates of the Arras *Passion*, see Traver, 78–82; also Grace Frank, 179–81.

[33]See my "Visions with Voices," 47–48.

creating a memorable image for the audience even before they acquire their own voices on stage:

> Cy est la Trinité en Paradis, c'est assavoir Dieu le pere assis en son
> throne et entour lui angles et archangles grant multitude qui font les
> aulcuns melodie, les aultres sont a genoulx par devant Dieu avec
> Misericorde qui tient ung ramisiel d'olivier en sa main. Et justice est
> empres ly toute droite qui tient une espée en sa main. Et avec Mis-
> ericorde sont a genoulx Verité, Sapience et Charité. Et commence
> Misericorde et dist einsi.   [After l. 82]

> Here is the Trinity in Paradise, to wit, God the Father seated on his
> throne, and around him a great multitude of angels and archangels,
> some of whom intone melodies; and the others are kneeling before
> God with Mercy, who holds a small olive branch in her hand. And
> directly behind her is Justice, who holds a sword in her hand. And
> kneeling with Mercy are Truth, Wisdom, and Charity. And Mercy
> begins, speaking thus.

As the audience is hushed (71–72) and the angels are invited to fill
the stage with appropriate melodies (74–75), these devotional images
come to life singing their own legal melodies.

Once again, the emotional Lady Mercy is moved by the pathos of
man's laments (99–103) to initiate the *procès de paradis*. But in the
Arras trial, the rigorous Lady Justice attempts to dismiss the entire
case even before it begins. Advocating not the regenerative memory
palace but the tabula rasa, she seeks to erase forever the very image
of fallen man: "Plus ne doit estre *memoire* / Del homme tant que
Dieu durera" (There must no longer be the memory of man for as
long as God shall live [132–33]). Distilling the principles of God's
sentence against man (169–88) into the same disputed question to
be addressed by Gréban, she argues that man is similar to Lucifer
and equally unworthy of forgiveness (197–203). There can be no
reunification of God and man and no harmony in the celestial memory palace. Man is in the "uncomfortable dwelling place" (*ottel mal*)
where he belongs (202).

However, Justice's juridical plan to erase the very images of
creation would constitute an artistic *mise en abîme* that is impossible for the Arras author: without the ensuing *procès de paradis*
there would be no redemption, no reconciliation, no fulfillment
of prophesy, and no play. Instead, she is drawn into the "genius
of the contest," insisting that eternal punishment be meted out
to man and his progeny (142–45). The agon of the *procès* thus

mirrors the internal struggle within Lady Justice, who desires two contradictory things: the utter disappearance of humankind from the collective memory, but also the eternal reminder of original sin through utter damnation. And as the daughters begin to verbalize their ordeal, their own legal *staseis* help to engender the dramatis personae of the Christian agon. When Lady Mercy uses assumptive issue to blame the devil for the Fall (204–97), for example, she refers to his having falsely presented a "portrait of the serpent" (232–34). It is those very *pourtraitures* that now populate the stage: the question of mnemonic images is also a question of law and of drama.

Mercy also introduces an argument for the redemption not seen in Gréban: because man repented immediately (254) and the Devil showed no remorse (276), the two crimes are of "diverse quality" (294). But Lady Justice is quick to perceive the momentous ramifications of that statement, asking if her loquacious sisters are really implying that the earlier judgment against man was the result of a "mistrial." Surely they are not imputing error to the deity by asking him to overturn his verdict, which would be "improper in a court of law" (312–14). Lady Justice agrees nonetheless to consider the feasibility of the redemption for the sake of argument (326–27), and in so doing she tacitly agrees to the Passion and the play. Lady Truth's subsequent speculations about how God might redeem his creatures by becoming a man (350–51) is actually a commentary on the entire dramatic enterprise, which stages human incarnations of divine beings. In order to inquire legally (and dramatically) into the question whether God will choose to be just or merciful, they must seek out the juridical assistance of Lady Wisdom. Their voyage for Wisdom and justice (432–35) becomes the voyage from law to drama.[34]

When the Arras daughters convene before God, Lady Wisdom presents him with a juridical fait accompli: he alone has the power to pardon man (413–18) if he is willing to find a redeemer (419–31). Initially, however, an Old Testament God of justice and vengeance rejects any notion of redemption (533–52); and in the debate that ensues, the dramatic agon resides in his own psyche. It is his own internal struggle between his just and merciful incarnations. Explaining that she will plead "al intercession / De ta fille Misericorde" (through intercession on behalf of your daughter Mercy [522–23]),

[34]Murphy makes a similar argument about the "pilgrimage" for justice in "Rhetoric and Dialectic in the *Owl and the Nightingale*," 229.

Wisdom begs that he mercifully undo the "vengeance" exacted upon humankind (492). If he shows "charity" (511) toward man, then a harmonious and fecund vision of unity between image and action will be restored to Paradise and to the stage, "affin qu'il ait la vision / De ta haulte fruicion" (that he may have the vision of your mighty fecundity [513–14]). Her rhetorical solution to the case is that God must assume dramatically a human incarnation in order to perform the redemption (598–600). But her line of argument is unexpected and complex: God, submits Wisdom, is actually denying (584) the great pain he expressed at the time of the Fall when he said *Me penitet fecisse hominem* (I regret having made man [587]). Through psychological cross-examination, she is actually encouraging God not only to fulfill earlier prophesy but to become who he is through the trial that is the play. Her veritable "psychoanalysis" of the deity allows the Arras author to exploit dramatic legal rhetoric as a mode of exploring the "character psychology" of God himself—a self-reflexive phenomenon that individualizes the dialogic conflict of the original *procès* in a way that suggests a further generic interplay between the forensic agon and the interior monologues of romance.[35] Indeed, one possible reading of the Arras trial is that the mnemonic visions that open the play are all *imagines agentes* within the divine psyche, verbalized and actualized during the process of legal *inventio* which is also the invention of drama.

In her own fascinating "ontological" argument (554–643), Wisdom now attempts to persuade God that the very genesis of Mercy as the allegorical benefactor of mankind incarnates his own merciful self: had he not wished to free man from his "horrible prison" (571), "il n'estoit pas necessité . . . / Que tu fisses misericorde, / C'est celle qui l'homme raccorde / A toy" (It was not necessary for you to create Mercy; she is the one who reconciles you with man [573–77]). This innovative argument (not seen in the other *procès*) underscores the remarkable power of logos in theology and drama alike. Wisdom's

[35]A similar phenomenon occurs with Jesus in Gréban: "En moy sens le plus fort debat / qu'oncques endurast crëature, / pour le fait d'umaine nature" (Within me, I feel the greatest debate that ever a creature endured because of human nature [18739–41]) and also in the *Mistére du Viel Testament*, discussed later in this chapter. I have argued the connection between forensics and the *roman* in "Memory and the Psychology of the Interior Monologue in Chrétien's *Cligés*"; see also Zink, "Allegorical Poem," 124–26; and Muscatine, "Emergence of Psychological Allegory," 1165–66. The psychological component of conflictual legal discourse is thus generically closer to the more self-reflexive structures of the *roman* than it might first appear. See, e.g., Kevin Brownlee, "Jean de Meun and the Limits of Romance," 128–30; and Karl Uitti, "Renewal and Undermining of Old French Romance," 135–37. I thank my colleague Marya Schechtman for sharing her work on the philosophy of psychology with me.

contention that God created Mercy as a symbol of hope in his divine plan parallels the author's creation of Mercy as a symbolic character in his own dramatic plan. And the divine will to bring man from darkness to light (629) further parallels the function of dramatic litigation, which is to restore man to the celestial *ostel*. Indeed, Wisdom emphasizes that mediatory function of law when she later describes her own status as mediator in much the same way Chambellan of the Parliament once proclaimed that an *"advocat n'est qu'interpretateur"* (a lawyer is but an interpreter).[36] Articulating the real dangers faced by medieval lawyers, Wisdom stresses that she is but the messenger (*"intercesseresse et message"* [738, 932]), as is the dramatist himself: "Je n'en suis riens que messaige / De Misericorde la saige / Pardonne moi se / j'ay mespris / Contre ta haultesse de pris" (I am nothing but the messenger for the wise Mercy. Forgive me if I have offended Your Mighty Highness [640–43]). She does, however, make a startling admission never recognized by Gréban: the redemption does not follow logically from the forensic premises advanced: "Non que je die toutes voies / Qu'en riens tu y soies tenu" (In any event, that is not to say that you are by any means obliged to do so [613–14]). God's sacrifice is a necessary conclusion only in the context of *caritas* and grace (618–25), the experience the narrator purported to demonstrate. If God consents, then grace remains immortal (635–36), and with any luck, so do the author's dramatic figures.

God, however, continues to refuse her request (644–742). And it is at that point that all present get into the legal act with effective (if unsolicited) interruptions. On bended knee, each daughter and each angel implore God to resolve his internal struggle on the side of mercy. Their solution is, in fact, that God do what the dramatist is doing: reconstruct the passage from remembrance to dramatic action. In a veritable litany to the power of memory, Charity, for example, begs for pity (651–97):

> *Souvienge* toy que tu l'as fait
> A ta *forme* et a ta *semblance*
> Et si prens en toy *remembrance*
> Que del ort limon de la terre
> Tu le fis sans autre *materre*.   [657–661; emphasis mine]

Remember that you made him in your image and likeness. And so recall unto yourself that you made him from the dust of the earth with no other material.

[36]See above, chap. 3, n. 33.

Her statement harks back to the very image of the Creation; but it also highlights the mnemonic function of any imagery used here to commemorate, imitate, and reenact dramatically the power of "divine speech" (677) or logos. Memory imagery is that which engenders the speech that in turn enables man to regain his place in the "celestial palaces" (686).

Gabriel too steps forward (698–742) to describe heaven as the ultimate mnemonic dwelling place and to urge God to restore man to his "blissful seat" there:[37]

> *Souviengne* toy des *mansions*,
> Des belles *habitations*,
> Des beaux *sieges celestiaux*
> Et des beaux *lieux* impériaux
> Qui sont wis et desemparés   [715–19; emphasis mine]

> Remember the dwelling places, the beautiful domiciles, the beautiful celestial seats, and the beautiful imperial places that are now vile and abandoned.

Unity was the original function of those palaces, and it may be reinstated through both the redemption and the dramatic commemoration of it. In fact, a strikingly similar vision of mnemonic mediation occurs in the heavenly trial of the English *Salutation and Conception* play.[38] It too dramatizes the trial that seeks to restore man to his original mnemonic station: "lete thi mercy make hym with Aungelys dwelle / of locyfere to restore the place" (47–48). And it too represents the fulfillment of prophesy as the actualization of God's own tendency to be merciful. Lady Truth, for example, cites God's words about his divine plan to dwell with man; as does Mercy, who argues against her "vengeabyl" sister (105) that "above all hese werkys god is mercyabyl" (107). He said "endlesly that mercy thou hast kept ffor man" (83). But, as Lady Truth recalls,

[37]It was too tempting to resist this reference to the first five lines of Milton's *Paradise Lost:* "Of Man's first Disobedience, and the Fruit / Of that Forbidden Tree, whose mortal taste / Brought Death into the World and all our woe, / With loss of *Eden,* till one greater Man / Restore us, and regain the blissful seat . . . "

[38]References are to K. S. Block's edition of the *Ludus Coventriae, or The Plaie called Corpus Christi,* which appears on pp. 97–109 of the volume, and are given by line number. The text also appears in Halliwell's edition of the *Ludus Coventriae,* 2:105–16, and excerpts may be found in Pollard's *English Miracle Plays.* Finally, Traver provides a line-by-line comparison of the *Salutation* with *The Charter of the Abbey of the Holy Ghost* in the context of other *procès de paradis* (126–35).

> Whan Adam had synnyd thou seydest thore
> That he xulde deye and go to helle
> And now to blysse hym to resstore
> twey contraryes mow not to-gedyr dwelle. [61–64]

Moreover, the clemency of God toward repentant humankind underscores his own humanity, as the Son voices heavenly disappointment with man in a manner similar to the *Me penitet fecisse hominem* of the Arras play (587):

> It peyneth me that man I mad
> That is to seyn peyne I must suffre fore
> A counsel of the trinite must be had
> Whiche of us xal man restore. [169–72]

And finally, like her Arras sisters, Lady Peace of the *Salutation* also rejects the notion of a mnemonic tabula rasa. Affirming that "yf mannys sowle xulde abyde in helle / be-twen God and man evyr xulde be dyvysyon / And than myght not I Pes dwelle" (118–20), she is also affirming her own existence. So, when the English daughters fulfill written prophesy in the kiss of peace (185–89) and re-engender the Annunciation, they too demonstrate that, as God the "makere" made man of clay (94), they, by virtue of their litigation, are the "makers" of drama.

In the Arras play, however, God agrees to the redemption more slowly, initially rejecting Gabriel's appeal (734). For what is truly at stake here—both legally and dramatically—is the transformation of the divine self from the incarnation of justice to the incarnation of mercy. Thus far, he is committed to the demonstration of the former, which has been confirmed by written authority: "Il est de moy escript / Ung grant et sumptueux escript, / Je suis juste, sy doy jugier / Justement sans riens espargnier" (A great and sumptuous scripture has been written of me: I am just, hence I must judge justly, sparing nothing [755–58]). Here Saint Michael appears to have the answer (765–90), implying that the nature of divine selfhood is to be found preserved in the memory loci of Paradise. Such a "lofty palace" (770), he asserts, was never to remain "deserted" (*dessertine* [771]); rather, it must be "filled" with all humankind (775–76) in the same way that memory is "filled" with an endless stock of materials for theological and dramatic invention. An empty memory palace would neither encourage drama nor fulfill oral and written prophecies of a merciful God: "Il est escript et dit de toy / Que la terre ou est gent

humaine / De ta misericorde est plaine" (It has been written and
said of you that the earth, where humankind dwells, is full of your
mercy [782–84]). By redeeming man, God would thus remain true
to his own nature (788–90) and to the means by which he is re-
membered here: in the passage from memory image to spoken and
written speech. Raphael then steps forward (791–818) to reinforce
that logic with a "great gloss" of his own (820): the redemption is
the only equitable verdict (813) of a merciful God, the proper dramatization of which may now begin.

Still insistent on retaining his just side (819–24), however, God
cannot yet abandon the legal rationale for his earlier verdict: since
man had free will, he *chose* to sin and is therefore the "cause of
the trouble" (829). A just God must exact appropriate punishment
for man's premeditated crime (830–32). At this point, Uriel can
only fall to his knees and implore God (833–74) to choose mercy
over justice "through ardent friendship" (835) and logos: "Si tu le
dis il sera fait" (If you speak it, it will be done [865]). By exercising
logos to transform *parole* into action, God may then restore unity
to the holy memory palace while the dramatist provides the commemorative imitation of that process: "affin que les sieges je voie
/ Remplis a grande multitude / D'esperis plains de beatitude" (that
I might see the seats filled with a great multitude of spirits full
of beatitude [872–74]). Even though Uriel specifies that God need
not perform the redemption "personnellement" (867), it is the
literal *images* of divine "personhood" that are at issue here. By
externalizing onstage a divine internal conflict between the opposing personae of God himself, the Arras author adds a level of
psychological complexity to the *procès de paradis* in a way that
recalls Burke's notion of the incantatory function of the image—
a "device for inviting us to 'make ourselves over in the image of
the imagery' " (*POLF*, 116). As the persons of the Trinity are then
explored as possible redeemers, as the person of God becomes more
humane, the dramatic personae of the Passion may take their places
onstage to resolve and commemorate the legal cause of action by
means of drama.

That abstract discussion of divine personhood continues in Cher-
ubin's speech (875–920) as the angel begs God to use his power
to restore man to the memory locus whence the dramatist has
regenerated him (887–96): "Faire le pues, se bien te plait, / Ainsi
sera finé le plait" (You can do it, if it please you; and thus our
trial will be over [905–6]). Here the pair of *plait* (please) and

plait (trial) celebrates the triumph of letter over spirit and the conflation of the rhetorics of pleasure and power. Such is the power of *actio*, as God now bends his will (938–78) to assume his merciful "incarnation": "Nous en personne de no fil / Prenderons incarnation / Pour humaine redemption / Dedans ung virginal autel" (In the person of our son, we will assume the incarnation for the redemption of humankind within a virginal altar [952–55]). The saddened Father is "humanized" (967–69), and Mary emerges as the memory "altar" where the humanity of Christ will be dramatized. She is the ultimate locus of mediation between God and man, memory and literary invention, rhetoric and drama (a status that is demonstrated more compellingly still in the *Advocacie Nostre-Dame*). Having prepared Gabriel for the rhetorico-dramatic manifestation of logos that will terminate the trial (983–89) and begin the play, God announces the Annunciation, that "grant signe d'amour / [que] tu me demonstres" (great sign of love that you demonstrate to me [1015–16]). Once again, that *demonstracion* is paralleled by that of the dramatist, who brings "before the very eyes" of the audience visible dramatic signs of his own. In the *modus dramatis* described by Origen,[39] Lady Wisdom directs both her sisters and the audience to open their eyes and ears (the traditional targets of *actio*) for the proof of her *"parolle"* (1040): "Regardez s'il vous plaist droit la, / Ve la Gabriel qui s'en va" (If you please, look right over there: there is Gabriel leaving [1041–42]).

As the Arras play runs it course, the role of the celestial court is reassigned to various "preachers" who supply exegetical commentary on the proceedings and metacommentary on a further interplay between drama and the *ars praedicandi*. The Second Day, for example, opens with a sermonic exhortation by John the Baptist that spectators seek salvation (6426) by translating the exemplary visions of the drama into "good works" (*bonnes muers* [6427]). The "signification" (6445) of his "collation" of sermonic "themes" (6437) is identical to that of forensic *demonstrance* in that both encourage the devoted public to "reap the fruits of our labors more *licitly*" (le fruit de no labourage / messonner plus *licitement* [13243–44]). And such a harvest is possible only at the mnemonic altar of the Virgin, the "gracious treasurer" (tresoriere de grace [13247; also 18603]). That regenerative vision of Mary now inspires the "virtuous signs" (13300) of drama as the narrators withdraw (much as they had done

[39]See Minnis, *Medieval Theory of Authorship*, 57–58.

in the Dionysian "origins" of drama), yielding their place to the visual experience:

> Verrez maint vertueulx signacle
> Maint bel et glorieux miracle
> Qui par moy ne seront contés,
> Car se no jeu bien entendés
> Vous en verrez entierement
> D'iceulx le propre experiment. [13300–13305]

You will see many a virtuous sign, many a beautiful and glorious miracle that I will not recount, because if you really understand our play, you will see fully the proper experience of them.

But if the *Passion* is to come to an end that is "convenable / Deue, licite et raisonnable" (due and proper, legal and reasonable [18592–93]), the public must commit to memory the "noble apparitions" (18725) of drama—a message that is reinforced in the final *determinatio*.

As in the quodlibet and as in Gréban, a detailed résumé of the initial *procès* (24632–42) is followed by a discussion of the visible evidence (*enseignes*) (24618) of the pathos of Christ's Passion (24619–30). He has "fulfilled" the prophesy of David as recorded (in Latin and French) in "a book he wrote" (24600–24606): "Or peulx tu voir qu'il est ainsi / que j'ay cest escrit acompli" (So you can see that it is thus that I have realized this scripture [24607–8]). Those *enseignes* are also the visible signs of drama, which God now calls upon all present to behold: "Les enseignes voir en pouez / Se bien sur lui vous regardez, / Ve cy ses plaies et son sang" (You can see the signs if you look closely upon him: here are his wounds and his blood [24737–39]). So when Lady Mercy praises the beauty of the *demonstracion*, she is also praising drama as the art form that similarly transforms prophetic speech inscribed within the memory into visible representations of actions (24755–64): "Car la chose est toute evidente, / J'en voy bien les propres enseignes / Que tu nous monstres et enseignes" (For the thing is fully evident; I see the proper signs of it, which you show and teach us [24770–72]). Those didactic signs (*enseignes/enseignes*) include such physical evidence as the stigmata, reminiscent here of the dramatic effects of bloodstained togas as described by Quintilian in reenactments of crimes:[40] "Je voy les playes et laidures, / Les angoisses griefves et dures, / Qu'il a souffert

---

[40]Quintilian, *Institutio oratoria*, VI, 1.31.

pour les humains" (I see the wounds and atrocities, the grievous and harsh anguish that he has suffered for humankind [24773–75]). Since Ladies Justice and Truth are also convinced by the evidence of their eyes (24785–826), the existence of charity as the fundamental principle of Christian law is confirmed rhetorically and dramatically: the daughters exchange the kiss of peace.

The forensic rhetoric of the *procès de paradis* has thus engendered the drama that has in turn transformed the law. In a final vision of legal and dramatic unity (24837–41), the play closes with "melodious songs" (24863–65) that suggest the music of forensic erudition, the *plaisir* of the *plait*. The public has now seen (*veu*), heard, and understood (*entendu* [24873–74]) that the legal evidence provided by Passion and play has reconciled God and man "in perpetuity" (24893–902). As mnemonic invocation of the *imagines agentes* of justice and mercy had hypostatized the litigious daughters of God onstage, so now memory demands that this dramatic commemoration be remanded to its own custody. There it may provide the stuff for future literary invention, and for future sermons as well—a possibility that is now confirmed by the returning preacher/narrator, who states that his own exegesis and sermonic "*theumes*" have been borne out by the play (24883–91). Performance has equated the Christian mediatory function of law and the *ars praedicandi* with that of drama. Performance has demonstrated that divine ideas may take on human incarnations to accomplish a religious and artistic mission.

Ultimately, the good works the public is encouraged to perform at the end of the play consist not only of the exercise of Christian charity but of the composition of new plays: "Doresnavant euvres faisons / Dont sa grace acquerir puissons" (Henceforth let us make works that will allow us to attain his grace [24921–22]). Man may thus remain forever in the "*glorieux firmament*" (24936) to which law and drama have restored him. In that way, the imitation of logos provided by the *procès de paradis* anticipates man's transformation of his life into an *imitatio Christi*. The Arras play thus reenacts the very process by which the dramatist turned to the *ars memorandi* as a source of literary invention, engendering the rhetorical *actio* of drama, a phenomenon that is particularly complex in the *Mistére du Viel Testament*.

The *Mistére du Viel Testament*

Nowhere is the importance of mnemonics as a precursor to rhetorico-dramatic delivery more remarkable than in the fifteenth-

century *Mistére du Viel Testament*.⁴¹ In yet another imitation of
the power of logos, images long preserved in oral and written memory come to life as a visible *demonstracion* (1:7) of how Old Testament justice anticipates New Testament mercy. In the *procès de
paradis* of this epic play of almost 50,000 lines, however, the trial
constitutes far more than a rhetorico-dramatic cause of legal action:
it is a veritable exegesis of equity. Consistently interspersed with
individual Old Testament crimes, the *procès* precipitates a relentless
series of individual verdicts that in turn advance ᵗhe drama and
literally *prefigure* the Passion (not staged in this play). It informs
the entire *Mistére* more compellingly than it does the other plays
studied thus far, recurring throughout as a rhetorical system of text
and gloss for the interpretation of "visible signs."⁴² As it inquires
into visual legal evidence, it simultaneously inquires into its own
epistemological, forensic, dramatic, and theological functions. And
by transforming its own mnemonic "figures" of equity into the
delivery of didactic drama, it clarifies visually and orally the epistemological foundations of Christian disputation.

Although the explicit authorial aim is to "produce divine and
virtuous [f]acts [*faictz*]" (4), what the mystery play actually produces
is an agonistic psychodrama waged within the divine psyche, the
two conflicting sides of which Justice and Mercy incarnate. When
Lady Justice demands retribution for the Fall, initially it is the venge-
ful Old Testament God she represents who calls upon his own rigorous laws for the immediate destruction of his traitorous creation
(1298–1303). But Lady Mercy's argument that God must be true to
the charitable nature that once prompted him to create her (1307–
11) provides the legal remedy that allows the deity to discover himself through drama. She initiates the *procès* that will allow the dramatic tale of humankind to unfold for six volumes—the space it
will take for the exegetical system of the play to be amply demonstrated. Contending that man's fall was due to his ignorant com-
pliance with the persuasive Devil (1395–1404), Lady Mercy offers a
veritable paraphrase of the qualitative *stasis:* in view of the "quality
of the crime" (*la qualité du malfaict* [1517]) and of man's immediate

⁴¹All references to *Le Mistére du Viel Testament* are to Rothschild's edition and
are given parenthetically by line number and, initially, volume number. The esti-
mated date for the play is the middle of the fifteenth century—the work appears to
have been widely known by 1480 (1:iv–ix)—although M. Ward, *History of English
Dramatic Literature*, has suggested that it might be as early as the late fourteenth
century. Translations are mine.
⁴²For rhetoric as the process by which signs are interpreted and glossed, see, e.g.,
Aristotle, *"Art" of Rhetoric*, 1402b–1403a.

repentance (1419–24), a "merciful God" (1439) has the power to remedy the inequities in the punishments and to forgive man's transgression. Here she has broached the issue that lies at the crux of Passion and play: the dramatic clarification that mercy is higher in God's psychic hierarchy than justice (1450–51). This *procès de paradis* functions as a kind of apocalyptic interior monologue and the mystery play itself as the dramatic commemoration of it. For example, when the two daughters of God emerge anew to interpret the theological, juridical, and dramatic signs of the Cain and Abel story, they hear the voice of Abel's blood crying out for Justice (2753–54)—a technique that recalls the mnemonic practice of "playing out" images of a crime in the mind in order to anticipate their reevocation and reenactment by personae during forensic delivery. So even though Lady Justice seeks to condemn all humankind with no "lengthy pleadings" (2793), the images of Cain and Abel and the forensic debates about them have prompted God to articulate his legal principle that good and evil must be punished accordingly (2387–88). Cain alone is punished (2839–48); and the court is in recess until Seth invokes Mercy (3878–79).

At that point, the rhetorico-dramatic function of the play is stated more explicitly still as God commits himself to the incarnation (3965–66): it will not take place until such time as the exemplary visions of Old Testament crimes have told their whole story (3929–36), until they have restaged for the audience the physical evidence of the divine hierarchy of virtues. When Lady Justice complains shortly before the Flood, for example, that God is "too full of clemency and sweetness toward humankind" (5074–75), her request that God (and the audience) behold the terrestrial *ordo vitiorum* is also a request for the interpretation of dramatic images: "Look at this sin here / Does it not require correction?" (5080–81). Lady Mercy objects, of course, that the innocent cannot be condemned with the guilty (5084–89), and that even Lady Justice cannot undermine her own existence by requiring something that is inherently unjust (5111–13). But at this point in the play, a just God can no longer endure the sight of his own creation (5114–17). As in the Arras play, however, he does not carry out his threat to "erase man from the face of the earth" (5126–27)—an act that would cause drama to undermine its own ontology. Instead, God dispatches an angel to Noah with news about the dramatic engenderment of one of the quintessential Christian mnemonic images: the ark.

"I give you the ark of Noah as a model of spiritual building," wrote Hugh of St. Victor, "which your eye may see outwardly so that your

soul may be built inwardly in its likeness."[43] A similar "building"
of the soul is now hypostatized as the mystery play recasts forensic
imagines agentes as dramatic characters to remind the devoted public that they too were created in God's "ymaige" (5616). In a fascinating recontextualization of the *ars memorandi*, God vows to save
Noah "in a secret place" not unlike Geoffrey of Vinsauf's "secret
places of the mind" (*en lieu segret preserveray* [5417].[44] The very
image of the ark thus defies the notion of a mnemonic tabula rasa:
it preserves the just from punishment and commemorates their
goodness onstage. As a Christian memory locus, it allows the continued revelation of a merciful God (5626–45) as it simultaneously
allows the play to continue. In fact, shortly thereafter God provides
a negative mnemonic example in the Tower of Babel (6753–802), a
memory building that signifies linguistic chaos and destroys the
monumentalization of man's iniquity (6769–79). Still, even after
leveling Sodom, God continues to foretell his own clemency toward
humankind (8304–66) in a way that is articulated most strikingly
by the figures of Abraham and Isaac.

   Their tale is introduced with the *engendrement* of a child for Sarah
(8345–50, 8790–801), which exemplifies the dramatic and exegetical
engenderments that will soon be revealed. In the most explicit gloss
offered thus far of the function of the mystery play, God explains
that the *visiones* onstage supply visible proof of a merciful God,
whose loving sacrifice was prefigured (*figurer*) by that of Abraham:
"Le pére me figurera" (The father is the figure of me [2:9470; also
9610–37]), as Christ's sacrifice was prefigured by Isaac (9870–73).
Quite literally, Old Testament images prefigure the Passion of Christ
through dramatic signs. And the prophetic dream "visions" that
enable Abraham to foresee the redeemer "spiritually" (8804) are also
prefiguracions of the New Testament and of its drama:

> Pour monstrer evidentement
> Que j'ay aymé parfaitement
> Et ayme humaine nature,
> Je vueil *prouver notérement*
> Qu'i sera prophetiquement
> Dit de mon filz en l'Escripture. [9435–40; emphasis mine]

[43]Hugh of St. Victor, "De arca Noe," in *Didascalicon*, as quoted in Carruthers,
Book of Memory, 44; also 231–39. In a fascinating discussion of the *arca* in mnemonic
theory, Carruthers notes that although traditionally an *arca* was a box, the word also
referred to the ark of the covenant: "as something to be built, the trained memory
is an *arca* in the sense understood by the Biblical object called Noah's Ark" (43).
[44]Geoffrey of Vinsauf, "New Poetics," trans. Kopp, 35.

> To show in an evident[iary] way that I have loved and love human
> nature perfectly, I wish to prove officially that which will be said
> prophetically of my son in the Holy Scriptures.

Even though Lady Mercy objects here to the violence of some of the
figures,[45] she advocates a totally mediated performance for both law
and the mystery play (so often characterized by actual violence). In
a theory that belongs to the history of aesthetics, she says that the
dramatic prefigurations of the *Passion* are so eloquent in themselves
that the act is no longer necessary: "car il peult souffire / De veoir
sa bonne voulenté" (because it may well suffice to see his goodwill
[9861–62; also 10288, 16740–41]). Once the "perfect obedience" of
both Abraham and Isaac has been commemorated visually (10304),
equity demands that the boy be spared (10343).

Through a forensic system of figurative, mnemonic writing (*figure monstrative* [10344]), dramatic images thus engender the legal
drama that in turn validates oral and written prophecy (les prophecies faictes / Et escriptes [10356–57]). Not only do they demonstrate the psychology of divine legal judgments; they illustrate an
epistemological system that is shared by biblical exegesis, law, and
drama: the proper reading of visible signs. Real/realistic visual
readings of the Bible and its drama (*"veoir reallement"* [10300])
are possible only when divine law has been made visible: "Or
regardés se loy divine / Est point plus ferme et plus certaine / En
ses faitz que nature humaine" (Thus look and see if divine law is
not more firm and certain in its deeds than human nature [10293–
95]). Figures and figurations provide the means by which Christian
rhetoric mediates between God and man, word and action, rhetoric
and drama, oral and written tradition, and, of course, the Old
Testament and the New.

Similar demonstrations occur later during the tale of the prose-
cutions and persecutions of Joseph, when God explains that "to show
by true appearance the effect of divine verdicts" (monstrer par vraye
apparence / L'effect de divine sentence), the Old Testament must
be read as "corresponding figuratively to the New" (figurativement
/ Et correspondant au nouveau [16955–59]). In the same way that
Gréban's *acteur* insisted that divine messages were to be demonstrated "generally and figurally" (grossement et figuraument [24]),
God maintains that *actio* is the only path to understanding, the only

---

[45]Certain figures seem more violent to the modern audience, as when they take
the insidious form of anti-Semitism in God's "prefiguration" of the "damnable Jews"
(16719, 16728–30, 16764–69, 16944–53).

way to reconcile prophetic speech (spoken, written, or sung) with dramatic action:

> Il fault *prefigurer*
> Ce qui est *dit* aux Escriptures;
> Quant il est baillé par *figures*
> En est beaucop mieulx entendu....
> L'Escripture *chante* en ce point.   [16746–51; emphasis mine]

What is uttered in the Scriptures has to be prefigured. When it is rendered by means of figures, it is far better understood, a point that is sung by the Scriptures.

When God confirms that Joseph too is the figure of Jesus (17213) and that his story "accomplishes" earlier prophecies (17229–30), the dramatic figures serve once again as the visual and auditory demonstration of what is legal: "il est *licite* / De *figurer* dessus son corps / Les grandes injures et tors / Que Jesus, mon filz, souffrera" (It is legitimate to figure upon his body the great injuries and wrongs that my son Jesus will suffer [17239–42; emphasis mine]). The figures of law have become the figures of drama as the mnemonic image is given a voice during delivery. Once the figure of the sale of God's son has been similarly "accomplished" (3:18255–57), once it is clear that God will allow his son to don the "cloak of humanity" (18270; also 1:8333, 6:49246–49), the dramatic characters of the *Viel Testament* begin to do the same; that is, with decreasing commentary from the celestial court, the characters begin to engender, interpret, and reenact the rhetorico-dramatic *figuracions*. Mnemonic *imagines agentes* have also donned the "cloak of humanity" in their own incarnations as dramatis personae.

Justice and Mercy appear for the last time at the tale of the burning bush (23389–552) to confirm that the play's semiotic system of figuration has been amply demonstrated. The successful consignment of Old Testament figures to the collective memory ("*perpetuelle memoire*" [26297; also 26430]) depends on the ability of the devoted public to "read" them as dramatic exempla of the Christian law of mercy: "Monstrer vous vueil bien choses telles. / Signifians ... / Que suis plein de misericorde" (Such things do I wish to show you: they signify that I am full of mercy [26300–26303]). As an astonished Moses now witnesses miracles "with eyes wide open" (*a oeul ouvert* [23389]), the audience sees, "discovers," the remainder of the play "directly," "uncovered" (*a descouvert* [23393]), with little or no expository intervention from the celestial court: "Et devant le peuple fera / Plusieurs miracles en publicque" (And before the people he will perform several miracles in public [23399–400]). In the same way, then, that the earliest dramas increasingly replaced narrative with dialogic representation,[46] God and his daughters here withdraw: their roles as litigants, expositors, and exegetes have been fulfilled and henceforth the exemplary tales can speak for themselves. At this point the *procès de paradis* takes its most interesting turn: it disappears.

In the astounding visions that close the *Mistére du Viel Testament*, the prophetic voice is transferred definitively to the stage. The trial has done more than populate the stage with dramatic Old Testament images: it has allowed itself to be replaced by them. After tens of thousands of lines devoted to the passage from forensic image to commemorative drama, the author now reverts to the regenerative mnemonic image, ending the play with a self-reflexive inquiry into the nature of artistic figuration in a Christian recontextualization of the Pygmalion myth. The penultimate scene places a sculptor onstage to refocus attention on the pictorial "effigy" of the beaux arts into which drama breathes new life. Like the dramatist, the sculptor is the creator of art that speaks—a veritable Pygmalion:

> j'ay une fois
> Tout l'art du grant Pigmalion.
> J'ay faict mainte portraction
> Mise dedans le Capitolle:
> Vifve sembloit sans fiction;
> Il ne restoit que la parolle. [6:48553–58]

For, once and for all, I have all the art of the great Pygmalion. I have fashioned many a portrait and had it placed inside the Capitol. Truly, it seemed alive, lacking only the power of speech.

Just as the lawyer drew upon *memoria* to reenact visions of crimes with his own voice during delivery, here the dramatist provides a final demonstration of how the same process engenders didactic drama: devotional images long preserved in the *"perpetuelle memoire"* (26297) wait only to be reendowed with speech by their own Pygmalions in future dramas.

The followers of Octavian have determined that in times of political trouble, the adoration of his "portraicture" will unify the

---

[46]See, e.g., Nicoll, *WD*, 4; Tydeman, *Theatre in the Middle Ages*, 28.

people (48459–63).[47] However, their extensive discussion of the "ymages" (48544), "coulonnes" (48617), and "pilliers" (48464, 48522) reveals that such unity is mnemonic. References to the traditional features of the pillared memory stage serve here to introduce questions of government, law, and idol worship that are also questions of Christian art. In fact, all the characters readily acknowledge that images have extraordinary didactic value: "Il peult de grans biens / Venir de faire telz ouvraiges" (Great profit can come from creating such works [48545–46]). And like the sculptor who "fashions with such authenticity that the statue seems lifelike" (48470–72), the Christian dramatist fashions didactic images for the stage. Indeed, as the sculptor hawks his artistic wares, he first generates the *portraicture* (48584) with words as he invites his interlocutors to a verbal sampling of his work (of the sort the dramatist provides).

After describing Octavian's face, eyes, forehead, nose, chin, and mien, he proceeds to costume—the "main thing" (c'est le principal [48589–602]); and their discussion shifts to the function of dress as a form of emblematic "denotance" (48608–10). The vivid verbal portrait of Octavian wearing a rich imperial robe and holding his sword serves as a *denotance seconde* (48603–13) of his authority, "for the one refers to the other" (car l'un a l'autre *se reffére* [48605]), as the Old Testament corresponds to the New. That mode of visual *denotance*, however, is immediately juxtaposed against the prophetic speech of a sybil who is simultaneously expounding her own version of the Pygmalion myth to her followers. The artist, she maintains, can but imitate God's power of logos to "form a creature" (48715)—and only through his grace. God alone is the authority, the giver of life: "En nature les vivifie; / Ainsi sont les hommes *parfaiz*" (He brings them to life in nature; thus have men been created [48723–24]). And as the verb *parfaire* indicates (it is the term that denotes the enactment of laws), he is also the giver of law. The creative and creational combination of law and invention in drama is the most perfect (*parfait*) artistic mimesis of logos the dramatist can provide. Indeed, drama is defined here as recreational re-creation during delivery of events preserved in the treasure house of memory.

Thus having advanced himself as a Christian Pygmalion, having refocused the audience's attention on the mnemonic origins of de-

---

[47]A similar representation of the Octavian story (minus the explicit references to Pygmalion) appears in *Wrightes Play* after l. 185. The text appears in *The Chester Mystery Cycle*, ed. Lumiansky and Mills, 1:97–124.

livered drama, the author of the *Viel Testament* now speaks through the prophetic voice of his own dramatic character: he has the sybil foretell in a final series of commemorative visions the ultimate legal/ dramatic resolution of the *procès de paradis.* She has been summoned to court by Octavian for a consultation about the interpretation of visible signs in law, rhetoric, theology, and drama. And in a visual and visional activity, she literally foresees how Christ will "assume his humanity" (48736), much as the dramatic characters have done throughout the play. Since the emperor has agreed to bow to her assessment of "what is legal [*licite*]" (48878), she proceeds to tell (and eventually to show) the dramatic signs of the Passion. Her references to the fact that Noah and Abraham have already "prefigured the new law" (49015) now constitute her *arguement* (49003) for the resolution of questions of law with questions of devotional imagery—and for the reenactment of law with dramatic imagery. The sybil anticipates the concordance between divine legal authority and the dramatic authority of the *Passion* as the play affirms what has been foretold: "C'est aprobacion certaine, / Ainsi que disent les *acteurs*" (This is sure and certain proof, as the authorities have stated [49022–23]). Those *acteurs*, however, are not only the Old Testament authorities; they are lawyers and actors (*actores*) and dramatic authors as well (*auctores*). The drama of law becomes the site of the passage from devotional image to prophetic speech as the sybil reminds Octavian of the figurative signification of the burning bush. The Virgin Mary too, she explains, will see a miraculous vision (49024–31) during the mystery of the Annunciation; indeed, so will the audience in what follows.

Octavian, however, is still unclear about the "great fantasy" that God might assume human form (49034–35), so in her final *demonstracion* of dramatic exegesis the sybil offers as proof the *fantasie* of speaking visible signs, of mnemonic *phantasmatae*. To persuade Octavian, she now directs his attention (along with that of the audience) to the sky. There he will "see visibly" (490451) the Virgin, who is about to speak. Like the medieval lawyer before his judge, Octavian removes his hat in deference to this "great and wondrous case" (49072):

Lors se desqueuvre Octovien et regarde au ciel; voit une grande clarté, et est en l'er une Vierge tenant ung enfant entre ses bras. . . . La Voix du ciel tonne, et se monstre encore plus apparement la Vierge et l'enfant, et resplendit grande clarté, tant que Octovien chet a terre

tout pasmé...et puis la Voix du ciel dit.../ "En ce lieu / Est le filz
de Dieu." [After l. 49052]

Then Octavian takes off his hat and looks up at the heavens. There
he sees a great light, and the Virgin in the sky holding a child in her
arms. The voice of the heavens resounds, and the Virgin and Child
appear still more clearly. And the light shines so brightly that Octavian
falls to the ground in a swoon. And the Voice of heaven speaks: "In
this place is the Son of God."

Utterly convinced, he vows henceforth not to be worshiped as a
god but to worship God as his loyal vassal, "kneeling with clasped
hands" (*a joinctes mains, a genoux* [49082]). The sybil's rhetorico-
dramatic meditation has thus served as mediation between the laws
of God and man. All present have witnessed the very genesis of the
holy mystery and mystery play in the probative value of the image,
which is now to be reconsigned to memory:

> Roy tout puissant, qui de vous
> Devons bien faire *memoire*,
> J'ay *veu* la parfaicte gloire....
> *Visiblement* je t'ay *veu*;
> Bien seroye despourveu
> Se ne pensoie au *mistére!*   [49084–91; emphasis mine]

Almighty King, whom all of us must remember clearly, I have seen
the perfect glory. I have seen you visibly. And I would surely be remiss
if I did not reflect upon this great mystery.

Though the Virgin and Child now disappear, their image will remain
in a collective *memoire* that generates and regenerates devotion and
drama.[48]

The play then draws to a close with a final dialogic vision of the
virgin birth that speaks simultaneously to the birth of drama. Twelve
prophetesses come forward to mediate between God and humankind
"in a prophetic manner" (*en maniére de pronostiquer* [after
l. 49146]). In this lengthy *ordo prophetessarum* (49147–386), the
sybils foretell the legal resolution of the *procès* by predicting another
sort of "germination"—that of Christ inside the Virgin: "Car La
Vierge son filz *germinera*, / Puis descendra pour nostre salut querre"
(For from the Virgin's gestation will be engendered a son, who will
descend to earth to seek our salvation [49152–53]). But this is also

---

[48]See also the reference in *Wrightes Play* to having "full memorye / of the angells
melodye" (707–8).

a reference to the germination of drama; for as Christ will light man's way out of darkness (49154), the prophetic visions of the play are as candles that illuminate the engenderment of drama from Christian mnemonic imagery. Themselves regenerated by the *procès de paradis*, they supply mnemonic foundations of Christian equity and Christian drama past and present:

> Une *chandelle*
> Vient par la quelle
> Tenébres en lueur seront....
>   *Ceulx qui ouront*
>   *Ou qui verront*
> Sa beaulté splendide, immortelle,
> Par admiracion diront:
> "Vecy les jours qui gueriront
> Adam et toute sa sequelle." [49180–91; emphasis mine]

A candle will come which will bring darkness into light. Those who will hear or those who will see its splendid and immortal beauty will say with admiration: "Here are the days that will cure Adam and all his lineage."

It is no coincidence that the dramatic equivalent here of "No mortal eye hath seen, no mortal ear hath heard such wondrous things" is also a juridical formula—that most pervasive of openings for French medieval legal documents: "A tous ceux qui ces presentes lettres verront ou orront." It is the vision of Christ resolving the *procès de paradis* (49158–69) that reconciles man with God, Old Testament with New, prophecy with action, law with drama, and ultimately drama with prayer as humankind is prompted to voice praise of the regenerative powers of Christ and his images: "Pour sa peine et sa souffréte / Nature en sera refaicte" (By his pain and suffering Nature will be regenerated [49288–89]). Similarly, by virtue of its own speaking dramatic images the *Mistére du Viel Testament* is equally regenerative and mediatory: "Par parolles tu le verras, / Dont en fin te resjouyras" (By words you will see it [the miracle of his birth] and finally rejoice in it [49300–49301]). Even though humankind is already "imagining" (49332) with horror the *disfigurement* of Christ's human incarnation (49336), the memory images provided by the play remain ever pure and perfect. All bless the Crucifixion as God's most holy and vivid sacrifice (49356–63)—a dramatic image now consigned to the memory of the audience (49378–86), who may reconstruct it through prayer. The future Pygmalions among them may reconstruct it through drama as well. It is they who are now responsible for preserving the dramatic imagery of Christian judgment in enduring art forms such as this play.

The Proof as Play

Since forensic rhetoric was not only a theme but a fundamental literary structure, its influence on the comic trial proves equally revealing. While radically different in context, such works as the *Pathelin*, the *Farce des drois de la Porte Bodès*, and the *Farce du pect* bespeak the consistent theatricalization of forensic rhetoric in a way that is no less stunning than in the *procès de paradis*. Analysis of these particularly litigious farces reveals that the *procès* is neither a stale formulaic entity nor the first step toward "psychological comedy," as Aubailly claims (*TM*, 151–60). Rather, when these disorderly courtrooms are called to "order," they recall Lucian's broadly sketched sophistic buffoon and Tacitus's traveling judge more than they do individual psychology. As the performance of forensic rhetoric is now assumed by such stock juridical characters as the *trompeur* and the *trompé*, they too participate in the aestheticization of the law. Drawn to the "spectacle of a fight," lawyer and client, actor and audience perpetuated a spectacle that had contagious popularity. And, like their dialectically inclined peers, the more rhetorically inclined dramatists discovered in legal mimesis a rich model for dramatic invention. Their own theatricalization of the law, however, had little to do with proof and everything to do with the pleasure and ostentation of the agon—a pleasure that the playwright had but to exploit onstage. In fact, the most dramatic feature of all these plays may well be the forensic rhetoric they stage so scrupulously.

The *Farce de Pathelin*

Down to the most minor detail of removing and replacing the furry hat during delivery (1218), *Pathelin* recreates the protodrama of law.[49] When the victimized Clothier indicates that he cannot

---

[49]All references to the mid-fifteenth-century *Farce de Maistre Pierre Pathelin* are to Pickford's edition and are given parenthetically by line number. The English translation is by Alan Knight and appears in Maddox's *Semiotics of Deceit*, 173–99. For an excellent analysis of elements of legal ritual in the *Pathelin*, see Harvey, 144–71, esp. his argument that late-medieval juridical practice would not have required lawyers to be present at such petty litigation (152–61).

proceed without the presence of counsel (1223–26), a hurried judge insists that the parties "deliver" immediately: "J'é ailleurs à entendre! . . . Délivrés-vous, sans plus d'atente" (I have cases to hear elsewhere. State the case yourself without delay [1227–29]). And as the Clothier/plaintiff begins his tale of legal woes (1237–49), Pathelin begins to flaunt his lawyerly talent for impersonation by hiding his identity through the subterfuge of a toothache (1255–56). A feigned malady will do quite nicely, thank you, in the juridical comedy he has "plotted" beforehand with Thibault L'Aignelet. The comic courtroom is then called to logical and theatrical disorder: "Avant, achevés de plaider! / Sus! Conclués appertement!" (Proceed! Finish your deposition. Come on, be brief about it [1261–62]). Irrelevant answer will counter irrelevant question, ad hominem attack will follow non sequitur as all are drawn into the genius of a confusing conflict about the theft of some cloth. Only the Judge is left to wonder aloud what fabric has to do with the case before him: "What's he saying about cloth?" (1267).

As the quintessential imitation of the degeneration of law from proving to pleading, the courtroom of the *Pathelin* becomes the locus for precisely the sort of ridiculous agon with which lawyers traditionally indulged their audiences: "Paix! De par le deable, vous [b]avés! / Et ne sçavés-vous revenir / A vostre propos sans tenir / La Court de telle baverie?" (Silence! The Devil take you for running off at the mouth! Can't you get back to your deposition without delaying the court with such drivel? [1283–86]). The scheming Pathelin could not agree more, amused by his success at casting the hapless Clothier as the fool in this trial: "Oh, my tooth aches, but I can't help laughing" (1287). Whence the celebrated response of the Judge: "Sus! revenons à ces moutons" (Come now, let's get back to those sheep [1291])—the terrestrial equivalent of God's insistence in the *procès de paradis* that the daughters return to the "main point" (*fait principal* [Gréban, 2225]). Despite the Judge's admonishment that the proper pasture of the attorney is truth, the litigants seem far more interested in presenting a *cause fictive:* "Sommes-nous becjaunes / Ou cornards? Où cuidés-vous estre?" (Do you take us for fools or simpletons? Where do you think you are? [1293–94]). But a fictional case engendered from the mimesis of legal rhetoric is exactly what this is. Still, is Pathelin simply continuing his masterly impersonation of a lawyer, finely honed during a lifetime of lawyering (*advocassaige* [7]), or is the lawyer imitating Pathelin? The legal grazing proper (*paistre* [1295]) then begins with the mimed spectacle of Thibault's characteristic "Baas" (1301).

The shepherd was initially identified by the Clothier as a silent party who "is not saying a word" (1233–34), but the court will in fact manage to get a single comic *mot* out of him. This is hardly Francis I changing the linguistic venue of his courtroom to impress Charles V with a forensic spectacle; this is a transformation of argument to nonsense designed to amuse the audience with the farce of the legal process itself. The shepherd's response to the Judge's query "Am I a goat?" (1302) is refusal to speak French, Latin, or any possible court language except that of impersonation. The frustrated Judge attempts to reinstitute forensic logic: "Et, taisés vous! Estes-vous nice? / Laissés en paix ceste assessoire, / Et venons au principal" (What! Hold your tongue! Are you dense? Set aside this accessory matter and let's get back to the principal [1311–13]). But the "principal" here is the courtroom histrionics that such theorists as Basin had endeavored to erase. Like the Judge and the audience, the Clothier has been ensnared in a legal farce. Despite his promise to keep to the putative subject of the trial (1315–16) and to "conclude quickly" (1366), the Clothier finds himself unable to indulge the Judge—but eminently able to indulge the audience. He continues to play the fool as he wanders from subject to subject, just as the Basochiens wandered physically about the space of the Grand' Chambre. Though the Judge claims that he will not tolerate such babbling and confusion ("There's neither rime [*sic*] nor reason in any of your railing and ranting" [1345–46]); in the end legal "reasoning" proves far more appealing for its poetry than for its logic: instead of pursuing truth, these characters play out a legal process that is pure mimesis.

Pathelin now comes forward with his finest impersonation yet: he is the master swindler when he plays the lawyer. Never the noble Ciceronian servant of the state, Pathelin resembles Lucian's singer of legal tales, an intoning "pleader" who took the low road to marry the actress Lady Rhetoric. Indeed, he boasts of just that to Guillemette at the beginning of the play, declaiming that he is as learned as any noble rhetorician, even with no formal training: "Si n'aprins oncques à lettre / Que ung peu. Mais je me ose vanter / Que je sçay aussi bien chanter / Ou livre avec nostre prestre / Que se j'eusses esté à maistre / Autant que Charles en Espaigne" (It's true I don't know much Latin, but when I chant with our priest from the massbook, it sounds like I've studied for as long as Charlemagne stayed in Spain [22–27]). The master of a variety of roles and tongues (as he demonstrates so eloquently in his polyglot delirium scene [5]), Pathelin even manages to counterfeit a description of the Christian mediatory function of the law by offering to take Thibault's case with no thought of personal gain (1367–82): "Ce bergier ne peult nullement / Respondre au fais que l'en propose / S'il n'a du conseil" (This shepherd cannot answer the charges against him without counsel [1367–69]).

What a performance! As Pathelin now mimics divine legal ministration in a staged conference with his client, the nonsensical drama plotted out earlier by lawyer and client unfolds. For surely if Francis I could prestage parliamentary hearings to impress visiting dignitaries, Pathelin could do so to amuse visiting spectators. After numerous bleatings, Pathelin effectively sums up the widespread degeneration of the juridical process, claiming that such folly has no place in the courtroom: "Or est-il plus fol qui boute / Tel fol naturel en procès!" (It takes a real ass to bring such a poor fool to trial [1393–94]). But the essence of this comedy is that just such folly utterly dominated the courtroom. In a comic version of the radical solutions proposed by Basin and Vives, Pathelin now suggests that the source of the folly—the *mimi*—be removed from the courtroom (an echo of the dubious edict in the Benedictus Levita?):[50] "Ha! Sire, renvoyés l'en à ses / Brebis. Il est fol de nature.... / Que mauldit soit-il qui ajourne / Telz folz, ne ne fait ajourner!" (Send him back to watch his sheep, *sine die*, never to return. A plague on him who brings charges against such natural-born fools [1395–1402]).

While the Clothier insists in vain that due process demands that he be heard (1403–4), he is helpless in this legalistic carnival.[51] His final attempt to present "conclusions" that are neither farce nor folly (1408–10) is immediately undermined as he resumes his role of the babbling *trompé*, still obsessed by the non sequitur of his stolen cloth (1423–26). For these stock characters of legal drama, there is no escape from their comic roles: "Je vous cognois à la parolle, / Et à la robe, et au visaige" (I recognize you by your speech, by your clothes, and by your face [1429–30]). *Moqueries* are the very foundation of this court: "Ce sont toutes tribouilleries / Que de plaider à folz ne à folles!" (Nothing but vexation comes of bringing suit against fools and simpletons [1411–12]). Even though the Clothier says that he is "not crazy" but sane (1431) and promises to analyze the entire case (1433), there are no *staseis* here, no syllogisms, no

[50]See Chambers, *Mediaeval Stage*, 1:37–38.
[51]Readers familiar with Bakhtin's discussion in *Rabelais and His World*, 5–8, will recognize the allusion; see also his remarks on the Fête des Fous in that context, 73–76.

enthymemes, no real argumentation: only Pathelin's request for silence—a request reminiscent of the one so often made of the noisy
Basochiens: "Hée, sire, imposés-leur silence! / N'av'ous honte de
tant débatre... / Veilz brebiailles ou moutons" (Please, Your Honor,
bring them to order. [To the Clothier.] Aren't you ashamed to haul
this poor shepherd into court for three or four grubby old sheep
[1436–38]). So like the authors of the *procès de paradis* who sub-
verted forensic rhetoric in favor of a noble transformation of devotional image to dramatic one, the comic author also subverts the
process—but in a different way: the image that dominates is that of
the histrionic lawyer himself, delivering the drama of law to please
the crowd.

Now it is the Clothier who inquires about the relevance of the
refrain about sheep: "Quelz moutons? C'est une viele?" (What
sheep? It's always the same old song! [1441]). A refrain (*viele*),
however, is exactly what it is, of the sort made (in)famous by
Lucian's legal song-and-dance man. The music of this legal erudition bears not the slightest resemblance to the *resonance* of
Gréban's *reson*. Indeed, the Judge has heard quite enough of this
asinine melody: "He won't stop braying for the rest of the day"
(1446). The beastly singing continues momentarily as the Clothier
makes a last futile attempt to make sense out of nonsense; but
he only compounds the nonsense by re-introducing the cloth he
has promised not to discuss: "Je luy parle de drapperie / Et il
respont de bergerie!" (I talk to him about cloth and he answers
me in sheep [1456–57]). At this point the rhetorico-dramatic *bergerie* has gone on long enough; it has truly fatigued the judge's
"stomach" (Quintilian, IV, 2.121) and he now desires another re-
past—dinner. So the Judge closes the case by sending Thibault back
to his ovine objects of imitation: "Je l'assolz de vostre demande
/ Et vous deffenz le procéder. / C'est ung bel honneur de plaider
/ A ung fol. Va-t-en à tes bestes" (I absolve him of your charges
and forbid you to proceed. A fine thing it is to bring suit against
a fool. Go back to your sheep [1471–74]).

Having profited from a legal system in which bleating is the most
effective mode of rhetorical proof, the shepherd offers a final *bée* of
thanks to the Judge as a defeated Clothier and a hungry Judge offer
the ultimate description of medieval legal practice: *fol* pleading
against *fol* about petty matters in a comic verbal battle that is as
appealing as any farce. In fact, the *Pathelin* has demonstrated that
the legal battle *is* a farce. Forensic rhetoric serves *tromperie* instead
of truth by means of its own spectacle: it is the quintessential por-

trait of its own *letteraturizzazione,* of the *affabulation* implied in Tacitus's description of how lawyers "chatted" *(fabulamur)* with judges.[52] It is the dramatic demonstration of how the beauty of legal language becomes its own reward, as Guillemette argued eloquently at the beginning of the play with her retelling of the fable of the crow and the fox (438–59): "Vous m'avéz trompé faulsement, / Et emporté furtivement / Mon drap, par vostre beau langage" (You tricked me with your eloquent speeches and carried my cloth away like a thief [1480–82]). And in the end that language serves the aesthetic needs of drama better than the juridical needs of equity. The *Pathelin* thus reenacts the transformation of the courtroom into a theater.

Now absolved (1490–92), Thibault departs over the Clothier's objections: "Es-se raison qu'il s'en aille / Ainsi?" (But is it right for him to go like that? [1495–96]). But clearly reason has little do with the drama of rhetoric or the rhetoric of drama. Justice? Righteousness? Logical argumentation? "Don't be ridiculous," implies the traveling judge, eager to depart before the curtain rises on his next legal drama (1496); because that is not what law is about. It is about *trompeur* and *trompé* sending each other "out to pasture" (1586) by means of clever rhetorical ruses. The fact that the *Pathelin* draws to a close outside the courtroom is thus eminently logical, given that law had retained its ties to an art whose legal value had long been questionable: mimicry. Pathelin implies as much when he compliments his pastoral client on a comic performance worthy of any histrionic lawyer: "Tu as très bien fait ton debvoir, / Et aussi très bonne contenance" (To tell the truth, you played your part very well; you looked good [1551–52]). The lesson Pathelin learns when he too receives bleating instead of cash is that in the widespread comedy of law, he is not the "master *trompeur*" (1587–88) or the king of *"bailleurs de parolles en payement"* (those who give their word in payment [1589–90]) because he has been bested by a simple shepherd (1592). Nevertheless, in the tradition of Quintilian, Tacitus, Lucian, and the Basoche, he and his cohorts were the *bailleurs* of comic *parole.* The curtain then falls with the promise of yet another legal farce: "Par saint Jacques, se je trouvasse / Ung bon sergent, je te fisse prendre!" (By Saint James, if I could find an officer, I'd have you arrested [1593–94]). And the implication is that lawyers (and dramatists) will continue to relish those roles.

[52]Tacitus, *Dialogus de oratoribus,* 39.

The *Farce des drois de la Porte Bodès*

Rhetorical exploitation of the protodrama of law is more striking still in the *Farce nouvelle très bonne des drois de la Porte Bodès et de Fermer l'huis*, a satirical portrayal of Basin's litigious people.[53] Though it's a far cry from the noble debates of the four daughters of God, this minor domestic dispute between a cobbler and his wife as to who should get up and close the door provides structural unity to the play as effectively as any *procès de paradis*. Most interesting of all is the fact that the legal bleating of this farce stages forensic rhetoric in order to recontextualize the law. Eventually, when the Cobbler's wife reaches into her rhetorical bag of tricks for a new legal authority, she too will transform the letter of the law into a new female spirit of the law.

The play opens with the pusillanimous Cobbler returning home after a hard day's work, afraid of drinking beer because of the noise it makes in his tummy (7–8). Little does he know that the "noise" that awaits him in his own *foyer* is legal noise: quite literally, his wife is about to "lui chercher des noises" (pick a [legal] fight with him). After the Cobbler purports to hear his wife braying (*braire*) in the distance (13–14), the juridical bleating begins almost immediately. She greets him with a dispute he has already staged in his mind (17–19), proceeding directly to the bone of contention: the open door, which she blames her "beast" of a husband for having left open (29–34). The game begins as the hapless husband attempts to give domestic orders to his better half: "Allés le fermer!" (Go on and shut it [35])—words he will live to regret. But his wife shuts neither the door nor her mouth; and she correctly identifies the legal issue at stake here: male versus female authority. She has better things to do than waste her time with household duties that are more properly his own: "J'ay bien autre besongne à faire, / Mais vous, c'est vostre droit affaire" (I have far better things to do; and besides, it's your own duty [36–37]). He asks again. She refuses again, thanking him not to put on airs: "Et cuidez-vous que je vous serve / Comme ung prince?" (And do you think I'm going to wait on you as if you were a prince? [41–42]).

The Cobbler's attempt at deductive logic proves equally ineffective. Clearly one of them has to get up, he argues, and as the man of the house, he may choose which one: "Il fault que l'ung de nous

[53]This fifteenth-century text appears in Cohen's *Receuil de farces françaises*, 159–64. Translations are mine.

y voise, / Ou certes, il y aura noyse" (One of us has to go or there will be trouble [48–49]). Since the wife has already rejected his major claim to *droits de seigneur* in the *foyer*, legal *noyse* there will be— noise that will help her to institute a new body of female law at the end of the play. Nor is she the least bit intimidated by the uncivilized principle on which her husband seeks to ground his authority—the threat of physical force: "And do you think you're going to scare me?" (52). After all, that was precisely what forensic language (as described by Cicero and Alcuin) was designed to mediate. Moreover, she counters, if anyone has *seigneurie* around the house, it is she. Her husband, of course, accepts her authority no more readily than she accepts his; and he continues his vain threats that "she will be sorry" (60). Still, she remains unmoved (and unwilling to move).

At this point the Cobbler resorts to the most ignoble of insults ad feminam: despite her assertions that she is in fact a noblewoman, entitled to servants to attend to such menial tasks as shutting the door (55–58), the Cobbler proffers the only logical explanation for her disrespect of his *seigneurie*. She is either too fat or too lazy: "Par ma foy, le cul trop vous poise / Ou c'est paresse qui vous tient!" (I dare say, either your ass is weighing you down too much or it's your own laziness). To her retort that if anyone has those problems, it's he ("What about you, anyway?"), the husband responds by articulating his own imperfect understanding of domestic law: "Pas n'apartient / Qu'ung homme s'abesse à sa femme. / On me reputeroit infame / Devant Dieu et devant le monde! / Vas le fermer!" (It's no man's business to humble himself before his wife. People would think me dishonored before God and everyone. Go on and shut it) (73–79). His command that she close the door is also a command that she abandon the conflictual language with which she is challenging his authority; that is, that she also shut her mouth.

Faced with her renewed refusal to bow to his renewed threats that "you will see whether or not you will be mistress of the house" (85– 86), the frustrated Cobbler attempts to buttress his view of conjugal law with the very "wisdom" that his wife will topple at the end of the play. Woman's duty is, of course, to please her husband: "En grant peine vit, par ma foy, / Qui ne peut jouir de sa femme, / Va tost fermer cest huis" (By God, it's a hard life when a man can't take pleasure in his wife. Now go and close that door [89–91]). He also abandons conflictual language in favor of the physical "mediation" that law was intended to replace: he strikes his wife (97–98), who strikes back immediately (101–2). This is scarcely Alcuin's civilized eloquence that had calmed the savage impulses of the first inhabitants of the earth. But eventually this violence does, in fact, elicit the more mediatory form of legal discourse in the form of an unscrupulous passing lawyer who is only too happy to offer his services for a fee. It is no coincidence that when the husband suffers the physical assault of his wife, he cries *haro*, the juridical plea for princely intervention cited in Basin's *Apologie* (259–61): "Haro! ma femme me veult batre, / Au meurdrier, à l'aide, bonnes gens!" (Haro! my wife is trying to beat me up! Murder! help! anybody! [103–4]).

While awaiting assistance, the Cobbler has no choice but to "surrender" temporarily and "beg for mercy," at least until he can plead his case in court. The temporary solution is drama, as he asks his wife's indulgence in putting on a little spectacle of his authority. She will pretend that it is he who is beating her by emitting a "most hideous scream" (ung cry treshideux) to convince their neighbors that he is master of the house, even though she will actually be beating him (106–14). Like Lucian's Professor, he seeks to maintain the appearance of authority—a favor his wife willingly grants in return for real authority. Victorious, she agrees to the farce with a convincing histrionic performance:

> Je vous entens bien: A la mort!
> Au meurdre! mon mary me tue,
> S'on ne m'aide, je suis perdue.
> Ha! le mauvais, ha! le truant!
> Me turas-tu, dy, chien puant!
> Helas! la teste il m'a assommée. [115–20]

I understand perfectly: Help! Murder! My husband is killing me! I'm lost if you don't help me! Ah, the fiend, ah! the criminal! Are you trying to kill me, you stinking dog? Alas! he has bashed my head in.

Still, though the Cobbler now sports the physical evidence of her "persuasion" all over his head and back, he continues to refuse to shut the door. Superior in physical "eloquence," his wife now tries her hand at verbal persuasion: Why should they both waste their time on such a minor matter? In all the time they have spent talking about the door, it could have been closed. Again the closed door emerges as a metaphor for the closed mouth: "C'est pour nostre huis qui n'est pas clos, / Vous en fault-il tant sermonner? / Jamais n'en deussiés mot sonner" (It's because our door isn't closed that you have to do all this pontificating? You should never have said a word about it). But the existence of both the dispute and the play depends on the difficulty in shutting either one. After all, extensive histrionic verbiage about ridiculous matters was the very essence of medieval law as the Basochiens practiced it. The Cobbler's wife then goes on to articulate what Quintilian and Lucian had stated long before her: by transforming law into a dramatic spectacle, male speakers had come to resemble women: "Vous dictes bien qu'entre nous femmes / Caquetons tousjours, mes vous-mesmes / Ne vous en povés pas tenir" (You say that we women are always yacking, but you yourselves can't keep from doing the same) [125–32]).

In a bizarre proposal for a "compromise," the Cobbler now suggests a game of silence that will reveal authority better than the game of words: whichever of the two of them speaks first will close the door (135–37). In other words, the outcome of the game of closed mouths will lead more effectively to a closed door. Initially, however, their subsequent dickering casts doubt on whether either one can remain silent long enough for the wager to begin. Each accuses the other of the kind of "chattering" and "debating" with which the Basochiens habitually disrupted the court. The Cobbler maintains that he has never seen a woman who could resist yacking and debating (caqueter ou de tencer [141–43]); she insists that he does twice the gabbing that she does (149–50). This is a description of the degeneration of law itself: too many words about nothing and too many words about words. When the couple finally stop talking after line 158, an expert in that particular area intervenes to mediate—a passing judge. Thus far, this farce has effectively transferred the histrionic spectacle of forensic rhetoric to the foyer, all the while suggesting that it has never left there. The contagious influence of litigation decried by Basin (Apologie, 262–63) might thus have been perpetuated by ordinary people as contentious as the Cobbler and his wife. What the comic foyer is to litigation the law is to farce, with lawyers imitating histrionic domestic disputers and domestic parties imitating lawyers in their own homes—an interplay that is clear as the Judge intervenes.

On his way to some unspecified revel, he asks directions to Saint-Lorens and is astonished that the two esbahis (170) answer his query with a veritable dumb show: "Le savetier luy fait des signes du doy" (the cobbler makes hand signals [after l. 169]). Having ruled out the Cobbler as a conversation-partner and source of information, the Judge now turns to the "sweet" and "mute" "little woman" (famelete [177–78]), flattering her with an invitation to a private interview (180–85). His compliments on her quiet discretion cause her to break her vow of silence with a vicious diatribe against her "crazy, nasty creep of a rogue" of a husband (*fol malostru, meschant coquart* [187]). Of course, the elated Cobbler points out immediately that she has lost the wager and must now close the door. It is when she refuses to honor their agreement that their domestic dispute is moved to the formal legal arena.

Now incredulous, the husband demands in vain that she keep her promise in good faith, obey his commands, and do what is right and proper by closing the door (208–11). Far from demurring to his view of the law, however, she reasserts her own authority. Not only does she refuse to obey him, she insists that he must obey her: "Ne jà n'obeiray à toy, / Ainçoys obeiras à moy" (Never will I obey you: in fact, it is you who will obey me! [221–22; also 212–13]). Domestic battle play becomes courtroom drama as the Cobbler's legal cause of action (failure to fulfill a contract) becomes clear. In order to vindicate his rights as master, he must haul her "before the judge" (224–27). As it happens, the opposite result will obtain: her reminder to her husband that she could still break his neck if she desired (245–46) will soon be buttressed by legal superiority as well.

When they arrive before the tribunal, the Cobbler (like Pathelin) greets the Judge with a *captatio benevolentiae*, and a duly flattered Judge invites him to speak first. After the Cobbler outlines the details of their dispute, the Judge confirms the existence of their contract, and the Cobbler demands swift judgment against his wife. Medieval justice swift? The Judge declines, of course, desirous of inquiring more thoroughly into this farcical cause of action. Elevating the *cause fictive* before him to the nobility of a Jean de Meun, the Judge requests legal and dramatic text and gloss: "Se seroit trop fait en bejaune / A moy de juger quelque chose, / Se je n'entens teste et glose" (It would be too *becjaune* of me to make a judgment about something without an understanding of text and gloss). The Cobbler is only too happy to oblige by glossing his very existence with an enumeration of the signs of his henpeckedness: his wife often curses him out, and she disobeys direct orders to close the door. Sympathetic to the plight of a member of his own gender, the Judge cajoles the poor fellow into articulating the crux of the case: this woman wants to be "mistress" of the house. Those words are sufficient cause for the Judge to bond forthwith with the complainant: "Elle est malle fame pour toy. . . . / il convient qu'elle soit pugnie" (She is no wife for you! She must be punished!) (250–85).

Be that as it may, the Cobbler's wife demands to be heard, and proceeds to manipulate the *stasis* of absolute issue in order to put a stop to this male fraternization. Stepping forward with a logic that rivals that of Lady Mercy, she readily admits that she broke their agreement, but claims that her actions are governed by "law and reason" and are not crimes. Furthermore, if criminality there be, it lies in the fallacious male domination of women: "Les hommes en toute saison / Doivent estre jugés à nous" (Men must be judged by us at all times). The Judge is stupefied by the notion that any man, no matter how unworthy, should obey his wife, and he asks by what body of law such principles of female equity have been authorized: "Et dea! desquelz droitz usés-vous? / Dictes-le-moy pour abreger, / Affin que je puisse juger" (What is this? What kind of laws are you invoking? Tell me briefly, so I can render judgment) (296–98). In his request for clarification, however, he has in fact made it possible for her to introduce a written document that will reverse his own authority. Forensic rhetoric is staged for the purpose of subverting itself as the Cobbler's wife responds by crowning the dramatic *letteraturizzazione* of eloquence with the "feminization" of the law. Spelling out the privileges that are woman's due, she becomes judge and jury over a submissive husband, meting out chores and punishments when appropriate: wife may chastise and correct husband when she is displeased, punish and beat him, and command him to perform all manner of household chores, which he must do without contradiction or complaint. That, she proclaims, is woman's legal due: "Velà les estatus entiers / Que les femmes doivent avoir" (And there you have all the rights to which women are entitled) (302–19).

Unfamiliar with those *ordonnances*, however, and dissatisfied with her evasive claim that her authority comes from "a certain place in this town" (320–23), the Judge demands to know the author of this outrageous doctrine that was "si liberal / De vous donner telle franchise" (so generous in according you such liberty). The Cobbler's wife complies immediately by citing the relevant source: it is none other than "les droits de la Porte Bouldès" (363), authored by "a certain provost prized by all" (327–30). Now producing documentary proof for the canonization of female authority, she commands him to read for himself that "nous en avons l'auctorité, / Lisés là tout le contenu" (we do have authority over all that. Read all the contents for yourself [333–34]). In a classic example of the interaction between oral and written transmission within the law, the Judge now reads the doctrine aloud. As he does so, his male voice affirms the constancy of female authority in the supervision of husbandly cooking, sewing, washing, spinning, baking, dish washing, bed making, house cleaning, extinguishing the candle before bed, and being beaten for disobedience (335–58): "Je treuve en escript

cy devant / Que l'homme doit estre servant / De sa femme en toutes
manières... / Et de ce ne soit point rebelle" (Herein I find written
that the man must be servant to his wife in all ways and not recal-
citrant in this) (336–45). Having thus sounded the death knell of
male rhetorical authority, the Judge resolves trial and play by cod-
ifying the "droits de la Porte Bouldès" as legal doctrine, dramatic
performance, and textual artifact. Himself bowing to its teachings,
he now orders the Cobbler (and all his male counterparts) to close
the door on their conception of their authority—legal, rhetorical,
domestic, or otherwise. That they will do every day, and willingly,
or risk prosecution. Future "lengthy trials" are unnecessary, given
the beautiful statutes to which men must submit. Needless to say,
in closing his mouth, the Cobbler must also close the door "par
nostre sentence et par droit" (by my verdict and by law) (359–72).

Gravely disappointed, the Cobbler has no choice but to renounce
his own authority in favor of that of womankind: "Chères dames,
par ma simplesse, / Il me conviendra fermer l'uys / Et ma femme
sera mestresse" (Dear ladies, because of my naiveté, it is up to me
to close the door and my wife shall be mistress [379–81]). The lawyer/
dandy of classical antiquity and the transvestite Basochien of the
Fête des Fous have given way to the feminine theatricalization of
the law. As the play draws to a close, an ungracious female victor
tells the impotent Cobbler that he had better respect the letter and
spirit of the new law or she will throw him into a well (382–83).
The Cobbler utters a final plea for indulgence from the female audience for the weaker male sex, and especially for the rhetorico-
dramatic spectacle that has finally placed legal authority in the
hands of those whom regenerate "pleaders" had resembled for centuries: women.

The *Farce du pect*

Finally, another particularly engaging trial serves as plot, comedy,
and commentary on the drama of law in the fifteenth-century *Farce
nouvelle et fort joyeuse du pect*.[54] In a new mediation of domestic
warfare, we find husband Hubert impatient for his supper, and wife
Jehannette needing a little help lifting a "burden" so she can set the
table. Since no assistance from Hubert is forthcoming (news of the
"droits de la Porte Bouldès" has apparently not yet reached him),

[54]The text of the play appears in Viollet-le-Duc, *Ancien Théâtre français*, 1:94–
110. References are to page numbers. See also Harvey's discussion of this play, 125–
29. Translations are mine.

she squats alone to attend to the task. And suddenly there is an audible sign to be interpreted. The nose now emerges as a more credible witness than the eyes or the ears, and the gloss of the fart begins: "Sus donc! O que ay-je ouy sonner?" (But lo! what was that I heard ring out? [95]).

While this is scarcely the noble imagistic *prefiguracion* of the *Viel Testament*, the *pect* serves this comic drama of legal exegesis in much the same way: the epistemological inquiry into its ontological status permeates the entire farce as the couple focus first on defining the sound. Jehannette speculates that the noise was probably due to something breaking or falling. But Hubert insists that he is quite expert in the interpretation of these phenomena and has no trouble identifying the sound: "it's a fart." The next step is to determine its locus of origin ("I know not whence it comes") and to affix blame. Rising to the argumentative challenge immediately, Jehannette hurtles her first enthymeme, deducing that the person who first smelt it is the responsible party: "Qui premier l'a sentu l'a faict. / Je n'en ay faict ne sentu nulz" (The one who first smelled it did it: I neither smelled nor did anything). Sniffing out that her logic is designed to mask guilt, Hubert tries another approach, refining and redefining his terms in order to attribute the crime, if not to her person, then to the offending anatomical part: "your asshole" (95).

Semantic precision notwithstanding, Jehannette still pleads innocent to the odorous crime. Surely it is impossible, she argues, that a body could commit such an act unknowingly. But Hubert is not so sure, inasmuch as the act originates "from behind," where it cannot be seen. In accordance with juridical issue, Jehannette continues to deny responsibility for the action, drawing upon the ethos of her own nobility: "I am of better lineage / and cleaner than you say." Hubert's continued badgering prompts her continued denials until the couple reach a stalemate that requires adjudication by a higher authority. Hubert will have his day in court: "Je entreray en jugement, / Affin que j'en aye justice" (I'll take you to court so I can be vindicated). And lo and behold, the Procureur is already there, eavesdropping outside the door to solicit this noteworthy case for his personal gain: "ung differend il a / Entre ces gens; il fault sçavoir / Se gaignage y pourroye avoir / En leur debast" (there's a quarrel between these folks: I must learn if there is anything to be gained from their dispute). Jehannette assures her husband that it is pointless to haul her before a judge without any proof, especially since she has every intention of lying under oath. Still, Hubert is undaunted, relying on her desire to avoid the embarrassment of public accusation of "such a huge fart." But Jehannette is not embarrassed and threatens to accuse him each time he accuses her in the "genius" of this weighty conflict. As a frustrated Hubert wonders aloud where a lawyer can be found when you need one, the fart-chasing Procureur appears hawking his legal wares: "Il est grant temps de me monstrer. / Çà, qui veult en procès entrer / Se vienne vers moy droicte voye" (It's high time I showed myself. Hear! hear! anyone wanting to go to trial, let them come straight to me! (96–98). The couple may come straight toward him, but there is nothing straight about the legal path all will follow.

At first the conjugal dispute becomes a battle for the ear of the unscrupulous lawyer—a sophistic fellow who seeks to engage both husband and wife as clients ("I will serve both one and the other well." As the accusations and denials fly, the lawyer asks to hear the husband first, dismissing Jehannette as unreliable: "Je croy que vous me bavez" (I think you're raving). Hubert now states the essence (as it were) of their domestic *différend*. Husband and lawyer join together to name the ill wind: "It's a fart." Even though this dispute should remain in the *mesnaige*, the Procureur is eager to litigate: "Il fauldroit bien des advocatz / Pour la matière disputer" (You have to have lawyers to dispute this matter). After all, much pleasure was to be derived from a legal war of words performed by histrionic *actores*. At this point, he attempts to "get to the bottom" of this litigious matter with Jehannette alone. Fearful at first of being the subject of mockery, Jehannette finally confesses the awful legal truth on which the *moquerie* of the farce revolves. All the while acknowledging that she committed the crime, she cites the assumptive issue in her defense, imputing blame to her husband as the responsible party: he rushed her so much that when she bent down, something "escaped her." An interested Procureur accepts the argument and the case, indicting Hubert for having placed Jehannette in an untenable legal/physical position: "Il a tort donc. / Car c'est peine extraordinaire" (Then he is wrong: for this is cruel and unusual). Jehannette is persuaded by his assurances of victory in court ("all such instances are punished") and engages him as her attorney (98–101). But the lawyer has not yet had his fill of money and possible glory: pleading two cases would double his pleasure, so he turns his attention to Hubert.

Poor Hubert! He now claims to have been sore afraid when he heard the incredible boom: "J'eus si peur / Que encores le cul me hallette" (I was so afraid that my butt is still quaking). Moreover, the disgusting act has soiled the propriety of his clean house and she must atone for it: "Je veuil qu'il [me] répare l'injure, / Que m'a faict[e] en ma maison" (I want the offense she committed against me in my own home to be atoned for). The crafty lawyer is delighted with his findings, and now proffers similar assurances of legal triumph to Hubert. With the second client as delighted as the first (and promising a fine fee), the trio set off for the mayor in search of a judgment. Once inside the disorderly courtroom described by Quintilian and Tacitus and made famous by the chattering Basochiens, each party nudges the Procureur to accuse the other. But at first it seems that neither will remain silent long enough for the *captatio benevolentiae* of "A Monsieur *bona vita*": "Merde! / Taisez-vous" (Shit! Shut up!). The Judge attempts to control all this legal noise about the other noise discovered by the nose with a request that the attorney "abbreviate," and the Procureur delivers. Hubert's complaint, he explains, is based on two important points: the unmerited trepidation Hubert was forced to suffer and the pollution of his home by his wife. In defense of Jehannette, however, the attorney advances an equally compelling juridical argument: Hubert is to blame for the ill wind, which was caused directly by his cruel and unusual treatment of his wife (*peine extraordinaire*) (102–5).

As the couple renew their squabbling with the winds of their own rhetoric, the Judge asks them to retire briefly while he consults with their attorney on the legalities of the matter. He is about to advance an argument of his own that will cause Hubert to lose the case on a technicality. With a logic that rivals Gréban's discussion of the persons of the Holy Trinity, he argues that Hubert must in fact endure the fart because of the spiritual communion of any married couple. Even though the lawyer protests that Hubert is not obliged to shoulder legal responsibility for an act he did not commit, the Judge rules that when he married the lovely Jehannette, "he took all of her," including the body part under litigation. He must therefore savor anything issuing from her, including farts. Here the clever lawyer perceives a final line of defense: he denies that Hubert ever married the *cul* and should thence be absolved from any ill effects issuing therefrom: "Il dit qu'il n'est prouvé de nul / Que jamais espousa le cul / De sa femme" (He says that there is no way to prove that he ever married his wife's asshole) (105–6).

This new development prompts the Judge to recall the litigants for further clarification from Hubert: did he or did he not take all of Jehannette for a wife? Far more savvy than the Cobbler, Hubert swears on his very baptism that he may well have married her body, "mais d'espouser son cul, arriere!" (but to marry her asshole, but[t] no!). The comedy of law has become the law of comedy as the legitimate juridical model serves to underscore the illegitimacy of the case it articulates. Here the Judge has no trouble wielding Ockham's razor to cut through that defective defense: "And if she had had no behind / Would you have taken her?" A confused Hubert does not perceive the impending syllogism, and confesses that he does not know. The author of the play has completely (and physiologically) reversed Plato's noble maieutics; for as the Judge ensnares Hubert in a dialectical exchange, the truth is revealed literally at the other end. And in this play, the other end of legal rhetoric is drama as Jehannette comes forward to reply. There can be little doubt, she argues, that Hubert married both *corps* and *cul* because he displayed a particular interest in the latter on their wedding night: "Mon cul fut la premiere pièce / Par ou il me print, somme toute" (Briefly, my asshole was the first place he took me). Her own body supplies irrefutable proof of her case, as the fumbling Hubert attempts to explain that, given the darkness of the room, he might well have become confused about which end was up: "Now, had it been daytime..." But the Judge has heard enough (106–7).

The legal issue of possession has been established on the most physiological level (an issue to which Coquillart devotes an entire series of *plaidoyés*), and the judgment is now "cler et notoire" (clear and evident). All parts of Jehannette are in Hubert's possession, including the one that gave rise to the fart. He must therefore acknowledge his own responsibility in the matter, since wife and husband form a single entity ("une mesme chose"). The judge has ensnared Hubert with his scatological version of Socratic dialectic, and has revealed the exquisite truth of the fart—a truth that resolves both the trial and the play. Anything passing from the *cul* of one into the nose of the other must be endured with patience—a charming metaphor indeed for the verbal pollution currently being perpetrated in the court. Now encouraged by both Judge and lawyer to embrace the connubial harmony that results from patient sharing of the fart, Hubert must yield to this noble *reson*. While its *resonance* is quite different from that of Gréban, its music is just as sweet. The Judge now codifies in writing a final verdict, ordering all spouses to "drink and share [the farts] equally," that all may live in conjugal, odorous accord. That is the legal sentence about scents: "Faictes tost la sentence escripre" (Record the verdict forthwith) (107–10).

As in the *Farce de la Porte Bodès*, the drama of law has engendered a new legal code as the play draws to its conclusion with a juridical version of a *silete* praising the sights, sounds, and smells of the *resonance* of rhetorico-dramatic *reson:* "Accordez les nez et les culz / Ensemble à tous sentemens. / Seigneurs, qui estes ici presens, / Prenez en gré le jugement" (Raise your noses and assholes together to all s[c]entences. My lords who are present, please accept our judgment [110]). Given that medieval audiences presumably left a mystery play with devotional images etched in their memories for the generation of silent prayer, one can only wonder what marvelous things are to be engendered in silence after the *Farce du pect*.

Dramatic Dialogue and Dialogic Drama

Given the adaptability of the forensic model to the most varied of dramatic contexts, it is equally fruitful to explore its role in the shifting generic interplay between dialogue and drama. The power of delivery to bridge the gulf between oral and written discourse does more than shatter the view that dialogues were "frozen" forms, generic anomalies or hybrids: it partially explains their tremendous popularity. Indeed, the theatricalization of forensic rhetoric suggests that in an oral culture where reading meant reading aloud, such dialogues might have moved from the protodramatic to drama proper simply by virtue of an oral reading. The histrionic register of legal *actio* thus allows us to piece together what Nicoll viewed as the generic "puzzle" posed by the "closet playwright." Nicoll's attempt to determine whether the plays of the younger Seneca were "intended for stage representation or whether they were designed merely as literary exercises suitable for private 'readings' " privileges an irrecuperable authorial intention that might readily have been harnessed to the performance agendas of a multiplicity of readers reading aloud, and hence histrionic transformations and even distortions (*WD*, 96). Moreover, any "mere" literary exercise recalls the rich declamatory tradition in which prosopopoeia was known to have been cultivated.

Still, despite such extraordinary instances of *mouvance* as that of the "Proces que a faict Misericorde," F. J. E. Raby maintained that "poetical debates are quite undramatic, even if the dialogue sometimes becomes convincingly lively and realistic" (308), and Young held that the performance of the elegiac comedies was at best "semi-dramatic." Though Young conceded the *possibility* that different voices might have delivered them and the *probability* that "the persons engaged in the recital sometimes used gestures and changes of voice by way of suggesting impersonation," he too concluded that there was "no assurance that even such compositions as *Pamphilus* and *Babio* were performed as plays, with complete use of impersonation and scenery" (1:8). Yet Young's veritable paraphrase here of the definition of delivery suggests that whether or not scenery, props, and actual staging were present, prosopopoeia could have rendered such works nascent dramas. If dialogue was "an accepted literary mode in which a man of learning could display his knowledge of and interest in religious and philosophical ideas," as Davenport maintains (96), then that display was clearly dramatic.

Both the *Advocacie Nostre-Dame* and Coquillart's *Plaidoyé d'entre la Simple et la Rusee* derive their protodramatic status from an overarching legal structure. They are literary trials that capture the legal mimesis in a way that is no less dramatic than it is in Gréban or the *farceurs*. To permit the freshness of their respective legal dramas to emerge anew, we have but to bridge the gulf between page and stage through delivery.

L'Advocacie Nostre Dame Sainte Marie

The subtitle of the *Advocacie Nostre Dame Sainte Marie* immediately underscores the juridical construction of the entire work: "et véz ci les rèsons pour quoy elle est apelée advocate de l'umain lignage" (and here are the reasons for which she is called lawyer for humankind).[55] Though by the fourteenth century the expression *véz ci* was becoming semantically close to the modern *voici*, the term still maintained much of its visual immediacy; and its presence here suggests a *demonstracion* as vivid and dramatic as that of any of the *procès* analyzed earlier. By placing a powerful visual representation of the gesticulating Virgin at center stage to plead the case for fallen humankind, the author commemorates simultaneously the passage from mnemonic to dramatic image and from histrionic legal delivery to drama. Though the *Advocacie* contains some narrative, those sections are no more intrusive than the extrapolations of Gréban's *acteur* or the Arras *prescheur* or the masked *exarchos* of the dithyramb. The work is a tribute to *mouvance* of genre, me-

---

[55] The *Advocacie Nostre-Dame*, often attributed to Jean de Justice, appears in excerpts (ed. Chassant) and in an unabridged edition by Raynaud. References are to the latter and are given parenthetically by line number; but both editions contain helpful introductions. Translations are mine. For the dating of the work in the first half of the fourteenth century, see Raynaud, ii–viii; and for brief discussions of it, see Fabre, *CP* (1882), 45–52, and Harvey, 158.

diating between Christian and secular traditions and, more important, between rhetoric, dialogue, and drama. Moreover, in its
feminization of forensic mediation, it suggests the devotional legal
ministration of Augustine and Alanus de Insulis, but also the history
of effeminacy in the regenerate rhetoric once described by Quintilian, Lucian, and the author of the *Drois de la Porte Bodès.*

This highly neglected work of some 2,500 lines begins with praise
of the Virgin, who dwells in a timeless realm of dramatic disputation.
Even if all past, present, and future creatures were to debate ad
infinitum (*respondre* and *opposer*), they could never sufficiently explain (*gloser*) her goodness, power, and grace (1–9). Forensic disputation and biblical exegesis are conflated as Mary emerges as the
ultimate locus of representation for both dramatic approaches to the
Christian agon. Whenever the hateful Devil initiates proceedings
against humanity, she is always available to effect the necessary
rhetorico-dramatic mediation: "El sçeit opposer et respondre / Pour
nostre adversaire confondre...;/ Et est advocat bon et sage / Et
souvent par plèt nous delivre" (She knows how to oppose and defend
in order to confound our adversary. And she is a good and wise lawyer
who often delivers us through litigation [93–101]). In other words,
what the Virgin accomplishes in the *Miracle de Théophile* by literally thrashing the Devil's *derrière*[56] she does here with a verbal
thrashing: she beats the Devil at his own legal game; and what she
delivers is the ennobled legal eloquence of female Christian equity
(as distinguished from the effeminate voice of such male sophists
as Lucian's). It is her skill in mimetic pleading that renders her
mistress not only of the court but of the stage.

The process of this *procès* resembles that of the Arras *Passion* in
that its dramatic business is not a pretrial about the redemption but
a retrial newly engendered from the contemplation of devotional
images. Like her merciful counterpart in the *procès de paradis*, Mary
has been moved by the vision of her son's crucifixion: "Quer il y
vient en *remembrance* / Qu'el le nourri en son enfance" (For there
comes to her a remembrance of how she nourished him in his child-
hood [85–86]). And it is her ability to "translate" the events inscribed
in her memory into persuasive legal language that transforms her
into an effective *avocate* for "l'Umaing Lignage" and into a player
in the dialogic drama. After a lengthy recapitulation of the Fall,
which establishes the legal foundation for the case at hand, the
"great drama" of Christianity is retransformed into a legal ordeal as

---

[56]I am referring to the final scene of Rutebeuf's play (2:102–3 in Jubinal's edition).

the Devil, "du fèz bien agregié" (well versed in the facts [283]), seeks to reopen his case against the souls liberated by Jesus. Still enraged by the "injustice" of the redemption, he marches off to appeal the case in celestial court before a God "full of justice" (305), whom the reader/spectator is enjoined to view as the sole juridical authority: "Cuidiez vous quil fust alegié / S'il iert devant le roy de France; / Nenil. Là meins n'auroit grevance" (Do you think he would have found relief had he gone before the king of France? Not at all. There he would have had less of a case [284–86]).[57]

At first, however, God patently refuses to recognize Satan's efforts to manipulate the letter of Christian law: "armed with his power of attorney" or not (de procuration garni [303]), the mendacious fallen angel has no case (325) and no credibility (341–42). But the litigious Devil knows full well how to take juridical and dramatic advantage of the fact that God is the incarnation of justice (as Isidore had once suggested [bk. 18, 15]). Insisting that his *procuration* is "without errors or defects" (355–56), he submits syllogistically that "you are the master of justice, / I want justice; you are justice,/ Render it unto me. Is that not your duty?" (344–46). As to the final outcome, Satan's scholastic bag of tricks and his mastery of forensic discourse in two languages will prove of no avail, even though he knows "franchoiz et latin / Et sceit respondre et opposer / Et toute Escripture gloser, / Et fallaces plus de cent a" (French and Latin, and knows how to oppose and defend, and to gloss the entire Scripture, and has more than a hundred ruses [448–51]). For the moment, however, the deity has no choice but to grant a plea for justice because "l'euvre est einsi attournée" (thus is the case regulated [348–49]). With those words the drama is *attourné* (arranged) as well.

Assured upon inspection that the *procuration* is "in good order" (*conforme*), God schedules the retrial for Good Friday (376–77)—a date to which Satan objects forthwith. Holding the trial on such a "solemn and renowned holiday" (382–83), he complains, would create a natural prejudice against his case and render any verdict "null and void" (385–86). But since Christ's Passion has already exemplified a Christian law dominated by the spirit of mercy, the Devil's case will only underscore the inefficacy of forensic rhetoric in the face of divine equity as it highlights the drama of the entire process (396–98). When Satan returns to court before the appointed time

---

[57]It is easy to see why such trials often precipitated accusations of lèse-majesté (again, see Delachenal, 203n). Indeed, the author goes on to assert that in comparison with God's divine justice, the "justice" of the king of France and even of the pope is as powerless as the justice now invoked by the Devil (see 439–44).

(421–38), God insists that he be patient. The injunction prompts renewed lamentations from the petitioner about the good old law of yesteryear: "Halas! où est Justice alée / Quand ès cyex à peine la treuve?" (Alas! where has Justice gone when she can scarcely be found in the heavens? [490–91]). Although the Devil's braying and wailing (494) will not prove as effective as that of Thibault L'Aignelet, he assures God that he will plead "courteously" and amiably (535–38). God then announces a demonstration of the principle that Gréban would theatricalize a century later—that divine equity is superior to terrestrial justice: "devant justice équité mètre... / Et d'équité vuil jeu user" (to place justice before equity. And I call upon equity [594–97]).

As gossip starts to fly in Heaven and Hell that the "entire world would have been lost had it not been for the mercy of God" (643–46), the news reaches the Virgin Mary, similarly poised to plead humanity's case (662–64). But in addition to being a trial about the Fall, this is also a trial about trials: Mary's first duty in the reconvened court is to establish her very right to be there. In fact, the Devil treats her and all women as invisible: "Fame ne puet fère demande / N'estre pour autre; c'est la somme; / Tel office appartient à homme" (Woman may not bring a complaint or represent another. That is the main point: such a role is the duty of man [860–62]). According to this diabolical logic, the Virgin's human client is not represented, and therefore is absent as well. Thus the Devil requests that the case be decided in his favor:

> Je ne voy à cuy je parole.
> Tu scéz qu'avoir doit vraiement
> .III. persones en jugement;
> L'auctour faut, et le deffendant,
> Et le juge, qui entendant
> Doit estre à jugier par rèson,
> Quant il en est tens et seson.
> Le deffendant ne voy je pas. [814–21]

I see not to whom I speak. You know, of course, that in any judgment, there must be three persons: the prosecution, the defense, and the judge, who, upon hearing the case, must judge according to reason at the proper time. I do not see the defendant.

But, despite Gaston Raynaud's contention that Mary triumphs over the Devil's "tight discussion" by virtue of "her cries and tantrums of the naïve woman" (iv), it is really her intelligent manipulation of rhetoric, and specifically of delivery, that wins the case. It is her legal rhetoric that establishes her own voice in opposition to the Devil's, confirming her dramatic visibility and juridical viability as she argues the consonance of equity and the female voice. In a feminization of the law (to say nothing of the principles of courtly love), Mary explains that women are the true "knights of law," having long been responsible for defending helpless widows and small children:

> Se fames tout généraument
> Ne pevent pour autres plèdier,
> Si pevent eulz de droit édier
> En aucuns cas especiaus
> Par devant touz officiaus,
> Et en ces cas ont avantage.
> Petiz enfans desouz aage,
> Véuves fames pitéables,
> Tiex gens maugré touz les Déables,
> Pevent fames par droit deffendre,
> Et le juge les y doit prendre.   [890–900]

If, generally speaking, women cannot litigate on behalf of others, nevertheless they have the right to intercede in certain particular cases before all courts, and in such cases they have priority. Small, under-aged children, piteous widows—such persons, confounding all the devils in the world, may women rightfully defend and the judge must accept them.

It follows, then, that her maternal duty is to protect her offspring in court: "A moy apartient à deffendre. . . . / Ce n'est pas droiz que je m'en tèse. . . . / Donc doy jeu, je n'en doute mie, / En moy deffendant estre oïe" (It is right that I defend. It is not right that I keep silent about this. Therefore, without a doubt, the defendant must be heard in me [916–26]). Having served as the "altar" for the virgin birth, she has devoted her whole life to mediating between God and man. She is therefore the true *advocat* described by Augustine and Alanus de Insulis and must be called thus ("Doy *advocat* estre appelée" [962]). And her literary duty is to interpret the dramatic agon of Christianity. God rules in her favor, and the Devil is ordered to provide her with "copies of all his letters" (977).

The "disloyal prosecutor" now begins what he believes to be a case of simple possession (983–1020)—the very question of *saisine* that will provide the stuff of Coquillart's satire. Citing the authority of God's own judgment against man for the Fall (elsewhere the province of Lady Justice), he seeks restitution of clear title to humankind, offering up a motion that the group of prisoners stolen from him during the Harrowing of Hell be "restitué de plein" (restored in full [999]). But Mary refutes him with traditional legal *staseis*, claiming that the felonious Devil and not man was the responsible party, the true "author of this thing." In a vehement ad hominem attack, the Virgin contends that since it was the Devil who perverted divine law, he has no right to invoke it now: "Il est mout bien acoustumé / De mentir, le fel enfumé. . . . / Il ment, le fel advocat ort" (He is very well accustomed to lying, the stinking criminal. He lies, the vile, dirty lawyer) (1027–35). Moreover, she continues, the Passion of Christ effectively nullified the Devil's legal title to man. Even by the strictest letter of the law, the "stinking boy" (1052) was never legally entitled to ownership, and his "squatter's rights" are not binding (1086–98): "Mès onques Sathan le traïtre / N'i out bonne foy, ne bon titre, / Ne il n'en a lètre ne chartre" (But never did Satan the traitor have good faith or clear title; nor has he deed or charter [1047–49]). Therefore, he has no legal right to reclaim title now (1072–76).

The crafty Devil, however, responds that if one were to believe "this lady," then "nary a soul would go to Hell" (1117–18). Surely, he insists, that cannot be the intent of divine law, however much God's traditional indulgence of the Virgin may cloud that intent (1122–23). Now brandishing his copy of the Bible, the perfidious Devil begins to read aloud from Genesis in support of his claim that God's own rigorous punishment of the vainglorious Adam validates his title to humankind (1140–78). But Mary has no difficulty refuting him with a text and gloss of her own. Restoring the sections of Genesis that the Devil has deceptively omitted, she completes the story of the temptation (1188–1214) to prove that "Satan was the cause of their sin." The Devil's arguments are about absence; Mary's arguments are about presence. Indeed, her very function here is to restore what is missing, whether the parts of Genesis deleted by Satan or humankind to its seat in paradise or the voice of woman in the courtroom. She now begs Christ to approve the use of "extraordinary means" in the case (1354–55), but it is Mary herself who provides them as she creates the most vivid dramatic image of the work.

In a lengthy description as vivid as many *didascalia*, the Virgin abandons argumentation in favor of gesture—the very conditions under which the theatricalization of the law had traditionally been nurtured. And while the narrator attributes her rhetorical shift to the popular wisdom that "woman is a frail creature" (frelle créature [1383–84]),[58] the Virgin's actions suggest otherwise. She is, in fact, about to persuade the court with a gesticular display of the pathos of her maternity, thus restoring the vivid images of the holy book with the dramatic reenactment of her own rhetoric. Although she is moved to the point of virtual speechlessness (1390), Mary's capacity for significative *actio* remains intact as voice and body become the dramatic exemplification of her soul. She wrings her hands, trembles, shakes, and sobs, becomes inflamed, and drips with sweat (1397–99). And while such crying and flailing in court was deemed aberrant conduct for male lawyers, it is the most crucial *demonstracion* of the *Advocacie*. Mary successfully proves her case (1505–25) by tearing open her garment to show (*demonstrant*) her breasts (1476): her own body displaces, replaces, and ennobles legal delivery as practiced by histrionic male lawyers:

> Lors la véist l'en souspirer
> Et puis sa robe dessirer
> Tout contre val vers les mameles,
> Que tant avoit tendres et beles,
> Et puis remonstroit sa poytrine
> A son filz, la douce royne,
> Et devant li tout à genous
> Se mètoit pour l'amour de nous,
> Puis se restendoit toute plate.   [1411–19]

You should have seen her lament about it and then rip open her dress all the way down to her breasts, so tender and beautiful. And then she showed her breast to her son, the sweet queen, and knelt before him for love of us all, and then she lay prostrate before him.

In much the same way that Caroline Walker Bynum has argued that Jesus was both father and mother,[59] here Mary is both male and female lawyer: "Onques *advocat* n'*advocate* / Sa cause si ne deffendi / Quant devant son filz s'estendi" (Never did a lawyer, male or female, uphold their cause in such a way as when she lay down before her son [1420–22]). The portrayal of the Virgin is as "profoundly dichotomous" as Bernard de Clairvaux's advice that priests be "mothers," not "masters" (*domini*): "Be gentle, avoid harshness,

---

[58]This description is remarkably similar to the Devil's description of Eve as a "*fieblette et tendre chose*" (weak and tender little thing) in the *Jeu d'Adam*, 227.

[59]See esp. Bynum's compelling analysis of maternal imagery in *Jesus as Mother*, 113–66; and her *Holy Feast and Holy Fast*, 277–88. My thanks to Marilyn Reppa for her research assistance on this subject.

do not resort to blows, expose your breasts...."[60] Classical rhetoricians had denounced the histrionic behavior of effeminate lawyers, and clergy advised women to "become 'male' or 'virile' in their rise to God," Bynum points out; whereas men "needed to become weak and human, yet spiritual, 'women' in order to proceed toward God;"[61] but Mary as *avocat/avocate* resolves those dichotomies. Now recreating Christ's suffering through her ennobled female *actio* (1427–72), she unites the two concepts of "the father as one who rules and produces" and "the mother as one who loves."[62] As the mediator between woman and man, humankind and God, and drama and rhetoric, she sanctifies forensic delivery and law itself, thus reuniting pleading and proving. And as she blurs the gender lines between male and female, she also helps to blur the genre lines between rhetoric, dialogue, and drama. The courtroom is exactly where Mary belongs; and it is her womanhood that resolves the moral and generic problematics of delivery.

The *Advocacie Nostre-Dame* constitutes a complex medieval reinterpretation of how the speaking rhetorical voice was literally engendered by intonation and by the gesticular language of the body: by rhetorical delivery. Compare Mary's performance with that of male attorneys who theatricalized the law through a form of rhetorical transvestism. There was nothing "false" about Mary's "resemblance to the female sex"; there was none of the transvestism that Quintilian decried, no loss of "purity and virility," no "castration" (V, 12.17–20). In view of the current swell of critical interest in the *Roman de Silence*, in which the generically ambiguous Silentius/Silentia manipulates law and society through deceit and disguise,[63] it is significant that the gender of the ideal practitioner of law in the *Advocacie* is not disguised but (quite literally) uncovered during delivery. In fact, the only character to complain bitterly about the Virgin's rhetorico-dramatic triumph is the Devil, who gripes that this is "some justice!" (1532) when a woman can prove a legal case by showing her bare breasts and by wailing and debating (*par crier et par tencier* [1539]). Hadn't he warned them all of the affront to logic that would be perpetrated by the dubious presence of women in court (1540–44):

> Tu pleures et plains et souspires,
> Tu sanglotes, tu te dessires;

[60]Bernard's Sermon 23, quoted in Bynum, *Jesus as Mother*, 118.
[61]Bynum, *Holy Feast*, 287–88.
[62]Bynum, *Jesus as Mother*, 113.
[63]See, e.g., Bloch, "Silence and Holes," and McCracken, "Poetics of Silence in the French Middle Ages," chap. 1.

Tu monstres à ton filz ton ventre,
Et tel pitié u cuer li entre
Que tu par *force l'amolies.*
Il prent à bon gré tes folies,
Quant tu li monstres ta mamèle....
Quant tu ris, il le convient rire;
Quant tu pleures, il veut pleurer;
Il te par veut trop hennourer. [2257–68]

You cry and wail and sigh, you sob, you flail, you show your bosom
to your son, and such pity enters his heart that you soften him with
your strength. He willingly accepts your folly when you show him
your breasts. When you smile, he must smile too; when you cry, he
is moved to tears. He seeks so much to honor you.

His real objection, however, speaks directly to the most stunning
conclusion of Mary's gesticular rhetoric: that power is female and
that it "softens" men. The histrionic delivery that was thought to
disempower male lawyers empowered such female voices as the
Virgin Mary's, helping to invent a new theatrical voice of female
authority in dramatic rhetoric and rhetorical drama.

After a snide query to the Virgin as to whether or not her crying
jag is finally over ("Aurez-vous huy assez plouré?" [1553]), Satan
attempts to silence Mary's voice by quoting the Gospel (1559–61)
in order to propose a settlement (1599–627): a reweighing of all the
souls that would allow him to keep the evil ones and Christ the
good ones (1614–16). Just as Jesus seems prepared to agree (1632),
Mary comes forward to demonstrate the pathetic proofs of the Crucifixion (1638–1703). All those souls, she reminds the court, were
equitably weighed and distributed during the Harrowing of Hell,
that supremely dramatic moment of the liturgy (*CRCD*, 139). And
the Passion already constitutes ample "satisfaction" for original sin
(2114, 2156–64). Nor does she accept the Devil's final legal ploy of
invoking himself as the ultimate negative exemplum: humankind
merits eternal damnation for having followed him (1713–26). Buttressed by the drama of her delivery, Mary's verbal manipulation of
the assumptive issue is as persuasive as her gestures. Any comparison of the two crimes, she argues, reveals very little similitude in
motive (1777): man was *de frelle nature* (frail in nature)—the same
term that the narrator had used to describe her (1383–84)—and the
Devil was divine (1811). Man sinned from *fragilité* (1823) and *ino-
bédience* (1852), whereas the Devil did so knowingly (1850) and with
a "pure malice" that was inconsistent with his divine nature (1825–

26). Mary then goes on to introduce a legal notion not seen in the *procès de paradis* studied thus far. Punctuating her speech with a series of angry commands that the Devil "shut up" (1884), she concludes that humankind requires a codified body of law, but divine beings endowed with "certain knowledge" (1874) do not. And humankind requires precisely the sort of dramatization of that body of law that she herself has provided. It is the Devil's voice that will eventually be silenced, not hers.

Despite Satan's assurance that he will "shut up" (1886), he does not—especially when the Virgin calls him horrible, evil, stinking, traitorous, disloyal, and stubborn (1895–97). And again, though Mary turns to Christ for mediation, it is she herself who instructs her son in the art of refuting faulty syllogisms (2223–41). Since Christ is "God and man together" (2161), he too is the incarnation of representative and representational mediation between God and man. And such representations provide both Mary and the author of the *Advocacie* with rich material for argumentative and dramatic invention in the images of the Passion. According to the Holy Scriptures, she recalls, God allows atonement to erase even the memory of evil: "Dieu tantost le péchié oublie... / Que jamès ne l'en souvendra" (God quickly forgets the sin, never to remember it again [2205–17]). That, she concludes, is "text and gloss" (2220) for the rhetorico-dramatic process by which images of crime are transformed into images of goodness—representations that in turn engender good works and good works of art.

Ultimately, the drama of the Virgin's rhetoric and the rhetoric of her drama reside in her ability to combine cries and gestures with subtle argumentation to confound evil: "non pas par plours tant soulement / Mès par aguèz et soutilment, / Doit son adversaire grever / Pour sa bonne cause achever" (not only by crying, but subtly and by cleverness, she must demolish her adversary in order to triumph in her good cause [2277–80]). She thus restores legal rhetoric to its noble Christian status as a mediatory force between man and a God who may always choose to restore his creation to the very *ostel* whence the Devil is now evicted (2287). Mary has demolished her adversary by pointing out that while both man and the Devil committed treason, only the Devil jeopardized the mnemonic station of the firmament (2360–72). That is, if God now fails to forgive man, his entire creation will be in vain—a logical, theological, and dramatic impossibility that now returns Satan disconsolate to Hell, his bestial moans and groans providing a final counterpoint to Mary's noble tears and cries: "Il souspira et s'estendi, / Et prist si forte fin à fère / Que d'Enfer l'oïst l'en bien brère" (He sighed and stretched out and carried on with such determination that you could hear him braying all the way from Hell [2398–400]). For all his knowledge of "all Law and Logic" (2391), he has "debated for nothing" (2438).

When Christ comes forward at his mother's request to render the "definitive ruling" (2410), he codifies the law of mercy that has now been demonstrated dramatically by Mary's *advocacie:* anyone present who repents of sin may rejoin God in his heavenly palace (2409–23). He also inscribes his mother in all the ludic/conflictual registers in which her *demonstracion* took place: oral and written legal tradition, *disputatio,* and, perhaps most interesting of all, musical antiphony. In a unified dramatic voice before a joyous celestial court (2442), the Trinity resolves the trial (2426–28) and engenders an antiphon that is still on the books: "Et adonc ceste antiène firent, / Que Sainte Eglise encor recorde" (And thus they made this antiphon, still recorded by Holy Church [2444–45]). Like Gréban, the author exploits all the connotations of *deduire* as the work draws to a close with the *resonance* of *reson,* the harmonious delivery of speech and song. In a prayer of thanks now offered to the Virgin (2446–52), speaking and singing fuse as they do in Saint Augustine's mnemonics (*Confessions,* bk. 10.8), and verbal forensic dialogue is replaced by the musical antiphony that once gave rise to liturgical drama:

> En Paradis se *déduisoient*
> Les Sains, qui l'*antiène disoient;*
> Le chief en *chantèrent et distrent,*
> Et tout le remanant *apristrent*
> A ceulz qui en char et en os
> Estoient.   [2453–58; emphasis mine]

In Paradise the saints who sang the antiphon rejoiced. They sang and proclaimed the beginning themselves, and the rest they taught to those made of flesh and bones.

Dramatic speech has been engendered from the devotional images and gestures of the *Advocacie,* which the author now closes with a regenerative prayer to be stored in memory. The Virgin remains the mnemonic "altar" where future rhetorico-dramatic language, music, imagery, and antiphons are stored and preserved. Indeed, she is remarkably similar to the perfect singer described by Aurelian of Reôme in the ninth century: "He cannot be perfect unless he has implanted by memory in the sheath of his heart the melody of all the verses through all the modes, and all the differences both of the modes and of the verses of the antiphons, introits, and of the responses."[64] But now Aurelian's *he* is a *she*. The long history of debate about the moral identity of forensic delivery has been resolved. Here the codification (*recorder* [2487]) of *actio* is not effeminate but feminine, exemplified by the "goodness, mercy, power, and pleadings" of the Virgin (2488–90). By identifying the Virgin as a locus of mnemonic inscription and inscribing her within a *livret* called *L'AD-VOCACIE NOSTRE DAME* (2494–95), the author stores the entire drama of her delivery for future generations, whom she will always defend "body and soul" (*le cors et l'ame* [2496]). Mary has provided a reminiscence that reenacts the Christian agon, transforms it into drama, and finally retransforms that drama into the written text of the *Advocacie*, collapsing the barriers of gender and genre.

Coquillart

In much the same way that the crazy courtroom of the *Pathelin* served as a terrestrial counterpart for the *procès de paradis*, Guillaume Coquillart's *Plaidoyé d'entre la Simple et la Rusee*[65] is an ignoble *Advocacie*. Though it is not normally classified as a drama, it too derives from the mimetic delivery of the trial. But instead of commemorating the reunion of God and man, Thibault L'Aignelet and his flock, or *corps* and *cul*, Coquillart provides a forensic and sexual reunion of women and their lovers. With no narrative sections, his *Plaidoyé* is not an *abrégé* but a "transcription" of the *plaidoiries*, a verbal reconstruction of the crowd-pleasing spectacle of a legal fight. In this lofty case about sexual/romantic possession, Coquillart represents a trial about a trial; and in staging forensic discourse, he discovers a panoply of dramatic characters and the essence of his dramatic plot. It is by "transcribing" the oral histrionics of forensic delivery that Coquillart rediscovers, reinvents, and reenacts the union of rhetoric and drama in a veritable chronicle of the *letteraturizzazione* of the law. In the same way that Geoffrey of Vinsauf, for example, employed rhetorico-poetic techniques to illustrate rhetorico-poetic techniques in the *Poetria nova*,[66] Coquillart dramatizes law to illustrate the dramatization of law.

---

[64]Aurelianus Reomensis, *Musica Disciplina*, 118, as translated by Treitler in "Reading and Singing," 160–61.

[65]References are to Freeman's edition of Coquillart's *Oeuvres* and are given parenthetically. Translations are mine.

[66]Woods advances this argument in "Unfashionable Rhetoric."

From the opening greeting by Maistre Simon, attorney for the Simple Girl, the *Plaidoyé* is pure histrionic dialogue, whose orality is emphasized from the outset: "*Oyés le plait* fort eschauffé / D'entre la Simple et la Rusee. / Que la cause soit cy traictee, / Affin que on *entende* le cas" (Hear ye! hear ye! this most heated trial between the Simple Girl and the Sneaky Girl. Let the case be treated here, that we may hear this trial [3–6]). The true "understanding" of this case resides in its status as protodramatic conflict. In fact, the two lawyers commence bickering even before the Judge calls the court to order: "Faictes paix la! / Acoup, que on entende a voz ditz" (Quiet over there, immediately, so that your speeches may be heard! [16–17]). The attorney for the defendant, Sneaky Girl (*Rusee*), comes forward immediately to proclaim his status as "interpreter" via *procuration* (11); and the named male lawyers—Simon for the Simple Girl, Olivier for the Sneaky Girl—now proceed to "represent" their unnamed female clients in this playful dispute about the stereotypical "possession/possessiveness" (*saisine*) of women. In a lengthy opening speech (18–313), Master Simon summarizes in pleading (*en plaidoiant*) the legal rationale for the complaint of the Simple Girl, "*demanderesse et complaignant*" (plaintiff and complainant [19]). There will be little rapid-fire dialogue between the two lawyers as each attempts to outdo the other with prolix displays. But in their histrionic efforts to establish the crucial premises of their respective deductive arguments, they also transform their discourse into impersonation as Coquillart transforms this dialogue into drama.

The entire case rests on divergent assumptions about the relationship between female sexual appetite and legal "possession" of a partner. True to her natural inclinations, argues Simon, the Simple Girl "acquired" a young man to satisfy (*assouvir*) her natural propensities (26–36). Legally speaking, she holds "clear title" to the Cutie (Mignon) (*juste tiltre et bon* [40]); and she holds it in "her own name" (*en son propre et privé nom* [37]). The irony, of course, is that she has no *propre et privé nom:* she is a stereotype as broadly sketched as any stock character type of drama or law. And so is the aforementioned Cutie, whose ontological status here is that of chattel. The two principals and the young man (all three absent) however, prove wonderful material for *inventio* that allows both attorneys to give the performances of their lives.

Master Simon, for example, calls upon all the dramatic resources of forensic oratory to paint a verbal picture of the Cutie, which he brings to life in a masterful display of prosopopoeia. Imitating the voices of several characters at once, he illustrates the Cutie's contentious character in a mimed spectacle. Not only does he imitate the Cutie fighting in unspecified *rixes*; he adds other voices to the dramatic legal dialogue and impersonates each imaginary protagonist:

> "Qui esce? Qui vive?" Et de combatre,
> Clif, clof, franchement et de hait,
> L'ung a la boue, l'aultre au plastre,
> "Demourés, ribault, pas ung pet...!"
> "Qui a ce fait?" "Je n'en sçay riens." [52–60]

"Who's that? who goes there?" Wham, bam, thank you ma'am! One in the mud, the other on the floor. "Halt, you punk! Not a fart out of you!" "Who did that? Beats me!"

And having "represented" his own version of battle play, Master Simon proceeds to another sort of play. When the Simple Girl first saw this fine strapping specimen of a dandy, she took immediate possession of the lad, "playing with him" as she saw fit: "ceste Simple en faisoit ses *jeux* / ... En tresbonne possession!" (that Simple Girl amused herself with him in fine possession indeed! [88–91]). Their sexual battle play is mirrored here by the dramatic battle play of a law court in which no one is particularly interested in "taming" bellicose (or any other) impulses. Indeed, legal battle play stands in for all sorts of pleasures and jousts, notably the Simple Girl's enjoyment of the Cutie's lance: whenever he returned from afar to do her bidding, he was "royde et bandé, / La lance au poing" (hard and erect, his lance in hand [97–99]). Their physical union is thus a literal, legal consummation of a contract that clearly establishes the Simple Girl's *saisine*. In a reversal of the noble feminization of the legal voice of the *Advocacie*, woman becomes *seigneur* over the effeminate Cutie (*Mignon*) (who seems *mignonne* enough as it is) in a series of obtrusive feminine terms for *seigneurie: droituriere, possesseresse, detenteresse, occupateresse, demanderesse* (102–9). The Cutie is rightfully hers—her possession, her beast, her chattel.

Therefore, concludes Simon, she must retain the right to effect her animal husbandry in whatever manner she sees fit: "de l'ediffier, labourer, / Luy faire prendre medicine / Pour plus amplement pasturer" (raise him, work him, administer medicine, the better to fatten him up [116–18]). She must also be assured perpetual enjoyment of all the fruits of her labors, collecting whatever "masculine revenue" (149) she may choose to levy, such as "baisiers, embrassemens / Aubades et cent mille bons jours / Et generalement tous biens / Qui pevent eschoir en amours" (kisses, caresses, serenades, and one hundred thousand sweet hellos, and, in general, all such goods that may occur in love [159–62]). Similarly, by virtue of his own legal training, Coquillart is entitled to harvest the fruits of the *cause fictive* by recapturing it as drama. Moreover, continues Simon, the Simple Girl is all the more entitled because she has proved a fine and noble owner of her property, dressing him up like a little doll (164–75) and reinforcing her *demaine* over the creature in bed: "Elle disposoit d'icelluy / Ainsi que de sa propre chose, / Et comme son privé amy / Le tenoit en sa chambre close" (She enjoyed the use of said item as if it were her own thing; and, as her personal consort, she kept it confined to her bedroom [184–87]). In the same way that the Simple Girl has squatter's rights to her man, having "enjoyed full possession" *(jouy et usé plainement)* for so many years that "there is no memory to the contrary" *(il n'est memoire du contraire* [266–71]), the histrionic attorneys have squatters' rights to drama, the memory of which has been inscribed in the collective *mémoire* for centuries. Indeed, the spectator/reader is entitled here to similar pleasures from this very dispute; and since Coquillart cannot take them to bed, he takes them to court for their fun.

Although Master Simon has promised to abbreviate the delicious tale (202), he is as verbose as he is dramatic, rattling on for some two hundred lines more before presenting his conclusion (287–313) that there can be no viable challenge to the Simple Girl's *saisine*. It thus behooves the court to rule that the Sneaky Girl has absconded with someone else's property, to order that she cease and desist (283–90), to return the Cutie to its rightful owner (291–97), and to assign her court costs as well (307–13). More important, given the rhetorico-dramatic body of law of *"la porte Baudet"* (229–30), it would be inequitable for the Simple Girl to take such good care of a beast and then see him graze elsewhere, for one woman to build the nest and another to take possession of the birds (225–26)—perhaps the *bec-jaunes*?

At this point the Judge turns the case over to the defense attorney, Olivier de Prés Prenant (314–17), who begins his counterattack after the ritual tipping and redonning of his hat (322–24). Though the Judge has asked him to be brief (321), brevity is, of course, impossible. He too will require some three hundred lines to disprove the Simple Girl's "rightful ownership" *(saisine et nouvelleté* [329]) and prove instead that it is the Sneaky Girl who has clear title to the Cutie. After all, he contends, nothing in the "law, statutes, or charters" *(loy, decretalle, ou chappittre* [344]) prohibits his crafty client from establishing squatter's rights of her own to the Cutie (334–45). To Master Simon's argument from popular wisdom about the nature of woman, Master Olivier opposes the equally notable doctrine about the insatiable sexual appetite of man. The litigation too is insatiable, and it proves equally effective in whetting the literary appetite of Coquillart's audience.

The Simple Girl, he argues, is either too "simple" or simply crazy (358–60) if she thinks it humanly possible for one woman to satisfy any one man (361–65). Happy to provide physical (in this case, physiological) evidence for that claim, he explains that all men seek to satisfy their carnal desires (362) wherever and whenever they see fit: "Il n'est homme qui ne se bende / Pour repaistre l'humanité, / Et n'y a celluy qui ne tende / A suivir la mundanité" (There is no man who fails to get hard in order to keep the species going, nor is there any one who doesn't tend to follow custom [379–82]). Now undercutting his opponent's argument (along with his own), he adds that it is always inadvisable to advance arguments based on human nature. They are never "binding" (as it were) because human nature is as inconstant as the wheel of fortune (383–94). Therefore, he concludes confusingly, the Simple Girl's juridical claim to sole ownership (398) is without legal foundation. The nature of any Cutie dictates that he will always have committed all sorts of follies (401–2). In fact, without such *folye*, where would the histrionic courtroom be?

Having denied the very ontology of "possession," Olivier then goes on to demand proof of possession. Where is the evidence of the Simple Girl's ownership? Where are the depositions? But what he is really requesting is the sexual equivalent of the histrionic display he himself has mastered as an actor in the courtroom: possession, he argues, must be public, never clandestine, if it is to have any legal weight at all. Since the Simple Girl used oblique means on her strange path (*voye oblicque*)—much like those of the forensic path (*voye*) of his own histrionic voice (*voix*)—her possession is not legal and binding. Nor, however, are his proofs, which speak to spectacle more than to equity:

> Il me semble que s'a esté
> Secrettement, par voye oblicque,
> Et est, selon bonne equité,
> Possession non juridique....
> N'est pas faicte tali modo
> Comme le droit le determine,
> Mais est secrette et claudestine. [415–31]

> It seems to me that this was done secretly and obliquely. Therefore, in proper accordance with equity, it is nonlegal possession. It was not done in a way that is established by law, but is secret and clandestine.

The Simple Girl is deluded in her claim to *seigneurie*, for it is the very nature of "rutting cuties" (459) to amuse themselves (*deduire*) with any woman they find in their pasture (460–62). While Master Olivier claims to be "returning to his point" (469), the point has in fact been lost in a concatenation of spectacularly delivered faulty premises. Having spent considerable time in his "brief" speech refuting the very existence of possession in matters of the heart and loins, he announces (contrary to his own logic) that his client alone holds title to the Cutie (488) as his "mistress" (476–78). Closing with his own requests for court costs for the Sneaky Girl (504–9), Master Olivier dismisses the Simple Girl's complaint as "illogical," "invalid," "false," "unreasonable," and "flimsy" (495–500).

What is illogical from a legal standpoint, however, is eminently logical in the context of dramatic rhetoric. Once again complainant and defendant, prosecutor and defense attorney have been drawn into the pleasing spectacle of a fight. As literary folly takes over in the courtroom, pleading engulfs proving and drama engulfs forensic rhetoric in *letteraturizzazione*. Even though the Judge has heard quite enough of this verbal "regurgitation," there is no stopping the lawyers' *cacquetz* (510–12). Simon, for example, now pontificates that his opponent's babbling has only proved what they knew all along: that the law creates nothing but adversarial relationships. "Il a dit chose bien diverse, / Et semble qu'il veulle ruer / Sur nous, pour tout controverse" (He has said many a contradictory thing; and it seems he wants to attack us for every little quarrel [526–28]). Now citing another popular diversion of his day that is as pleasing as that very *controverse*, Master Simon speculates about the frightful ramifications of Olivier's theory about man's eternal quest for greener sexual pastures (533–37). Just think of the rampant sexual anarchy that would be the order of the day, he muses: sexual freedom would result in communal play; any man could take possession of any woman on the streets on a mere whim (543–47). What would become of courtly love? and the language and gestures of love? The answer is clear: the semiotics of amorous discourse would undergo a transformation reminiscent of that of forensic delivery. Noble intentions would again disappear in favor of pleasure; but more alarming still, "rubies, diamonds, and turquoises" would no longer be necessary, nor would any other *langaige* beyond "Let's do it" (561–65). What anarchy indeed! Flowery language, conspicuous gestures, and conspicuous consumption thereof would be replaced by straightforward requests! What would become of the histrionic lawyer's forte in a society where people all came straight to the point? And what is more, continues the prophetic Simon, think of the disastrous consequences to lyric poetry alone if solely public possession of objects of desire were authentic (568–75). Why, soon enough, the only legitimate evidence of an act of amorous possession would be the *losengiers* broadcasting it to everyone within earshot (590–98) with "trumpeting" as loud as that of the Basochiens taking their own possession of the Grand' Chambre. If Master Olivier truly espouses that doctrine, insists Simon, let him be the first to submit to its rigors by revealing all his own secrets (610).

Thus demolishing Olivier's argument about possession, secret or otherwise (587–88), Simon concludes by launching a lengthy argumentum ad feminam against the Sneaky Girl herself, who is not even present. In reality, she is the mirror image of the histrionic, effeminate attorney; and what follows is a veritable panorama of medieval French legal performance: the wandering, chattering Basochiens, their mordant wit, their dissembling and impersonation, their ridiculous language, their satire, their outrageous dress, disorder, and immorality, and the mimetic pleasures of all that degeneration:

> Ceste Rusee, par *soy distraire,*
> Par tant d'*allees et de venues,*
> Par trop penser, par soy forfaire,
> Les *mordans parolles* aguës,
> Nouvelletés, *choses indeues...*
> Prieres, *persuasions;*
> Par faintises, *derisions,*
> Par motz dorés, par joncherie,
> *Sornettes,* adulations,
> Malices, façons rencheries,
> *Langaige affaictié, railleries...,*
> Par desordonnees *fringueries*
> Et par *manieres dissolues,*
> Par telles *faulsettés* a eues
> Ses droictz, ses acquisitions. [618–35; emphasis mine]

That Sneaky Girl, in order to divert herself by so many comings and goings, by too much thinking, by acting illicitly, [by] mordant and bitter words, transfers of title, improper things, prayers and persuasion, tricks and derision, polished words, camouflage, riddles, adulation, malice, disdainful ways, affected speech, mockery, revealing clothing, and dissolute ways: by such dishonesty she acquired her rights and possessions.

The Sneaky Girl "makes faces and shows her uncovered breasts" (*tetins descouvers* [641]), but she is no Virgin Mary. Rather, her ruses (represented here by men) are those of the "effeminate" sophist described by Lucian, who had once aided and abetted the advent of drama itself.[67] They have little to do with truth and everything to do with mimesis of the sort that Coquillart continues to engender from the law. In fact, Master Simon has provided an eloquent summation of the aestheticization of his own discipline: once the histrionics of delivery overshadow proof, once pleading engulfs proving, juridical authority is more literary than legal. The *voyes indeuez* (undue paths [279, 631]) are actually the paths taken by lawyers from legal rhetoric to dramatic performance, as he is about to demonstrate in a compelling display of impersonation. As rhetorico-dramatic proof for his assertion that the Sneaky Girl took physical possession of the Cutie through the false and seductive charms of language and dream visions (*songes*), he reenacts and recreates both parts of a representative dialogue between them:

> "Que vous en semble il d'icelluy?"
> "C'est il, c'est mon"...
> "Estes vous bien?" "Oil, nenny"...
> Elle estoit si rusee et faicte
> Qu'elle luy disoit franchement:
> "Je vous songe, je vous souhaite,
> Je pense a vous incessaument."
> Par telle mine et tel semblant,
> Et par tel langaige trouvé
> L'a faulsement, maulvaisement,
> Seduit et aussy suborné. [652–68]

"What do you think of this one?" "He's the one, all right." "Are you OK?" "Yes, no." She was so sneaky and polished that she used to tell him openly, "I dream of you, I want you, I think of you incessantly." With such a mien and appearance and with such [richly] invented language did she seduce and abscond with him falsely and with malice aforethought.

Master Olivier objects, of course, demanding witnesses, testimonials, and depositions (717–23) of the sort Coquillart provides in his

---

[67]Lucian, "Professor of Public Speaking," 23.

Nouveaulx droictz. And he insists that his opponent has done a ludicrous thing in advocating silence about love and sex. Where, then, would the *bec-jaune* be if he were unable to charm the court-room with the music of his own erudition? The silence and secrecy suggested by Simon would silence their own legal drama. Indeed, the literary authority cited by Simon is "faulse et *variable* / Et au droit prejudiciable" (false and variable and prejudicial to the law [715–16]) in the sense that courtly silence hinders the delivery of forensic spectacle. Once the whole discussion is recontextualized within the oral drama of legal language, however, Coquillart can illustrate a far more illuminating theory of "versions," or what Cerquiglini called *variance* and Zumthor *mouvance*.[68]

As Olivier rests his case with an indictment of Simon's "excess of folly" (725), he implies that such *folies* are actually the most entertaining aspect of their profession. There was nothing untoward in the Sneaky Girl's behavior: no sexual/juridical deviant is she in her manipulation of *motz couvers* and *jousteries* (735). Far from it, argues Olivier; she resembles the lawyer in a virtuous, industrious, and directed quest for pleasurable *seigneurie* of bedroom and court-room (731–32, 736–38). As Coquillart is about to show in the bizarre final outcome of this rhetorical seduction, all the "disguised words" and "jousting" of law and love are far more pleasurable when they record the battles of their own process rather than verdicts deter-mined by equity. For even though all possession has been declared null and void, the court is about to rule in favor of the Simple Girl— a verdict that is remarkably similar to that of the *procès de paradis* in that it has nothing to do with the arguments presented. Master Simon remands the trial to the hurried Judge (748): "Je demande la recreance, / Je m'en rapporte aulx assistens" (I seek custody, and place myself in the hands of the spectators [749–50]). And the Judge remands it to the spectators.

What follows is a recreational *ordo actorum* in which each mag-istrate comes forward to pronounce a ridiculous juridical opinion. Rapidly dispatched through his hat-tipping and *exordium* by the increasingly irritable Judge (755–57), a certain Happart asks the court to undergo the ultimate mimesis. In a move that even Lucian's Professor could not have anticipated, Happart proclaims that the most important thing is not legal equity or even the appearance of legal equity; it is the mimetic value of the appearance of the litigants. The Simple Girl must prevail, he affirms, because they have wit-

[68]Cerquiglini, *Eloge de la variante;* Zumthor, *Essai,* 65–72.

nessed an impersonation of her that is more pleasurable: "A la Simple la recreance, / Car elle a plus belle apparence / Que la Rusee"
(Custody goes to the Simple Girl, because her appearance is more
beautiful than that of the Sneaky Girl [761–63]). Master Oudard de
Main Garnie concurs (perhaps hoping that his hands will soon be
full of something else), as do his colleagues. The shocking triumph
of the Simple Girl (792–95) has nothing to do with logic and everything to do with theater.

Delighted with their rulings, the Judge now proposes to codify in
writing (795–801) the theatricalization of forensic rhetoric in his
own outrageous verdict. In this fictional travesty of the fictionalization of legal rhetoric, all notions of equity disappear as justice
becomes the *recreance* of pleasure and literature becomes recreation.[69] It is the Acteur who emerges to close the curtain with the
praise of juridical folly, declaiming eloquently on the transformation
of law into a gloriously bellicose spectacle performed by the barking
dogs (*abayans* [809]) once described by Ockham. Like Coquillart
himself, the gifted *acteur* (lawyer-author-actor-authority) can plead
one side as readily as the other, as long as he is well paid (*la main
garnie* [808]). How could the lawyer/author do otherwise in support
of his own cast of dramatic characters?

Now bidding adieu to all, the Acteur remands his legal play to
the custody of the audience's memory: "Et, vous en veulle souvenir"
(May you remember it well [811]). In this sexual comedy about legal
possession, law and literature, law *as* literature have been engendered from the primordial struggle for justice—a struggle that had
been transmuted by histrionic practitioners of the law into an end
in itself. Once again a legalistic dispute has led medieval sophists
to the most logical arena for the linguistic medium in which the
medium was everything: devoid of philosophical or legal truth, their
legal discourse was drama, and in this "case," farce. Imitating the
imitation of justice, Coquillart's legal dialogue is a rhetorical drama.

In the final analysis, the distinctions between Coquillart and the
Advocacie and between all the dramatic *procès* studied here are
better attributed to the interplay between dialectical and rhetorical
visions of drama than to the traditional polarities of "popular" versus
"learned" and "comic" versus "serious." Both visions are dramatic,
and both chronicle the aestheticization of the law. Each work speaks
eloquently to the artistic exploitation of the legal protodrama. Where

[69]See esp. Olson's "Medieval Fortunes," 265–66, and his *Literature as Recreation*,
64–77.

the authors of the *procès de paradis* (re)presented a devotional reflection on the nature of law, Coquillart and other farceurs staged
the intrinsic delights of the legal process itself. Given the remarkable
endurance of the rhetorical tradition in medieval European education, our understanding of the pervasive popularity of the agon in
medieval law, literature, theology, and pedagogy is greatly enhanced
by a revitalized appreciation of the importance of disputation as a
crucial medium and of delivery as the medieval performative method
par excellence. After all, even though the critics who rediscovered
the "origins" of liturgical drama in the Mass never referred to *actio*
as such, their rereadings of veritable stage directions encouraged us
to imagine how the ecclesiastical protodrama was brought to life
through reenactment before the medieval public. The power of *actio*
to mediate even today between histrionic performance and the written legal/literary text thus proves an invaluable hermeneutic framework by which to contextualize disputational discourse and to
restore its lost dynamism. By reintegrating delivery into literary
criticism we rediscover a crucial means of bridging the gulf between
oral and written discourse and, in this case, between rhetoric and
the very "origins" of medieval drama.

Though it is always tempting to propose sweeping and definitive
conclusions, it is doubtless more appropriate to raise more questions
than one answers. Among the questions that I relinquish to others
for more complete answers are these: Why is it that fifteenth-century
France saw so rich an aestheticization of legal discourse? Can a more
intensive study of the history of the interrelations of law and literature in France and in other countries provide partial answers to
that question? Surely the variegated medieval and Renaissance manifestations of that interplay will have significant ramifications for
the connections between medieval English drama, the Inns of Court,
and the rhetorical exercises practiced in universities. While forensic
rhetoric cannot account for all of the structural, stylistic, and tonal
variations in every work, nevertheless its dialogic imitation of conflict is so reminiscent of the dramatic enterprise that it provides
abundant and abundantly complex testimony about the shifting interplay between medieval genres: it exemplifies *mouvance.*

As our twentieth-century legal system grapples with such issues
as whether or not to permit executions to be televised, it is equally
tempting to submit that contemporary society also participates in
the dramatic continuum of legal rhetoric in ways that are no less
compelling, no less inherently "literary," and occasionally no less
frightening than the phenomena described by the earliest theorists

of rhetoric. To say that we have come full circle would be false, for
the route has been neither circular nor circuitous. Plato's condemnation of sophistry, Tacitus's critique of the mania for gladiatorial
display, and Vives's indictment of audience's fascination with the
spectacle of a fight might just as readily have been launched against
the plethora of agonistic and even newly "gladiatorial" entertainments that crowd the airwaves and other media today. Future his-
tories will surely provide insights as to why the 1980s and 1990s
gave rise to all manner of courtroom dramas, from the patently
fictive to the semirealistic to the video "transcription" of actual
courtroom proceedings. In short, all the human vices once denounced by Tacitus are really not so "peculiar" to his "metropolis"
(29) after all. Quite to the contrary, it seems that the enormous
complexity of a notion such as the "natural drama of law" has been
camouflaged by our ready acceptance of those "vices"—in this case,
in the critical arena. Despite Rainer Warning's observation that "religious drama is perhaps the genre which demonstrates most forcefully the alterity of the Middle Ages," the dramatic continuum of
the agon suggests that many sorts of medieval performance genres
are far less "other" than they have long appeared.[70] Our recognition
of the similarities along with the differences thus forces a revision
of our very conception of the celebrated and often daunting "alterity"
of the Middle Ages.

But perhaps the most significant consequence of the critical
reevaluation of *actio* is the notion that the *letteraturizzazione* of
rhetoric was limited neither to the theater nor to the Middle Ages.
I have focused here on forensic rhetoric, but all three rhetorical
genres—including deliberative and epideictic—were inherently performative. For centuries the entire rhetorical tradition offered a paradigm for the dramatization of the images and *imagines agentes* of
its memory stages. Since it retained its integrity as the cultural
institution that ensured the vivification of the "images" and "effigies" of written discourse, its mnemonic protodramas might just as
readily have been enacted literally and literarily by means of
impersonation, in compatible ways in other discourses. While the
presence of impersonation essentially closes the case for the commingling of forensic rhetoric and drama, it also instigates a larger
discussion about the interplay between other rhetorics and other
medieval literary genres. Indeed, it seems fitting that a book whose
purpose is to recast the terms of the debate about origins should

[70]Rainer Warning, "On the Alterity of Medieval Religious Drama," 266.

close not by resting its case but by initiating further debate. Training in all three rhetorical genres or exposure to them in such displays of eloquence as political speeches, Sunday sermons, proclamations, and funeral orations might thus be echoed in diverse literary forms: the *tenso* and *joc-partit* of lyric poetry, the moral dialogues that unfold within the walled city of Christine de Pizan's *Cité des Dames* and the immoral ones in Chaucer's equally mnemonic "House of Fame," the interior monologues of Chrétien de Troyes, the allegorical dream visions of the *Roman de la rose*, the great debates of *The Owl and the Nightingale* and the *Celestina*, even the visual dramas committed to the custodianship of the illuminated manuscript page.[71] Similarly, the history of delivery promises to prove equally compelling in the Renaissance, not only in theatrical productions but also in the interaction between speech and image in the emblem book, the famous declamatory performance of Erasmus's Folly, the personal voices heard by essayists, the dialogic interaction of Marguerite de Navarre's *devisants*, and the performative imagery of Shakespeare, and even in the possibility of reading all those elusive Rabelaisian lists aloud. Wherever and whenever *rhetorica* appeared, the memory of delivery inhered, and performance was as imminent as it had been in the mnemonic exercises once described by the pseudo-Cicero, Augustine, and Martianus. There was no origin of medieval drama, only origins of medieval dramas and dramatic genres. Once the rhetoric of performance and the performance of rhetoric have been allowed to participate anew in the critical idiom, the study of *actio* supplies fresh insights into the aestheticization of many sorts of ritual and ritualized discourse. As the crucial conduit between institutions and their discourses, delivery offers an eternally variegated scenario not only for dramatic productions but for medieval literary production, thus prompting a redefinition of how oral and literate discourses interacted in early cultures.

[71]I refer here esp. to Sylvia Huot's compelling argument about the "performative quality" of the manuscript book in *From Song to Book*, 3–4.

Bibliography

Primary Sources

Abelard, Peter. *Historia calamitatum.* Ed. J. Monfrin. Paris: Vrin, 1967.
———. *The Story of Abelard's Adversities.* Ed. and trans. Etienne Gilson. Toronto: Pontifical Institute, 1964.
L'Advocacie Nostre-Dame et La Chapelerie Nostre-Dame de Baiex: Poème normand du XIVe siècle. Ed. Gaston Raynaud. Paris: Académie des Bibliophiles, 1899.
L'Advocacie Notre-Dame ou La Vierge Marie plaidant contre le Diable. Ed. Alphonse Chassant. Paris: August Aubry, 1855.
Alanus de Insulis [Alain de Lille]. "A *Compendium on the Art of Preaching:* Preface and Selected Chapters." Trans. Joseph M. Miller. In *Readings in Medieval Rhetoric,* ed. Joseph M. Miller, Michael H. Prosser, and Thomas W. Benson, 228–39. Bloomington: Indiana University Press, 1973.
———. *Summa de arte praedicatoria.* In *Patrologia Latina,* ed. J. P. Migne, vol. 210, cols. 110–98. Paris: Vrin, 1855.
Alcuin. *The Rhetoric of Alcuin and Charlemagne.* Ed. and trans. Wilbur Samuel Howell. Princeton: Princeton University Press, 1941.
Andeli, Henri d'. *The Battle of the Seven Arts.* Ed. Louis John Paetow. Berkeley: University of California Press, 1914.
Aristotle. *The "Art" of Rhetoric.* Ed. and trans. John Henry Freese. Loeb Classical Library. 1926; rpt. Cambridge: Harvard University Press, 1975.
———. *De anima.* Ed. and trans. W. S. Hett. Loeb Classical Library. Cambridge: Harvard University Press, 1935.
———. *De poetica liber Graece et Latine.* Ed. T. C. Harles. Leipzig: Siegfried Lebrecht Crusius, 1780.
———. *Poetics.* Ed. and trans. W. Hamilton Fyfe. In *Aristotle, Longinus, Demetrius.* Loeb Classical Library. 1927; rpt. Cambridge: Harvard University Press, 1946.
———. *The Poetics of Aristotle: Translated from Greek into English and from*

Arabic into Latin. Ed. and trans. D. S. Margouliouth. London: Hodder & Stoughton, 1911.
——. *Posterior Analytics and Topica.* Ed. and trans. Hugh Tredennick and E. S. Forster. Loeb Classical Library. 1960; rpt. Cambridge: Harvard University Press, 1966.
Augustine of Hippo. *Confessions.* Trans. R. S. Pine-Coffin. 1961; rpt. London: Penguin, 1974.
——. *Confessions.* Ed. William Watts. 2 vols. London: Heinemann, 1912.
——. *On Christine Doctrine.* Trans. D. W. Robertson, Jr. 1958; rpt. Indianapolis: Bobbs-Merrill, 1980.
Aurelianus Reomensis. *Musica Disciplina.* Ed. Lawrence Gushee. Corpus Scriptorum de Musica, 21. Rome: American Institute of Musicology, 1975.
Basin, Thomas. *Apologie, ou Plaidoyer pour moi-même.* Ed. Charles Samaran and Georgette de Groër. Classiques de l'histoire de France au Moyen-Age, 31. Paris: Belles-Lettres, 1974.
——. *Histoire des règnes de Charles VII et de Louis XI.* Ed. J. Quicherat. 4 vols Paris: Renouard, 1859.
Boethius. *De topicis differentiis.* Trans. Eleonore Stump. Ithaca: Cornell University Press, 1978.
Boutillier, Jean. *Somme rural[e] tres utille en toutes cours de pratiques.* Paris, ca. 1515.
Brunetto Latini. *Li Livres dou Trésor.* Ed. Francis J. Carmody. Berkeley: University of California Press, 1948.
Bullaire de l'Inquisition française au XIVᵉ siècle et jusqu'à la fin du grand schisme. Ed. J.-M. Vidal. Paris: Letouzey et Ané, 1913.
Chartier, Alain. *Le Quadrilogue invectif.* Ed. Eugénie Droz. Paris: Champion, 1923.
Chartularium Universitatis Parisiensis. Ed. Henricus Denifle and Aemilio Chatelain. Paris, 1891.
Chaucer, Geoffrey. *Canterbury Tales.* In *The Riverside Chaucer,* ed. Larry D. Benson. 3d edition. Boston: Houghton Mifflin, 1987.
[Cicero]. *Ad C. Herennium.* Ed. and trans. Harry Caplan. Loeb Classical Library. 1954; rpt. Cambridge: Harvard University Press, 1977.
Cicero. *Brutus* and *Orator.* Ed. and trans. G. L. Hendrickson and H. M. Hubbell. Loeb Classical Library. Cambridge: Harvard University Press, 1952.
——. *De inventione and Topica.* Ed. and trans. H. M. Hubbell. Loeb Classical Library. 1949; rpt. Cambridge: Harvard University Press, 1968.
——. *De oratore and De partitione oratoria.* Ed. and trans. E. W. Sutton and H. Rackham. 2 vols. Loeb Classical Library. 1942; rpt. Cambridge: Harvard University Press, 1976.
Cohen, Gustave, ed. *Mystères et moralités de MS 617 de Chantilly.* Paris: Champion, 1920.
——, ed. *Receuil de farces françaises inédites du XVᵉ siècle.* Cambridge: Mediaeval Academy of America, 1949.
Coquillart, Guillaume. *Plaidoyé d'entre la Simple et la Rusée.* In *Oeuvres,* ed. Michael J. Freeman. Geneva: Droz, 1975.
Corpus iuris civilis. Vol. 1: *Institutiones,* ed. P. Krueger; *Digesta,* ed. T. Mommsen; *Codex Iustinianus,* ed. P. Krueger. Berlin, 1877.
Daniel of Morley. "Prefatio ad Librum de naturis superiorum et inferiorum." In

Rara Mathematica, ed. James Orchard Halliwell. London: John William Parker, 1839.

Demetrius. "On Style." Ed. and trans. W. Rhys Roberts. In *Aristotle, Longinus, Demetrius*. Loeb Classical Library. 1927; rpt. Cambridge: Harvard University Press, 1946.

Du Breuil, Guillaume. *Stilus Curie Parlamenti*. Ed. Félix Aubert. Paris: Picard, 1909.

——. *Style du Parlement de Paris*. Paris: Gouverneur, 1877.

La Farce de Maistre Pierre Pathelin. Trans. Alan Knight. In Donald Maddox, *Semiotics of Deceit: The Pathelin Era*, 173–99. Lewisburg, Pa.: Bucknell University Press, 1984.

La Farce de Maistre Pierre Pathelin. Ed. C. E. Pickford. 1967; rpt. Paris: Bordas, 1977.

Fournier, Edouard, ed. *Le Théatre français avant la Renaissance*. 1972; rpt. New York: Burt Franklin, 1965.

Fulbert of Chartres. *The Letters and Poems of Fulbert of Chartres*. Ed. and trans. Frederick Behrends. Oxford: Clarendon, 1976.

Geoffrey of Vinsauf. "The New Poetics (*Poetria nova*)." Trans. Jane Baltzell Kopp. In *Three Medieval Rhetorical Arts*, ed. James J. Murphy, 27–108. Berkeley: University of California Press, 1985.

——. *Poetria nova*. In Edmond Faral, *Les Arts poétiques du XIIᵉ et du XIIIᵉ siècle*, 194–262. 1924; rpt. Paris: Champion, 1958.

——. *Poetria nova*. In *The "Poetria nova" and Its Sources in Early Rhetorical Doctrine*. Trans. Ernest Gallo. The Hague: Mouton, 1971.

Gerard de Frachet. *Lives of the Brethren of the Order of Preachers, 1206–1259*. Trans. Placid Conway. London: Burns, Oates & Washbourne, 1924.

Gréban, Arnoul. *Le Mystère de la Passion*. Ed. Omer Jodogne. Brussels: Académie Royale, 1965.

——. *Le Mystère de la Passion*. Ed. Gaston Paris and Gaston Raynaud. 1878; rpt. Geneva: Slatkine, 1970.

——. "Arnoul Gréban's *The Mystery of the Passion*: The Third Day." Trans. Paula Giuliano. Ph.D. dissertation, City University of New York Graduate Center, 1991.

Gringore, Pierre. *Oeuvres complètes*. Ed. Charles d'Héricault and Anatole de Montaiglon. 2 vols. Paris, 1858, 1877.

Hauréau, B. *Notices et extraits de quelques manuscrits latins de la Bibliothèque Nationale*. Paris: Klincksieck, 1893.

Heldris de Cornuälle. *Le Roman de Silence*. Ed. Lewis Thorpe. Cambridge: Heffer, 1972.

Hicks, Eric, ed. *Le Débat sur le "Roman de la rose."* Paris: Champion, 1977.

Hugh of St. Victor. *Didascalicon: De studio legendi: A Critical Text*. Ed. Charles Henry Buttimer. Washington, D.C.: Catholic University Press, 1939.

——. *The Didascalicon of Hugh of St. Victor*. Trans. Jerome Taylor. 1961; rpt. New York: Columbia University Press, 1991.

Hugo, Victor. *Poésies*. Ed. Bernard Leuilliot. Vol. 1. Paris: Seuil, 1972.

Isidore of Seville. *Etymologías*. Ed. José Oroz Reta and Manuel A. Marcos Casquero. 2 vols. Madrid: Biblioteca de Autores Cristianos, 1982.

——. *Isidori Hispalensis Episcopi Etymologiarum sive Originum Libri XX*. Ed. W. M. Lindsay. 2 vols. 1911; rpt. London: Oxford University Press, 1962.

Jacques de Thérines. *Quodlibets I et II.* Ed. Palémon Glorieux. Paris: Vrin, 1958.
Le Jardin de Plaisance et Fleur de Rhétorique. Ed. Eugénie Droz and A. Piaget. 2 vols. 1925; rpt. New York and London: Johnson, 1968.
Jean de Meun. *Le Roman de la rose.* Ed. Daniel Poirion. Paris: Garnier-Flammarion, 1974.
John of Garland. *The "Parisiana poetria" of John of Garland.* Ed. Traugott Lawler. Yale Studies in English, 182. New Haven: Yale University Press, 1974.
John of Salisbury. *The Metalogicon.* Trans. Daniel McGarry. 1955; rpt. Gloucester, Mass.: Peter Smith, 1971.
Journal d'un bourgeois de Paris, 1405–1449. Ed. A. Tuety. Paris, 1881.
Langlois, Ernest. *Recueil d'arts de seconde rhétorique.* 1902; rpt. Geneva, 1974.
Le Roux de Lincy, Antoine and Francisque Michel, eds. *Receuil de farces, moralités et sermons joyeux.* 4 vols. Paris: Techener, 1837.
Lesage, Jean. *Quodlibets I.* Ed. Palémon Glorieux. Paris: Vrin, 1958.
Las Leys d'amors. Ed. Joseph Anglade. 4 vols. Toulouse, 1919.
Las Leys d'amors. Ed. M. Gratien-Arnoult. Toulouse, Privat, 1841–43.
Longinus. "On the Sublime." Ed. and trans. W. Hamilton Fyfe. In *Aristotle, Longinus, Demetrius.* Loeb Classical Library. 1927; rpt. Cambridge: Harvard University Press, 1946.
Lucian of Samosata. "A Professor of Public Speaking." Ed. and trans. A. M. Harmon. In *Works of Lucian,* vol. 4. Loeb Classical Library. 1925; rpt. Cambridge: Harvard University Press, 1969.
———. "Saltatio." Ed. and trans. A. M. Harmon. In *Works of Lucian,* vol. 5. Loeb Classical Library. 1936; rpt. Cambridge: Harvard University Press, 1972.
Ludus Coventriae. Ed. James Orchard Halliwell. 1841; rpt. Nendeln, Liechtenstein: Kraus, 1966.
Ludus Coventriae, or The Plaie called Corpus Christi. Ed. K. S. Block. Early English Text Society. London: Oxford University Press, 1922.
Machaut, Guillaume de. *Le Remède de Fortune.* Ed. Ernest Hoeppfner. In *Oeuvres,* vol. 2. Paris, 1908–1921.
Mahieu le Poirier. *Le Court d'Amours: Suite anonyme de la "Court d'Amours."* Ed. Terence Scully. Waterloo, Ont.: Wilfrid Laurier University Press, 1976.
Maistre Pierre Pathelin (Farce). Ed. Richard T. Holbrook. 2d ed. Classiques Français du Moyen Age, 35. Paris: Champion, 1962.
Martial d'Auvergne. *Les Arrêts d'amour.* Ed. Jean Rychner. Société des Anciens Textes Français, 141. Paris: Picard, 1951.
Martianus Capella. *De nuptiis Philologiae et Mercurii.* Ed. Adolfus Dick. Liepzig, 1925.
———. "De nuptiis Philologiae et Mercurii, V: 'The Book of Rhetoric.' " Trans. Joseph M. Miller. In *Readings in Medieval Rhetoric,* ed. Joseph M. Miller, Michael H. Prosser, and Thomas W. Benson, 1–5. Bloomington: Indiana University Press, 1973.
Matthew of Vendôme. *Ars versificatoria.* In *Les Arts poétiques du XIIe et du XIIIe siècle,* ed. Edmond Faral, 106–93. 1924; rpt. Paris: Champion, 1958.
———. *The Art of Versification.* Trans. Aubrey E. Galyon. Ames: University of Iowa Press, 1980.
Milton, John. *Paradise Lost.* Ed. Merritt Y. Hughes. New York: Odyssey, 1935.
Le Mistére du Viel Testament. Ed. James de Rothschild. 6 vols. 1878; rpt. New York and London: Johnson, 1966.
Montaiglon, A. de, and Gaston Raynaud, eds. *Receuil général et complet des*

fabliaux des XIIIe et XIVe siècles. Vol. 2. 1877; rpt. New York: Burt Franklin, 1964.

Le Mystère d'Adam (Ordo representationis Ade). Ed. Paul Aebischer. Geneva: Droz, 1964.

Le Mystère de la Passion: Texte du Manuscrit 697 de la Bibliothèque d'Arras. Ed. Jules-Marie Richard. 1891; rpt. Geneva: Slatkine, 1976.

Le "Mystère de la Passion" de Troyes. Ed. Jean-Claude Bibolet. 2 vols. Geneva: Droz, 1987.

Picot, Emile, ed. *Receuil général des sotties*. 3 vols. Paris: Firmin Didot, 1902–1912.

Plato. *Gorgias*. Trans. Benjamin Jowett. In *The Dialogues of Plato*, vol. 1. 8th ed. New York: Random House, 1937.

——. *Phaedrus*. Trans. R. Hackforth. 1952; rpt. Cambridge: Cambridge University Press, 1972.

——. *The Sophist and the Statesman*. Trans. A. E. Taylor. London: Thomas Nelson, 1961.

——. *Theaetetus*. Trans. Francis MacDonald Cornford. 1957; rpt. Indianapolis: Bobbs-Merrill, 1977.

Pollard, Alfred W., ed. *English Miracle Plays, Moralities, and Interludes*. 1890; rpt. Oxford: Clarendon, 1954.

Procès de condamnation de Jeanne d'Arc. Ed. Pierre Champion. 2 vols. 1920, 1921; rpt. Geneva: Slatkine, 1976.

"Proces que a faict Misericorde contre Justice." Bibliothèque Nationale, Rés. Yf101.

"Processus iuris ioco-serius." 1611. Bibliothèque Nationale, 12396.

Quintilian. *Institutio oratoria*. Ed. and trans. H. E. Butler. 4 vols. Loeb Classical Library. 1920; rpt. Cambridge:Harvard University Press, 1980.

Le Recueil Trepperel: Les Sotties. Ed. Eugénie Droz. Paris: Droz, 1935.

Le Registre d'Inquisition de Jacques Fournier (Evêque de Pamiers). Ed. Jean Duvernoy. 3 vols. Paris: Mouton, 1978.

Richard, son of Nigel [Fitzneale], Treasurer of England and Bishop of London. *De necessariis observantiis scaccarii dialogus*. Ed. and trans. Charles Johnson. London: Thomas Nelson, 1950.

Robert of Basevorn. *The Form of Preaching*. Trans. Leopold Krul. In *Three Medieval Rhetorical Arts*, ed. James J. Murphy, 109–215. Berkeley: University of California Press, 1985.

Rutebeuf. *Le Miracle de Théophile*. In *Oeuvres complètes*, ed. Achille Jubinal, 2:79–105. Paris: Edouard Pannier, 1839.

Seneca the Elder. *Controversiae*. Ed. and trans. M. Winterbottom. 2 vols. Loeb Classical Library. Cambridge: Harvard University Press, 1974.

Tacitus. *Dialogus de oratoribus*. Ed. and trans. Sir W. Peterson; rev. M. Winterbottom. Loeb Classical Library. 1914; rpt. Cambridge: Harvard University Press, 1980.

Tertullian. *De spectaculis*. Ed. and trans. T. R. Glover. Loeb Classical Library. 1931; rpt. Cambridge: Harvard University Press, 1977.

——. *"De spectaculis" suivi de Pseudo-Cyprien "De spectaculis."* Ed. André Boulanger. Paris: Belles Lettres, 1933.

Thomas Aquinas, Saint. *Summa theologica*. Pt. 1, vol. 2. London: R. & T. Washbourne, 1912.

Thomas de Bailly. *Quodlibets*. Ed. Palémon Glorieux. Paris: Vrin, 1960.

Viollet-le-Duc, M., ed. *Ancien Théâtre français.* Vols. 1–3. 1854; rpt. Nendeln, Liechtenstein: Kraus, 1972.
Vives, Juan Luis. *Adversus pseudodialecticos* and *De causis corruptarum artium,* Book III. In *Juan Luis Vives against the Pseudodialecticians: A Humanist Attack on Medieval Logic,* ed. and trans. Rita Guerlac. Boston: D. Reidel, 1979.
——. *Vives: On Education [De tradendis disciplinis].* Trans. Foster Watson. 1913; rpt. Totowa, N. J.: Rowman & Littlefield, 1971.
Wrightes Play. In *The Chester Mystery Cycle,* ed. R. M. Lumiansky and David Mills, 1:97–124. Early English Text Society, S. S. 3. London: Oxford University Press, 1974.

Secondary Sources

Accarie, Maurice. *Le Théâtre sacré de la fin du Moyen Age: Etude sur le sens moral de la "Passion" de Jean Michel.* Geneva: Droz, 1979.
Akehurst, F. R. P. "Seeing Justice Done." Paper presented at conference, "City and Spectacle in Medieval Europe," Minneapolis, 1 March 1991.
Alexander, Michael. *Trials in the Late Roman Republic.* Toronto: University of Toronto Press, 1990.
Alton, R. E., ed. "The Academic Drama in Oxford: Extracts from the Records of Four Colleges." *Malone Society Collections* 5 (1960).
Anglo, Sydney. *Spectacle, Pageantry, and Early Tudor Poetry.* Oxford: Clarendon, 1969.
Arden, Heather. *Fools' Plays.* Cambridge: Cambridge University Press, 1980.
Arnold, Carroll C. "Oral Rhetoric, Rhetoric, and Literature." In *Rhetoric in Transition: Studies in the Nature and Uses of Rhetoric,* ed. Eugene E. White, 157–73. University Park: Pennsylvania State University Press, 1980.
Artaud, Antonin. *Le Théâtre et son double.* Vol. 4 of *Oeuvres complètes.* Paris: Gallimard, 1964.
Arts libéraux et philosophie au Moyen-Age. Actes du 4ᵉ Congrès International de Philosophies Médiévales, 27 August–2 September 1967. Montreal: Institut d'Etudes Médiévales, 1969.
Aubailly, Jean-Claude. *Le Monologue, le dialogue et la sottie.* Paris: Champion, 1976.
——. *Le Théâtre médiéval profane et comique.* Paris: Larousse, 1975.
Auerbach, Erich. *Literary Language and Its Public in Late Latin Antiquity and in the Middle Ages.* New York: Pantheon, 1965.
——. *Mimesis: The Representation of Reality in Western Literature.* Trans. Willard R. Trask. 1953; rpt. Princeton: Princeton University Press, 1974.
Austin, J. L. *How to Do Things with Words.* Ed. J. O. Urmson and Marina Sbisà. 2d ed. Cambridge: Harvard University Press, 1978.
Axer, Jerzy. "Tribunal-Stage-Arena: Modelling of the Communication Situation in M. Tullius Cicero's Judicial Speeches." *Rhetorica* 7 (1990): 299–311.
Axton, Richard. *European Drama of the Early Middle Ages.* London: Hutchinson, 1974.
Baker, Donald C. "When Is a Text a Play? Reflections upon What Certain Late Medieval Dramatic Texts Can Tell Us." In *Contexts for Early English Drama,*

ed. Marianne G. Briscoe and John C. Coldewey, 20–40. Bloomington: Indiana University Press, 1989.

Bakhtin, Mikhail. *The Dialogic Imagination: Four Essays by M. M. Bakhtin.* Ed. Michael Holquist; trans. Caryl Emerson and Michael Holquist. Austin: University of Texas Press, 1981.

——. *Rabelais and His World.* Trans. Hélène Iswolsky. Bloomington: Indiana University Press, 1984.

Baldwin, Charles Sears. *Medieval Rhetoric and Poetic.* New York: Macmillan, 1928.

——. *Renaissance Literary Theory and Practice: Classicism in the Rhetoric and Poetic of Italy, France, and England, 1400–1600.* New York: Columbia University Press, 1939.

Barish, Jonas. *The Anti-Theatrical Prejudice.* Berkeley: University of California Press, 1981.

Barricelli, Jean-Pierre, and Joseph Gibaldi, eds. *Interrelations of Literature.* New York: MLA, 1982.

Barry, Jackson G. *Dramatic Structure: The Shaping of Experience.* Berkeley: University of California Press, 1970.

Barthes, Roland. "L'Ancienne Rhétorique." *Communications* 16 (1970): 172–229.

——. *Mythologies.* Paris: Seuil, 1957. Published in English under the same title, trans. Annette Lavers. New York: Hill & Wang, 1987.

Baty, Gaston, and René Chavance. *Vie de l'art théâtral des origines à nos jours.* Paris: Plon, 1932.

Bernstein, Alan E. "The Exemplum as 'Incorporation' of Abstract Truth in the Thought of Humbert of Romans and Stephen of Bourbon." In *The Two Laws,* ed. Laurent Mayali and Stephanie Tibbetts, 82–96. Washington, D.C.: Catholic University Press, 1990.

Bevington, David. *Action Is Eloquence: Shakespeare's Language of Gesture.* Cambridge: Harvard University Press, 1984.

——. *From "Mankind" to "Marlowe."* Cambridge: Harvard University Press, 1962.

——. *The Medieval Drama.* Boston: Houghton Mifflin, 1975.

Birch, Walter De Gray. *On a Thirteenth Century Service Book of Strasbourg with Dramatic Representations.* Transactions of the Royal Society of Literature, 10. London, 1874.

Blackstone, William. *Commentaries on the Laws of England.* Ed. Robert Kerr. 1811; rpt. Boston: Beacon, 1962.

Bliese, James. "The Study of Rhetoric in the Twelfth Century." *QJS* 63 (1977): 364–83.

Bloch, R. Howard. *Medieval French Literature and Law.* Berkeley: University of California Press, 1977.

——. "Silence and Holes: The *Roman de Silence* and the Art of the Trouvère." *YFS* 70 (1986): 81–99.

Boas, Frederick S. *University Drama in the Tudor Ages.* Oxford: Clarendon, 1914.

Boglioni, Pierre. "Some Methodological Reflections on the Study of Medieval Popular Religion." *Journal of Popular Culture* 11 (1977): 697–705.

Bolgar, R. R. "The Teaching of Rhetoric in the Middle Ages." In *Rhetoric Re-*

valued, ed. Brian Vickers, 79–86. Binghamton, N.Y.: Medieval and Renaissance Texts and Studies, 1982.

Bongert, Yvonne. *Recherches sur les cours laïques du Xe au XIIIe siècle*. Paris: A. & J. Picard, 1949.

Bonner, Robert J. *Lawyers and Litigants in Ancient Athens: The Genesis of the Legal Profession*. Chicago: University of Chicago Press, 1927.

Bonner, S. F. *Roman Declamation in the Late Republic and Early Empire*. Berkeley: University of California Press, 1949.

Bossy, Michel-André. "Medieval Debates of Body and Soul." *Comparative Literature* 28 (1976): 144–63.

Bourgeault, Cynthia. "Liturgical Dramaturgy." *Comparative Drama* 17 (1983): 124–40.

Bowen, Barbara C. *Les Caractéristiques essentielles de la farce française et leur survivance dans les années 1550–1620*. Champaign: University of Illinois Press, 1964.

Branham, R. Bracht. *Unruly Eloquence: Lucian and the Comedy of Traditions*. Cambridge: Harvard University Press, 1989.

Brault, Gerald J., ed. *The Song of Roland: An Analytical Edition*. 2 vols. University Park: Pennsylvania State University Press, 1978.

Brehaut, Ernest. *An Encyclopedist of the Dark Ages: Isidore of Seville*. Studies in History, Economics, and Public Law, 48. New York: Columbia University Press, 1912.

Breisach, Ernst, ed. *Classical Rhetoric and Medieval Historiography*. Kalamazoo: Medieval Institute Publications, 1985.

Briscoe, Marianne G. "Preaching and Medieval English Drama." In *Contexts for Early English Drama*, ed. Briscoe and John C. Coldewey, 151–72. Bloomington: Indiana University Press, 1989.

———. "Some Clerical Notions of Dramatic Decorum in Late Medieval England." *Comparative Drama* 19 (1985): 1–13.

Briscoe, Marianne G., and John C. Coldewey, eds. *Contexts for Early English Drama*. Bloomington: Indiana University Press, 1989.

Bristol, Michael D. *Carnival and the Theatre: Plebeian Culture and the Structure of Authority in Renaissance England*. New York: Methuen, 1985.

Brown, Cynthia. *The Shaping of Poetry and History in Late Medieval France*. Birmingham, Ala.: Summa, 1985.

Brown, Frederick. *Theater and Revolution: The Culture of the French Stage*. New York: Viking, 1980.

Brown, Howard Mayer. *Music in the French Secular Theater, 1400–1550*. Cambridge: Harvard University Press, 1963.

Brownlee, Kevin. "Jean de Meun and the Limits of Romance." In *Romance*, ed. Kevin Brownlee and Marina Scordilis Brownlee, 114–34. Hanover, N.H.: University Press of New England, 1985.

Brownlee, Kevin, and Marina Scordilis Brownlee, eds. *Romance: Generic Transformation from Chrétien de Troyes to Cervantes*. Hanover, N.H.: University Press of New England, 1985.

Brownstein, Oscar L. "Plato's *Phaedrus*: Dialectic as the Genuine Art of Speaking." *QJS* 51 (1965): 392–98.

Brundage, James A. *Law, Sex, and Christian Society in Medieval Europe*. Chicago: University of Chicago Press, 1987.

Bryant, Donald C. "Aspects of the Rhetorical Tradition: The Intellectual Foundation." *QJS* 36 (1950): 169–76.

Burke, Kenneth. *The Philosophy of Literary Form: Studies in Symbolic Action.* 3d ed. 1941; rpt. Berkeley: University of California Press, 1973.

——. *The Rhetoric of Religion: Studies in Logology.* Boston: Beacon, 1961.

——. "Rhetoric—Old and New." *Journal of General Education* 5 (1951): 203–9.

Burks, Don M. *Rhetoric, Philosophy, and Literature: An Exploration.* West Lafayette, Ind.: Purdue University Press, 1978.

Bynum, Caroline Walker. *Holy Feast and Holy Fast: The Religious Significance of Food to Medieval Women.* Berkeley: University of California Press, 1987.

——. *Jesus as Mother: Studies in the Spirituality of the High Middle Ages.* Berkeley: University of California Press, 1982.

Caillois, Roger. *L'Homme et le sacré.* Paris: Gallimard, 1950.

——. *Les Jeux et les hommes: Le Masque et le vertige.* Paris: Gallimard, 1967.

Camargo, Martin. "Rhetoric." In *The Seven Liberal Arts in the Middle Ages,* ed. David L. Wagner, 96–124. Bloomington: Indiana University Press, 1986.

Camille, Michael. "The Book of Signs: Writing and Visual Difference in Gothic Manuscript Illumination." *Word and Image* 1 (1985): 26–49.

Campbell, Paul Newell. "Elements of Rhetorical Form in Dramatic Discourse." Paper presented at SCA convention, New York, 15 November 1980.

Caplan, Harry C. "Classical Rhetoric and the Mediaeval Theory of Preaching." In *Historical Studies of Rhetoric and Rhetoricians,* ed. Raymond F. Howes, 71–89. 1961; rpt. Ithaca: Cornell University Press, 1965.

——. "Memoria: Treasure-House of Eloquence." In *Of Eloquence: Studies in Ancient and Mediaeval Rhetoric,* 196–246. Ithaca: Cornell University Press, 1970.

Cargill, Oscar. *Drama and Liturgy.* New York: Columbia University Press, 1930.

Carlson, Marvin. *Places of Performance: The Semiotics of Theatre Architecture.* Ithaca: Cornell University Press, 1989.

——. *Theories of the Theatre: A Historical and Critical Survey, from the Greeks to the Present.* Ithaca: Cornell University Press, 1985.

Carnahan, David H. *The Prologue in the Old French and Provençal Mystery.* New Haven: Tuttle, Morehouse & Taylor, 1905.

Carruthers, Mary. *The Book of Memory.* Cambridge: Cambridge University Press, 1990.

Cerquiglini, Bernard. *Eloge de la variante: Histoire critique de la philologie.* Paris: Seuil, 1989.

Chaignet, A. E. *La Rhétorique et son histoire.* Paris, 1888.

Chambers, E. K. *The Mediaeval Stage.* 2 vols. Oxford: Oxford University Press, 1903.

Chaytor, H. J. *From Script to Print.* 1945; rpt. Cambridge: Heffer, 1950.

Chenu, Marie-Dominique. "Auctor, actor, autor." *Bulletin du Cange—Archivium Latinitas Medii Aevi* 3 (1927): 81–86.

Chodorow, Stanley. *Christian Political Theory and Church Politics in the Mid-Twelfth Century: The Ecclesiology of Gratian's "Decretum."* Berkeley: University of California Press, 1972.

Clanchy, M. T. *From Memory to Written Record: England, 1066–1307.* Cambridge: Harvard University Press, 1979.

——. "Remembering the Past and the Good Old Law." *History* 55 (1970): 166–72.

Clark, Donald Lemen. *Rhetoric and Poetry in the Renaissance.* New York: Columbia University Press, 1922.

——. *Rhetoric in Greco-Roman Education.* New York: Columbia University Press, 1957.

Clerval, Jules Alexandre. *Les Ecoles de Chartres au Moyen-Age du Vᵉ au XVIᵉ siècle.* Chartres: Selleret, 1895.

Clopper, Lawrence M. "Lay and Clerical Impact on Civic Religious Drama and Ceremony." In *Contexts for Early English Drama,* ed. Marianne G. Briscoe and John C. Coldewey, 102–36. Bloomington: Indiana University Press, 1989.

——. "*Miracula* and *The Tretise of Miraclis Pleyinge.*" *Speculum* 65 (1990): 878–905.

Coffman, George Raleigh. *A New Theory Concerning the Origin of the Miracle Play.* Menasha, Wis.: Collegiate Press, 1914.

Cohen, Gustave. *La Comédie latine en France au XIIᵉ siècle.* Paris, 1931.

——. *Histoire de la mise en scène dans le théâtre religieux français du Moyen-Age.* 2d ed. Paris: Champion, 1951.

——. *Le Théâtre en France au Moyen-Age.* Vol. 1, *Le Théatre religieux;* vol. 2, *Le Théâtre profane.* Paris: Rieder, 1928, 1931.

Coldewey, John C. "Plays and Play in Early English Drama." *RORD* 18 (1975): 103–21.

——. "That Enterprising Property Player: Semi-Professional Drama in Sixteenth-Century England." *Theatre Notebook* 31 (1977): 5–12.

Colie, Rosalie L. "Literature and History." In *Relations of Literary Study,* ed. James Thorpe, 1–26. New York: MLA, 1967.

Colish, Marcia L. *The Mirror of Language: A Study in the Medieval Theory of Knowledge.* New Haven: Yale University Press, 1968.

Collins, Fletcher. *The Production of Medieval Church Music-Drama.* Charlottesville: University Press of Virginia, 1972.

Conley, Thomas. "Some Significant Contributions to the History of Rhetoric." *Rhetorica* 1 (1983): 93–108.

Conte, Gian Biago. *The Rhetoric of Imitation: Genre and Poetic Memory in Virgil and Other Latin Poets.* Trans. Charles Segal. Ithaca: Cornell University Press, 1986.

Copeland, Rita. *Rhetoric, Hermeneutics, and Translation in the Middle Ages: Academic Traditions and Vernacular Texts.* Cambridge: Cambridge University Press, 1991.

Craig, Barbara. "Didactic Elements in Medieval French Serious Drama." *L'Esprit Créateur* 2 (1962): 142–48.

Craig, Hardin. *English Religious Drama of the Middle Ages.* 1955; rpt. Oxford: Clarendon, 1964.

Creizenach, W. *Geschichte des neueren Dramas.* 4 vols. Halle, 1893–1910.

Croll, Morris W. *Style, Rhetoric, and Rhythm.* Ed. J. Max Patrick and Robert O. Evans. Princeton: Princeton University Press, 1966.

Crosby, Ruth. "Oral Delivery in the Middle Ages." *Speculum* 11 (1936): 88–110.

Curtius, Ernst Robert. *European Literature and the Latin Middle Ages.* Trans. Willard R. Trask. Bollingen, 36. 1952; rpt. Princeton: Princeton University Press, 1973.

Davenport, W. A. *Fifteenth-Century English Drama: The Early Moral Plays and Their Literary Relations.* Cambridge, Eng.: D. S. Brewer, 1982.

Davidson, Clifford. "Gesture in Medieval Drama with Special Reference to the Doomsday Plays in the Middle English Cycles." *EDAM Newsletter* 6 (1983): 8–17.

——. "Positional Symbolism and English Medieval Drama." *Comparative Drama* 25 (1991): 66–76.

——. "Space and Time in Medieval Drama: Meditations on Orientation in the Early Theater." In *Word, Picture, Spectacle,* 39–93. Early Drama, Art, and Music, 5. Kalamazoo: Medieval Institute Publications, 1984.

——, ed. *A Middle English Treatise on the Playing of Miracles.* Washington, D.C.: University Press of America, 1981.

Davidson, Clifford, and John H. Stroupe, eds. *Iconographic and Comparative Studies in Medieval Drama.* Kalamazoo: Medieval Institute Publications, 1991.

Davidson, Hugh M. *Audience, Words, and Art: Studies in Seventeenth-Century French Rhetoric.* Columbus: Ohio State University Press, 1965.

Davies, Wendy. "People and Places in Dispute in Ninth-Century Brittany." In *The Settlement of Disputes in Early Medieval Europe,* ed. Wendy Davies and Paul Fouracre, 65–84. Cambridge: Cambridge University Press, 1986.

Davies, Wendy, and Paul Fouracre, eds. *The Settlement of Disputes in Early Medieval Europe.* Cambridge: Cambridge University Press, 1986.

Davis, Nathalie Zemon. *The Return of Martin Guerre.* Cambridge: Harvard University Press, 1983.

Delachenal, Roland. *Histoire des avocats au Parlement de Paris (1300–1600).* Paris: Plon, 1885.

Delhaye, Philippe. "L'Organisation scolaire au 12ᵉ siècle." *Traditio* 5 (1947): 211–68.

De Man, Paul. "Semiology and Rhetoric." *Diacritics* 3 (1973): 27–33.

Denny, Neville. "Arena Staging and Dramatic Quality in the Cornish Passion Play." In *Medieval Drama,* ed. Neville Denny, 125–53. Stratford-upon-Avon Studies, 16. London: Edward Arnold, 1973.

Derrida, Jacques. *De la grammatologie.* Paris: Minuit, 1967.

Diderot, Denis. *Paradoxe sur le comédien.* In *Oeuvres esthétiques,* ed. Paul Vernière, 299–381. Paris: Garnier, 1968.

Diehl, Patrick S. *The Medieval European Religious Lyric: An Ars Poetica.* Berkeley: University of California Press, 1984.

Dockhorn, Klaus. "Rhetorica movet: Protestantischer Humanismus und Karolingische Renaissance." In *Rhetorik,* ed. Helmut Schanze, 17–42. Frankfurt am Main: Athenaion, 1974.

Dondis, Donis A. *A Primer of Visual Literacy.* Cambridge: MIT Press, 1973.

Dubech, Lucien, J. de Montbrial, and M. Horn-Monval. *Histoire générale illustrée du théâtre de Paris.* Vol. 2. Paris: Librairie de France, 1931.

Duby, George. *De l'Europe féodale à la Renaissance.* Vol. 2 of *Histoire de la vie privée.* Paris: Seuil, 1985.

Dunn, E. Catherine. "French Medievalists and the Saint's Play: A Problem for American Scholarship." *Medievalia et Humanistica* 6 (1975): 51–62.

——. *The Gallican Saint's Life and the Late Roman Dramatic Tradition.* Washington, D.C.: Catholic University Press, 1989.

——. "Gregorian Easter Vespers and Early Liturgical Drama." In *The Medieval Drama and Its Claudelian Revival.* Washington, D.C.: Catholic University Press, 1970.

——. "Popular Devotion in the Vernacular Drama of Medieval England." *Medievalia et Humanistica* 4 (1973): 55–68.

——. "Voice Structure in the Liturgical Drama: Sepet Reconsidered." In *Medieval English Drama*, ed. Jerome Taylor and Alan Nelson, 44–63. Chicago: University of Chicago Press, 1972.

Durand, Gilbert. *Les Structures anthropologiques de l'imaginaire.* Paris: Presses Universitaires de France, 1960.

Durkheim, Emile. *L'Evolution pédagogique en France.* 2d ed. Paris: Presses Universitaires de France, 1969. Published in English as *The Evolution of Educational Thought* trans. Peter Collins. London: Routledge & Kegan Paul, 1977.

Dutka, JoAnna. "Mystery Plays at Norwich: Their Formation and Development." *Leeds Studies in English* n.s. 10 (1978): 107–20.

Duvignaud, Jean. *L'Acteur: Esquisse d'une sociologie du comédien.* Paris: Gallimard, 1965.

——. *Sociologie du théâtre.* Paris: Presses Universitaires de France, 1965.

Eco, Umberto. *Semiotics and the Philosophy of Language.* Bloomington: Indiana University Press, 1984.

Eden, Kathy. *Poetic and Legal Fiction in the Aristotelian Tradition.* Princeton: Princeton University Press, 1986.

——. "The Rhetorical Tradition and Augustinian Hermeneutics in *De doctrina christiana.*" *Rhetorica* 8 (1990): 45–63.

Eisenbichler, Konrad, ed. *Crossing the Boundaries.* Kalamazoo: Medieval Institute Publications, 1991.

Eisenbichler, Konrad, and Amilcare A. Ianucci, eds. *Petrarch's "Triumphs": Allegory and Spectacle.* Ottawa: Dovehouse, 1990.

Elam, Kier. *The Semiotics of Theatre and Drama.* New York: Methuen, 1980.

Eliot, T. S. *Selected Essays.* New York: Harcourt Brace, 1932.

Elliot, John R., Jr. "Medieval Acting." In *Contexts for Early English Drama*, ed. Marianne G. Briscoe and John C. Coldewey, 243–44. Bloomington: Indiana University Press, 1989.

Enders, Jody. "Delivery and the Emasculation of Eloquence." Paper presented at SCA convention, Chicago, 1 November 1990.

——. "Memory, Allegory, and Medieval Generic Structures." Paper presented at MLA convention, New Orleans, 28 December 1988.

——. "Memory and the Psychology of the Interior Monologue in Chrétien's *Cligés.*" *Rhetorica* 10 (1992): 3–21.

——. "Music, Delivery, and the Rhetoric of Memory in Guillaume de Machaut's *Remède de Fortune.*" Forthcoming in *PMLA.*

——. "The Theatre of Scholastic Erudition." Forthcoming.

——. "Visions with Voices: The Rhetoric of Memory and Music in Liturgical Drama." *Comparative Drama* 24 (1990): 34–54.

Enos, Richard Lee. *The Literate Mode of Cicero's Legal Rhetoric.* Carbondale: Southern Illinois University Press, 1988.

Erlich, Howard S. "The Congruence of Aristotle's *Rhetoric* and *Poetics.*" *SSCJ* 38 (1973): 362–70.

Evans, Gillian R. "*Argumentum* and *Argumentatio:* The Development of a Technical Terminology up to c. 1150." *Classical Folia* 30 (1976): 81–93.
———. *The Language and Logic of the Bible: The Earlier Middle Ages.* Cambridge: Cambridge University Press, 1984.
Fabre, Adolphe. *Les Clercs du Palais.* 2d ed. of *Etudes historiques sur les clercs de la Bazoche.* Lyon: N. Scheuring, 1875.
———. *Les Clercs du Palais: La Farce du cry de la Bazoche.* Vienne: Savigné, 1882.
———. *Etudes Historiques sur les clercs de la Bazoche.* Paris: Potier, 1856.
Faral, Edmond. *Les Arts poétiques du XIIe et du XIIIe siècle.* 1924; rpt. Paris: Champion, 1958.
———. *Les Jongleurs en France au Moyen Age.* Paris: Champion, 1910.
Febvre, Lucien, and Henri-Jean Martin. *L'Apparition du livre.* Paris: Albin Michel, 1950.
Fichte, Jörge O. *Expository Voices in Medieval Drama: Essays on the Mode and Function of Dramatic Exposition.* Nuremberg: Hans Carl, 1975.
Flanigan, C. Clifford. "The Liturgical Drama and Its Tradition: A Review of Scholarship, 1965–1975." *RORD* 18 (1975): 109–36.
Fleischman, Suzanne. "Philology, Linguistics, and the Discourse of the Medieval Text." *Speculum* 65 (1990): 19–37.
———. *Tense and Narrativity: From Medieval Performance to Modern Fiction.* Austin: University of Texas Press, 1990.
Fleming, John. *Reason and the Lover.* Princeton: Princeton University Press, 1984.
———. *The "Roman de la Rose."* Princeton: Princeton University Press, 1969.
Florescu, Vasile. "Rhetoric and Its Rehabilitation in Contemporary Philosophy." *Philosophy and Rhetoric* 3 (1970): 193–224.
———. *La Rhétorique et la néo-rhétorique: Genèse-Evolution-Perspectives.* Trans. Melania Munteanu. 2d ed. 1973; rpt. Bucharest: Editura Academiei, 1982.
Foley, John Miles. *The Theory of Oral Composition: History and Methodology.* Bloomington: Indiana University Press, 1989.
Fortenbaugh, W. W. "Aristotle's *Rhetoric* on Emotions." *Archiv für Geschichte der Philosophie* 52 (1970): 40–70.
Foucault, Michel. *Les Mots et les choses.* Paris: Gallimard, 1966.
France, Peter. *Rhetoric and Truth in France.* Oxford: Clarendon, 1972.
Frank, Grace. *The Medieval French Drama.* Oxford: Clarendon, 1954.
Frank, Robert Worth, Jr. "The Art of Reading Medieval Personification Allegory." *English Literary History* 20 (1953): 237–50.
Frappier, Jean. *Le Théâtre profane en France au Moyen Age.* Paris: Centre de Documentation Universitaire, 1960.
Frappier, Jean, and A. M. Gossart. *Le Théâtre comique au Moyen Age.* Paris: Larousse, 1935.
Frazer, Sir James George. *The Scapegoat.* Vol. 6 of *The Golden Bough.* 3d ed. 1913; rpt. London: Macmillan, 1920.
Frye, Northrop. *Anatomy of Criticism.* 1957; rpt. Princeton: Princeton University Press, 1973.
Fumaroli, Marc. *L'Age de l'éloquence: Rhétorique et "res literaria."* Hautes études médiévales et modernes, 43. Geneva: Droz, 1980.
Gallo, Ernest. "The *Poetria nova* of Geoffrey of Vinsauf." In *Medieval Eloquence,* ed. James J. Murphy, 68–84. Berkeley: University of California Press, 1978.

Garner, Richard. *Law and Society in Classical Athens*. New York: St. Martin's Press, 1987.

Garvin, Harry R. *Rhetoric, Literature, and Interpretation*. Lewisburg, Pa.: Bucknell University Press, 1983.

Gastier, René. *Nouveaux styles des cours de Parlement, des aides, de la Chambre des Comptes, etc.* Paris, 1668.

Gelis, M. F. de. *Histoire critique des Jeux-Floraux*. Toulouse, 1912.

Gellrich, Jesse M. *The Idea of the Book in the Middle Ages: Language Theory, Mythology, and Fiction*. Ithaca: Cornell University Press, 1985.

Gellrich, Michelle. *Tragedy and Theory: The Problem of Conflict since Aristotle*. Princeton: Princeton University Press, 1988.

Genty, Lucien. *La Basoche notariale: Origines et histoire du XIVe siècle à nos jours de la cléricature notariale*. Paris: Delamotte, 1888.

Gibson, Gail McMurray. *The Theater of Devotion: East Anglian Drama and Society in the Late Middle Ages*. Chicago: University of Chicago Press, 1989.

Giles, B. "Medieval Latin Translations of Aristotle's *Art of Rhetoric.*" *Transactions of the American Philological Association* 65 (1934): 37–38.

Gilson, Etienne. *La Philosophie du Moyen Age: Des origines patristiques à la fin du XIVe siècle*. Paris: Payot, 1952.

Girard, René. *Violence and the Sacred*. Trans. Patrick Gregory. Baltimore: Johns Hopkins University Press, 1977.

Glorieux, Palémon. *La Littérature quodlibétique de 1260–1320*. 2 vols. Bibliothéque Thomiste, 5 and 21. Vol. 1: Le Saulchoir, Kain, Belgium, 1925; vol. 2: Paris: Vrin, 1935.

——. *Robert de Sorbon: L'Homme, le Collège, les documents*. Vol. 1 of *Aux origines de la Sorbonne*. Paris: Vrin, 1965.

Goebel, Julius, Jr. *Felony and Misdemeanor: A Study in the History of Criminal Law*. Philadelphia: University of Pennsylvania Press, 1976.

Gombrich, Ernst. *Art and Illusion: A Study in the Psychology of Pictorial Representation*. Princeton: Princeton University Press, 1961.

Gouron, André. "Court Proceedings in the Public Sphere." Paper presented at conference, "City and Spectacle in Medieval Europe;" Minneapolis, 1 March 1991.

Grafton, Anthony, and Lisa Jardine. *From Humanism to the Humanities: Education and the Liberal Arts in Fifteenth-Century Europe*. London: Duckworth, 1986.

Gravdal, Kathryn. *Ravishing Maidens: Sexual Violence in Medieval French Literature and Law*. Philadelphia: University of Pennsylvania Press, 1991.

Green, Richard Firth. *Poets and Princepleasers: Literature and the English Court in the Late Middle Ages*. Toronto: University of Toronto Press, 1980.

Guenée, Bernard. *Tribunaux et gens de justice dans le baillage de Senlis à la fin du Moyen Age*. Paris: Belles Lettres, 1963.

Guenée, Bernard, and Françoise Lehoux. *Les Entrées royales françaises de 1328 à 1515*. Paris: Centre National de la Recherche Scientifique, 1968.

Gunn, Alan. *The Mirror of Love: A Reinterpretation of "The Roman de la Rose."* Lubbock: Texas Tech Press, 1952.

——. "Teacher and Student in the *Roman de la Rose:* A Study in Archetypal Figures and Patterns." *L'Esprit Créateur* 2 (1962): 126–34.

Hadas, Moses. *Ancilla to Classical Reading*. New York: Columbia University Press, 1954.

Hagen, Susan K. *Allegorical Remembrance: A Study of "The Pilgrimage of the Life of Man" as a Medieval Treatise on Seeing and Remembering.* Athens: University of Georgia Press, 1990.

Hagstrum, Jean H. *The Sister Arts: The Tradition of Literary Pictorialism and English Poetry from Dryden to Gray.* Chicago: University of Chicago Press, 1958.

Hajdu, Helga. *Das mnemotechnische Schrifttum des Mittelalters.* Vienna, 1936.

Hajnal, Istvan. *L'Enseignement de l'écriture aux universités médiévales.* Budapest: Academia Scientiarum Hungarica Budapestini, 1954.

Harding, Harold F. "Quintilian's Witness." In *Historical Studies of Rhetoric and Rhetoricians,* ed. Raymond F. Howes, 90–106. 1961; rpt. Ithaca: Cornell University Press, 1965.

Hardison, O. B., Jr. *Christian Rite and Christian Drama in the Middle Ages: Essays in the Origin and Early History of Modern Drama.* Baltimore: Johns Hopkins University Press, 1965.

——. *The Enduring Moment: A Study of the Idea of Praise in Renaissance Literary Theory and Practice.* 1962; rpt. Westport, Conn.: Greenwood, 1973.

Harvey, Howard Graham. *The Theatre of the Basoche.* Cambridge: Harvard University Press, 1941.

Haskins, Charles Homer. *The Renaissance of the Twelfth Century.* New York: New American Library, 1927.

Havelock, Eric A. *The Muse Learns to Write.* New Haven: Yale University Press, 1986.

Herington, John. *Poetry into Drama: Early Tragedy and Greek Poetic Tradition.* Sather Classical Lectures, 49. Berkeley: University of California Press, 1985.

Heuzé, Philippe. "Le Plaisir de la parole: Le Témoignage de Sénèque le Père." Paper presented at seventh conference of ISHR, Göttingen, 27 July 1989.

Horner, Olga. "Manifestations of Medieval Law in Early English Drama." Paper presented at ICMS, Kalamazoo, 10 May 1990.

Horner, Winifred Bryan. *Historical Rhetoric: An Annotated Bibliography of Selected Sources in English.* Boston: G. K. Hall, 1980.

Howell, Wilbur Samuel. "Classical and European Traditions of Rhetoric and Speech Training." *SSCJ* 23 (1957): 73–78.

——. *Logic and Rhetoric in England, 1500–1700.* Princeton: Princeton University Press, 1956.

——. *Poetics, Rhetoric, and Logic: Studies in the Basic Disciplines of Criticism.* Ithaca: Cornell University Press, 1975.

Howes, Raymond F., ed. *Historical Studies of Rhetoric and Rhetoricians.* 1961; rpt. Ithaca: Cornell University Press, 1965.

Hudson, Hoyt. "Rhetoric and Poetry." In *Historical Studies of Rhetoric and Rhetoricians,* ed. Raymond F. Howes, 369–79. 1961; rpt. Ithaca: Cornell University Press, 1965.

Huizinga, Johan. *Homo Ludens: A Study of the Play Element in Culture.* 1950; rpt. Boston: Beacon, 1972.

——. *The Waning of the Middle Ages.* 1924; rpt. Garden City, N.Y.: Anchor/Doubleday, 1954.

Hult, David F. "The Limits of Mime(sis): Notes Toward a Generic Revision of Medieval Theater." *L'Esprit Créateur* 23 (1983): 49–63.

Hummelen, W. M. H. "The Dutch Rhetoricians' Drama." Paper presented at ICMS, Kalamazoo, May 1979.

——. *Repertorium van het Rederijkersdrama, 1500–c. 1620.* Assen: Van Goroun, 1968.

Hunt, R. W. *The History of Grammar in the Middle Ages.* Ed. G. L. Bursill-Hall. Amsterdam: Benjamins, 1980.

Hunt, Tony. "Rhetoric and Poetics in Twelfth-Century France." In *Rhetoric Revalued,* ed. Brian Vickers, 165–71. Binghamton, N.Y.: Medieval and Renaissance Texts and Studies, 1982.

Huot, Sylvia. *From Song to Book: The Poetics of Writing in Old French Lyric and Lyrical Narrative Poetry.* Ithaca: Cornell University Press, 1987.

Iser, Wolfgang. *The Act of Reading: A Theory of Aesthetic Response.* Baltimore: Johns Hopkins University Press, 1978.

Jackson, Bernard. *Semiotics and Legal Theory.* London: Routledge & Kegan Paul, 1985.

Jager, Eric. "Speech and the Chest in Old English Poetry: Orality or Pectorality." *Speculum* 65 (1990): 845–59.

James, Mervyn. "Ritual, Drama and Social Body in the Late Medieval English Town." *Past and Present* 98 (1983): 3–29.

Jauss, Hans-Robert. "The Alterity and Modernity of Medieval Literature." *NLH* 10 (1979): 181–227.

——. "Littérature médiévale et théorie des genres." *Poétique* 1 (1970): 79–101.

Jeanroy, Alfred. "Sur quelques sources des mystères français de la Passion." *Romania* 35 (1906): 365–78.

——. *Le Théâtre religieux en France.* Paris, 1923.

Jeffrey, David L. "Franciscan Spirituality and the Rise of Early English Drama." *Mosaic* 8 (1975): 17–46.

Jodogne, Omer. "Recherches sur les débuts du théâtre religieux en France." *CCM* 124 (1965): 179–89.

——. "Le Théâtre français du Moyen-Age: Recherches sur l'aspect dramatique des textes." In *The Medieval Drama,* ed. Sandro Sticca, 1–21. Albany: State University of New York at Albany Press, 1972.

Johnston, A. F. "The Plays of the Religious Guilds of York: The Creed Play and Pater Noster Play." *Speculum* 50 (1975): 55–90.

Jonsson, Ritva. *Tropes du propre de la messe: Cycle de Noël,* Corpus Troporum, 1. Stockholm: Almqvist & Wiksell, 1975.

Jubinal, Achille, ed. *Jongleurs et trouvères.* Paris: J. A. Merklein, 1835.

Kahrl, Stanley J. "Medieval Staging and Performance." In *Contexts for Early English Drama,* ed. Marianne G. Briscoe and John C. Coldewey, 219–37. Bloomington: Indiana University Press, 1989.

——. *Traditions of Medieval English Drama.* London: Hutchinson's University Library, 1974.

Katzenellenbogen, Adolf. *Allegories of the Virtues and Vices in Medieval Art: From Early Christian Times to the Thirteenth Century.* Medieval Academy Reprints for Teaching, 24. 1939; rpt. Toronto: University of Toronto Press, 1989.

Kelley, Michael R. *Flamboyant Drama: A Study of "The Castle of Perseverance," "Mankind," and "Wisdom."* Carbondale: Southern Illinois University Press, 1979.

Kelly, Douglas. "The Contextual Environment of the Medieval Arts of Poetry and Prose." Paper presented at MLA convention, New Orleans, 28 December 1988.

——. *Medieval Imagination: Rhetoric and the Poetry of Courtly Love.* Madison: University of Wisconsin Press, 1978.

——. "The School Arts of Poetry and Prose." Paper presented at ICMS, Kalamazoo, 6 May 1988.

——. "The Scope of the Treatment of Composition in the Twelfth- and Thirteenth-Century Arts of Poetry." *Speculum* 41 (1966): 261–78.

——. "Theory of Composition in Medieval Narrative Poetry and Geoffrey of Vinsauf's *Poetria Nova.*" *Medieval Studies* 31 (1969): 117–48.

——. "Topical Invention in Medieval French Literature." In *Medieval Eloquence,* ed. James J. Murphy, 231–51. Berkeley: University of California Press, 1978.

——. "*Translatio Studii:* Translation, Adaptation, and Allegory in Medieval French Literature." *Philological Quarterly* 57 (1978): 287–310.

Kendall, Calvin B. "Bede's *Historia ecclesiastica:* The Rhetoric of Faith." In *Medieval Eloquence,* ed. James J. Murphy, 145–72. Berkeley: University of California Press, 1978.

Kendrick, Laura. *The Game of Love: Troubadour Wordplay.* Berkeley: University of California Press, 1988.

Kennedy, George A. *The Art of Persuasion in Greece.* Princeton: Princeton University Press, 1963.

——. *Classical Rhetoric and Its Christian and Secular Tradition from Ancient to Modern Times.* Chapel Hill: University of North Carolina Press, 1980.

——. "Forms and Functions of Latin Speech, 400–800." In *Medieval and Renaissance Studies,* vol. 10, ed. G. M. Masters, 45–73. Chapel Hill: University of North Carolina Press, 1984.

Kennedy, William J. *Rhetorical Norms in Renaissance Literature.* New Haven: Yale University Press, 1978.

Kenny, Anthony, and Jan Pinborg. "Medieval Philosophical Literature." In *The Cambridge History of Later Medieval Philosophy,* ed. Norman Kretzmann, Anthony Kenny, and Jan Pinborg, 11–42. Cambridge: Cambridge University Press, 1982.

Kenyon, Frederic. *Books and Readers in Ancient Greece and Rome.* 2d ed. Oxford: Clarendon, 1951.

Kernodle, George R. *From Art to Theatre.* Chicago: University of Chicago Press, 1943.

Kerr, Walter. *Tragedy and Comedy.* New York: Simon & Schuster, 1967.

Kibédi Varga, Aron. "L'Histoire de la rhétorique et la rhétorique des genres." *Rhetorica* 3 (1985): 201–22.

——. *Rhétorique et littérature: Etudes de structures classiques.* Paris: Didier, 1970.

Kimminich, Eva. "The Way of Vice and Virtue: A Medieval Psychology." *Comparative Drama* 25 (1991): 77–86.

Kinneavy, James L. *Greek Rhetorical Origins of Christian Faith: An Inquiry.* New York: Oxford University Press, 1987.

Kintgen, Eugene R., Barry M. Kroll, and Mike Rose, eds. *Perspectives on Literacy.* Carbondale: Southern Illinois University Press, 1988.

Kipling, Gordon. "The Idea of the Civic Triumph: Drama, Liturgy, and the Royal Entry in the Low Countries." *Dutch Crossings* 22 (1984): 60–83.

Kirby, E. T. *Ur-Drama: The Origins of the Theatre.* New York: New York University Press, 1975.

Kittay, Jeffrey. "Utterance Unmoored: The Changing Interpretations of the Act of Writing in the European Middle Ages." *Language in Society* 17 (1986): 209–30.

Knight, Alan E. *Aspects of Genre in Late Medieval French Drama.* Manchester: Manchester University Press, 1983.

———. "From the Sacred to the Profane." *Tréteaux* 1 (1978): 41–49.

———. "The Medieval Theater of the Absurd." *PMLA* 86 (1971): 183–89.

Knox, Bernard. *Word and Action: Essays on the Ancient Theater.* Baltimore: Johns Hopkins University Press, 1979.

Kolve, V. A. *The Play Called Corpus Christi.* Stanford: Stanford University Press, 1966.

Kors, Alan C., and Edward Peters. *Witchcraft in Europe, 1100–1700: A Documentary History.* Philadelphia: University of Pennsylvania Press, 1972.

Kristeller, Paul Oskar. "Renaissance Aristotelianism." *Greek, Roman, and Byzantine Studies* 6 (1965): 157–74.

Lang, Robert A. "The Teaching of Rhetoric in French Jesuit Colleges, 1556 to 1762." *Speech Monographs* 19 (1952): 286–98.

Lanham, Richard A. *A Handlist of Rhetorical Terms.* Berkeley: University of California Press, 1968.

———. *The Motives of Eloquence: Literary Rhetoric in the Renaissance.* New Haven: Yale University Press, 1976.

Lanson, Gustave. *Histoire de la littérature française.* 21st ed. Paris: Hachette, 1929.

Lauvergnat-Gagnière, Christiane. *Lucien de Samosate et le Lucianisme en France au XVIe siècle.* Travaux d'Humanisme et Renaissance, 227. Geneva: Droz, 1988.

Lebègue, Raymond. *Etudes sur le théâtre français.* Vol. 1 of 2. Paris: Nizet, 1977.

———. "La *Passion* d'Arnoul Gréban." *Romania* 60 (1934): 218–31.

———. *Le Théâtre comique en France de Pathelin à Mélite.* Paris, 1972.

———. *La Tragédie religieuse en France: Les Débuts (1514–1573).* Paris: Champion, 1929.

Lecoy de La Marche, A. *La Chaire française au Moyen Age.* Paris: Renouard, 1886.

Lefebvre, Léon. *Histoire du théâtre de Lille de ses origines à nos jours.* 5 vols. Lille: Lefebvre-Ducrocq, 1901–1907.

Leff, Michael C. "In Search of Ariadne's Thread: A Review of the Recent Literature on Rhetorical Theory." *CSSJ* 29 (1978): 73–91.

———. "The Topics of Argumentative Invention in Latin Rhetorical Theory from Cicero to Boethius." *Rhetorica* 1 (1983): 23–44.

Le Goff, Jacques. *La Civilisation de l'Occident médiéval.* Paris: Arthaud, 1967.

Lentz, Tony M. *Orality and Literacy in Hellenic Greece.* Carbondale: Southern Illinois University Press, 1989.

Lerer, Seth. *Boethius and Dialogue.* Princeton: Princeton University Press, 1985.

Le Roux de Lincy, Antoine, and L. M. Tisserand. *Paris et ses historiens aux XIVe et XVe siècles.* Paris: Imprimerie Impériale, 1867.

Leupin, Alexandre. *Barbarolexis: Medieval Writing and Sexuality.* Trans. Kate M. Cooper. Cambridge: Harvard University Press, 1989.

Lewalski, Barbara Kiefer. *"Paradise Lost" and the Rhetoric of Literary Forms.* Princeton: Princeton University Press, 1985.

Lewicka, Halina. *Etudes sur l'ancienne farce française.* Paris: Klincksieck, 1974.

Lewis, C. S. *The Allegory of Love: A Study in Medieval Tradition.* 1936; rpt. London: Oxford University Press, 1976.

Lewry, P. Osmund. "Rhetoric at Paris and Oxford in the Mid-Thirteenth Century." *Rhetorica* 1 (1983): 45–64.

Little, A. G., and Pelster, F. *Oxford Theology and Theologians, c. A. D. 1282–1302.* Oxford Historical Society, 96. Oxford: Clarendon, 1934.

Löhr, G. M. *Die theologische Disputationem und Promotionem an der Universität Köln.* Liepzig, 1926.

Looze, Laurence de. "The Gender of Fiction: Womanly Poetics in Jean Renart's *Guillaume de Dole.*" *French Review* 64 (1991): 596–606.

Lord, Albert. *The Singer of Tales.* Harvard Studies in Comparative Literature, 24. Cambridge: Harvard University Press, 1960.

Lucas, Robert H. "Medieval French Translations of the Latin Classics to 1500." *Speculum* 45 (1970): 225–53.

Luscombe, D. E. *The School of Peter Abelard: The Influence of Abelard's Thought in the Early Scholastic Period.* London: Cambridge University Press, 1969.

Lyons, John D., and Stephen G. Nichols, eds. *Mimesis: From Mirror to Method, Augustine to Descartes.* Hanover. N.H.: University Press of New England, 1982

Lyotard, Jean-François, and Jean-Loup Thébaud. *Just Gaming.* Minneapolis: University of Minnesota Press, 1985.

McCracken, Peggy. "The Poetics of Silence in the French Middle Ages." Ph.D. dissertation, Yale University, 1989.

MacGregor, Alexander P. *Manuscripts of Seneca's Tragedies: A Handlist.* Aufstieg und Niedergang der römischen Welt, 32.2. Berlin: De Gruyter, 1985.

MacKendrick, Paul. "The Classical Origins of Debate." *CSSJ* 12 (1961): 16–20.

McKeon, Richard. "Rhetoric in the Middle Ages." *Speculum* 17 (1942): 1–32.

McLaughlin, Megan. "The Woman Warrior: Gender, Warfare, and Society in Medieval Europe." *Women's Studies* 17 (1990): 193–209.

McLuhan, Marshall. *The Gutenberg Galaxy.* 1962; rpt. Toronto: Toronto University Press, 1967.

Maddox, Donald. *Semiotics of Deceit: The Pathelin Era.* Lewisburg, Pa.: Bucknell University Press, 1984.

Mâle, Emile. *The Gothic Image: Religious Art in France of the Thirteenth Century.* Trans. Dora Nussey. New York: Harper & Row, 1958.

Mandonnet, P. "Chronologie des questions disputées de Saint Thomas d'Aquin." *Revue Thomiste* 23 (1928): 267–79.

Marcel, Gabriel. *Théâtre et religion.* Lyon: Vitte, 1958.

Mayali, Laurent, and Stephanie Tibbetts, eds. *The Two Laws: Studies in Medieval Legal History Dedicated to Stephan Kuttner.* Washington, D.C.: Catholic University Press, 1990.

Meredith, Peter, and Lynnette Muir. "The Trial in Heaven in the Eerste Bliscap and Other European Plays: A Question of Relationships." *Dutch Crossings* 22 (April 1984).

Meredith, Peter, and John E. Tailby, eds. *The Staging of Religious Drama in Europe in the Later Middle Ages: Texts and Documents in English Translation.* Early Drama, Art and Music, 4. Kalamazoo: Medieval Institute Publications, 1983.

Meyer, Michel, ed. *De la métaphysique à la rhétorique: Essays in Honour of Chaïm Perelman*. Brussels: Editions de l'Université de Bruxelles, 1986.
Meynet, Roland. "Histoire de 'l'analyse rhétorique' en exégèse biblique." *Rhetorica* 8 (1990): 291–320.
Michael, W. F. *Das deutsche Drama des Mittelalters*. Berlin, 1971.
Michel, Alain. *La Parole et la beauté: Rhétorique et esthétique dans la tradition occidentale*. Paris: Belles Lettres, 1982.
Miles, Margaret R. *Image as Insight: Visual Understanding in Western Christianity and Secular Culture*. Boston: Beacon, 1985.
Miller, Joseph M., Michael H. Prosser, and Thomas W. Benson, eds. *Readings in Medieval Rhetoric*. Bloomington: Indiana University Press, 1973.
Minnis, A. J. *Medieval Theory of Authorship: Scholastic Literary Attitudes in the Later Middle Ages*. London: Scholar Press, 1984.
Miraulmont, Pierre de. *De l'origine et établissement du Parlement et autres jurisdictions royales estans dans l'enclos du Palais royal de Paris*. Paris: Chevalier, 1612.
Moore, R. I. *The Origins of European Dissent*. New York: St. Martins Press, 1977.
Morrison, Karl F. "The Church as Play: Gerhoch of Reichersberg's Call for Reform." In *Popes, Teachers, and Canon Law in the Middle Ages*, ed. James Ross Sweeney and Stanley Chodorow, 114–44. Ithaca: Cornell University Press, 1989.
Morse, Ruth. *Truth and Convention in the Middle Ages: Medieval Rhetoric and Representation*. Cambridge: Cambridge University Press, 1991.
Mortensen, Jean. *Le Théâtre français au Moyen-Age*. Trans. Emmanuel Philipot. 1903; rpt. Geneva: Slatkine, 1974.
Motter, T. H. Vail. *The School Drama in England*. London: Longmans, 1929.
Muir, Lynette. *Liturgy and Drama in the Anglo-Norman Adam*. Oxford: Basil Blackwell, 1973.
——. "Medieval English Drama: The French Connection." In *Contexts for Early English Drama*, ed. Marianne G. Briscoe and John C. Coldewey, 56–76. Bloomington: Indiana University Press, 1989.
Mullini, Roberta. *La scena della memoria: Intertestualità nel teatro Tudor*. Bologna: Cooperativa Libraria Universitaria Editrice Bologna, 1988.
Murphy, James J. "Aristotle's *Rhetoric* in the Middle Ages." *QJS* 52 (1966): 109–15.
——. "The Historiography of Rhetoric." *Rhetorica* 1 (1983): 1–8.
——. "The Influence of Quintilian in the Middle Ages and Renaissance." Paper presented at ISHR conference, Göttingen, Germany. 27 July 1989.
——. *Medieval Rhetoric: A Select Bibliography*. Toronto: University of Toronto Press, 1971; 2d ed., 1989.
——. "New Elements in Traditional Rhetoric, 1450–1650." Paper presented at SCA convention, New York, 15 November 1980.
——. *Renaissance Rhetoric: A Short-Title Catalogue of Works on Rhetorical Theory from the Beginning of Printing to A. D. 1700*. New York: Garland, 1981.
——. "Rhetoric and Dialectic in *The Owl and the Nightingale*." In *Medieval Eloquence*, ed. James J. Murphy, 198–230. Berkeley: University of California Press, 1978.
——. *Rhetoric in the Middle Ages: A History of Rhetorical Theory from Saint*

Augustine to the Renaissance. 1974; rpt. Berkeley: University of California Press, 1981.

——. "The Scholastic Condemnation of Rhetoric in the Commentary of Giles of Rome on the *Rhetoric* of Aristotle." In *Arts Libéraux et philosophie au Moyen Age*, 833–41. Montreal: Institut d'Etudes Médiévales, 1969.

——. *A Synoptic History of Classical Rhetoric.* New York: Random House, 1972.

——, ed. *Medieval Eloquence: Studies in the Theory and Practice of Medieval Rhetoric.* Berkeley: University of California Press, 1978.

——, ed. *Three Medieval Rhetorical Arts.* Berkeley: University of California Press, 1985.

Murray, Alexander. *Reason and Society in the Middle Ages.* Oxford: Clarendon, 1978.

Muscatine, Charles. "The Emergence of Psychological Allegory in Old French Romance." *PMLA* 68 (1953): 1160–82.

Nagler, A. M. *The Medieval Religious Stage: Shapes and Phantoms.* New Haven: Yale University Press, 1976.

——. *A Source Book in Theatrical History.* 1952; rpt. New York: Dover, 1959.

Nelson, Alan H. "Contexts for Early English Drama: The Universities." In *Contexts for Early English Drama*, ed. Marianne G. Briscoe and John C. Coldewey, 137–49. Bloomington: Indiana University Press, 1989.

——. *The Medieval English Stage: Corpus Christi Pageants and Plays.* Chicago: University of Chicago Press, 1974.

Nelson, Janet. "Dispute Settlement in Carolingian West Francia." In *The Settlement of Disputes in Early Medieval Europe*, ed. Wendy Davies and Paul Fouracre, 45–64. Cambridge: Cambridge University Press, 1986.

Neuss, Paula. *Aspects of Early English Drama.* Cambridge, Eng.: D. S. Brewer, 1983.

Nichols, Stephen G. "Fission and Fusion: Mediations of Power in Medieval History and Literature." *YFS* 70 (1986): 21–41.

——. "A Poetics of Historicism? Recent Trends in Medieval Literary Study." *Medievalia et Humanistica* 8 (1977): 77–101.

——. *Romanesque Signs: Early Medieval Narrative and Iconography.* New Haven: Yale University Press, 1983.

Nicoll, Allardyce. *Masks, Mimes, and Miracles.* New York: Cooper Square, 1963.

——. *The Theatre and Dramatic Theory.* New York: Barnes & Noble, 1962.

——. *World Drama from Aeschylus to Anouilh.* 1949; 2d ed. New York: Harper & Row, 1976.

Olson, Glending. *Literature as Recreation in the Later Middle Ages.* Ithaca: Cornell University Press, 1982.

——. "The Medieval Fortunes of 'Theatrica.' " *Traditio* 4 (1986): 265–86.

O'Malley, John W. *Praise and Blame in Renaissance Rome: Rhetoric, Doctrine, and Reform in the Sacred Orators of the Papal Court, c. 1450–1521.* Durham: Duke University Press, 1979.

Ong, Walter J. *Interfaces of the Word: Studies in the Evolution of Consciousness and Culture.* Ithaca: Cornell University Press, 1977.

——. *Orality and Literacy.* New York: Methuen, 1982.

——. *Ramus, Method, and the Decay of Dialogue.* 1958; rpt. Cambridge: Harvard University Press, 1983.

——. *Rhetoric, Romance, and Technology: Studies in the Interaction of Expression and Culture.* Ithaca: Cornell University Press, 1971.

Osborn, Michael. "The Rhetoric of Theatre." Paper presented at SCA convention, Louisville, November 1982.

Owst, Gerald R. *Literature and Pulpit in Medieval England.* 1933; rev. ed. Oxford: Basil Blackwell, 1961.

Padley, G. A. *Grammatical Theory in Western Europe, 1500–1700: The Latin Tradition.* Cambridge: Cambridge University Press, 1976.

Paetow, Louis John. *The Arts Course at Medieval Universities with Special Reference to Grammar and Rhetoric.* Champaign: University of Illinois Press, 1910.

Panofsky, Erwin. *Gothic Architecture and Scholasticism.* 1951; rpt. New York: New American Library, 1976.

Paris, Gaston. *La Littérature française au Moyen Age (XIe–XIVe siècle).* 5th ed. Paris: Hachette, 1914.

Parry, Milman. "Studies in the Technique of Oral Verse-Making." *Harvard Studies in Classical Philology* 41 (1930): 73–147.

Partner, Nancy. "The New Cornificus: Medieval History and the Artifice of Words." in *Classical Rhetoric and Medieval Historiography,* ed. Ernst Breisach, 5–59. Kalamazoo: Medieval Institute Publications, 1985.

Payne, Robert O. "Chaucer's Realization of Himself as Rhetor." In *Medieval Eloquence,* ed. James J. Murphy, 270–87. Berkeley: University of California Press, 1978.

——. *The Key to Remembrance: A Study of Chaucer's Poetics.* New Haven: Yale University Press, 1963.

Pellegrini, Angelo M. "Renaissance and Medieval Antecedents of Debate." *QJS* 28 (1972): 14–19.

Perelman, Chaïm. *L'Empire rhétorique: Rhétorique et argumentation.* Paris: Vrin, 1977.

Perret, Donald. *Old Comedy in the French Renaissance: 1576–1620.* Geneva: Droz, forthcoming.

Peters, Edward. *The Magician, the Witch, and the Law.* Philadelphia: University of Pennsylvania Press, 1978.

Petit de Julleville, L. *Les Mystères.* Vol. 1 of *Histoire du théâtre en France.* 1880; rpt. Geneva: Slatkine, 1968.

——. *Répertoire du Théâtre comique en France au Moyen Age.* 1886; rpt. Geneva: Slatkine, 1967.

——. *Le Théâtre en France: Histoire de la littérature dramatique.* Paris: Armand Colin, 1923.

Picot, Emile. *Les Moralités polémiques.* 1887; rpt. Geneva: Slatkine, 1970.

——. *Pierre Gringore et les comédiens italiens.* Paris: Morgan et Fatour, 1878.

Pitts, Brent A. "Absence, Memory, and the Ritual of Love in Thomas's *Roman de Tristan.*" *French Review* 63 (1990): 790–99.

Pizarro, Joaquín Martínez. *A Rhetoric of the Scene: Dramatic Narrative in the Early Middle Ages.* Toronto: University of Toronto Press, 1989.

Plucknett, T. F. T. *Early English Legal Literature.* Cambridge: Cambridge University Press, 1958.

Posner, Richard A. *Law and Literature: A Misunderstood Relation.* Cambridge: Harvard University Press, 1988.

Postelwait, Thomas, and Bruce A. McConachie, eds. *Interpreting the Theatrical*

Past: Essays in the Historiography of Performance. Iowa City: University of Iowa Press, 1989.

Potter, Robert. "Public Execution as a Moral Spectacle." Paper presented at conference, "City and Spectacle in Medieval Europe," Minneapolis, 1 March 1991.

——. "The Unity of Medieval Drama: European Contexts for Early English Dramatic Traditions." In *Contexts for Early English Drama*, ed. Marianne G. Briscoe and John C. Coldewey, 41–55. Bloomington: Indiana University Press, 1989.

Price, Glanville. *The French Language.* 1971; rpt. London: Edward Arnold, 1975.

Prosser, Eleanor. *Drama and Religion in the English Mystery Plays.* Stanford: Stanford University Press, 1961.

Purcell, William M. "*Identitas, Similitudo,* and *Contrarietas* in Gervasius of Melkley's *Ars poetica:* A *Stasis* of Style." *Rhetorica* 9 (1991): 67–91.

Quicherat, J. *Histoire du costume en France.* Paris, 1875.

Quilligan, Maureen. *The Language of Allegory: Defining the Genre.* Ithaca: Cornell University Press, 1979.

Raby, F. J. E. *A History of Secular Latin Poetry in the Middle Ages.* 2 vols. Oxford: Clarendon, 1934.

Radding, Charles M. *The Origins of Medieval Jurisprudence: Pavia and Bologna, 850–1150.* New Haven: Yale University Press, 1988.

Rashdall, Hastings. *The Universities of Europe in the Middle Ages.* Ed. F. M. Powicke and A. B. Emden. 3 vols. 1895; rpt. London: Oxford University Press, 1964.

Rawson, Elizabeth. *Intellectual Life in the Late Roman Republic.* Baltimore: Johns Hopkins University Press, 1985.

Rey-Flaud, Henri. *Le Cercle magique: Essai sur le théâtre en rond à la fin du Moyen Age.* Paris: Gallimard, 1973.

——. *Pour une dramaturgie du Moyen-Age.* Paris: Presses Universitaires de France, 1980.

Robertson, D. W., Jr. *A Preface to Chaucer: Studies in Medieval Perspectives.* Princeton: Princeton University Press, 1962.

Robinson, Christopher. *Lucian and His Influence in Europe.* Chapel Hill: University of North Carolina Press, 1979.

Robinson, J. W. *Studies in Fifteenth-Century Stagecraft.* Early Drama, Art, and Music, 14. Kalamazoo: Medieval Institute Publications, 1991.

Rodríguez Adrados, Francisco. *Fiesta, comedia y tragedia: Sobre los orígenes griegos del teatro.* Barcelona: Planeta, 1972.

Romilly, Jacqueline de. *Magic and Rhetoric in Ancient Greece.* Cambridge: Harvard University Press, 1975.

Roy, Emile. *Le Mystère de la Passion en France du XIVe au XVIe siècle.* 1903–1904; rpt. Geneva: Slatkine, 1974.

Russell, Jeffrey Burton. *Dissent and Reform in the Early Middle Ages.* Berkeley: University of California Press, 1965.

Saenger, Paul. "Silent Reading: Its Impact on Late Medieval Script and Society." *Viator* 13 (1982): 367–414.

Schaefer, Ursula. "Material Possession and Memory: The Vocal World of Books." Paper presented at ICMS, Kalamazoo, 10 May 1990.

Schlauch, Margaret. "Rhetorical Doctrine and Some Aspects of Medieval Narrative." *Kwartalnik Neofilologiczny* 18 (1971): 353–64.

Schoor, J. Van. *La Basoche*. Brussels, 1892.

Schouler, Bernard. "La Classification des personnes et des faits chez Hermogène et ses commentateurs." *Rhetorica* 8 (1990): 229–54.

Sepet, Marius. *Le Drame chrétien au Moyen Age*. Paris: Didier, 1878.

——. *Le Drame religieux au Moyen Age*. Paris: Bloud, 1908.

——. *Origines catholiques du théâtre moderne*. 1901; rpt. Geneva: Slatkine, 1975.

——. *Les Prophètes du Christ: Etude sur les origines du théâtre au Moyen Age*. 1878; rpt. Geneva: Slatkine, 1974.

Sheingorn, Pamela. "The Visual Language of Drama: Principles of Composition." In *Contexts for Early English Drama*, ed. Marianne G. Briscoe and John C. Coldewey, 173–91. Bloomington: Indiana University Press, 1989.

Shergold, N. D. *A History of the Spanish Stage from Medieval Times until the End of the Seventeenth Century*. Oxford: Clarendon, 1967.

Siraisi, Nancy G. *Arts and Sciences at Padua: The "Studium" of Padua before 1350*. Toronto: Pontifical Institute, 1973.

Smith, G. C. More. "Academic Drama at Cambridge: Extracts from College Records." Malone Society *Collections* 2, pt. 2 (1923).

Smith, P. J. "Memoria et actio dans l'oeuvre de Rabelais." Paper presented at ISHR conference, Göttingen, 28 July 1989.

Sorabji, Richard. *Aristotle on Memory*. London: Duckworth, 1972.

Southern, R. W. *The Making of the Middle Ages*. London: Hutchinson, 1953.

——. *Medieval Humanism and Other Studies*. Oxford: Basil Blackwell, 1970.

Southern, Richard. *The Medieval Theatre in the Round*. London: Faber & Faber, 1957.

——. *The Seven Ages of Theatre*. New York: Hill & Wang, 1961.

Spiegel, Gabrielle. "History, Historicism, and the Social Logic of the Text in the Middle Ages." *Speculum* 65 (1990): 59–86.

Squires, Lynn. "Law and Disorder in *Ludus Coventriae*." In *The Drama of the Middle Ages: Comparative and Critical Essays*, ed. Clifford Davidson, C. J. Gianakaris, and John H. Stroupe, 272–85. New York: AMS Press, 1982.

Stahl, William Harris, Richard Johnson, and E. L. Burge. *Martianus Capella and the Seven Liberal Arts*. 1971; rpt. New York: Columbia University Press, 1991.

Steenberghen, Fernand van. *Aristote en Occident: Les Origines de l'Aristotélisme parisien*. Louvain: Editions de l'Institut Supérieur de Philosophie, 1946.

Steiner, George. *The Death of Tragedy*. New York: Knopf, 1961.

——. *Language and Silence: Essays on Language, Literature, and the Inhuman*. New York: Atheneum, 1967.

Stevens, John. *Words and Music in the Middle Ages: Song, Narrative, Dance, and Drama, 1050–1350*. Cambridge: Cambridge University Press, 1986.

Sticca, Sandro. "Drama and Spirituality in the Middle Ages." *Medievalia et Humanistica* 4 (1973): 69–87.

——. *The Latin Passion Play: Its Origins and Development*. Albany: State University of New York at Albany Press, 1970.

——., ed. *The Medieval Drama*. Albany: State University of New York at Albany Press, 1972.

Stock, Brian. "History, Literature, and Medieval Textuality." *YFS* 70 (1986): 7–17.

——. *Implications of Literacy: Written Language and Models of Interpretation in the Eleventh and Twelfth Centuries.* Princeton: Princeton University Press, 1983.

——. *Listening for the Text: On the Uses of the Past.* Baltimore: Johns Hopkins University Press, 1990.

Strong, Roy. *Art and Power: Renaissance Festivals, 1450–1630.* Berkeley: University of California Press, 1985.

Styan, J. L. *Drama, Stage, and Audience.* London: Cambridge University Press, 1975.

——. *The Elements of Drama.* London: Cambridge University Press, 1969.

Sweeney, James Ross, and Stanley Chodorow, eds. *Popes, Teachers, and Canon Law in the Middle Ages.* Ithaca: Cornell University Press, 1989.

Tade, George T. "Rhetorical Aspects of the *Spiritual Exercises* in the Medieval Tradition of Preaching." *QJS* 51 (1965): 409–18.

Taylor, Jerome, and Alan Nelson, eds. *Medieval English Drama: Essays Critical and Contextual.* Chicago: University of Chicago Press, 1972.

Theiner, Paul. "Medieval English Literature." In *Medieval Studies,* Ed. James M. Powell, 239–75. Syracuse: Syracuse University Press, 1976.

Thurot, Charles. *De l'organisation de l'enseignement dans l'Université de Paris au Moyen-Age.* 1850; rpt. Minerva, 1967.

Traver, Hope. *The Four Daughters of God: A Study of the Versions of This Allegory with Especial Reference to Those in Latin, French, and English.* Philadelphia: John C. Winston, 1907.

Treitler, Leo. "Oral, Written, and Literate Process in the Transmission of Medieval Music." *Speculum* 56 (1981): 471–91.

——. "Reading and Singing: On the Genesis of Occidental Musical Writing." *Early Music History* 4 (1985): 135–208.

Treitler, Leo, and Ritva Jonsson. "Medieval Music and Language: A Reconsideration of the Relationship." In *Studies in the History of Music,* 1:1–23. New York: Broude, 1983.

Trimpi, Wesley. *Muses of One Mind: The Literary Analysis of Experience and Its Continuity.* Princeton: Princeton University Press, 1983.

Troll, Denise. "Monastic Silence and Sign Language: Medieval Prerequisites for Modern Literacy?" Paper presented at ICMS, Kalamazoo, 4 May 1989.

——. "The Role of Medieval Manuscript Technology and Monastic Silence in the Development of Literate Habits." Ph.D. dissertation, Carnegie Mellon University, in progress.

——. "The Role of Monastic Silence in the Development of Literate Consciousness." Paper presented at ICMS, Kalamazoo, 6 May 1988.

Tunison, Joseph S. *Dramatic Traditions of the Dark Ages.* Chicago: University of Chicago Press, 1907.

Tuve, Rosemond. *Allegorical Imagery: Some Mediaeval Books and Their Posterity.* 1966; rpt. Princeton: Princeton University Press, 1977.

——. *Elizabethan and Metaphysical Imagery.* Chicago: University of Chicago Press, 1947.

——. "Imagery and Logic: Ramus and Metaphysical Poetics." *Journal of the History of Ideas* 3 (1942): 365–400.

Tydeman, William. *The Theatre in the Middle Ages: Western European Stage Conditions, c. 800–1576.* Cambridge: Cambridge University Press, 1978.

Uitti, Karl D. "Foi littéraire et création poétique: Le problème des genres littéraires en ancien français." In *Acts of the Fourteenth International Congress of Romance Linguistics and Philology*, 165–76. Naples: Gaetano Macchiaroli and John Benjamins B. V., 1974.

———. "Renewal and Undermining of Old French Romance." In *Romance*, ed. Kevin Brownlee and Marina Scordilis Brownlee, 135–54. Hanover, N.H.: University Press of New England, 1985.

———. *Story, Myth, and Celebration in Old French Narrative Poetry: 1050–1200*. Princeton: Princeton University Press, 1973.

Vance, Eugene. *From Topic to Tale: Logic and Narrativity in the Middle Ages*. Theory and History of Literature, 47. Minneapolis: University of Minnesota Press, 1987.

———. *Mervelous Signals: Poetics and Sign Theory in the Middle Ages*. Lincoln: University of Nebraska Press, 1986.

———. "Roland, Charlemagne, and the Poetics of Memory." In *Textual Strategies*, ed. Josué Harrari, 374–403. Ithaca: Cornell University Press, 1978.

Ventrone, Paola. "On the Use of Figurative Art as a Source for the Study of Medieval Spectacles." *Comparative Drama* 25 (1991): 4–16.

Vernant, Jean-Pierre. *Mythe et société en Grèce ancienne*. Paris: François Maspero, 1974.

Vickers, Brian. *Classical Rhetoric in English Poetry*. New York: Macmillan, 1970.

———, ed. *Rhetoric Revalued: Papers from the International Society for the History of Rhetoric*. Binghamton, N. Y.: Medieval and Renaissance Texts and Studies, 1982.

Vince, Ronald W. *Ancient and Medieval Theatre: A Historiographical Handbook*. Westport, Conn.: Greenwood, 1984.

Viollet-Le-Duc, Eugène-Emmanuel. *Dictionnaire raisonné de l'architecture française du XIe au XVIe siècle*. 10 vols. Paris: Morel, 1867–1870.

Wagner, David L., ed. *The Seven Liberal Arts in the Middle Ages*. Bloomington: Indiana University Press, 1986.

Walther, H. *Das Streitgedicht in der lateinischen Literatur des Mittelalters*. Quellen und Untersuchungen zur lateinischen Philologie des Mittelalters, 5. Munich: Beck, 1920.

Ward, John O. "The Commentaries on Ciceronian Rhetoric." Paper presented at ICMS, Kalamazoo, 7 May 1988.

———. "Education in the Middle Ages and Renaissance: Ritual, Celebration, or Performance? Rhetorical Theory and Practice in the Time of Thierry of Chartres and Guarino da Verona." Paper presented at ISHR conference, Göttingen, 27 July 1989.

———. "From Antiquity to the Renaissance: Glosses and Commentaries on Cicero's *Rhetorica*." In *Medieval Eloquence*, ed. James J. Murphy, 25–67. Berkeley: University of California Press, 1978.

———. "Some Principles of Rhetorical Historiography in the Twelfth Century." In *Classical Rhetoric and Medieval Historiography*, ed. Ernst Breisach, 103–65. Kalamazoo: Medieval Institute Publications, 1985.

Ward, M. *History of English Dramatic Literature*. London, 1875.

Warning, Rainer. "On the Alterity of Medieval Religious Drama." *NLH* 10 (1979): 265–92.

Weaver, Richard. M. *The Ethics of Rhetoric*. Chicago: Henry Regnery, 1953.

———. *Language Is Sermonic.* Ed. Richard L. Johannesen, Rennard Strickland, and Ralph T. Eubanks. Baton Rouge: Louisiana State University Press, 1970.

Weber, Alison. *Teresa of Avila and the Rhetoric of Femininity.* Princeton: Princeton University Press, 1990.

Weber, Joseph G. "The Poetics of Memory." *Symposium* 33 (1979): 293–98.

Weinberg, Bernard. *A History of Literary Criticism in the Italian Renaissance.* 2 vols. Chicago: University of Chicago Press, 1961.

Weisberg, Richard, and Jean-Pierre Barricelli. "Literature and Law." In *Interrelations of Literature,* ed. Jean-Pierre Barricelli and Joseph Gibaldi, 150–75. New York: MLA, 1982.

Welch, Kathleen. *The Contemporary Reception of Classical Rhetoric: Appropriations of Ancient Discourse.* Hillsdale, N. J.: Lawrence Erlbaum, 1990.

Wenzel, Siegfried. *Preachers, Poets, and the Early English Lyric.* Princeton: Princeton University Press, 1986.

Wetherbee, Winthrop. *Platonism and Poetry in the Twelfth Century: The Literary Influence of the School of Chartres.* Princeton: Princeton University Press, 1972.

Whorf, Benjamin Lee. *Language, Thought, and Reality.* Ed. John B. Carroll. Cambridge: MIT Press, 1956.

Wickham, Glynne. *The Medieval Theatre.* 3d ed. Cambridge: Cambridge University Press, 1987.

Wieruszowski, Helene. *Politics and Culture in Medieval Spain and Italy.* Rome: Edizioni di Storia e Letteratura, 1971.

Wilcox, S. "The Scope of Early Rhetorical Instruction." *Harvard Studies in Classical Studies* 53 (1942): 121–55.

Winn, James Anderson. *Unsuspected Eloquence: A History of the Relations between Poetry and Music.* New Haven: Yale University Press, 1981.

Winterbottom, Michael. "Schoolroom and Courtroom." In *Rhetoric Revalued,* ed. Brian Vickers, 59–70. Binghamton, N.Y.: Medieval and Renaissance Texts and Studies, 1982.

Woods, Marjorie Curry. "A Medieval Rhetoric Goes to School—and to the University: The Commentaries on the *Poetria nova.*" *Rhetorica* 9 (1991): 55–65.

———. "Teaching the Tropes: The Theory of Metaphoric Transference in School Commentaries on the *Poetria nova,*" Paper presented at MLA convention, New Orleans, 28 December 1988.

———. "An Unfashionable Rhetoric in the Fifteenth Century." *QJS* 75 (1989): 312–20.

Wright, Stephen K. "Records of Early French Drama in Parisian Notary Registers." *Comparative Drama* 24 (1990): 232–54.

Yates, Frances A. *The Art of Memory.* Chicago: University of Chicago Press, 1966.

York, R. A. *The Poem as Utterance.* New York: Methuen, 1986.

Young, Karl. *The Drama of the Medieval Church.* 2 vols. Oxford: Clarendon, 1933.

Zink, Michel. "The Allegorical Poem as Interior Memoir." *YFS* 70 (1986): 100–126.

———. *La Prédication en langue romane.* Paris: Champion, 1976.

———. *La Subjectivité littéraire.* Paris: Presses Universitaires de France, 1985.

Zumthor, Paul. *Essai de poétique médiévale.* Paris: Seuil, 1972.

———. "From Hi(story) to Poem, or the Paths of Pun: The Grands Rhétoriqueurs of Fifteenth-Century France." *NLH* 10 (1979): 231–63.

———. *La Poésie et la voix dans la civilisation mediévale.* Paris: Presses Universitaires de France, 1984.

———. "Rhétorique médiévale et poétique." *Poetics* 1 (1971): 46–82.

Zumthor, Paul, and Bruno Roy, eds. *Jeux de mémoire: Aspects de la mnémotechnie médiévale.* Paris: Vrin, 1985.

Index

Quodlibet, 2–3, 10–12, 17, 38, 70, 72, 77, 88, 91, 97, 102, 106–8, 111, 114–16, 119–20, 130, 133, 148–49, 153, 159, 162, 165–67, 169n, 171, 180n, 183, 192. *See also* Disputation, scholastic

Raby, F. J. E., 14n, 164n, 168n, 221
Raynaud, Gaston, 13, 166n, 169–70, 222n, 225
Reenactment, 52–53, 61, 77, 113, 128, 172, 174, 183, 188, 192–93, 195, 201, 209, 228, 240, 243
Rey-Flaud, Henri, 5n, 10, 46n, 52–53, 60n, 66n, 72, 73, 88, 103, 104, 110n, 111–12, 136, 183n
Rhetorica ad Herennium, 4n, 6n, 20n, 21, 24, 34, 44, 46–47, 49, 52, 92, 100, 174–78, 180, 245
Ritual: legal, 2, 10–11, 16, 20, 42, 61–62, 66–67, 69, 71–76, 87, 98, 102–4, 107, 128–29, 139, 141, 145, 154, 164–65, 174, 176; religious, 7, 10, 61, 75, 77n, 80–81, 103n, 111, 165. *See also* Liturgy; *Spectaculum crudelitatis*
Rixa, 72, 100–103, 112, 132, 144, 146–47, 235
Robertson, D. W., 164n, 167n, 168
Romance (*roman*), 37n, 43–45, 53, 109n, 128, 186, 229
Roman de la Rose, 168, 186n, 214, 245
Roy, Emile, 171n

Salutation and Conception, 188–89
Satire, 2, 10, 22, 61, 95–96, 108, 128–29, 152, 155, 162, 210, 239
Scholasticism. *See* Disputation, scholastic
Seneca the Elder, 16, 20–21, 24, 34, 91–92, 94, 100–101, 106, 168
Seneca the Younger, 40–41, 221
Sepet, Marius, 5n, 65n, 66, 169–70
Sermon, 10, 38, 115, 157, 191, 193, 212, 228, 245. *See also Ars praedicandi*
Song, 1, 22, 26, 33, 34, 45, 64, 73, 85–88, 180–81, 184, 193, 198, 202, 206, 208, 232–33. *See also* Lyric poetry; Music
Sophistry, 2, 29–30, 69, 72, 87, 89, 94–95, 116, 155, 204, 218, 223, 240, 242
Sorbonne. *See* Theology, Faculty of; University of Paris
Spectaculum crudelitatis, 87–88, 102, 105, 107, 111, 148
Sports, 72, 74, 78, 80–85, 88, 102, 106,

110, 144–45, 147. *See also* Amphitheater; Gladiators; Wrestling
Stage directions. *See* Didascalia
Staging. *See* Costume; Props; Reenactment; Theatrical space; *Theatrum*
Stasis theory (*status*), 79, 174, 176, 180, 185, 194–95, 207, 214, 217–18, 227
Steiner, George, 10n, 36n, 166
Stock, Brian, 5n, 6, 16n, 20n, 36n, 37, 43, 110n
Styan, J. L., 16, 22, 34, 75, 110, 113
Style. *See Elocutio*
Syllogism. *See* Dialectic; Logic; Proofs

Tacitus, 23, 24, 26, 62–64, 69–70, 73, 75, 84, 88, 89, 91, 96, 101, 106, 108, 110, 113, 115–22, 126–28, 133, 139–40, 146–47, 149, 204, 209, 219, 244
Temenos, 72, 74–79, 81, 115, 129, 133, 135, 138, 141, 164. *See also* Theatrical space
Tenso. *See* Lyric poetry
Tertullian, 32, 81, 97
Theatrical space, 4, 17, 46–53, 70–72, 74–89, 131, 134–41, 206
Theatrum, 23, 55, 84–85
Theology, Faculty of, 2, 38, 66, 72, 77, 82, 95, 97, 101, 119–20, 141, 149, 152, 159, 164, 166–67, 170. *See also* University of Paris
Thespis, 50, 65, 154
Thomas Aquinas, 91, 93, 108, 171
Topos, 10, 13, 44, 63, 162–63, 167n, 173
Tragedy, 10, 23, 24, 28–29, 33–34, 55–58, 60, 69, 74–75, 85–86, 105, 109, 125–26, 146, 154, 165–67, 169n
Translation, 9n, 43, 109–10, 153–54, 178, 180–81, 183, 223
Traver, Hope, 170, 171, 181, 183n, 188n
Treitler, Leo, 26n, 38n, 43n, 66n, 233n
Trivium, 3n, 91
Troping, 10, 56–57, 65, 67. *See also* Antiphony; Liturgy: Christian
Tuve, Rosemond, 7, 50
Tydeman, William, 77n, 88, 102n, 103n, 104, 107, 112, 199n

University of Paris, 12, 77, 90, 93n, 94–95, 101, 108n, 115, 119–21, 147, 153n, 157, 166n. *See also* Theology, Faculty of

Vance, Eugene, 30n, 53, 164n
Varro, 80

Library of Congress Cataloging-in-Publication Data

Enders, Jody. 1955–
    Rhetoric and the origins of medieval drama / Jody Enders.
        p.   cm.—(Rhetoric & society)
    Includes bibliographical references and index.
    ISBN 0-8014-2655-3 (alk. paper)
        1. Drama, Medieval—History and criticism.   2. Forensic oratory—
    History.   3. Law in literature.   4. Theater—History—500–1500.
    I. Title.   II. Series.
    PN1751.E5   1992
    809.2'02–dc20
                                                            92-2798